Cavell on Film

THE SUNY SERIES

HORIZONS OF CINEMA

MURRAY POMERANCE | EDITOR

Cavell on Film

Edited and with an Introduction by

William Rothman

STATE UNIVERSITY OF NEW YORK PRESS

Published by
State University of New York Press, Albany

For information, address State University of New York Press,
194 Washington Avenue, Suite 305, Albany, NY 12210-2365

Production by Marilyn P. Semerad
Marketing by Susan M. Petrie

Library of Congress Cataloging-in-Publication Data

Cavell, Stanley, 1926–
    Cavell on film / edited and with an introduction by William Rothman.
        p. cm — (SUNY series, horizons of cinema)
    Includes bibliographical references and index.
    ISBN 0-7914-6431-8 (alk. paper)—ISBN 0-7914-6432-6 (pbk. : alk. paper)
    1. Motion pictures—Philosophy. I. Rothman, William. II. Title. III. Series.
PN1995.C396 2005
791.43′01—dc22   2004010302

10 9 8 7 6 5 4 3 2 1

Contents

Illustrations

Acknowledgments

EXCEPT FOR MINOR REVISIONS TO assure consistency of format, and the addition of a number of frame enlargements, I have not altered the writings in this volume.

"*Prénom:* Marie" was originally published in Maryel Locke and Charles Warren, editors, *Jean-Luc Godard's* Hail Mary: *Women and the Sacred in Film* (Southern Illinois University Press, 1993); "Words of Welcome" appeared in Charles Warren, editor, *Beyond Document* (Wesleyan University Press, 1996), "After Half a Century" was the epilogue to Robert Warshow, *The Immediate Experience: Movies, Comics, Theatre, and Other Aspects of Popular Culture* (Cambridge and London: Harvard University Press, 2001). All are reprinted by permission of these publishers.

I am grateful to Stanley Cavell for permission to include all the other materials in the present collection, for the unfailing support, encouragement, and friendship he has offered at every stage of this project, and for the inspiration his writing and teaching have provided to me—as to so many—over the years.

Introduction

WILLIAM ROTHMAN

WRITING ABOUT MOVIES HAS BEEN strand over strand with Stanley Cavell's philosophical life from his earliest to his latest writings. As he observes in the preface to *Contesting Tears: The Hollywood Melodrama of the Unknown Woman*, Cavell's thinking about film has for four decades been bound up with his thinking "about most of whatever else I have been thinking about in what may be called philosophy or literature."[1] *Contesting Tears*, which follows *The World Viewed: Reflections on the Ontology of Film* and *Pursuits of Happiness: The Hollywood Comedy of Remarriage*, is his third book devoted to the subject of film—or third and a half, if we include the four essays on film (and one on television and its relation to film) in his 1984 collection of essays, *Themes Out of School: Events and Causes. Cities of Words: Pedagogical Letters on a Register of the Moral Life*, whose chapters alternate between readings of movies and of classic texts of moral philosophy, makes it an even four. In addition to these books, he has also written a substantial number of other pieces on film, in a diversity of formats—some ambitious theoretical statements, others apparently slight "occasional pieces"—originally presented to a diversity of audiences, on a diversity of occasions, and published, if at all, in a diversity of journals and anthologies.

In "The World as Things: Collecting Thoughts on Collecting," one of the chapters in the present collection, Cavell remarks that "every collection requires an idea," and that this "seems to presage the fact that collections carry narratives with them, ones presumably telling the point of the gathering, the source and adventure of it." The idea of the present collection is, quite simply, to gather under one cover all of Cavell's writings on film—including the material from *Themes Out of School*—other than *The World Viewed*, *Pursuits of Happiness*, *Contesting Tears*, and *Cities of Words*.

The idea of such a collection is mine, not Cavell's. He has never chosen to isolate his writings on film in this way. Nor is it my wish, in putting together this collection, to suggest that the writings it contains, or Cavell's writings on film in general, stand apart in their concerns, or in their status as philosophy, from his other writings.

In his preface to *Themes Out of School*, Cavell finds value in the fact that it is a collection of writings that address a wide range of topics. By focusing on only one topic, film, the present collection may seem to be denying that value. But that is not really the case. The pieces in this volume address "classical" Hollywood movies, such as *Mr. Deeds Goes to Town*, *Now, Voyager*, *North By Northwest*, and the films of Fred Astaire and the Marx Brothers; European "art" films, such as Ingmar Bergman's *Smiles of a Summer Night* and Luis Buñuel's *Belle de Jour*; documentaries, such as Robert Gardner's *Forest of Bliss*; iconoclastic modernist films, such as Dusan Makavejev's *Sweet Movie* and Jean-Luc Godard's *Hail, Mary*; postmodernist films, such as Andy Warhol's *Sleep* and *Empire*; and popular movies as current, or nearly current, as, among others, *The Matrix*, *American Beauty*, and *Being John Malkovich*. The writings gathered in this collection also address film's relation to other media, such as television, opera, and the novels of Jane Austen and George Eliot. They address the ideas and intellectual procedures of such major thinkers as Nietzsche, Freud, Heidegger, Wittgenstein, Austin, and, on this side of the Atlantic, Emerson and Thoreau. And they address, philosophically, such diverse concepts as medium, art, language, reading, collecting, and America, to name only a few. Taken together, these writings reflect, and illuminate, the major developments that have marked Cavell's thinking over the years. These include the emergence, as central themes, of such matters as the problematic of skepticism (which links the beginning of modern philosophy in Descartes with Shakespearean tragedy and romance); voice; the ways skepticism and voice are inflected by gender; and the outlook on morality—embraced both by Cavell and by the films he cares most about—that he calls moral perfectionism or Emersonian perfectionism.

In all the writings collected in this volume, in other words, Cavell is thinking about film, but he is also thinking about topics no less diverse and wide ranging than those addressed in the essays that comprise *Themes Out of School*, or, for that matter, in the totality of his work. Indeed, the writings collected in this volume are noteworthy not only for the range and diversity of the topics they address, but also for the range and diversity of the audiences that attended their original presentations, the range and diversity of the institutions that have invited this American philosopher to share his thoughts on the subject of film.

And yet all of these writings are also of a piece. Every one participates, in its own way, in furthering Cavell's philosophical enterprise as a whole. It is, indeed, a defining feature of that body of work that it aspires to *be* a whole, an *oeuvre* in the fullest sense of the word, even as all his individual writings undertake to acknowledge, as he puts it in *Themes Out of School*, "the autonomy of their separate causes."[2]

Cavell is the only major American philosopher who has made the subject of film a central part of his work. Yet to many philosophers, the relation of Cavell's writings on film to his explicitly philosophical writings remains perplexing. And within the field of film study the potential usefulness of Cavell's writings—the potential usefulness of philosophy, as he understands and practices it—remains generally unrecognized. It has long been one of Cavell's guiding intuitions that a marriage between philosophy and film is not only possible but also necessary. To illuminate why Cavell's work aspires to such a marriage, and how it achieves it, is a central goal of *Cities of Words* and of the course of lectures, which he gave several times toward the end of his teaching career at Harvard, on which it is based. And it is the "point," the "source and adventure," of the present collection.

When Marian Keane and I published *Reading Cavell's* The World Viewed: *A Philosophical Perspective on Film*, our book promised a companion volume, a retrospective of Cavell's previously unpublished and uncollected writings on film. Such a collection, we argued, would help readers grasp the trajectory of Cavell's writing about film in the thirty years subsequent to *The World Viewed*, all of it marked by that book's initial articulation of film's philosophical importance. It would also illuminate the relation of his writings on film, as they developed in those years, to the development of his philosophical enterprise as a whole. At the same time, it would illuminate the relation of Cavell's practice of philosophy, as it developed in the same years, to the institution and development of film study as an academic field in America and throughout the world.

The potential value of Cavell's work to the serious study of film is a function of the fruitfulness of his intuitions. It is no less a function of the exemplary discipline by which his writing—word by word, sentence by sentence, page by page, essay by essay—"follows out in each case the complete tuition for a given intuition," as Cavell puts it in an Emersonian mood, so that "this prose just here, as it's passing before our eyes," is capable of achieving conviction.[3] Cavell's writings on film incorporate insights about a diversity of matters pertaining to film's origins; its historical development; its characteristic forms and genres; the myths and the human types around which those genres revolve; the medium's ability, until recently, to stave off modernism, to continue to employ without self-consciousness traditional techniques that tap naturally into the medium's powers; and so on. In addressing such matters, those writings incorporate equally insightful remarks about particular films, genres, stars, and cinematic techniques.

Although Cavell's writings on film address issues (for example: what film is; film's origins and history; film's relation to other arts, and to modernism; the conditions of film theory and criticism) fundamental to the field of film study since its inception, his perspective on such issues diverges in virtually every respect from the succession of theoretical positions that have gained most prominence in the field. Within academic film study, for example, it remains an all but unquestioned doctrine that "classical" movies systematically subordinate women, and, more generally, that movies are pernicious ideological representations to be decoded and resisted, not treated as works of art capable of instructing us as to how to view them. Film students are generally taught that in order to learn to think seriously about film, they must break their attachments to the films they love. Cavell's writings on film, by contrast, bespeak "a sense of gratitude for the existence of the great and still-enigmatic art of film, whose history is punctuated, as that of no other, by works, small and large, that have commanded the devotion of audiences of all classes, of virtually all ages, and of all spaces around the world in which a projector has been mounted and a screen set up."[4]

It remains another largely unquestioned doctrine, within academic film study, that the stars projected on the movie screen are "personas," discursive ideological constructs, not real people; that the world projected on the screen is itself an ideological construct, not real; and, indeed, that the so-called real world is such a construct, too. By providing convincing alternatives to such skeptical positions, Cavell's writings on film are capable of helping academic film study free itself to explore regions that have remained closed to it, capable of inspiring the field to think in exciting new ways about film and its history.

The academic study of film had reached a point, Marian and I felt as we were writing our book on *The World Viewed*, at which the field could no longer move forward without revisiting its own history. Looking back on that history from the philosophical perspective exemplified by *The World Viewed*, it became clear to us that at each stage of the field's development there were alternative paths that were not taken, paths of discovery that have remained unexplored. Thus, we felt, together with a reading of *The World Viewed* that undertook to introduce or reintroduce that book to the field of film study (and to introduce or reintroduce it to the field of philosophy, as well), a complete retrospective of Cavell's writings on film—

including material unknown even to most readers of his books on the subject—could help the field to achieve a new perspective on its own origins
and development, hence a new understanding of the possibilities, and challenges, that remain for those who are committed to thinking seriously
about film, about our experience of film.

   Cavell on Film is that promised retrospective. It contains the four
essays on film and the essay on television—all written between 1978 and
1983—that were reprinted in *Themes Out of School*, as well as six additional pieces from the 1980s, and sixteen written since the early 1990s. As luck
would have it, however, the present volume is also something other, something much more, than the retrospective Marian and I envisioned when we
began composing our book on *The World Viewed*. In the past several years,
Cavell has been enjoying a period of remarkable productivity, and film has
been looming more prominently than ever in his thoughts. As it turns out,
more than half of this collection consists of recent writings, many of them
previously unpublished. This new material includes "Nothing Goes without Saying: Reading the Marx Brothers"; "Seasons of Love: Bergman's
Smiles of a Summer Night and *The Winter's Tale*"; "Something Out of the
Ordinary"; "The World as Things: Collecting Thoughts on Collecting";
his remarks presented at the Paris Colloquium occasioned by the publication of *The World Viewed* in French translation; "The Image of the
Psychoanalyst in Film"; "Opera in (and As) Film"; "Philosophy the Day
after Tomorrow"; "The Good of Film"; "Moral Reasoning: Teaching from
the Core"; "Crossing Paths," a version of a paper he presented at a colloquium on Arthur Danto's work; and "After Half a Century," his epilogue
to a new edition of Robert Warshow's *The Immediate Experience*.

   The fact that so much of this volume is "all new," as television networks like to put it, gives it a quite unanticipated richness and contempo-
raneity. That it gathers Cavell's current thoughts as well as his thoughts from
earlier periods, however, might seem to make my task all the more daunting
in penning a narrative that tells the "point" of this collection. In truth, however, it makes it easier for me to introduce this volume to its potential audience, or audiences. For Cavell has already done most of the hard part in the
most recent of the writings on film gathered in this collection. With that
lucidity that is the wonder of so many late works by great authors, those
recent writings, even as they blaze new paths, look back on his lifetime of
writing on film, speak to its "point," its "source," its "adventure."

   In looking back in order to move forward, Cavell's recent writings on
film bear the mark of his turning to autobiography—and to autobiography's relation to philosophy—in his recent book *A Pitch of Philosophy*. This
turning was already adumbrated in *Contesting Tears*, whose final chapter,
"Stella's Taste," begins and ends with moments of autobiography. Then

again, it is an idea that has always figured prominently in Cavell's work that
in philosophy it is necessary to look back if one is to move forward. As
early as the introduction to *Must We Mean What We Say?* he had argued
that innovation in philosophy has traditionally gone together with a repudiation of most of the history of the subject. For a philosopher like Cavell
who understands himself to be writing within a modernist situation, however, the repudiation of the past has a transformed significance, "as though
containing the consciousness that history will not go away except through
our perfect acknowledgment of it (in particular, our acknowledgment that
it is not past), and that one's own practice and ambition can be identified
only against the continuous experience of the past."[5]

  In innumerable ways, the writings gathered in this volume illuminate, and are illuminated by, Cavell's books on film, and thereby help clar-
ify the overall trajectory of his thinking. It will be helpful to recount a few
of those ways.
  Cavell can quite accurately say, as he does in one of the most recent
pieces in the present collection (remarks he presented in Paris at
a colloquium occasioned by the publication of *The World Viewed* in
French translation):

> The theoretical concepts put in play in *The World Viewed* have seen
> me . . . through two further books about film, the one on comedy and
> a companion volume on Hollywood melodrama . . . and a number of
> further essays on the subject.

And yet in those "two further books," and in *Cities of Words* as well, references to *The World Viewed* are few and far between. In *Pursuits of Happiness*
and *Contesting Tears* it goes almost without saying, whether in their introductions or in the readings that make up the body of each book, the extent
to which the theoretical concepts put in play in *The World Viewed*, indeed
"see those readings through," to use Cavell's terms.
  Then, too, although it is the central thrust of *The World Viewed* that
it is not possible to think seriously about film apart from the perspective of
self-reflection only philosophy is capable of providing, and that philosophy for its part cannot avoid the subject of film, the kinds of remarks about
philosophy that are everywhere to be found in *Must We Mean What We
Say?* are all but absent in Cavell's first book on film. In *The World Viewed*,
it goes almost without saying the extent to which his reflections on the

ontology of film derive philosophically from the "theoretical concepts put in play" in *Must We Mean What We Say?*.

Must We Mean What We Say? is curiously submerged within *The World Viewed*, in other words, even as *The World Viewed* is curiously submerged within Cavell's other books about film. *The World Viewed* is not comparably submerged, however, in the writings gathered in the present collection. Just as Wittgenstein's writings from the period between the *Tractatus* and *Philosophical Investigations* illuminate both books by helping readers to trace the paths between them, an essay like "What Becomes of Things on Film?" for example—written more or less simultaneously with "More of *The World Viewed*" and the foreword to the "Enlarged Edition" of *The World Viewed*—illuminates the continuities between *The World Viewed* and *Pursuits of Happiness* and *Contesting Tears*.

In the little introduction to "What Becomes of Things on Film?" that Cavell composed for its reprinting in *Themes Out of School*, Cavell observes that this piece

> played a role in my further thinking about film out of proportion to its small size. . . . A principal place these thoughts are picked up explicitly is in the *Adam's Rib* chapter of . . . *Pursuits of Happiness*, where I read the presence of its film-within-the-film (fictionally a home movie) as a demonstration that "no event within a film (say no gesture of framing or editing) is as significant (as 'cinematic') as the event of film itself."[6]

"What Becomes of Things on Film?" anticipates *Pursuits of Happiness* and *Contesting Tears* in other ways, as well. For one, those books take the form of readings of individual members of the genres Cavell names the "comedy of remarriage" and "the melodrama of the unknown woman," respectively (the latter derived from the former, in his view), while "What Becomes of Things on Film?" raises the question of what "any reading of a film must do" if it is to count as a serious act of film criticism. And it anticipates those books by the twin answers it gives to this question: A reading of a film must "account for the frames of the film being what they are, in the order they are in," and it must accurately state the film's subject. It also anticipates *Pursuits of Happiness* and *Contesting Tears* by its linking of philosophical skepticism and Shakespearean Romance (which *Pursuits of Happiness* finds a crucial source of remarriage comedies, hence of the melodramas that, according to *Contesting Tears*, are derived from them). And by its discovery that such masterpieces of film as *Belle de Jour, Persona, Ugetsu, Vertigo,* and *It's a Wonderful Life* share, as a common subject, "the meaning, or limits, or conditions, of female identity, hence . . . of human identity."

At the same time, "What Becomes of Things on Film?" emphatically declares its continuity with *The World Viewed*. It does so, for example, by its suggestion that what it is about film that lends itself to such a subject as female identity or human identity is a question that demands "so solemn a topic as 'the ontology of film.' "

When *Pursuits of Happiness* was first published, sympathetic readers were struck by Cavell's vision of a constellation of Hollywood genres logically related to the remarriage comedy, and to each other. Yet we were at a loss to identify groups of films that constituted other comparable genres. Once the essays that were to comprise *Contesting Tears* began to appear, we had, thanks to Cavell, a second such genre to think about. Comprised of films such as *Blonde Venus, Stella Dallas, Now, Voyager, Gaslight*, and *Letter from an Unknown Woman*, the melodrama of the unknown woman, as Cavell names the genre, is, he claims, derived from the remarriage comedy (by an operation of negation) as opposed to the operation by which members of a genre "compensate" for the apparent lack of a particular feature; for example, *It Happened One Night* appears to lack a place that functions—like Connecticut in *The Lady Eve*—as the equivalent of the "green world" in Shakespearean Romance, but it compensates for this by taking place on the road.

Even attentive readers of *Pursuits of Happiness* and *Contesting Tears* may find these operations perplexing, though. They may also find it a perplexing question what other genres there may be that are comparable to the two that proved so fruitful as subjects for Cavell's readings. The chapter in the present volume called simply "*North by Northwest*," written between *Pursuits of Happiness* and *Contesting Tears*, finds Hitchcock's great film to exemplify a kind of romantic thriller intimately related to the romantic comedies of remarriage, yet essentially different from them in structure. Cavell elegantly sums up the difference:

> The goal of the comedies requires what I call the creation of the woman, a new creation of a new woman. This takes the form in the comedies of something like the woman's death and revival, and it goes with the camera's insistence on the flesh-and-blood reality of the female actor. When this happens in Hitchcock, as it did in *Vertigo*, the Hitchcock film preceding *North by Northwest*, it is shown to produce catastrophe: the woman's falling to her death, precisely the fate *averted* in *North by Northwest*. Here, accordingly, it is the man who undergoes death and revival (at least twice, both times at the hands of the woman) *and* whose physical identity is insisted upon by

the camera. Hitchcock is thus investigating the point that the comedies of remarriage are least certain about, namely, what it is about the
man that fits him to educate and hence rescue the woman, that is, to
be chosen by the woman to educate her and thereby to achieve happiness for them both.[7]

By studying in considerable detail a third instance of a film genre,
Cavell's reading of *North by Northwest* complements *Pursuits of Happiness*
and *Contesting Tears*, enabling readers to achieve a perspective on the
remarriage comedy and the melodrama of the unknown woman that those
two books, even joined by *Cities of Words*, cannot provide.

✧

    The World Viewed, *Pursuits of Happiness*, *Contesting Tears*, and *Cities of
Words* all reflect on ways film is different from other artistic media (for
example, still photography, painting, poetry, music). In "The Fact of
Television," Cavell considers a medium whose relationship with film is
especially intimate. This important essay illuminates both *The World
Viewed* and *Pursuits of Happiness*, and their relation to each other, by explicitly addressing the ways television's ontological conditions differ from
those of film, and by considering television's leading genres in light of
those differences.
    Similarly, "Opera in (and As) Film," one of the recent pieces in the
present collection, illuminates the relation between film and opera.
"Seasons of Love: Bergman's *Smiles of a Summer Night* and *The Winter's
Tale*" and "Eric Rohmer's *A Tale of Winter*," two other recent pieces,
further illuminate the relation—ontological, historical—between Shakespearean theater and the Hollywood comedies and melodramas Cavell
studies in *Pursuits of Happiness*, *Contesting Tears*, and *Cities of Words*. And
"Philosophy the Day after Tomorrow," yet another recent piece, explores
the relation between those genres of film and the novels of Jane Austen
and George Eliot. (In Cavell's writing, it had long been a guiding intuition
that film has special affinities with opera and with Shakespearean theater.
It had largely gone without saying, however, that film has comparable
affinities with the nineteenth-century English novel, affinities it promises
to be equally fruitful to explore. Although it is only occasionally that
"Philosophy the Day after Tomorrow" explicitly raises the subject of film,
film is everywhere in its thoughts.)

✧

The World Viewed was written long before most of today's college students were born. It can leave contemporary readers quite in the dark as to what, if anything, its author might have to say about more recent films. So can Cavell's subsequent books on film, which focus on genres of "classical" Hollywood movies of the 1930s and 1940s.

In this regard, a chapter like "On Makavejev on Bergman" (1979), which contains an extended reading of Dusan Makavejev's *Sweet Movie*, a major modernist film made more than a decade after the latest films referred to in *The World Viewed*, is instructive. Written during the period Cavell was composing the readings of remarriage comedies that were to comprise *Pursuits of Happiness*, "On Makavejev on Bergman" is illuminating, among other reasons, for affirming—at a moment when Cavell's readers might have thought he had turned his back on current films—that works such as Makavejev's, which he accepts as a "significant present in the history of the art of film," were still being made. And for reaffirming that such works constitute "a place in which the future of filmmaking, hence of significant film theory and of film studies generally, will have to work itself out."[8]

In "*Prénom*: Marie," his foreword to *Jean-Luc Godard's* Hail Mary: *Women and the Sacred in Film*, an anthology of essays edited by Maryel Locke and Charles Warren, Cavell is led by his experience of *Hail Mary*—an even more recent film whose claim to seriousness he finds himself prepared to accept—to revise his perhaps too harsh judgment of Godard in *The World Viewed*. Godard's films of the mid-1960s, Cavell had charged, criticized our culture for treating people as if they had no souls, yet that seems to be precisely how the filmmaker himself treated his subjects—and his viewers. From so compromised a position, how can an artist achieve an authentically radical critique of our culture? How is the world's dehumanizing of its inhabitants to be distinguished from Godard's depersonalizing of them? Those inclined to side with Godard's earlier Marxist politics, Cavell observes in "*Prénom*: Marie," are "apt to sense a falling off, or backing off," in Godard's late films. Yet Cavell thinks of *Hail Mary* "not as an evasion of politics, but as a critique of politics, of what he had once named politics." And he recognizes Godard's self-criticism, in this film, "as a continuation of a mode of criticism internal to his work from the beginning."[9] Godard is thinking about film and about films, about their origins, the conditions of their possibility. Wasn't he always?

And in "Eric Rohmer's *A Tale of Winter*," whose ideas are further elaborated in the concluding chapter of *Cities of Words*, Cavell addresses a yet more recent film he accepts as a "significant present in the history of the art of film," taking seriously the film's invocations of Shakespeare's *The Winter's Tale*, which *Pursuits of Happiness* identifies as a source for the Hollywood remarriage comedies of the 1930s and 1940s. If the Shakespeare play is about "an art / which does mend nature—change it rather—but / The art itself is nature" (Act IV, sc. Iv), Rohmer's film, in Cavell's view, is in part a meditation on the fact that Shakespeare's words, when applied to film—"writing in light and motion"—"take on an uncanny literalness."[10]

No less illuminating are the pieces that incorporate Cavell's thoughts on recent American movies and their relation to "classical" Hollywood genres. These range from his tiny piece on *Groundhog Day* (which in sixty-two words suggests that this "small film that lives off its wits and tells a deeply wonderful story of love" poses the question—highly resonant in the context of Cavell's work—"how, surrounded by conventions we do not exactly believe in, we sometimes find it in ourselves to enter into what Emerson thought of as a new day")[11] to "The Good of Film," one of the most recent of the essays in the present volume, and among the most ambitious. In the course of its extended meditation on film's affinity with Emersonian perfectionism, the over-riding concern of *Cities of Words*, "The Good of Film" considers a wide range of recent movies (among them: *As Good as It Gets, Clueless, Groundhog Day, The Savage Heart, Inventing the Abbotts, Four Weddings and a Funeral, My Best Friend's Wedding, Everyone Says I Love You, Cookie's Fortune, Say Anything, Grosse Point Blank, Good Will Hunting, The Matrix, Fight Club, Being John Malkovich, Dogma, Waking the Dead, American Beauty, The Sixth Sense,* and *The Cider House Rules*). These films differ from remarriage comedies of the 1930s and 1940s in a number of ways the chapter explores (for example, the couples in the recent films tend to be, or to seem, much younger than their counterparts). How could today's films not differ from those of the 1930s and 1940s, Cavell observes, since "the fear of divorce has changed, the threat of pregnancy has changed, the male and female stars and the directors and writers who put them in action are gone?" Nonetheless, he argues, "there do seem to me a remarkable number of new films (within my limited experience)" that have something of the "feel" of classical remarriage comedies, provide interpretations of some of their features, and, like them,

> concern a quest for transcendence, a step into an opposite or transformed mood, not so much by becoming another person, or taking a further step in attaining an unattained self, or becoming who you are, as by being recognized as the one you are by having, or giving, access to another world.[12]

In "*North by Northwest*," Cavell writes:

What I found in turning to think consecutively about film a dozen or so years ago was a medium which seemed simultaneously to be free of the imperative to philosophy and at the same time inevitably to reflect upon itself—as though the condition of philosophy were its natural condition.[13]

In almost every one of the writings in the present volume, as in all of his books on film, Cavell reflects on the affinity he finds between film and philosophy, an affinity that makes the marriage between them, exemplified by his own writings on film, possible—and necessary. In "The Thought of Movies," for example, he poses the question: What does it reveal about movies, and what does it reveal about philosophy, that "the same sensibility that is drawn to and perplexed about philosophy is drawn to and perplexed about movies"?[14] Cavell's thoughts on this affinity and its implications, both for philosophy and for the serious study of film, become deeper and more complex as he ponders, in the writings collected in this volume, the role movies played in his own philosophical education.

During the period he was writing *The World Viewed*, it had not yet fully dawned on Cavell the extent to which the unique combination of popularity and artistic seriousness of American movies, especially of the 1930s and 1940s, was a function of their inheritance of the concerns of American transcendentalism. Not coincidentally, during the period he was writing *The World Viewed*, the extent to which Cavell's own way of thinking inherited Emerson's understanding and practice of philosophy also had not yet fully dawned on him.

In the writings collected in the present volume, however, Cavell's intuition that Hollywood movies have inherited the philosophical concerns of American transcendentalism, conjoined with his intuition that he has inherited these concerns, too, leads to the astonishing further intuition that his own philosophical procedures are underwritten by the ways American movies think about society, human relationships, and their own condition as films. It is in the very movies that were for so many years a normal part of Cavell's week that Emerson's ways of thinking remained alive within American culture, available as an inheritance. Apart from the role Hollywood movies played in Cavell's education, it would not have been possible for a philosopher who received his professional training within an Anglo-American analytical tradition that has never acknowledged Emerson as a philosopher to have inherited Emerson's ways of thinking at all.

By comparison with *The World Viewed*, *Pursuits of Happiness*, *Contesting Tears*, and *Cities of Words*, some of the writings contained in the present volume may, as we have suggested, appear to be relatively slight, mere occasional pieces. Yet Cavell's occasional pieces bring home, with special vividness, a crucial feature of his aspiration and achievement as a writer; namely, that every one of his writings is an occasional piece. Every one of Cavell's writings responds to, acknowledges, its particular occasion, an occasion inseparable from the writing's "cause." This brings home, in turn, that any and every occasion may be found to call for philosophy. And it is in itself an occasion whenever philosophy finds itself answering to its calling. Some of those occasions—the writing of *The Claim of Reason*, for example—are of extraordinary magnitude within Cavell's career as a whole. Others are more . . . everyday or ordinary. Cavell, like Emerson, is capable of finding something out of the ordinary in the most ordinary of occasions. Philosophy, for Cavell, is not a realm of abstract thought. It is an activity performed by human beings *in* the world, an activity best performed in a spirit of adventure. Philosophy is a way of rising to its occasion.

Even when in a particular piece of writing Cavell may seem only to be reiterating an idea or argument he has already articulated elsewhere, his recounting on this new occasion always constitutes a new accounting, a revision that creates a new thought from the old, enables a new aspect to dawn. Every piece of his writing questions every other, acknowledges every other, is as capable as any other of revealing, and teaching, something about philosophy as Cavell understands and practices it. Attentive readers of this collection can expect the pleasure of discovering, or rediscovering, that every one of Cavell's writings, even those that may seem the slightest, contains at least one new idea or thought, an idea or thought so astonishing that it illuminates the entirety of his work, and which he expresses, puts into words, more fully here, on this occasion, than anywhere else in his writings.

The remarks by Cavell at the Paris Colloquium that we have already had occasion to cite, for example, are studded with such revelatory ideas or thoughts. One is his intuition that thinking about film has had an effect on his "ambitions for philosophical prose." In particular, as he puts it, the "necessity to become evocative in capturing the moods of faces and motions and settings, in their double existence as transient and as permanent," has left "permanent marks" on the way he writes. "It was, I believe," he adds, "more than any other ambition I held, a basis of freedom from the guarded rhythms of philosophy as I had inherited it."[15]

In thinking about film, Cavell is saying with these words, he recognized the need for prose capable of evoking the evanescence of the world on film, the ever-shifting moods of "faces and motions and settings," and capable of capturing, as well, what remains inflexible, fixed, in the physiognomy of the world on film (what in *The World Viewed* he calls the "reality of the unsayable," the "unmoving ground" that makes film capable of exhibiting the world).[16] Then the double existence—the transience and permanence—that is automatically possessed by the world on film, vouchsafed by the ontological conditions of the medium, became an aspiration of Cavell's philosophical prose.

Part of what this means can be registered by saying that each of Cavell's writings (this Paris talk, for example) aspires to permanence (it lives on in these pages). Yet it also aspires to acknowledge, to rise to, the transient occasion that gave rise to it. But the point is also, I take it, that "the moods of faces and motions and settings, in their double existence as transient and permanent," are the stuff of philosophy, as Cavell aspires to practice it, no less than the stuff of film. The originality and power of Cavell's view of skepticism, for example, resides in the way he envisions the onset of skeptical doubt as a scene—not a scene from a stage play, but a scene that happens in the world, like a scene from a movie. For Cavell, writing philosophical prose that is capable of achieving conviction, like writing about film that is capable of achieving conviction, requires the ability, and willingness, to be evocative.

Thus it is quite characteristic and instructive that Cavell's way of contesting the philosophical position staked out by Saul Kripke, in his influential book *Wittgenstein on Rules and Private Language*, is by taking issue with the way Kripke "reads" a particular "scene" from Wittgenstein's *Philosophical Investigations*. (From *PI*, Section 217: "If I have exhausted the justifications [for following the rules of mathematics or of ordinary language as I do] I have reached bedrock, and my spade is turned. Then I am inclined to say, 'This is simply what I do.' ") Hence the following passage from "Philosophy the Day after Tomorrow" (yet another of the recent pieces in the present collection), which provides a perfect illustration of the way Cavell's thinking about film has empowered his prose, freed it to be evocative, helped liberate it from the "guarded rhythms" that keep most philosophical writing from swinging, or soaring. (Writing powerful, evocative prose like this is simply what Cavell does.)

> Kripke . . . takes the teacher's (or speaker's) gesture of showing what he does to be meant as a show of power. . . . I have taken the gesture oppositely, as acknowledging a necessary weakness, I might call it a creative limitation, in teaching (or socialization), stressing

that the arrival at an impasse between teacher and pupil also threatens, and may enlighten, the teacher. This difference of interpretation demands a long story (which I undertake to tell in *Conditions Handsome and Unhandsome*). At the moment I wish to be as uncontroversial as possible and draw a moral from the fact that, whichever way you take the scene of instruction, when the teacher recognizes that she or he has exhausted the justifications, he becomes silent and waits. Satisfaction eludes him, but more words are pointless. Wittgenstein anticipates this inevitable moment of silence in teaching—that the student must at some point go on alone—in the very opening section of the *Investigations*, where he notes, casually but fatefully, "Explanations come to an end somewhere." The moral I draw for Wittgenstein is that an utterance must have a point, whether to inform, amuse, promise, question, insist, beseech—in that sense must be worth saying; and that the point will exceed the saying, is inherently vulnerable, as human action is, to misfortune. . . . And the moral of silence in teaching at the same time implies a task of teaching, namely to demonstrate that informing, amusing, promising, questioning, insisting, beseeching, etc., must themselves be seen to be worth doing. Quite as if teaching must, as it were, provide a reason for speaking at all. As if we might become appalled by the gift of language, the fatedness to speech, the condition Wittgenstein describes as the life form of talkers, of us.[17]

Within the field of film study, it is sometimes supposed that Cavell's writing is impressionistic, unrigorous, self-indulgent. And yet Cavell's ambition is ultimately to be known as a writer. His prose is the measure of his achievement It is, to be sure, unsystematic. That is, Cavell—like Emerson, like Thoreau, like Nietzsche, like Wittgenstein—is not a philosopher who strives to construct a *system* of thought. As a consequence, his writing, like theirs, can be difficult.

Insisting on the difficulty can make it seem—and sometimes it can seem—that reading Cavell is a painful matter. There are times when Cavell's writing is painful. For example, *Contesting Tears* dwells on films, such as *Gaslight*, which in their own ways are as great as the comedies of remarriage Cavell writes about in *Pursuits of Happiness*, but which are at times not pleasurable, are even painful, to view. Cavell's writing does not shrink from this pain. *Pursuits of Happiness* itself, however, is altogether pleasurable to read, to savor. Most of the pieces in the present collection are closer to *Pursuits of Happiness*, in this regard, than to *Contesting Tears*. In them, Cavell generously shares pleasures movies in his experience have given him, as well as pleasures philosophy alone is capable of providing. (Are they the same pleasures?)

Another way to put this is to say that there is poetry to Cavell's writing. In his writings on film, as in the films that move him to write this way about them, art and philosophy cannot be separated. "Unlike the prose of comic theatrical dialogue after Shakespeare," Cavell writes,

> film has a natural equivalent for the medium of Shakespeare's dramatic poetry. I think of it as the poetry of film itself, what it is that happens to figures and objects and places as they are variously molded and displaced by a motion-picture camera and then projected and screened. Every art, every worthwhile human enterprise, has its poetry, ways of doing things that perfect the possibilities of the enterprise itself, make it the one it is. . . . You may think of it as the unteachable point in any worthwhile enterprise. I understand it to be, let me say, a natural vision of film that every motion and station, in particular every human posture and gesture, however glancing, has its poetry, or you may say its lucidity. . . . Any of the arts will be drawn to this knowledge, this perception of the poetry of the ordinary, but film, I would like to say, democratizes the knowledge, hence at once blesses and curses us with it. It says that the perception of poetry is as open to all, regardless as it were of birth or talent, as the ability is to hold a camera on a subject, so that a failure so to perceive, to persist in missing the subject, which may amount to missing the evanescence of the subject, is ascribable only to ourselves . . . , as if to . . . fail to trace the implications of things . . . requires that we persistently coarsen and stupefy ourselves.[18]

We "coarsen and stupefy" ourselves insofar as we think about film, write about film, in ways that miss the poetry of the subject. The study of film cannot be a worthwhile human enterprise insofar as it isolates itself from the kind of criticism Walter Benjamin had in mind when he argued, as Cavell paraphrases him, that "what establishes a work as art is its ability to inspire and sustain criticism of a certain sort, criticism that seeks to articulate the work's idea; what cannot be so criticized is not art."[19] And yet, as Cavell reminds us, Benjamin himself developed "his famous speculations concerning the technological medium of film . . . without consulting a film's idea of itself, or undertaking to suppose that one or another may have such a thing." Contrast *Pursuits of Happiness*, say, in which Cavell treats "the seven films principally studied in that book both as representative of the best work of Hollywood's classical period and (hence) as works capable of reflecting critically on the cultural conditions that make them possible."

Marrying film and philosophy, the writings gathered in the present collection do not miss the poetry of either subject, and thinking about film emerges as a worthwhile human enterprise, indeed. In these writings, the study of film achieves its own poetry, its own "ways of doing things that perfect the possibilities of the enterprise itself, make it the one it is." That is the "unteachable point" of this collection, the lesson it above all aspires to teach.

Notes

1. Stanley Cavell, *Contesting Tears: The Hollywood Melodrama of the Unknown Woman* (Chicago and London: University of Chicago Press, 1996), xi–xii.

2. Stanley Cavell, *Themes Out of School: Effects and Causes* (San Francisco: North Point, 1984), xi.

3. "An Interview with Stanley Cavell (with James Conant)," in Richard Fleming and Michael Payne, editors, *The Senses of Stanley Cavell, Bucknell Review*, Lewisburg, Pa.: Bucknell University Press, 1989, 59.

4. From Cavell's remarks at the Paris Colloquium on *La Projection du Monde* (French translation of *The World Viewed*), 1999.

5. Stanley Cavell, *Must We Mean What We Say?* (New York: Scribner, 1969), xix.

6. From "What Becomes of Things on Film."

7. From "*North by Northwest*."

8. From "On Makavejev on Bergman."

9. From "*Prénom*: Marie."

10. From "Eric Rohmer's *A Tale of Winter*."

11. From "*Groundhog Day*."

12. From "The Good of Film."

13. From "*North by Northwest*."

14. From "The Thought of Movies."

15. From the Paris Colloquium.

16. Stanley Cavell, *The World Viewed: Reflections on the Ontology of Film* (New York: Viking, 1971; Enlarged Edition, Cambridge, Mass.: Harvard University Press, 1979), 148.

17. From "Philosophy the Day after Tomorrow."

18. From "The Thought of Movies."

19. From the Paris Colloquium.

1

What Becomes of Things on Film?

These remarks, more or less, were read at one of the symposia of the Modern Language Association Annual Convention held in Chicago, in December 1977. The title of the symposium was "*Chosisme* and the Cinema: The Perception of Physical Reality in Cinema and Literature." Its idea, as well as the invitation to me to comment on the papers submitted to it, was the work of Professor Terry Comito. The thoughts I put together for my contribution to that occasion have played a role in my further thinking about film out of proportion to its small size (it first appeared in *Philosophy and Literature,* vol. 2 no. 2, fall 1978). A principal place these thoughts are picked up explicitly is in the *Adam's Rib* chapter of my book *Pursuits of Happiness,* where I read the presence of its film-within-the-film (fictionally a home movie) as a demonstration that "no event within a film (say no gesture of framing or editing) is as significant (as 'cinematic') as the event of film itself."

ND DOES THIS TITLE EXPRESS a genuine question? That is, does one accept the suggestion that there is a particular relation (or a particular system of relations, awaiting systematic study) that holds between things and their filmed projections, which is to say between the

First published in *Philosophy and Literature*, fall 1978; reprinted in *Themes Out of School* (North Point Press, 1984; reprinted by University of Chicago Press, 1989.

originals now absent from us (by screening) and the new originals now present to us (in photogenesis)—a relation to be thought of as something's becoming something (say as a caterpillar becomes a butterfly, or as a prisoner becomes a count, or as an emotion becomes conscious, or as after a long night it becomes light)? The title is, at any rate, the working formulation I have given myself for the guiding question of this discussion. Of the many issues and many levels of issue raised by the papers I have been invited to comment upon, I have picked two moments at which work of my own about film has been referred to, wishing to contribute to a conversation in the territory of film study.

The first moment is one in which I am quoted (or Heidegger and I jointly quoted) as saying that "The cinematic image accentuates the conspicuousness, obtrusiveness and obstinacy of things." I am sorry to have given such an impression. The background of what I said[1]—in the course of giving some examples of how thinking about films and thinking about philosophy have drawn upon one another in my work—was this: early in *Being and Time*, Heidegger characterizes the specific way in which the phenomenon occurs, in his terms, of the "worldhood of the world announcing itself"; it is a phenomenon in which a particular mode of sight or awareness is brought into play. What brings this mode of sight into play is a disruption of what Heidegger calls the "work-world," a disruption of the matters of course running among our tools, and the occupations they extend, and the environment which supports these occupations. It is upon the disruption of such matters of course (of a tool, say by its breaking; or of someone's occupation, say because of an injury; or of some absence of material) that the mode of sight then brought forth discovers objects in what Heidegger notes as their conspicuousness, their obtrusiveness, and their obstinacy. Now the foreground of what I said was this: it struck me that this perception or apprehension of the things of our world is part of the grain of silent film comedy; and, more particularly, that Buster Keaton is the silent comic figure whose extraordinary works and whose extraordinary gaze, perhaps the fundamental feature of his character, illuminate and are illuminated by the consequent concept of the worldhood of the world announcing itself.

While I take even this bare broaching of this idea to formulate one possibility of cinematic images of the things of our world, it is no more to be expected that *all* cinematic images carry this force, than it is to be expected that all are in the service of Keaton's species of comedy; any more than the idea of such images exhausts what there is to say about Keaton, or about Heidegger, or about any further relations between them. What the idea ought to do is to help us to see and say at once what it is Keaton permits us to laugh about and what concretely the nature is of the mode of sight from which Heidegger begins his analysis of Being-in-the-world.

This laughter is not defined, for example, by a Bergsonian suggestion that the human being has become machine-like, or vice versa. Keaton is as flexible, as resourceful, as Ulysses, and his giant machines do exactly what they might be expected to do under their circumstances. We have here to do with something about the human capacity for sight, or for sensuous awareness generally, something we might express as our condemnation to project, to inhabit, a world that goes essentially beyond the delivery of our senses. This seems to be the single point of agreement throughout the history of epistemology, at least throughout the modern history of the subject, say since Descartes. The most common conclusion among epistemologists has been some kind of skepticism—a realization that we cannot, strictly speaking, be said to know, to be certain, of the existence of the world of material things at all. I understand Buster Keaton, say in *The General*, to exemplify an acceptance of the enormity of this realization of human limitation, denying neither the abyss that at any time may open before our plans, nor the possibility, despite that open possibility, of living honorably, with good if resigned spirits, and with eternal hope. His capacity for love does not avoid this knowledge, but lives in full view of it. Is he dashing? He is something rarer; he is undashable. He incorporates both the necessity of wariness in an uncertain world, and also the necessary limits of human awareness; gaze as we may, there is always something behind our backs, room for doubt.

Quickly compare Chaplin's knowledge and his world of things, say in *The Gold Rush*, made the same year as *The General* (1925). And take just the two most famous set routines from that film, the Thanksgiving dinner of roast shoe, and the dream-dance of the rolls on forks. In both cases one object is taken as, treated as, something it is not in fact. The ability so to regard objects is studied in Part II of Wittgenstein's *Philosophical Investigations*, through the concept of "seeing as," the concept Wittgenstein takes as the topic of his study of interpretation. To this human capacity for seeing or for treating something *as* something, Wittgenstein attributes our capacity for intimacy in understanding, for what we might call the innerness of the meaning we attach to words and gestures. That the Chaplin routines are in a sense opposites of one another allows them to suggest a complete world of such understanding—in the one case a shoe is treated as a food (a case of dire necessity), in the other a food is treated as a shoe (a case of dire luxury); in both, his imagination gives habitation to his ecstasy and to his grief. The madness of his meaning keeps him sane. (One could say that the worldhood of the world never reveals itself to the little man; he is both too far inside the world for that, and too far outside.)

Say that Keaton and Chaplin make a comedy of the fact that such a creature as a human being is fated to pursue happiness, and that they undertake to demonstrate that such a creature is after all, and to a certain extent, under very exacting conditions, capable of happiness. Then Keaton shows these conditions to be essentially those of virtuousness, or of conscientiousness—for example, of courage, of temperance, of loyalty, and of an aptness of the body that Spinoza calls wisdom; an ability to maintain your poise no matter what happens to your plans (the outside of you). Chaplin shows these conditions to be those of free imagination, especially the imagination of happiness itself—an ability to gather your spirits no matter what has happened to them (the inside of you).

The logic of skepticism requires two things chiefly: that knowledge be discovered to fail in the best cases—in knowing, for example, that I am seated before my fire, or that two plus three is five—and that this failure be discovered in ways open to any normal human being, not something knowable only by experts. It requires only the willingness to know. The logic of the comedy that absorbs skepticism (in opposite ways in Keaton and in Chaplin) requires that we discover outer and inner aptnesses with objects to succeed in the worst cases, and by means of a precision and beauty of conduct in principle open to any normal human being. It requires only the willingness to care.

A second moment at which work of mine is mentioned occurs in Elliot Rubinstein's valuable discussion of Buñuel, when he questions Robbe-Grillet's remark that "the cinema knows only one grammatical mode: the present tense of the indicative."[2] Others, including myself, have in effect questioned what "present" means applied to filmed objects. Rubinstein interestingly extends the worry to the idea of the "indicative mode" more generally, characterizing *Belle de Jour* as exploring "the camera's possibilities in the realm of the subjunctive." What Rubinstein is registering here is not simply the general truth, shown since the beginning of cinema, that the camera can lend itself to the projection of fantasy as readily as of reality; but, more specifically, the discovery that screened events remain intelligible to us if, even without conventional (or grammatical?) warning—specifically, without changes in the sound track, or the acting, or the modes of filming—they alternate between the depiction of the real and of the fantasized, call it the alternation between the indicative and the subjunctive.

Rubinstein claims distinctly more than this minimal intellectual or technical amount; he claims that Buñuel's discovery in *Belle de Jour* constitutes an artistic triumph. Going on my memory of the film from one distant viewing, and guided by Rubinstein's shaping of it, I am inclined to agree with him. But I put the point minimally first to emphasize that the intellectual or technical discovery, and the artistic achievement, do not assure one another. This is the sort of very primitive point of aesthetics that has to be made again and again in speaking of the modern in art, where artistic achievement does so often seem to be a function of some intellectual or technical discovery. An instance at hand is provided by Robbe-Grillet's *Trans-Europe Express*. It was taken by one of the panelists of this session as exemplifying roughly the procedure under discussion in *Belle de Jour*, that of unmarked juxtapositions of the actual and the . . . what? Call it the imaginary. (One already senses such a distinction giving way. And what it should give way to is a set of ideas I expressed in *The World Viewed* by saying: "It is a poor idea of fantasy which takes it to be a world apart from reality, a world clearly showing its unreality. Fantasy is precisely what reality can be confused with" [p. 85].) But *Trans-Europe Express* is, I find, a more or less uninteresting piece of work. And it is, for me, a matter of aesthetic logic that no procedure discovered in a particular work can be proven by that work to have greater artistic point than the work itself achieves, or some relevant part of it. (Of course the work may inspire a better or different artist to look more deeply into that procedure's possibilities. And of course we must not suppose ourselves to know yet whether, nor how, the procedures in question really are the "same.") Then shall we say that *Belle de Jour's* superiority is not a function of any such procedure, but is due rather to the presence of such phenomena as Catherine Deneuve, and the camerawork of Sacha Vierney, and the genius of Buñuel? But I think one feels immediately that such an alternative is false to one's experience of the film, that the procedure in question is indeed integral to the artistic achievement of the film, and that the phenomena of actress, camera, and director are to be accounted for by determining how the procedure lends itself to them, and contrariwise. I would like to say: in Buñuel's film the procedure has found its natural subject, which, if we accept this film as a masterpiece of the medium of film, means: in *Belle de Jour* film has found one of its master subjects. What is this subject?

Buñuel says, or someone says for him: the masochistic nature of a woman's impulses.[3] Rubinstein says, or suggests: the balance between sadism and bourgeois domesticity. How could we convince ourselves that these are answers, good answers, to the question I formulated?

I note that there is another masterpiece of film made within a year of *Belle de Jour* that employs the procedure of unmarked juxtapositions of reality with some opposition to reality, and which maintains their balance, the irresolution of them, through to the end: I mean Bergman's *Persona*. And that film, too, has as what we might call its subject something about the imagination of a woman, or of a beautiful woman, or perhaps of two women; which no doubt in part means: a man's imagination of the imagination of women, or perhaps a man's compulsion to imagine the imagination of a woman. More particularly, both films concern the meaning, or limits, or conditions, of female identity, hence no doubt of human identity. (I do not wish to disguise that I take the accurate statement of a work's subject to be an obligation of criticism.)

What is it about film that lends itself to such a subject? (The validity and pressure of such a question is what I take to demand so solemn a topic as "the ontology of film.") Two further films—masterpieces of their own kind—might be allowed to have a bearing on the further specification of the subject we are seeking to formulate: Hitchcock's *Vertigo*,[4] from a decade earlier; and Capra's *It's A Wonderful Life*, from a decade before that. The climax of the Capra is as subjunctive as a stretch of film can be, the realization of the wish that one had never been born; and it is filmed and acted in no special way and with no conventional marks to indicate its break with the larger body of the film. It is true that we as viewers are not in doubt about the shift of the plane of reality, but the character with whom we identify is tortured by exactly this doubt; it is an expression of this character's self-doubt, doubt about the worth of his existence. And since this worth is explicitly characterized as a matter of the difference his existence has made in the world, the doubt can be said to be about his identity—something amply registered at the climax of the climax as he turns in anguish from friends to mother to wife, accosting them with the demands: Don't you know me? Tell me who I am. In *Vertigo* we do not exactly move from a real place to a projected place, but we are made to share the hero's quasi-hallucinatory, quasi-necrophilic quest in the realm of the subjunctive for the woman he imagines dead. The confusion over the question whether there is one woman or two, or whether one woman is alive or dead, feels like a confusion within his own identity. His existence takes place elsewhere than in the world we see.

The point, at once critical and theoretical, of considering the procedure of juxtaposed realities is to enable us to do what any reading of a film must do—account for the frames of the film being what they are, in the order they are in; for example, to say what motivates the camera to look and to move as and where it looks and moves. The Capra and the Hitchcock films make nakedly clear the power of film to materialize and to satisfy (hence to dematerialize and to thwart) human wishes that escape the satisfaction of the world as it stands; as perhaps it will ever, or can ever, in fact stand. (Whose wishes, a character's, or the viewer's? We would, I think, like to say both. But the justification of this answer will require an understanding of the nature of a viewer's "identification" with screened characters.) I think it cannot be an accident that the actor in both films is James Stewart, that both Capra and Hitchcock see in Stewart's temperament (which, of course, is to say, see in what becomes of that temperament on film, its photogenesis) the capacity to stake identity upon the power of wishing, upon the capacity and purity of one's imagination and desire—not on one's work, or position, or accomplishments, or looks, or intelligence. Call the quality Stewart projects a willingness for suffering—his quality Capra also records in *Mr. Smith Goes to Washington*, and that John Ford used in *The Man Who Shot Liberty Valance*. It is the quality that would admit him to the company of the women whose search for their identities seems to have traced the contours of the subject of film to which I have been wanting to give expression. Then call the subject the identifying or the inhabitation of a feminine region of the self, whether the person whose self it is be male or female.

(A comparison seems immediately called for with Mizoguchi's *Ugetsu*. I do not feel that I know the temperament or the environment of this male well enough to assay his photogenetic possibilities—for example, his femininity. But I note that his wish, anyway his final wish, is not for translation into an opposed habitation, but for a particular figure to inhabit, or reinhabit, his own. This wish seems to me to have its source not in the woman in him, but in the child in him. Its materialization is of a woman moving about his familiar room, and it occurs as he is curled on the floor; our response to it is not that of a cry in the throat but of a break in the heart.)

That to be human is to have, or to risk having, this capacity to wish; that to be human is to wish, and in particular to wish for a completer identity than one has so far attained; and that such a wish may project a complete world *opposed* to the world one so far shares with others: this is a way of taking up the cause of Shakespearean Romance. If so, it is not surprising that a filmic procedure which taps this cause is one that juxtaposes modes and moods of reality as a whole, taunts them with one another. So romance in turn shares with skepticism the realization, in the terms of Descartes's *First Meditation*, that "there are no conclusive indications by which waking life can be distinguished from sleep." The consequence of this realization, Descartes goes on to say, is that "I am quite astonished, and my bewilderment is such that it is almost able to convince me that I am sleeping." In both skepticism and romance, knowledge, call it consciousness as a whole, must go out in order that a better consciousness can come to light. (The idea of modes and moods of reality altering together as totalities, or the idea that the concepts of consciousness and of the world as such are made for one another, in one another's image, is epitomized in Wittgenstein's remark near the end of the *Tractatus*: the world of the happy is quite another than that of the unhappy. To this remark we might add that the worlds may be juxtaposed within the same breast.)

With one final film admitted to this discussion I will be ready to draw a moral. Rubinstein quotes Susan Sontag on Godard's films as follows: "In Godard's films things display a wholly alienated character. Characteristically, they are used with indifference, neither skillfully nor clumsily; they are simply there. 'Objects exist,' Godard has written, 'and if one pays more attention to them than to people, it is precisely because they exist more than these people. Dead objects are still alive. Living people are often already dead.' " I know this quotation from Godard only from his voice, or half-voice, as narrator of *Two or Three Things I Know about Her.* We know that we are to be wary of granting the whole truth to any remark of this narrator, for at least the reason that he recurrently questions his own remarks. *Two or Three Things*, made the same year as *Belle de Jour*, is also a film about a bourgeoise who spends afternoons as a prostitute, and also explicitly links questions about her identity with speculations about the nature and existence of the external world. This film contains a juxtaposition of filmed objects to whose extraordinariness the filmmaker Alfred Guzzetti has called special attention.[5] With shots of the woman, and certain others, in a cafe-bar, the camera alternates, with progressively closer shots, a cup of coffee just stirred, and at last peers over the cup's rim until the bubbling liquid swirling as a whole fills the cinemascope rectangle; the sound track rises to a poeticizing meditation that fits our willingness to endow this image with the power to invoke the swirling of the universe, and hence the question of its origin and ending.

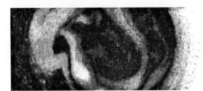

Figure 1.1

Whereupon we cut to an image of the rough barman filling a shot glass, then drawing a beer from a machine of pull faucets which now fills the rectangle.

Figure 1.2

Figure 1.3

One possible reading of the juxtaposition of the cup-universe and the barman is as a rebuke to our willingness for a poetic meditation on universal origins when we do not even know where the beer and the coffee we drink on earth come from—that we drink them in real places made by real people for just this purpose; and that they are handed to us by real people whose livelihoods depend upon their being bought. We might speculate, among other things, upon whether the gleaming beer dispenser, worked by the barman as he observes the scene of meditation, is a comment on the idea of a movie camera.

The moral I draw is this: the question what becomes of objects when they are filmed and screened—like the question what becomes of particular people, and specific locales, and subjects and motifs when they are filmed by individual makers of film—has only one source of data for its answer, namely the appearance and significance of just those objects and people that are in fact to be found in the succession of films, or passages of films, that matter to us. To express their appearances, and define those significances, and articulate the nature of this mattering, are acts that help to constitute what we might call film criticism. Then to explain how these appearances, significances, and matterings—these specific events of photogenesis—are made possible by the general photogenesis of film altogether, by the fact, as I more or less put it in *The World Viewed*, that objects on film are always already displaced, *trouvé* (i.e., that we as viewers are always already displaced before them), would be an undertaking of what we might call film theory.

Notes

1. In "Leopards in Connecticut," *The Georgia Review* 30 (1976): 233–62. The passage now appears in the appendix to *Pursuits of Happiness*.

2. Rubinstein's "Buñuel's World, or The World and Buñuel" also (with this of mine) appears in *Philosophy and Literature*, fall 1978.

3. Cf. the Introductory Note to the English presentation of *Belle de Jour*, prepared by Robert Adkinson (New York, 1971).

4. Robin Wood cites *Vertigo* as a touchstone for assessing certain matters of the viewer's distance or involvement with the events of *Persona* in "The World Without, The World Within," reprinted in *Ingmar Bergman: Essays in Criticism*, ed. Stuart M. Kaminsky (Oxford, 1975). Reprinted in this same collection, Susan Sontag's essay on *Persona* momentarily contrasts, hence compares, that film with *Belle de Jour*.

5. In a long study of this film prepared for a meeting of the American Film Seminar in 1975. Revised, and with a full body of frame enlargements, Guzzetti's study of Godard's film was published by Harvard University Press in 1980.

$ $

2

On Makavejev on Bergman

In our times, from the highest class of society down to the lowest, every one lives as under the eye of a hostile and dreaded censorship. Not only in what concerns others, but in what concerns themselves, the individual, or the family, do not ask themselves—what do I prefer? or, what would suit my character and disposition? or, what would allow the best and highest in me to have fair play, and enable it to grow and thrive? They ask themselves, what is suitable to my position? what is usually done by persons of my station and pecuniary circumstances? or (worse still) what is usually done by persons of a station and circumstances superior to mine? I do not mean that they choose what is customary, in preference to what suits their inclination. It does not occur to them to have any inclination, except for what is customary. Thus the mind itself is bowed to the yoke: even in what people do for pleasure, conformity is the first thing thought of; they live in crowds; they exercise choice only among things commonly done: peculiarity of taste, eccentricity of conduct, are shunned equally with crimes: until by dint of not following their own nature, they have no nature to follow: their human capacities are withered and starved: they become incapable of any strong wishes or native pleasures, and are generally without either opinions or feelings of home growth, or properly their own. Now is this, or is it not, the desirable condition of human nature?

—John Stuart Mill, *On Liberty*

First published in *Critical Inquiry*, winter 1979; reprinted in Vlada Petric, editor, *Film and Dreams: An Approach to Bergman* (Redgrave, 1981) and in *Themes Out of School*.

These remarks were occasioned by an experiment and a paper presented by the Yugoslavian filmmaker Dusan Makavejev to a conference entitled "Bergman and Dreams" held at Harvard University in January, 1978. The experiment consisted of a screening made entirely of material from the films of Ingmar Bergman, chosen and arranged with the following ideas in mind:

> At times, Bergman's films look more like a book than a movie. Often, they can be reduced to "talking heads" moving through rooms. However, the nonverbal sequences in Bergman's films are replete with inner meaning and dreamlike atmosphere. It is in these sequences that Bergman tells us of many subliminal processes occurring beneath the level of the verbal interaction
>
> The original intention for the format of the presentation was to compose a single reel of the strongest nonverbal sequences from several of Bergman's most famous films, arrange them in some meaningful order, and screen them without any introductory explanation at the conference. The order of the sequences was worked out so that various events would not only relate to and resonate with each other, but also that parts of a sequence would have significant juxtapositions with other parts of the same sequence.
>
> I decided to project alongside the black and white sequences two more recent films of Bergman that were photographed in color. Not only were these additional sequences in color, but they were also widescreen, thus producing a stunning visual collage. Thus, the schematization of the program is . . . : I. A single-screen projection of eleven black and white nonverbal sequences (thirty minutes). II. A three-screen simultaneous projection of black and white sequences flanked by color sequences (twenty-five minutes). III. A single-screen projection of the final minute and a half of *Persona*.

These descriptions are taken from the paper Makavejev, in association with his student Matthew Duda, prepared for the publication of the proceedings of the conference. However, it was expressly not to be read at the conference. On the contrary, Makavejev wished to manifest his healthy doubts about the primacy, or say authority, of the verbal. In fact the similar document that appears in the proceedings is a later version of that paper, together with other matters, put together by Duda, who had also assisted in the selection and screening of the Bergman sequences. While my remarks were not written for the conference, they are included (reprinted from the winter 1979 number of *Critical Inquiry*), along with other postconference papers, as part of its proceedings, issued in *Film and Dreams: An Approach to Bergman,* edited by Vlada Petric (Redgrave Publishing Company, South Salem, N.Y., 1981). I am, I trust, still learning from the talks I have had with Makavejev about his work and from the times I have listened to and watched him speak publicly about his films and about film generally—about the practical, artistic, political, intellectual, moral (though he may distrust that word) contexts of their making. I am also indebted to Vlada Petric, who organized the conference as well as edited its proceedings, for many exchanges about Makavejev's work as well as about other names and topics in the history and theory of film.

I HAD BEEN DELAYED AND ONLY arrived at Makavejev's Bergman compilation as the lights were going down for the screening to begin. I would not be surprised later to learn that Makavejev had, to deliver a few words of introduction, put on a black cape and a woman's bright red hat. I mean that while I was taken by surprise in learning of the particular objects he sported, I might have known that he had found at hand some way of putting a seam in our experience, of joining it, hence differentiating it, to and from what was to succeed our arrival in the basement auditorium of the Carpenter Center; some way of acknowledging that his experience was about to intervene, along certain lines, in ours.

That opening acknowledgment was in effect continued by the beginning of his presentation at the close of the film, presenting himself for discussion, no hat and cape now, no words either, no business at all, just standing at the front of the room, looking over the lectern at us, awaiting our pleasure, or whatever it would be. When it dawned on me that he would not speak first, and that I might have known that too (since I had come to accept, over the previous couple of years, a philosophical ambition in his work), I tried both to stay in the experience and to be aware of the length of time lapsing. Makavejev later said that it had been three minutes, but in a group of some three hundred souls, at attention, the resulting magnification of time was immeasurable. So I might itemize for future reference the elements of Makavejev's presentation in this way: (1) his verbal/visual introduction; (2) the screening; (3) his silent introduction, or invitation to discussion; and his two documents, one of which preceded the former items, one of which followed, call them (0) and (4) respectively. Document (4) is the earlier version of the Makavejev-Duda paper from which my introductory note quotes; document (0) is interpolated, explicitly as such, into the later, published version of (4).

Makavejev variously declares his intention in running together non-verbal sequences from Bergman's films. For example, in the conference paper that I quoted from in my introductory note (document [4]) he says it is "to produce a singular experience for the participants at the conference"—quite as if he were composing his own film for them. I can testify that for this viewer the intention to provide a singular experience was realized. Makavejev goes on to say that his experiment addresses the question Is it possible to construct a Bergman film that Bergman never made? I cannot testify to the answer to this question because I still do not know what constitutes, that is, what individuates, "a Bergman film." Maybe Makavejev could make one; maybe out of images Bergman would or could not use; and maybe another filmmaker could not.

The question Is it possible to construct a Bergman film . . . ? serves to make us think again about the relation of film and theater, about the fact that plays have productions and performances whereas films, by comparison, have their awful integrity or finality: modifying them feels like mutilating them. I suppose this is the feeling that, at best, could have produced the outraged question that at last broke the silence following the screening. It was a question, a comment rather, rebuking Makavejev's irresponsibility toward the prints he would have used in order to piece together ("re-edit" would hardly have been the word) his Bergman film ("his" "Bergman" "film"). The outrage rather takes it that Bergman's films are (or had been) identical with the prints Makavejev used, and that those prints were not Makavejev's to use, and hence that Makavejev's artistic probing suggested that he may not know his social obligations toward the property of others.

Having reassured the group that the prints he used of the Bergman films are fully intact, Makavejev addressed the feeling I imagined to underlie the outraged question by heading it in the direction, as in his films, of the question of outrage. He proposed that an accurate description of what he had done to Bergman was to excerpt him, thus allowing us to think how little control film audiences have over the conditions in which they view films—almost as little as over the events they view on the screen, thus perfecting the state of passivity in regarding them. In contrast, members of an audience of a (live) performance are participants in it in varying degrees; writing can be read at any tempo, at any length, in any order, and a passage reread at will; music can in addition be practiced, for example, hands separately. Those who praise film as the realization of the idea of a total art work, incorporating the other arts, appear to me to miss the equally obvious fact that film does not reciprocate; it does not lend itself—with but minor exceptions—to incorporation by the other arts. It is the perfect consumer, with a stomach for anything.

The matter of passiveness in viewing films must be an especially poignant matter for Makavejev, partly because he is so natural a maker of film, so generous a lover of film, that film's liabilities are his natural inheritance; and partly because, no doubt for this reason, one of the great subjects of his films is the variety of human passiveness, as if his interest in making his Bergman film is to say to his *semblable*, and to say it in the form of an *hommage*: Yes, the passiveness of your men and women is one revelation of the nature of film (of viewing and being viewed, of victimization), but further revelations are possible. You may have discovered only the passiveness of revenge, and revenge itself may be causing this discovery. But who says that revenge is the last of human possibilities?

Something Makavejev calls a hypothesis about his experiment is this: "A film in which all the images are . . . [Bergman's] own but put into a different structure would offer to the viewer a possibility of exploring the inner meaning of Bergman's narrative." When later he finds the experiment to have succeeded, he accounts for the success more specifically, or practically, by claiming again that his reconstruction stayed within Bergman's imagination while at the same time it "[destroyed] the most important features of Bergman's narrative films—the plot structure, forcing the audience to perceive other components of his directorial style, such as camera movement, light impulses, *mise-en-scène*, shot composition, use of objects as symbols, faces in close-up, and color interactions." Nothing, I feel, is more important—who could deny it?—than to get an audience to perceive the specific events on the screen. (To have to insist on something like this is an indictment of our film culture. Surely serious readers of novels or audiences of plays know that things beyond what you may call their plots go to make up their art. Do they not?) But to effect the perception of specific events in a human work, with the goal of offering a possibility of exploring the inner meaning of, let us say, a narrative, is just something I understand the work of criticism to be.

Then let us call Makavejev's screening experiment a work of criticism. (His suggestion that it may be called a film is apt to beg a significant question of criticism.) The liability of criticism in words is that words can be cheap, the product of what Makavejev in his opening sentence calls "talking heads": mere critics using themselves only from the neck up. The liability of criticism in images is that the juxtaposition of images can be cheap, the product of mumbling bodies: mere entertainers using themselves only from the neck down. In any case the point of criticism lies in its fruitfulness. Criticism in words might take you away from the object under attention, say by avoiding everything but plot, as though everything else were ornamental or arbitrary. Criticism in images might take you away from the object by avoiding the plot, suggesting that it is arbitrary or incidental (or worse: it may encourage a perpetual assumption of poor criticism itself, that you know what the plot is, and how to assess it, apart from the specific events on the screen). So the fruitfulness of criticism depends upon how it is taken, what appropriation is made of it. What is the plot of *Persona*? And is it useful to assume that the brilliance of its exploration of the hunger for words and the hunger for silence, or for emptiness and fullness, or for absence and existence, or for otherness and oneness, would have been feasible for Bergman apart from the banality and evanescence of what we may call its plot? Are banality and stultification of plot Bergman's price for his art, or essential ingredients of its medium? Or both? What form of criticism is best placed to give us an answer here?

How was Makavejev's experiment in criticism appropriated by its audience? The claim I remember being made out loud most frequently during the discussion was that the experiment was not shocking, as though there were some honor in not being shockable. Makavejev says that for the three minutes of silence that unpredictably greeted the end of his screening it seemed to him that the audience was still dreaming. I do not find this quite fits my experience of that silence. I was grateful for Makavejev's power in having created this experience, and while at first I was tempted to embarrassment, I was drawn back into the experience by the candor and interest I felt in Makavejev's presence as he looked silently back at us. It was a therapeutic passage, a time in which one's experience of another and of oneself seemed fresh, seemed capable of surprise, of instruction; in which one's experience of time seemed fresh.

There were, to my mind, two primary pieces of instruction in the freshness of the inner voices made audible in that silence. One voice spoke simply of the power and energy brought to one's experience by the sheer fact of being a member of something to call an audience—a massive fact that systematic study of film, with its enforced isolation and registered audiences, is prompted to ignore. Here was a chance, exactly because no one could predict what the normal reaches of the experience would be nor what the discussion might sound like, to discover or construct an experience in common; or, perhaps I should say, to possess not only an experience in common but a certain spiraling of interpretations around it; a chance, as with old comedies, to be grateful to one's strangers rather than resentful of their intrusions, their differences from us. While this opportunity was not improved, a chance for something else almost as good might have occurred to one, namely to recognize by oneself that one may have nothing to say in a given moment and that this need be no disgrace; a chance to see that it is no point of honor to make oneself a talking head, or machine, or monkey merely because someone (perhaps oneself) cannot bear silence and gives you a penny of attention.

A related voice of instruction spoke not exactly of having nothing to say but eloquently of not wanting to say anything, of wanting not to speak. This is another creative possibility that normal routines of education ignore or suppress. It may be true of any experience of significance that one is reluctant in a given moment to try to form words for it. Sometimes one feels violated in having to produce words that one is years away from being ready to say; sometimes one may be only minutes away, but that time is no less decisive for being short. Naturally such facts may serve as excuses for someone for whom the time for words never comes, for whom the cry for change is always awkwardly too soon, for whom discussions always end before the propitious moment for satisfaction (as though others somehow exist in different circumstances). If the audience of Makavejev's experiment was really still doing something like dreaming and for that reason silent, I would accept this as good evidence that the experiment had constituted the showing of a film, because a natural experience of involvement in a film (inhabiting in its own way the realm of art) is that afterwards one has to awaken to the world.[1]

While Makavejev offers his experiment as "not a definitive product, but only a research . . . a new kind of evidence in film studies," it should help us to perceive that an immediate kind of evidence for studying a film, a kind taking the form of what I earlier called "criticism by images," is the use of other films: significant films are inherently criticisms of other films. Otherwise, of course, Makavejev could not have conceived of his research experiment as itself a film. But then it is worth going over again one's experience of the experiment to discover whether it is right to say that "the audience followed and accepted the new structure [of the single-screen projection] as a unique continuity, that is, as a 'single' film" (perhaps as in certain kinds of musical medleys, generally comic), or whether it is better to say that the single-screen projection rather worked like vertically "compressed cinema" in which the nine films, represented in the twenty-five sequences, each maintains an autonomy that works upon one another associatively as well as reflexively; that is, both as separate films may work upon one another and as the parts of a single film work upon one another.

The nature or natures of autonomy is something Makavejev's procedures as a filmmaker depend upon and reflect upon. He declares himself to be the author of *Sweet Movie* in the statement distributed beforehand to the participants at the conference (document [0])—written to "trigger the audience's thinking about the real meaning of Bergman's films." The statement was itself triggered, evidently, by Makavejev's having had to think about the real meaning of *Sweet Movie*. (It begins: "Recently, after a screening of my film, *Sweet Movie*, someone asked me. . . .") I might add that even should some segment of the audience respond to these events as forming a single continuity, this would not prove that they have on their hands, in Makavejev's words, "a kind of psychological Frankenstein." The Frankenstein in question may rather be, to correct a familiar mistake here where it may make all the difference, not the depicted monster but the (in the case of film, generally undepicted) maker of the monster, a role we are thus invited to project ourselves into, or rather to incorporate, in order to be in a position to ask ourselves in the right way, Why are the events on the screen as they are?

It was also the author of *Sweet Movie* who was capable of the most memorable set of critical observations made in the course of my attendance at the sessions of the conference. During a discussion of the opening sequence of more or less explicitly autobiographical images and reflexive cinematic preoccupations that form the authorial prologue to *Persona*, Makavejev interrupted from the floor, saying, in effect, "Why speculate here? Science can be brought to bear and we can look at what the actual images show us. From Tausk's 1919 paper 'On the Origin of the Influencing Machine' we learn that each schizophrenic has his own all-powerful dictating machine. This machine is our genitals, projected and seen as foreign, determining our lives, the source of life. Bergman's depiction of the parts of a projector is his declaration of his machine, so conceived. Now by editing, the old woman becomes (is replaced by) the live young boy. The woman is magnified and blurred. In relation to her the boy is the size of a fetus. But what is the blurring for? The capacity for sight matures in the womb at about five or six months. So blurring suggests that the child in question is yet unborn." If you can think like this, nothing is beyond mattering to you. The implication I draw is not that it is necessary to be a significant filmmaker in order to be capable of such remarks but rather that some significant filmmakers are also born teachers and that this fact about them may enter into the experience of their films, yielding the ecstatic experience—perhaps therapeutic—of being encouraged genuinely to think.

I take this as my cue for saying that my appropriation of Makavejev's experiment was and remains determined by my acceptance of his corpus of films as a significant present in the history of the art of film, a place in which the future of filmmaking, hence of significant film theory and of film studies generally, will have to work itself out. I do not propose to discuss this achievement at much length here, but I wish to give a concrete sense of Makavejev's remarks about his experiment as issuing from an experience of, especially, *Sweet Movie*.

Makavejev's recurrence to the ideas of death and birth, in his critical remark about the opening of *Persona* and in his quoting (in document [0]) of Bergman's statement "Each film is my last" (commenting about this that "it is not only a statement about imminent death, but a testimony of an obsessive need to be reborn over and over again"), recalls the recurrence of the ideas of death and birth in *Sweet Movie*. The sound track opens with a song asking "Is there life after birth?" and the images end with a corpse coming to life; in between, the film is obsessed with images of attempts to be born. The question about life after birth—posing the question whether we may hope for mortality as prior to the question whether we may hope for immortality—has the satisfying sound of one of Feuerbach's or the early Marx's twists that turn Christianity upside down into socialism. (Compare this from Marx's "A Contribution to the Critique of Hegel's 'Philosophy of Right': Introduction": "Luther, to be sure, overcame servitude based on devotion, but by replacing it with servitude based on conviction. He shattered faith in authority by restoring the authority of faith. . . . But if Protestantism was not the real solution it at least posed the problem correctly. Thereafter it was no longer a question of the layman's struggle with the priest outside of him, but of his struggle with his own inner priest, his priestly nature. And if the Protestant transformation of the German laity into priests emancipated the lay popes—the princes together with their clergy, the privileged and the philistines—so the philosophical transformation of the priestly Germans into men will emancipate the people.") It is the great concluding moments of *Sweet Movie*, however, which bear direct comparison with the great opening moments of *Persona*. But even to describe those concluding sonorities relevantly requires a general idea of the film as a whole.

Sweet Movie is, at a minimum, the most original exploration known to me of the endless relations between documentary and fictional film, incorporating both; hence in that way an original exploration of the endless relations between reality and fantasy. Its use of documentary footage declares that every movie has a documentary basis—at least in the camera's ineluctable interrogation of the natural endowment of the actors, the beings who submit their being to the work of film. My private title for Makavejev's construction of *Sweet Movie* (his fifth film) and of (his third and fourth films) *Innocence Unprotected* and *WR: Mysteries of the Organism* is "the film of excavation." (WR means Wilhelm Reich, on whom the film is a meditation.) I mean by this of course my sense of his work's digging to unearth buried layers of the psyche but also my sense that these constructions have the feeling of reconstruction—as of something lost or broken. The search at once traces the integrity (you might say the autonomy) of the individual strata of a history and plots the positions of adjacent strata. I accept as well the implied sense—something the experience of Makavejev's last three films conveys to me—that these constructions are inherently the working out of a group's genius, its interactions, not of one individual's plans; though it is true and definitive of Makavejev's work that a group's interactions, or those of shifting groups, work themselves out into comprehensible forms because a given individual is committed to seeing to it that they may.

This so far says nothing at all about how these autonomies, adjacencies, and interactions are devised and directed. But all I wish to convey here is an intuition of the kind of differences there will be between works made by the director of excavation sites and by, let us say, the operator of a switchboard (I take the title of Makavejev's second film—*Love Affair; or, The Case of the Missing Switchboard Operator*—to give one description of the director of a film, hence to name his relation to this work). And I would like to encourage as well an intuition of the differences there may be between works made on the principles of Eisensteinian montage or of Surrealist juxtapositions and those which are made on the principle of what I am thinking of as the aligning of adjacent strata. The former seek to fix or to flout significance, perhaps to suggest that significance is necessarily private or public or arbitrary or infinite or nonexistent. The latter propose significance as the intersection of nature and history, as a task of a continuous and natural unfolding of interpretations, each felt as complete and each making possible the next, until a human form of life fits together. (This is how classical narrative may be understood to direct itself.) The analogue of archeological excavation would accordingly realize what Bazin wanted from continuous shooting and deep focus without having to invoke an a priori or fixed understanding of the general differences between montage and continuity. (Of course all these modes of abutment are employed by Makavejev. Just as any good film may be expected to require authors who are, in varying degrees, both excavators and switchboard operators. And of course I am not prepared to define what a continuous and natural unfolding of interpretations is. I propose an intuition for investigation, of which the discovery and justification of this phrase is a proposed first step.)

The conscience of *Sweet Movie* is most hideously captured in a sequence of literal excavation—the Nazi documentary footage of German troops exhuming bodies from mass graves in the Katyn Forest. A lifelong participant in a society of declared socialist aspirations, Makavejev is asking: Was my revolution capable even of this? Has it cannibalized everything that has touched it? Is it true that the Red Army committed a mass murder of the Polish officer corps? The film shows a card which contains Anthony Eden's response to this news: "Let us think of these things always. Let us speak of them never." For Makavejev, that conspiracy of silence, call it mass hypocrisy, is a prescription for self-administered mass death. Mere film alone cannot prove who caused and buried the corpses in the Katyn Forest, but this film directly refuses the conspiracy of silence about it.

The focal characters of *Sweet Movie* are two women, Miss World and Captain Anna Planeta, who respectively represent, more or less allegorically, the Americanized and the Sovietized forms of contemporary existence; though, as their names suggest, they are to be found everywhere. These women never meet, but their conditions intertwine under the tension of the representations and ideas of the film, especially of birth and death, of sexuality and seduction, and of food, of eating and being eaten. The muse of old revolutions, Captain Anna, living on memories, presides over a drifting boat named Survival; the North American Miss World, figure of an early republic and living on anticipation, is presided over successively by a mother-in-law, a husband, and a Latin lover, types from farce and romance let loose. The film opens on the North American side with a burlesque beauty or sweetness contest and continues with a satiric honeymoon trip about Niagara Falls and a wedding night of apparently Swiftian ambition. The first problem with the film, for me, is in understanding why this ambition is so weakly realized; the opening jokes on America are too broad, too abstract. The beauty contest in the form of competitive pelvic examinations seems too corny an idea to bear the weight of the themes it takes upon itself. Anyone who has given a thought to beauty contests knows that the plain facts about them must be more fantastic than a ribald allegory will capture and knows most particularly that beauty contests are burlesque shows. Then perhaps the real target of this satire is the real burlesque show. But the pleasures, the sweetness, no doubt somewhat uneducated, in either the real or the artificial exhibition is not something one can imagine a thinker of Makavejev's aspirations criticizing by making abstract fun of them, distancing himself from such expressions of needfulness, from the victims and the victimizers in these entertainments. Indeed, one of the qualities you come to depend upon in his work is its generosity toward pleasures and aspirations not exactly his own. (The failure of this generosity may even be derived as a characteristic of what he would mean by tyranny.) This is especially true in his feeling for popular entertainments or exhibitions, represented in his first film, *Man Is Not a Bird*, and in his third, *Innocence Unprotected*, in images of the circus. But then here is a first answer to this problem of *Sweet Movie*: images of circus acts (of all but inhuman acrobatic feats; of the things human beings can train themselves to swallow—swords, snakes, fire) together with vaudeville science (sometimes a sensational lecture, sometimes a demonstration of the powers of hypnosis) at once represent the degree to which society trains us to be freaks and form Makavejev's declarations of the powers or sources or responsibilities of the fact and the art of film. Makavejev cannot then be exempting himself from the worlds he departs from and depicts. But I knew that without such evidence. The therapeutic effect that watching and thinking about his films seems to have upon me is possible only as a function of the sense of inclusion in an enterprise honestly in search of self-understanding.

Of course if those opening sequences are badly done, without interesting ideas or true feelings, then these considerations of mine will not save them. But these considerations do make me want to see those sequences again. Then I would ask what the participating gynecologist, and the instrument, I mean the camera, his interest directs, are looking for up there: a hymen? a fetus? a penis? Makavejev credits Bergman with having been "the first major contemporary filmmaker who publicly raised the essential question: 'Am I, indeed, a woman?' " Is the pelvic examination a way of confessing that we do not know what a woman, in oneself or others, is?

The film fully begins for me (the three times I have seen it) when the second narrative focus—the boat of the drifting revolution—begins being cut in periodically with the first. This experience suggests an asymmetry of interest between the external depiction of Americanization and the internal expression of Sovietization and suggests that the tissue of cliche in which the opening sequences are wrapped is itself a perception or confession that socialist criticisms of cliched Americanized aspirations are themselves cliches. This is a problem for a socialist; for a liberal, let us say, it may be a relief. But why isn't the issue for both of them to understand what happened to the fact and the idea of liberty under Americanization and to understand what happened to the idea and fact of community under Sovietization? Why isn't it?

Simultaneous issues of individual liberty and of true community, issues forever compromising one another in liberalism and in socialism, come to a crisis in *Sweet Movie* in the documentary or quasi-documentary footage of members of the Muehl commune—the film's best-remembered feature—where individuals who claim to witness the absolute bondage in which social existence has secured them band together to permit one another something you might see as absolute freedom. This freedom is to be achieved by a transgression of social taboos as specific and systematic as Freud's transgressions of defense mechanisms when he accompanied his patients on their journeys back. Expressing themselves in spitting food on one another, in vomiting at will, pissing, shitting, in mock self-castrations, the members of the commune go further than one might have expected to see in turning themselves inside out. They regress to the condition of birth as if to give birth to themselves from their otherwise dead bodies, the group assisting as anagogic midwives, oiling, wiping, and powdering their huge, bouncing babies and praising their performances of the natural functions of living things. Thus is Makavejev's opening question of life after birth given one answer, and Bergman's opening fantasy of the dead woman and the fetus given one natural realization.

The center of the action of the commune sequence is a communal meal, a feast whose ritualization strikes me as possessing, for all its confusion of tongues, a working solemnity. I think of Marx's characterization of religion as the heart of a heartless world, and I ask myself what the things of acceptance and redemption might look like to those who would actually bring such concepts to earth—as if inventing them and giving them a heart. I had not liked Makavejev's complaint that Bergman's "conception of God, especially, the God who does not love people and who makes them unexplainably miserable, seems to me incomprehensible and gratuitous for a serious artist." If this is bad for a serious artist, I felt, it is bad for any human being; but is it a matter over which human beings have a choice? But I also felt that Makavejev is meeting Bergman at once on Bergman's ground and on Marx's: "The critique of religion is the prerequisite of every critique." What Makavejev sees in religion and how he effects his critique of it will come up again.

(Since in the working of this film and in the mode of thinking it exemplifies, apt conjunction is everything, allowing the mutual excavation of concepts, I shall quote from the early pages of C. G. Jung's autobiography, *Memories, Dreams, Reflections*, without comment (as if one might use a quotation within the body of a text, that is, after the text has begun, as what you may call an internal epigraph), some fragments from his interpretation of "the earliest dream I can remember, a dream which was to preoccupy me all my life": "At all events, the phallus of this dream seems to be a subterranean God 'not to be named,' and such it remained throughout my youth, reappearing whenever anyone spoke too emphatically about Lord Jesus. . . . The fear of the 'black man,' which is felt by every child, was not the essential thing in that experience; it was, rather, the recognition that stabbed through my childish brain: 'That is a Jesuit.' So the important thing in the dream was its remarkable symbolic setting and the astounding interpretation: 'That is the man-eater.' . . . In the dream I went down into the hole in the earth and found something very different on a golden throne, something non-human and underworldly, which gazed fixedly upward and fed on human flesh. It was only fifty years later that a passage in a study of religious ritual burned into my eyes, concerning the motif of cannibalism that underlies the symbolism of the Mass. . . . Through this childhood dream I was initiated into the secrets of the earth. What happened then was a kind of burial in the earth, and many years were to pass before I came out again. Today I know that it happened in order to bring the greatest possible amount of light into the darkness. It was an initiation into the realm of darkness. My intellectual life had its unconscious beginnings at that time.")

The sequences in the commune are, among other things, revolting. Placed in general adjacency with the sequences of the Katyn massacre, which is also revolting, we are asked to ask ourselves what we are revolted by. What is the meaning of revulsion? If rotting corpses make us want to vomit, why at the same time do live bodies insisting on their vitality? But the members of the commune themselves display images of revulsion, as if to vomit up the snakes and swords and fire the world forces down our throats. It is on this understanding that the sequence strikes me as one of innocence, or of a quest for innocence—the exact reverse of the unredeemable acts of tyrants, under whatever banner. (Look at this from *Walden*, the penultimate chapter entitled "Spring": "We need to witness our own limits transgressed, and some life pasturing freely where we never wander. We are cheered when we observe the vulture feeding on the carrion which disgusts and disheartens us, and deriving health and strength from the repast. There was a dead horse in the hollow by the path to my house, which compelled me sometimes to go out of my way, especially in the night when the air was heavy, but the assurance it gave me of the strong appetite and inviolable health of Nature was my compensation for this. I love to see that Nature is so rife with life that myriads can be afforded to be sacrificed and suffered to prey on one another; that tender organizations can be so serenely squashed out of existence like pulp,—tadpoles which herons gobble up, and tortoises and toads run over in the road; and that sometimes it has rained flesh and blood! With the liability to accident, we must see how little account is to be made of it. The impression made on a wise man is that of universal innocence." Our wisdom is being put to the test here, along with Makavejev's. For the commune can give an impression of innocence, and achieve it, only if the work it is doing is the work of nature. Yet just that claim of obeying nature is the perennial claim of the de Sades of history.)

The commune is perfectly or purely indecent. I recall that to allegorize modern totalitarianism, Camus wrote *The Plague*, claiming that the only power sufficient to rid us of plagues is ordinary decency. Makavejev, through the commune, suggests that our strategy against emotional plague will have to be or to include indecency. I recall as well that the original title of Camus's book translated as *The Rebel* is *L'Homme revolté*, man revolted. Camus speaks of every form of revolt save, apparently, the one Makavejev takes as fundamental, physiological revolt. This means something for which I take Zarathustra to have laid down the logic or prescription: "You say 'I' and you are proud of this word. But greater than this—although you will not believe in it—is your body and its great intelligence, which does not say 'I' but performs 'I' " ("Of the Despisers of the Body"). Beyond the images of the commune, the emotion in the film as a whole, in its horrors, in its longing, in its laughter, is to have us become less proud of saying No in order to let the intelligence of the body perform No—in preparation, of course, of finding something, that is, creating something, to which Yes can be said and be done. I think of this No in terms of Zarathustra's parable in "Of the Three Metamorphoses": "I name you three metamorphoses of the spirit: how the spirit shall become a camel, and the camel a lion, and the lion at last a child. There are many heavy things for the spirit, for the strong weight-bearing spirits in which dwell respect and awe: its strength longs for the heavy, for the heaviest. . . . To create freedom for itself and a sacred No even to duty: the lion is needed for that, my brother. . . . Why must the preying lion still become a child? The child is innocence and for-getfulness, a new beginning, a sport, a self-propelling wheel, a first motion, a sacred Yes."

This combination of physiological revolt, of revoltedness, of disgust, together with the quest for innocence which forms a particular epistemo-logical access to the state of the world, is something I broached in an essay that introduces a reading of *Othello* with a letter addressed to Molière's Alceste, the misanthrope.[2] In that letter I tell Alceste of some later writers who have shared his revulsion with the ways of the world, his finding the world uninhabitable. The immediate cause for linking Alceste and Othello is that each, because of his perceptions of certain distasteful, metaphysical facts about human existence, demands to be the whole world to the woman he loves—which really means, demands that she provide an entire world for him. One woman declines and is abandoned; the other accepts and is suffocated. I tell Alceste that I mean to write to him about *Sweet Movie* as in effect the most concentrated work I know that follows out the idea that the way to assess the state of the world is to find out how it tastes (a sense modality not notably stressed by orthodox epistemologists but rather con-signed to a corner of aesthetics)—which means both to find out how it tastes to you and how it tastes you, for example, to find out whether you and the world are disgusting to one another. Such an assessment is partic-ularly suited to a time at which the individual is asked to consent to his or her world, to take his or her place in society, that is, to take responsibility for it. It is the time at which adolescence and adulthood are discovered, the one as what you are asked to forgo, the other as what you are asked to accept instead. I claim that Alceste, and Hamlet before him (with his sen-sitivity to odor, to the rotting) and the romantics and the existentialists after him, represent this discovery of adolescence.

The discovery of adulthood through disgust was something acted out in the student movement in the time of our war in Vietnam. To perform ugly and indecent acts was an expression of the rejection of a world that asked for consent to its disgusting deeds. This was not my way of expression, partly because I had already given my consent to this world and partly because I do not understand myself as performing ugly and indecent acts. But I understand that way, I felt the exactness of its spiritual accuracy. To say so was my way, and it has its own price. This is or was so obvious that serious films made during that period did not so much need to assert disgust with the world as to ask for its assessment, to acknowledge this fact of the world without letting it sap the motivation to work at this art, even if the art itself was the best context for the assessment. Makavejev's way in *WR* is to follow a sole poet-actor dressed in mock battle gear down New York streets, a diminished Quixote bringing the war home. Makavejev is letting the war show its threat to drive one crazy. Bergman's way in *Persona* is to have the woman of silence see on a television screen the unforgettable footage of a priest immolating himself in protest; as if she were witnessing an image of a dream of herself, as if she were the origin of the craziness of the world.

Alceste's interpretation of the uninhabitability of the world, that is, of his distaste, is to see the world as a scene of universal hypocrisy. *Sweet Movie* interprets this hypocrisy, as it were, by picturing the earth as full of corpses—buried evidence of mass murder, rotting ideals, corpses with souls still in them. The film attempts to extract hope—to claim to divine life after birth—from the very fact that we are capable of genuine disgust at the world; that our revoltedness is the chance for a cleansing revulsion; that we may purge ourselves by living rather than by killing, willing to visit hell if that is the direction to something beyond purgatory; that the fight for freedom continues to originate in the demands of our instincts, the chaotic cry of our nature, our cry to have a nature. It is a work powerful enough to encourage us to see again that the tyrant's power continues to require our complicitous tyranny over ourselves. (In the early paragraphs of *Walden*: "It is hard to have a Southern overseer; it is worse to have a Northern one; but worst of all when you are the slave-driver of yourself." That was never easy to say. It is always in danger of a merely literary appropriation.) In my earlier essay I more or less accuse both Alceste and Othello of inviting Montaigne's terrible rebuke to mankind in "On some verses of Virgil": "What a monstrous animal to be a horror to himself, to be burdened by his pleasures, to regard himself as a misfortune!" But I go on to say—something I take *Sweet Movie* to be saying—that the world during my lifetime rather shows that it is yet more horrible to lose this capacity for horror.

It is to the anarchic commune that the American Miss is brought (some successor of what in *The Philadelphia Story* is called the married maiden, the American female), in a wheelbarrow, as if we are to discover that there may be something beyond the rubbish heap of history. She proves unable, however, to participate in this invitation to rebirth, and in the next and final sequence that we see her (as in her first sequence and in her central scene of copulation and cramp on the Eiffel Tower with El Macho), she is in front of a camera, enlivened, say animated, by the condition of exhibition. (Is this all a camera can do after human birth—create animation, or liveliness, not life?) Her inability to participate is shown as an inability to be nourished. A lifelong force-fed consumer, she becomes anorexic, and she swiftly winds up as a piece of chocolate. (Sorority girls in my youth used to announce their engagement to their sorority sisters by passing around a box of chocolate-covered cherries.) As she writhes and then drowns in the vat of chocolate-mud-excrement, like an isolated female wrestler, we can see at last, though filtered through a film of chocolate, a sweet movie, the genitals denied our sight when she was first introduced to us. She is again food for the hungry movie camera, a responsibility accepted by Makavejev as his depicted cameraman says an excited "Beautiful!" in response to her dying. And the insatiable and deadly voyeurism of the camera is then more amply declared by alluding—in an extreme close-up of this woman's profile as her head touches the floor of the vat and we see one eye caught open by death—to the shower murder of *Psycho*.

The anorexia of Miss World is linked to Captain Anna Planeta's cannibalism, suggesting that this figure of the revolution is a further surrogate for this movie director and this director's camera; at once the projection of human desire and the potential death of it. The women are also linked, also in counterpoise, by the idea and representations of corpses, the one seduced into becoming a corpse, the other producing corpses of those she has seduced. We see Captain Anna kill only once, the sailor from *Potemkin* whom she has bathed like a child; she bites him to drink blood and then stabs him to death in a bed of sugar. We are given to believe that this is her habitual treatment of those to whom she grants her favors.

We are also given to believe that she kills the four barely pubescent boys whom she invites into her hold and seduces in a scene of private striptease that forms the most difficult passage, from the perspective of ordinary moral sensibility, of this difficult film. The primary direction or object of moral outrage here is the reverse of what it is in the commune sequence. There we must wonder what the justification is for Makavejev's subjecting his audience to these scenes; the actors are unharmed, they self-evidently are behaving in ways no one has dictated to them; the struggle of their freedom with the power of the camera is an equal one. In the seduction of the children, both actors and audience are being subjected to something that requires justification, but one's first concern is for the actors, I mean the children. The question of this concern is opened to criticism (treated dialectically, its question subjected to a question) by our finding that the experience of the scene contains tenderness and elicits from us a reluctant excitement preserved under its anxiety. We recognize our complicity in finding in a world of corpses a world whose common coin of relationship is seduction, and we recognize our complicity as seducer and as seduced. But is this lesson sufficient justification for subjecting these young boys to this treatment? The scene is also a brilliant and inescapable declaration of a fact essential to anything I have recognized as a movie I have cared about—that it contains projections of (photographic displacements of) real human beings, human beings subjected to the interrogations and the imposing transformations of the camera. But is the declaration of this fact sufficient justification for subjecting just these real young male human beings to exactly these ways of this particular older woman's presenting herself to them? She really is taking off her stocking for this boy; really placing her naked leg over his shoulder, her pubic hair tufting beyond the edges of the strip of fabric hanging loosely down her front; she really is unzipping his fly. . . . No serious artist could have risked this sequence who did not know in his or her bones that eleven- or twelve-year-old boys have already been seduced over and over and more intractably than any way in which this nice lady will affect them in providing them and herself for the camera. The artist knows this not in a spirit which would say that a little more seduction won't hurt but knows it out of a conviction that the process of going through these gestures—with friendly preparation and with explicit delimitations, for the comprehensible purpose of producing the communication in these matters for a film—is, on the contrary, potentially therapeutic. (It was perhaps not surprising that freedom in the direction of what will still be called the pornographic has made possible a further region in which film may acknowledge the human individuality of its human subjects. I believe some people have felt that the softcore freedom of *Last Tango in Paris* did this for Marlon Brando. I do not so much wish to deny this as to say that it seems to me to underrate other of Brando's self-revelations—from as early as the t-shirt in *Streetcar*. An altogether more important revelation of *Last Tango*, to my mind, lies in its softcore limitation. Given what this film seems to be about, this limitation acknowledges not a freedom but a limitation that we understand will persist however far the camera will be permitted to go with stars in the future. The camera's metaphysical limitation is that it cannot provide unshakable evidence of the satisfaction of desire any more than the plain eye or ear can provide it—not of the woman's and not, if you are serious about it, of the man's either. A realization of this limitation must have contributed to turning the camera to greater feats of violence.)

The therapeutic effort in reenactment conjoins the seduction dance with the project of the commune; so does the mood it reaches of attentive solemnity, another invocation of the religious. The sound track—a male chorus singing something I recall Makavejev's identifying as a piece of Russian Orthodox liturgical music—does not impose the idea of the religious on this dancing but reveals it there, shows that it is naturally to be taken there, however unpredictably. (Exactly what creates this experience is an obligation of criticism to discover.) This experience—call it an experience of seeing something as something, witnessing its presence— acknowledges a clear indebtedness to Surrealism's experiments in cinema but simultaneously acknowledges an absolute break with, or reinterpretation of, Surrealism's experience and ambition. The sequence is equally conjoined, by opposition, to two features in the opening sequences with Miss World: first, the striptease is another direct borrowing from burlesque; second, Captain Anna is dressed, to the extent she is dressed, as a bride, so this is a honeymoon for her. In comparison with the honeymoon to which the first woman is subjected—her brutish and foul husband, wishing to sully her, obsessed with his personal hygiene, urinates at her from his metallic penis (bronzed or gilded, I imagine, as if in sentimental and detached memory of itself)—Anna's dance for the young boy is progressive, humanizing, and gives seduction due praise as an origin and consequence of the human craving for beauty, for a genuine cleansing of the spirit.

One more identification within the complex crossroads of the seduction sequence and I can make good—as good as I can—on my claim concerning the richness of the ending of *Sweet Movie*. Children led into an out-of-the-way dwelling, made of and covered with sweets, by an old witch who means to roast them for a meal, is the story of Hansel and Gretel, hardly the only fairy tale in which children are in danger of being eaten. When the sailor from the *Potemkin* says poignantly, "I'm starved for love," Anna buries the image, which is true of her, under a callous ideological rhetoric: "Only those who starve know how to love." The film is about how children come to be eaten and thereby about how witches are created, with their terrible, human emptiness. (That the failure to acknowledge children, to grant them an autonomous existence, may present itself in consciousness as their being eaten by their parents, is attested to twice in *King Lear*, once by each father.)

It is in light of this fairytale allusion that I call attention to one of Makavejev's perceptions of Bergman's silences: "The nonverbal sequences in Bergman's films are replete with inner meaning and dream-like atmosphere. . . . [They], however, are often 'covered over' by the banality of the plot, creating an ambiguous understanding of the characters' psychic tension. . . . This tension is presented in a dreamlike way, possessing that 'tender insecurity' which always appears when the unreal is presented as absolutely real. It seems to me that Bergman's frequent use of nonverbal sequences is due to his fear of laying bare this insecurity in a direct verbal manner." *Sweet Movie* contains three extended nonverbal sequences, the dance of seduction, the communal feast, and the Katyn Forest footage. The seduction is the most dreamlike, the commune the least, and that documentary footage somewhere between dream and reality. To think through this variation is an obligation for those who believe in the value of this film and in the value of the consideration of dreams. The seduction could be read as a dream, but it need not. How is this different from our less luxurious, hence less noticeable, waking seductions? If we dream of such seduction, what is our complicity in the trance of our waking life? Again, if the reality of Katyn Forest is unbearable, then what happens if we cannot put it out of our dreams? Isn't that forest a name for the region inhabited by regimes who no longer know that there is a difference between dream and reality, acting out the one, wiping out the other? Again, if the members of the commune so directly express their wishes, destroying for one another the censorship that comes between us and ours, then what need would they have to dream? Can they? Is the vanishing of dreams something that frightens us? And are we to be likened, as Freud implies and as Descartes says at the close of his First Meditation, to slaves who are struggling not to awaken from a dream of liberty?

All I call attention to here is that in each of these three sequences the cause or occasion of the silence—or rather of the absence of words—is clear, as clear as an initial broaching of the situations can make them; and the issues within the situations are clear, anyway clear enough to begin a course of thinking about them; and the demand for thinking is urgent, as urgent as this master of excavation and conjunction can make it; and the evidence we are given for thinking through our silences and our conjunctions—for supporting a course of meditation—is complete, anyway as complete as the movie is, yielding significance to genuine interest and meditation, perhaps willing to be known better than it knows itself, an inspirer of thought.

It seems to me a reasonable hypothesis (which I will not attempt to test here) that Makavejev's films are less closely related to the dreams of sleep than they are to the dreams of what we call waking life, to trances. We might call the former restoring dreams (stocking our memories); and the latter guiding dreams (stocking us with what we call perceptions). The former emphasize the private and hallucinatory quality of dreaming; the latter emphasize the public and hypnotic character of dreaming. The former relate dreaming, anyway something less than waking, to religion; the latter relate dreaming to politics.

The final sequence of *Sweet Movie* opens, tinted blue, with five corpses (the sailor and the four boys) wrapped in plastic shrouds and laid neatly side by side on a river bank. We got there this way: We had earlier seen the police board the Survival, take Captain Anna into custody, and lay the wrapped bodies on this bank. Then after the American Miss fails to find another birth of freedom in the continent of the commune, we find her succeeding in becoming a chocolate corpse. From there we cut for a moment back to the exhumations of the bodies in the Katyn Forest, the footage tinted blue as it was in its original occurrence for us; and it is from here, retaining the monochrome blue tinting, that we cut back to those corpses on the bank. I remember what then happens this way: The wrapped corpses, shot so as to recede from us, begin to stir, and the human beings we knew to be inside, call them the actors, begin removing themselves from their cerements or cocoons, exhuming themselves. The figure nearest us proves to be the boy who was the main object of the seduction dance. He turns his face toward the screen and looks out, toward the (invisible) camera, toward us. An elevated train enters the background of the frame, from right to left, its high whistle blowing. The boy's look, perhaps in conjunction with this intervention of the train, freezes the frame, which thus preserves the looking and stops the train in midpassage; the whistle continues to blow for a moment, from nowhere to nowhere. Then gradually the blue tint gives way and color comes back to the frame, upon which the film ends.

These final moments form a further nonverbal sequence which epitomizes the film's perception of the world as full of corpses and in need of salvation—call it unfreezing, or metamorphosis, or coming to life, or call it the possibility of putting off the old man, the possibility of being born. The sequence, as well, claims for itself the classical alliance of sleep with death, so that the boy, in shedding his character and being (re)born as the actor he is in actuality, seems to be awakening, as from a dream, as from a film. In this absence of words, Makavejev acknowledges himself as the maker of this film by declaring his choice over a procession of what I have called automatisms of cinema. He is implied by whether a particular image moves, by its duration, by exactly what is allowed inside any frame and what is excluded, by what is heard, its duration and whether it is in synchrony, by the relations achieved between characters and the live actors they inhabit for the film, by whether color is wished for.

Significant films are those which give significance to the conditions of the medium of film. These conditions cannot be known a priori but must be worked out in acts of criticism which undertake to derive the significance of particular automatisms, undertake even to say that a particular set of events constitutes a significant automatism. But deriving significance is a matter of seeing how just this automatism is invited by just this subject, given significance by its place in this film—for the subject is not defined before the way of discovering it is defined. To get these matters together for a particular film is to give a reading of it. I read the concluding sequence as follows.

The boy looks out. Which is to say, Makavejev directs the boy to look out, at him; not exactly in accusation, rather as with a question. Makavejev is asking himself: Is there life after the birth of my film? Am I, at the end of what I have made here, to see that I have given life to this creation, or have I worked with live human beings only to choke off their voices in midpassage, only to turn them into dead replicas of themselves, mummies wrapped in celluloid? The boy looks out at the man who has interrogated his life and subjected it to new seductions and interrogates him in turn: If I am the innocence from which your experience has grown, the ambition along which your art has developed, you, who are now a consenting adult in a world of horrors, what world have you made for me to want, or in what way have you instructed me in what to want and in how to want, or what beauty and honesty have you provided for me to tide me over into my own consent? That Makavejev risks his work by giving it over to these questions and that the boy accepts the bequest and forgives the older self that he has become is expressed by the flowering of the film from its ambiguous tint back into color. It is being returned back to life and to its author. To see that the actor forgives the director is to see that Makavejev is forgiving himself—for the fact that the world is not better than it is and the fact that those who would make it better have only themselves, products of such a world, to work with. It is the best basis in the world from which to look for a new beginning, a first motion.

I have said little about Makavejev's sense of humor, but that sense is as active throughout *Sweet Movie* (and *WR*) as its sense of outrage. Indeed his good humor and his outrage make one another possible. I do not know that I can yet say anything useful by way of characterizing his particular cast of humor, but I feel sure that the commune sequence, for example, hasn't done what work it can until we can see, for example, the fat rosy man, who is being bounced and oiled and powdered and who then, while lying on his back, pisses a mighty arc into the air—not at all to sully anyone—and thereupon rises to take a bow, as someone being accepted back into a condition of playfulness.

Sweet Movie's conjunctions of ideas and moods invokes *The Gold Rush*, which extracts hilarity from a threat of cannibalism. Chaplin contrasts the imagination of his brutish cabinmate, who hallucinates the little man to be a Thanksgiving turkey, with the imagination of that little man himself, who can turn a shoe into a piece of food and turn pieces of food into a pair of shoes, actions which prove genuinely life sustaining. The former dreams as we imagine the brutes dream, as the dog dreams of the rabbit. Judging from *The Gold Rush*, to dream the dream of civilization, to elaborate dire necessity into a ceremonial feast and into art, requires an openness to one's childhood, or childlikeness, and an openness to the distance and the splendors of others. The art of the little man's dream here is depicted as dancing (making rolls dance), but the self-reflexive references in the concluding sequence (where the little man is told, by a man behind a camera, that he has ruined the picture, apparently by expressing his desire before the camera) make it clear that the actual work of art in question is this film. So this film, as explicitly as *Sweet Movie* but less concretely, accounts for its origins. The cabin fever of the brute expresses itself as cannibalism not simply because he is starving but because he cannot tolerate the incomprehensible imagination of the one he is starving with, the mystery of that other's difference from him. He would incorporate the difference.

The conjunction of hilarity with human nature stripped away occurs, again, in the figure of Harpo Marx, another type of the artist (depicted as a virtuoso on the instrument of angels). Here cannibalism seems bypassed in a general condition of insatiability—an id somehow escaped intact. Groucho's acceptance and appreciation of Harpo establishes one of the tenderest relationships in the history of theater and exacts of him a pure commitment to anarchy. I do not quite wish to say that Harpo and Groucho would be at home in the Muehl commune but rather that they treat so-called civilized persons as if those persons were living in the commune without knowing it or knowing much—not because Harpo and Groucho impose their imaginations upon others but because they can respond accurately to the veneer of hieroglyphs the others put upon their desires. Their humor would then represent an effort not to die of pity for the world. Wit, by contrast, is conservative, not penetrating the hieroglyphs of society but perpetuating their mode. And here one should recognize that Groucho's commitment to the pun is a profound trait of his character not because his puns are always funny (often they are not), but because it is a commitment, a pure commitment to his response, refusing the coin of what the world has given him to mean. Thus is humor a moral equivalent of heroism. (I think of two fine songs that treat the knowledge of our wish to incorporate others not with horror but with particular good humor: "Sweet Georgia Brown" ("She ain't colored, she was born that

way") and "Honeysuckle Rose" ("You're confection, goodness knows . . .").
I come from a culture in which a preoccupation of Montaigne's is brought
momentary peace in the strains of Fats Waller.)

I know of no one who has found humor in anorexia, unless Kafka's
"Hunger Artist" can be seen to be funny. (Though it occurs to me that I
do not understand why an impulse to vomit, the hand over the mouth and
a hasty exit, is found funny [in America; in English-speaking theater more
generally?], whereas an urge to defecate, to lose control that way, is not. In
France, *On purge bébé*, but in America it is *Bringing Up Baby*.) The most
explicit anorexic I know in film is the woman in Antonioni's *Red Desert*,
whose refusal to partake appears as something between a fear of being pol-
luted or poisoned, a terror of trusting, and a wish not to have a body. It
also goes with difficulty in taking care of a child, as if this obligation
blocked a wish to become small or thin enough to be seen to need taking
care of. I find myself thinking in this connection also of the woman in
Godard's *Two or Three Things I Know about Her*, who consumes or swallows
everything but what requires literal eating. Does the fact that, after our
American Miss fails to be taught by the commune to admit nourishment
or comfort by her mouth, she then exposes her genitals to a camera mean
that she has been brought to ask: "Am I, indeed, a woman?" (She has identified with an earlier aggressor, the chocolate man who carried her to a
cave of milk, exposed himself to her, knocked her out, and then packed her
off to let her see if she could be born. Her identification, though mistak-
en, was a sign of a will to health, since she knew this man to be real, knew
what he was made of, having licked his cheek and found it tasted sweet, the
last taste in her mouth. But she found out from this empirical investigation
only what the world had already forced down her throat, that the darkness
of his skin was not merely a color but a matter of substance.) Is this question of identity something a camera can answer? I have said that it seems
to me a question the camera is asking—of her, of itself.

What is the question? Am I, indeed, . . . since I do not know the difference between men and women—or perhaps between activity and passivity—and hence can imagine that there is none? Am I, indeed, . . . since
I am castrated (I lack something)? Am I, indeed, . . . since I am not castrated (there is nothing I lack; I was born this way)? This sequence represents
Miss World's active participation in the reality of theater. It links her with
the theater of the seduction dance and with the enactments of the commune. It also dissociates her, since the origin of her act lies in the old food
for peep show booths, and hence isolates her rather than initiates her.

The image of an anorexic woman exposing her genitals—anyway, a
woman who refuses the world without letting it go—takes me to the image

of Ingrid Thulin in *Cries and Whispers*; it is I guess the most shocking moment of Makavejev's compressed Bergman film. To the conjunction of spiritual starvation and of exhibition, Bergman adds the woman's explicit cutting of something inside her vagina and then licking the blood from her fingers. Are we to be disgusted by this? Is she? Is her husband meant to be—the fictional audience for whose benefit this set of actions has been undertaken? She is, let us say, eating her heart out. Cannibalizing herself. She is perhaps doing this as a sign of remorse and surely as an expression of rage, of revenge. To wish to harm another by a gesture of self-castration, to bloody one's mouth as if it were a replication of the castrated genitals, is to turn oneself into Medusa. Then this woman means to turn her husband to stone, perhaps by demonstrating to him that he is stone. And since Bergman's screen in this film fades into red at the close of its sequences, we may take Bergman to be declaring his film screen to be a version or container of the severed head of the Gorgon, to contain that kind of assault upon us. But what would be his attitude to this possibility? We are quite certain that we are not turned to stone, are we not? If we are not stone, and if the power of the film image is nevertheless what I say it is, then the screen we see it on is a version of the shield of Perseus. Then a film director, like Perseus flying through the air, looking down upon the earth, has in his hands the power to put halls full of people to instant death, or to preserve them.

Am I man or woman? is characterized, by Deleuze and Guattari in their *Anti-Oedipus*, as "the hysterical 'question' " and is paired with "the obsessional 'question' " "Am I dead or alive?" (They refer at this point to an essay by Serge Leclaire which I have not read.) The *Othello* material alluded to earlier represents the closing pages of my book *The Claim of Reason* (Oxford, 1979), the fourth part of which contains certain lines of meditation on what philosophers in the English-speaking tradition of philosophy call the problem of (how I know) (the existence of) other minds. These meditations can be said, I believe, to discover this problem to raise the question Am I a human being or a monster? They also suggest that the problem of the existence of the other can be seen to derive from or to replace an earlier philosophical stake in the problem of the existence of God. This would provide a conceptual realm within which to grasp the progress of a Bergman character as he or she moves from a quarrel with God to a quarrel with the existence of others. Could we come to understand this final narcissism as an analogue of the initial narcissism sought by the commune, even as a step toward it? After all, it attaches ultimate importance to ultimate matters. And it is equally unreceptive to the further corruption of the world.

I understand there to be two modes of sweetness of which *Sweet Movie* speaks and which it embodies; they project alternatives for us. Either to continue to anesthetize the world, put that form of distance between it and our experience of it, say by converting all our experience into a mode of viewing. Or to learn to taste again, so that we can learn to maintain our disgust more easily than we learn to maintain what disgusts us. But this will require a transformation of the five senses, a new perspective, a new aesthetics. For mankind, to adapt a form from Nietzsche, would rather take Nothingness to be sweet than find nothing sweet.

Take the idea of film as producing, or making possible, a particular form of distance—let me call this the distance of something which makes its presence felt only through absence, as absence; together with the idea that this distance makes possible a particular mode of sweetness or nearness—let me call this seductiveness (or suggestiveness, to capture the neighboring sense of the hypnotic); together with an awareness that a filmmaker is raising the question whether he or she is indeed a woman— and let me now specify this as a speculation that the screen acts as a woman acts. This crossroads of ideas I find summarized in a passage from Nietzsche's *The Gay Science* in which he specifies the particular action of women (I dare say he is reporting on the feminine side of human character,[3] as that has so far unfolded itself) in the following terms: "When a man stands in the midst of his own noise, in the midst of his own surf of plans and projects, then he is apt also to see quiet, magical beings gliding past him and to long for their happiness and seclusion: women. He almost thinks that his better self dwells there among the women, and that in these quiet regions even the loudest surf turns into deathly quiet, and life itself into a dream about life. Yet! Yet! Noble enthusiast, even on the most beautiful sailboat there is a lot of noise, and unfortunately much small and petty noise. The magic and the most powerful effect of women is, in philosophical language, action at a distance, *actio in distans*; but this requires first of all and above all—distance" (section 60).

In claiming Nietzsche's figuring of action at a distance as a kind of mythological description of the action of film on a screen, I invite for consideration the consequent ideas that our Newtonian universe required the discovery of gravity as magnetism, call it mutual attraction, and that the Cartesians, battling Newtonianism, found such a property, invoking action at a distance, to be occult, that is, extrascientific or magical. It is as if the philosophers who invented psychology as a metaphor or allegory of Newtonianism somehow took it that if you got laws of association in the role of laws of motion, the idea and fact of universal attraction—you may say libido—would take care of itself. From which perspective Freud and his predecessors in hypnotism and animal magnetism, looking as it were for the gravity in human constellations, are felt to be dealing in occult or magical properties. And in a sense that is true, too—so long as society remains a field of occult forces.

A chain of ideas reaching throughout this essay is condensed or displaced in the final image of the woman in *WR*. The last of her we see is her severed head, brought into an autopsy room and placed in a white tray.

Figure 2.1

The facts are quickly told: "DOCTOR: 'No sign of a struggle. Therefore she received the semen willingly. Better check mental hospitals in case some sex-starved patient has escaped. Find the murder weapon?' INSPECTOR: 'Yes, these nickel-plated Champions. They're the finest made.'" While he unwraps the silvery skates from a newspaper, the head begins to speak. Now when she begins to speak we have before us a literalization of the "talking head" that Makavejev finds characters in a Bergman movie often look like. I take the image in *WR*, accordingly, as an acknowledgment of a condition of movie making, more specifically as a danger of movie making that serious filmmakers must face or outface. But for a filmmaker to acknowledge this in this way requires him or her to acknowledge that it is he or she who has called for the severance of this head from its body and directed its placement into just this white tray. But how has this Perseus received the authorization for such an act, the sword necessary to accomplish it (call it the camera) and the shield necessary to bear up under its consequences (call it the screen)? In the absence of gods, what *WR* tells us is that this woman lost her head to love because of a mortal who had already been turned to stone; that she was made a monster, a talking head without a body, or confirmed in monstrousness, by a man who interpreted his purity as demanding that he exempt himself from ordinary human desires, save himself for something higher. The woman's words for this—that is, the talking head's words, I mean of course Makavejev's words—are "He's romantic, ascetic, a genuine Red Fascist," a patriot. Makavejev's further identification with this murderousness, his refusal to exempt himself from recognizing it in himself (in accordance, no doubt, with his own romanticism and asceticism and his patriotism toward a still invisible fatherland) is his further interpretation of the man's self-exemption as the capacity for art. This is shown in the man's beautiful song of prayer as he walks lost along the river, comprising the closing sequence of this film. Makavejev thus discovers further adjacencies in the concept of art as we have it, art as decapitation or renunciation or alienation; and he bears out the knowledge that this art is at the same time the victim or martyr of the very circumstances that produce it. I take the implication to be that this condition of what we know as art is also a condition of what we know as thinking, or philosophy; or might know. (An image of the kind of art that adapts to this condition, extracting no acknowledgment or autonomy of its own, is something I see in *WR*'s footage of the plaster-caster of erections, whose object or product is a tinted plaster phallus, a sort of life mask, which I read as a further stand-in for a certain kind of film image and filmmaking and film viewing (and by no means only or especially a stand-in for the obviously pornographic).)

The head of the woman, smiling, succeeding or surviving the man's song, retakes the field of the screen; she is displaced by the smiling head of Wilhelm Reich or absorbed by it. In bequeathing the film to these figures, Makavejev acknowledges further his identification with the muse and the presiding genius of his film, that he speaks from them, for them, in the excavation of their visions, and like them executes nothing of which he is not also the victim. So Makavejev declares himself indeed both a man and a woman. And, like all of them, a talking head. How could it be otherwise? The possibilities of film in any period can reach no higher or lower than the possibilities of humanness in that period, no higher or lower than the possibility of using talking heads therapeutically. To the extent that our heads and our bodies are not joined, we are Gorgons. Like the gods, we precede the human.

Notes

1. I see no help whatever in thinking about Makavejev's experiment in the light of a remark—which seemed to gain some currency at the conference—to the effect that "the primary motivating force for dreaming is not psychological but physiological since the time of occurrence and duration of dreaming sleep are quite constant, suggesting a preprogrammed, neurally determined genesis." You might as well conclude that the primary motivating force for kissing is not psychological but physiological on the ground that the places of occurrence and the duration of kisses are quite constant. (This vaguely sounds like something Chamfort might actually have said.)

2. "A Cover Letter to Molière's Misanthrope," *Themes Out of School*: 97–102.

3. The feminine side of human character is something I found (in "What Becomes of Things on Film?") to be "a natural subject of film." It is to be discovered in certain films (among them *Persona*) that are built upon a particular procedure of conjoining waking with dreaming life.

$$3$$

North by Northwest

Printed in *Critical Inquiry,* Summer 1981, this represents my contribution to a colloquium on Hitchcock's film held at the English Institute in Cambridge, Massachusetts, August 31, 1980. The other participants were Professors William Rothman (who organized the colloquium) and Geoffrey Hartman.

P HILOSOPHY'S ALL BUT unappeasable yearning for itself is bound to
seem comic to those who have not felt it. To those who have felt it, it
may next seem frightening, and they may well hate and fear it, for the
step after that is to yield to the yearning, and then you are lost. From such
a view of philosophy I have written about something called modernism in
the arts as the condition of their each yearning for themselves, naming a
time at which to survive, they took themselves, their own possibilities, as
their aspiration—they assumed the condition of philosophy. What I found
in turning to think consecutively about film a dozen or so years ago was a
medium which seemed simultaneously to be free of the imperative to philosophy and at the same time inevitably to reflect upon itself—as though the
condition of philosophy were its natural condition. And then I was lost.

But this is said after the fact. Over and over I have had to find again
my conviction in these matters, to take my experience over the same path,

First published in *Critical Inquiry,* summer 1981; reprinted in *Themes Out of School* and in
Marshall Deutelbaum and Leland Poague, editors, *A Hitchcock Reader* (Iowa State University
Press, 1986).

finding the idea of film's philosophical seriousness first to be comic, then frightening, then inescapable. To achieve this conviction in the films of Alfred Hitchcock is not something I can imagine apart from a continuing conversation about film and about philosophy with William Rothman, whose conviction in the precision of Hitchcock's self-consciousness and passionate exploration of that self-consciousness in his films has convinced me to find this for myself. My remarks on *North by Northwest* are guided, more specifically, by two ideas from Rothman's book on Hitchcock, *The Murderous Gaze: Readings of Five Hitchcock Films*: first, that Hitchcock's interpretation of the power of the movie camera—for example, its power of interrogation of its human subjects—is something Rothman calls its murderousness; and second, that the Hitchcock film, hence Hitchcock, is first fully formed in *The Thirty-Nine Steps*, in its weaving of Hitchcock's interest in his themes of the murder thriller together with the themes of romance.[1]

In *Pursuits of Happiness* I put together seven Hollywood romances of the thirties and forties and claim that they define a particular genre, something I call the comedy of remarriage. It happens that Cary Grant is in four of the seven; Katharine Hepburn is the only other principal to appear in more than one. In my account of Howard Hawks's *Bringing Up Baby* (one of the seven films in question), I claim that Grant's saving Hepburn from falling, at the close of the film, by hoisting her hand in hand onto the ledge of a scaffold, a place that also looks like a crib or treehouse, upon which they embrace, is alluded to by the conclusive hoisting in *North by Northwest* from a ledge onto an upper berth. If I will not ask you out of the blue to believe this connection, still less will I ask you to believe an allusion from *North by Northwest* to *The Philadelphia Story*, another of the seven films with Cary Grant, when Grant (or rather, Thornhill) early in *North by Northwest* tries to make the police and his mother believe what happened to him at the mansion in Glen Cove, and the place of liquor bottles is shown to be occupied by books. Thornhill's drinking is the subject of much attention in the opening sequences of *North by Northwest*—that is, as long as his mother is present—and C. K. Dexter Haven (Grant's role in *The Philadelphia Story*) cured himself of alcoholism by reading books, a process apparently from which he acquired the authority to affect the destiny of his love. I will wind up saying that *North by Northwest* derives from the genre of remarriage, or rather from whatever it is that that genre derives from, which means to me that its subject is the legitimizing of marriage, as if the pair's adventures are trials of their suitability for that condition. Perhaps this only signifies that *North by Northwest* is a romance. It is in any case the only one of Hitchcock's romantic thrillers in which the adventurous pair are actually shown to have married. It is also the only one in which the man of that pair is shown to have a mother—a mother, needless to say, whom he is shown to leave, and to leave running (out of the Plaza Hotel, away from his abductors, but at the same time away from his mother, who shouts after him to ask whether he will be home for dinner). The fate of the mother in *The Birds* will complicate this story. And naturally certain of Hitchcock's villains, and certain of his heroines, are allowed to have mothers.

But let us begin as uncontroversially as we can. *North by Northwest* contains as one of its stars Cary Grant. It underscores this uncontroversial fact in two principal ways: first, by remark after remark about his nice-looking, vaguely familiar face and about his being irresistible and making women who don't know him fall in love with him, together with several double takes when strangers look at his face (a man going into a phone booth Grant is leaving, a woman who, after as it were seeing who he is, wants him to stop in her hospital room); and second, by allusions to each of the other films Hitchcock made with Grant. *To Catch a Thief* also has him at the end holding a woman by the hand over a precipice, and in that film he is comically shown to be irresistible; *Suspicion* climaxes with a wild ride down a coast road in a convertible driven by Grant, from which he seems to shove someone out and from which someone who might be poisoned almost falls over a cliff into the sea; and the basic situation of *Notorious* is gone over again (a loose woman's liaison with something like a foreign agent is exploited by an American intelligence agency; the assignment thwarts Grant's desire; it leads to the woman's mortal danger from which Grant rescues her).

There seem to be two immediate reasons in *North by Northwest* for insisting upon the presence of Cary Grant; first, to redeem him from certain guilts acquired in those earlier environments, especially in allowing him to overcome the situation of *Notorious*, as if film actors and their characters get stuck to one another, and as if he is being readied for something purer in this context; and second, to inscribe the subject of film acting, and acting generally, as a main topic of this film, which is to say, a main branch of its investigation of the nature of film. The topic is invoked over and over in *North by Northwest*: Philip Vandamm (James Mason) hardly says a word to Grant that does not comment on his acting; the Professor (Leo G. Carroll) asks him to act a part; Eve Kendall (Eva Marie Saint) compliments him on his performance in the scene they have just acted out for Vandamm's benefit. The theme of theatricality is generalized by the fact that the part Thornhill is asked and forced to play is that of someone named George Kaplan, who doesn't exist; but to play the part of a fictional character is just what actors normally do. It happens that in the fiction of this film this new fictional identity is imposed by reality, thus generalizing the theme further into the nature of identity and the theatricality of everyday life.

It is, I think, part of Hitchcock's lingo to be referring to these facts, and more, in the exchange on the train between Thornhill and Eve about the monogram on his matchbook.

Figure 3.1

"Rot," he says, "it's my trademark." She asks what the *O* stands for. "Nothing," he replies. In a Hitchcockian context this means both that this man knows that the advertising game (and the modern city generally which it epitomizes) makes up words that are rot and also that it would be rot to think this is all he means. Thornhill and Eve have already questioned his identity and spoken about his familiar face. So in part what or who is "nothing" is the film character (here, Roger Thornhill) in comparison to the film actor playing him. Cary Grant would be more or less who he is if Roger Thornhill had never existed, whereas Roger Thornhill would be nothing apart from Cary Grant (a form of consideration broached as long ago as Erwin Panofsky's "Style and Medium in the Motion Pictures"), "Nothing" equally means that the film actor is nothing in comparison to the power of the camera over him. This is not so much in need of argument as of interpretation. *North by Northwest* interprets the actor as a victim, as if of foreign views of himself. This thought puts two figures in the film in the role of directors, the Professor and Vandamm, who create scenarios and make up parts for people.[2] On Vandamm's first encounter with Thornhill he draws some theatrical curtains across proscenium-sized windows, shutting the world out, and arranges for Thornhill to be killed, as if punishing him for acting; the Professor lets this go on until forced for the sake of his own script to intervene.

The "nothing," or naught, in the ROT monogram equally appropriately stands for origin, so its simultaneous meaning is that the actor is the origin of the character and also the origin of what becomes of himself or herself on film. The further thought that the human self as such is both an origin and a nothing is a bit of Cartesianism that is conceivably not called for in the context of this film. (To say that Hitchcock is up to it if he wants it is to say that Hitchcock is as intelligent as, say, Samuel Beckett and that he is as good at what he does as Beckett is at what he does.)

But I was trying to begin uncontroversially. The film is called *North by Northwest*. I assume that nobody will swear from that fact alone that we have here an allusion to Hamlet's line that he is but mad north-northwest; even considering that Hamlet's line occurs as the players are about to enter and that *North by Northwest* is notable, even within the oeuvre of a director pervaded by images and thoughts of the theater and of theatricality, for its obsession with the idea of acting; and considering that both the play and the film contain plays-within-the-play in both of which someone is killed, both being constructed to catch the conscience of the one for whose benefit they are put on. But there are plenty of further facts. The film opens with an ageless male identifying himself first of all as a son. He speaks of his efforts to keep the smell of liquor on his breath (that is, evidence of his grown-up pleasures) from the watchful nose of his mother, and he comes to the attention of his enemies because of an unresolved anxiety about getting a message to his mother, whereupon he is taken to a mansion in which his abductor has usurped another man's house and name and has, it turns out, cast his own sister as his wife. (The name, posted at the front of the house, is Townsend, and a town is a thing smaller than a city but larger than a village, or a hamlet.) The abductor orders the son killed by forcing liquid into him. It is perhaps part of the picture that the usurper is eager to get to his dinner guests and that there is too much competitive or forced drinking of liquor. Nor, again, will anyone swear that it is significant that the abductor-usurper's henchmen are a pair of men with funny, if any, names and a single man who stands in a special relationship with the usurper and has a kind of sibling rivalry with the young woman that this son, our hero, will become attracted to and repelled by. These are shadowy matters, and it is too soon to speak of "allusions" or of any other very definite relation to a so-called source. But it seems clear to me that if one were convinced of *Hamlet* in the background of *North by Northwest*, say to the extent that one is convinced that Saxo Grammaticus's *Danish History* is in the background of *Hamlet*, then one would without a qualm take the name Leonard as a successor to the name Laertes.

We have further to go. In Saxo Grammaticus's telling of the story the son's enemies send a beautiful woman to seduce him; he is to believe that he and the woman meet by chance. When questioned about what happened between them he says he raped her; she has agreed to back his story since they had known one another in the past. This figure is, as editors have noted, a peculiar prototype for Ophelia, but we can take her as near perfect for Eve Kendall. Thornhill does not, it is true, say that he raped her, but he describes something happening between them, in the name of love, that they both call murdering her. Hitchcock here is following one of his favorite identifications, that of killing with intercourse, the other side of a metaphysical wit's identification of dying with orgasm. It is also to the point, thinking of Thornhill's attention to his clothes, that Hamlet's prototype in Saxo Gramrnaticus is pictured as covering himself with dirt. That Hitchcock has gone back to the source or origin of the story of *Hamlet*, as well as to the play, is a reason not to have the title exactly from *Hamlet*.[3]

I note two or three further echoes of the play. Thornhill's problem begins when he is confused with, so to speak, someone who doesn't exist, let us say it is a nothing, or let us say a ghost; and when the woman betrays him he finds her out by following the itinerary dictated by the ghost. And then the son protects himself, saves his life, by what I would like to describe as feigning madness—in the auction scene in which he pretends not to know how you join in bidding for things. The auctioneer at one stage says, "Would the gentleman please get into the spirit of the proceedings?" that is, be decorous, be socialized; but society has been forcing an identity and a guilt upon him that he does not recognize as his own, so the natural hope for a way out is to abdicate from that society. Thornhill's identifying "rot" as his trademark by now irresistibly suggests to me Hamlet's sense of something rotten.

Allow for the sake of argument that *Hamlet* is present in the film in some fashion. Of what interest is this, I mean of what interest to Hitchcock? I have various speculations about this based on my claim that *North by Northwest* invokes *Hamlet* in conjunction with the source of the story of *Hamlet* and on my sense that *North by Northwest* plays a special role in Hitchcock's oeuvre, a summary role. I take Hitchcock, as it were, to be saying something like the following. Granted that it is not necessary for anyone, let alone a filmmaker, to disclaim the intention of trying to compete with the quality and the importance of *Hamlet*, it is nevertheless my intention, as the filmmaker I am, to compete with Shakespeare in his handling of sources and in this way, or to this extent, to show myself to do whatever it is I do as well as Shakespeare does whatever it is he does. It is with sources as Coleridge famously remarked about Shakespeare's stories: "My belief is that he always regarded his story, before he began to write, much in the same light as a painter regards his canvas, before he begins to paint—as a mere vehicle for his thoughts—as the ground upon which he was to work." But then of course (still speaking for Hitchcock) the question is what one means by "sources." The story is one source, lifted often from indifferent places that would not constitute sources unless I had been inspired to make them such. So is the past body of my work a source, as

North by Northwest makes explicit. So are what some people call "locations," which for me are places whose genius I wish to announce or to become. So are what other people call "actors," whereas for me what is called "Cary Grant" is considerably more than what that may be taken to mean. So is what you might call the camera a source . . . You see the point. But why is it *Hamlet* about which this is all, according to my speaking for Hitchcock, being said? I think there are two reasons. First, *Hamlet* is perhaps the most popular, or famous, of the greatest works of world literature; the man who on the basis of his kind of thriller became perhaps the most famous director of films in the world, and for a longer period than any other, and whom just about any critic recognizes as in some sense brilliant, may well be fascinated by and wish to comprehend this fact. Surely the play's fame cannot be the result of its actually being understood. Second, *Hamlet* is the subject of what is still probably the most famous Freudian interpretation of a work of art, Ernest Jones's *Hamlet and Oedipus.*

Given the blatant presence of Freudian preoccupation and analysis in Hitchcock's work I see in his allusion to *Hamlet* a kind of warning to Freudians, even a dare, as if to say: of course my work, like any art, is subject to your interpretations, but why are these interpretations so often so obvious, unable to grasp the autonomy, the uniqueness, of the object? (Hitchcock would not be the first artist of this century to feel he has to pit his knowledge of human nature against the thought of the man who is said to have invented its science.)[4]

The origin of Eve Kendall in Hitchcock's own past work is explicit enough. She succeeds another good-looking, blonde stranger in *The Thirty-Nine Steps* whom an earlier Hitchcock hero also met on a train, also as he was eluding the police to get to a person who could clear him of the suspicion of having put a knife in someone's back; and at the end of that train ride there was also a professor. But this time, over twenty years later and in another country, the woman offers rather than refuses him help. This proves initially to be treachery rather than salvation, but it affords a picture of a relationship to women that this man, now and in the past, had not known. This woman's apparent faith in him succeeds both Madeleine Carroll's early skepticism about his predecessor (Robert Donat), who spends much of *The Thirty-Nine Steps* trying to overcome it; and her faith succeeds more immediately the skepticism of his mother, to whom he had said goodbye just before encountering Eve on the train. The effect of these substitutions is elaborate and paradoxical, and all in favor of Eve.

Aligning, in retrospect, the Madeleine Carroll figure with the present mother, doubt is cast on the picture of marriage in the final shot of *The Thirty-Nine Steps;* the man puts his arm around the woman with the handcuffs still dangling from his wrist, a picture suggesting that marriage is a kind of voluntary handcuffing (a portable version of the ball and chain). On the other hand Eve is made to incorporate both the good woman and the adventuress of *The Thirty-Nine Steps*, that is, both the marriageable and the unmarriageable woman. The most delicious linking of them is made openly by Eve when she explains her interest in Thornhill to him by saying, "It's going to be a long night and I don't particularly like the book I've started. Know what I mean?" The Madeleine Carroll figure had been reading a book when Donat burst in on her. Thornhill knows what she means, as if seeing a dream coming true. And in that dream, and its responsibilities, the man's task will be not just to save himself and save his country's secrets from leaving it and thus win himself a suitable mate. He has first of all to save the bad woman, to rewrite the earlier plot which in effect began by killing her off, to rescue or redeem or resurrect her, that is to say, to put the good and the bad together. This is rather more like creating a suitable mate for himself.

Why is she his to rescue? Both the Professor and Eve tell him he is responsible for her condition, the one because he has cast suspicion on her, the other because men like him don't believe in marriage. But I think the film shows two further causes. First, in addition to her incorporating at least two of the women from *The Thirty-Nine Steps* she also incorporates the mother, perhaps the mother he never had, protecting him from the police by hiding him in a bellying container that shows she holds the key to his berth. (This wasn't necessary: the fact that she subsequently hides him from the porter sufficiently well in the washroom proves that.) It is every bit this birth he is reciprocating in his closing gesture of the film. Second, he has passed some kind of ordeal at her hands in the crop-dusting sequence, and his survival here somehow entitles them to one another—as if his survival, or revival from a Frazerian cornfield, had given them the key piece of knowledge with which to overcome their unlucky erotic pasts, which accordingly would be the knowledge that ecstasy such as she invites is not necessarily death dealing. I am taking it that she is not purely reluctant to send him to meet Kaplan. She is not worried that he is a murderer but that she is. They are both about to undergo an education in these matters. Redemption for them both is underway. But it is not a simple matter to put such knowledge into the world—say, in the form of marriage—and there is danger ahead.

How is it that he is equipped to meet the danger, I mean how does he know that the attempt is the most important thing in the world? I must now put the uncontroversial aside and put forward a bunch of assertions.

I begin by reinterpreting, or interpreting further, Thornhill's survival of the attack by the plane. The attack is the central image of his victimization. I said earlier that this is the form in which his being an actor is to be declared; and just now I said that his sexual redemption depended on what you might call his survival of a kind of victimization by, or a willing subjection to, an assault of feeling. Something cataclysmic happened to Thornhill and Eve the night before, and I understand the attack the next day to be simultaneously a punishment for the night and a gaudy visual equivalent of it. Then I understand the crop-dusting plane, instrument of victimization, as a figure for a movie camera: it shoots at its victims and it coats them with a film of something that both kills and preserves, say that it causes metamorphosis. I claim evidence for the association of the prairie with the, let us say, inner landscape of the train compartment, in the way a medium close-up of Eve's face at the Chicago train station dissolves into the establishing aerial shot of the road and fields of the plane attack.

Figure 3.2   Figure 3.3

Figure 3.4

That conjunction of color and mood I claim asks for an allegorical identification of the woman and this stretch of land, but this is just something further each viewer must try out on his or her own. It is on this ground that the man undergoes his Shakespearean encounter of nothings—the nothing of Thornhill meeting the nothing of Kaplan—the attack on his identity, as it were, by itself. The recognition of the plane sent by Vandamm as a figure for the camera accounts satisfactorily for his gathering his stolen secrets on microfilm. This, in turn, would be a way

Hitchcock has of saying that film—anyway in his camera—is the recorder
of state secrets.

     Put this together with the other overt declaration of the movie cam-
era, this time by synecdoche rather than metaphor: I mean the telescope
on the terrace of the Mount Rushmore Memorial focused on the faces of
the presidents. A lot is being woven together here. We have cut to the
presidents' faces from a close-up of Grant's face, turned toward us and suddenly illuminated as for examination by a harsh light from what we understand fictively to be a plane turning in his direction, hence what we understand literally and figuratively as a piece of photographic apparatus.

Figure 3.5

We are being told that this face belongs to just one person on earth and
that we are going to have to think about what that means. The cut from
that image to the image of the presidents evidently poses some matching
of Grant's face with the faces of stone, a matching generally prepared of
course by the insistent references to the familiarity of his face but prepared
more specifically by his having shaved with the minuscule razor and brush.
Letting the phallic symbolism alone for a while, the question is certainly
being posed about the sizes things are. Thornhill and Eve have had an
exchange about whether he is a little boy or a big boy, and now the issue
is about what size the human face of flesh and blood is in comparison with
faces on the face of a granite mountain and the size of both in comparison
with the photographic projection of the human face. A question is thus
raised about what Grant is (made of), about what it means that he has
become a national monument, and hence about what a monument is. So
at the same time a question is raised about what presidents are and about
what it means to know and remember them. These comparisons are
underscored when it turns out, directly, that our initial view of the presidents' faces is an image of them as seen through a telescope set up for the
pleasure and instruction of tourists. The image is possessed for us by, let

us say, Thornhill, but there is no reason to think that anyone present wouldn't see the same image, the one we have now.

Figure 3.6

Figure 3.7

Its being Grant who looks through the telescope at the famous stone faces identifies the conditions of his existence as a screen actor and thus identifies the mode in which we see him and think we know him. And I would be willing to swear from the fact alone of the way Grant is standing behind that telescope that he is also meant as a surrogate for the one who is capturing these images for our pleasure arid instruction. But the Professor is there with Thornhill as we cut to him standing before the telescope, so the matter of directorial surrogates must be complicated.

Let us run through the evidence for Grant/Thornhill as surrogate for Hitchcock. There is, first of all, the hint laid down by Hitchcock's having autographed himself in this film as someone who misses a bus: Thornhill is the only (other) character in the film before whom a bus shuts its doors and drives off. Again, however we are to understand Thornhill's participation in the killing of the real Lester Townsend in the United Nations building, we must understand him as what this moment visually declares him to be, someone who betrays by showing a picture; that is, a picture which is, or which causes, a knife in the back—a reasonable, or anyway Hitchcockian, description of Hitchcock's narrative procedure. Now take the telescope and the two men on the terrace. Thornhill's initial reaction to the view through the telescope is to say "I don't like the way Teddy Roosevelt is looking at me." And he will say, "I think he's telling me not to go on with this harebrained scheme." This could be a line Hitchcock is allowing Grant to use about himself, perhaps about his role in this strenuous film, perhaps about his career as an actor. (I wouldn't put it past Hitchcock to be alluding to the fact that Grant shares a name with a president of the United States, one famous for drinking, and one in particular that only Teddy Roosevelt among the four presidents figured at Mount Rushmore would have known was a president.) But the professor's response suggests something else first: "He's telling you to walk softly and carry a big stick." This makes a certain amount of sense said either to Grant or to Thornhill. It makes much better sense said to Hitchcock, hence said as it were to himself, that is, by one directorial surrogate to another. The exchange about a harebrained scheme and walking softly, as behind a big camera, would express a moment of self-doubt on Hitchcock's part to be overcome by the course of this film; and since this film is a kind of summary or anthology of his mature career as a whole, the doubt must be about the course of his mature career as a whole. If one were prepared to believe this, one would be encouraged to take the title *North by Northwest* not as naming some unheard of direction but as titling a search for directedness, or sanity, a claim to have found it, as of the course of a career. (We will come to a more general reason for taking the title this way.) Hitchcock's identifying himself with the actor figure permits him a certain opposition to the two more explicit director figures, that is, permits him to claim opposition to the way other directors operate; his testimony is to show himself the victim as well as the inquisitor of his trade, the pursued as well as the pursuer, permitting himself to be looked back at.

This prompts me to collect one of the last of Hitchcock's inclusions in his anthology: his reference to *Rear Window*, whose hero (James Stewart) also looks through a telescope, now explicitly a telescopic camera lens and thus more explicitly conferring an identification as a film director, and whom someone or something eventually also looks back at through his telescope in a way he does not like. The Stewart figure has a kind of comic Hamlet derivation in that he sees everything and is debarred from taking action (by a broken leg in a cast). The thing that looks back at him, locking gazes with him, is the man whose murdering of his wife and dismemberment and disposition of the pieces of the body Stewart's camera has divined; and this too feels like an act of identification, between viewer and viewed, between director and subjects. Hitchcock's confession is a terrible one. (It may just be worth remembering that the Hamlet figure in Saxo Grammaticus dismembered the body of the figure that became Polonius and disposed of the parts in a sewer; and just worth putting this together with Thornhill's early dictation to his secretary of a note to accompany a gift of gold-wrapped candy: "This is for your sweet tooth, and all your other sweet parts.") The brighter side of Hitchcock's sensing an identification of himself with Hamlet claims his position as that of an intellectual, as possessed of a metaphysical imagination, and as unknown (partly because of the antic disposition he puts on).

What I just called Hitchcock's terrible confession—it is something I understand by Rothman's detection of Hitchcock's murderous camera—was going to be the guiding subject of these remarks, the thought that filming inevitably proceeds by severing things, both in cutting and, originally, in framing, and that Hitchcock is fully sensible of this fact and responsible to it. While it is buried in *North by Northwest* in the rarified reference to the original Hamlet story it is, if you allow the subject, blatantly posed by the gigantic heads of the monument and by the matching of Grant's head with them. The suggestion is that these memorializations have required acts of severing. This would be something else Grant does not like when he sees something looking back at him through the telescope. And it is this fate that Thornhill is saved from in earning the rescue from the faces of the monument. So when I say that Grant's looking through the telescope represents our perception of film, of something I mean by viewing, I am proposing that a theory of this mode of perception will be given in a theory of the perception of part-objects, as this is broached in the work of Melanie Klein. Such a theory should be able to help account for a pair of familiar facts in looking at film: that there may apparently be the most fantastic disproportion between what is actually shown on the screen and the emotion this elicits; and that this disproportion can be resisted, the emotion fail to appear. After all, many people think, or think they think, that *North by Northwest* is a light comedy. But while I have left the theme of severed objects as an undercurrent of these remarks I decided against making it explicit (then I partly changed my mind).

What is it that looks back through the telescope at Thornhill, who presumably has no special relation to those heads (anyway not Grant's relation)? It is puzzling that he should say it is Teddy Roosevelt since that head is, from the angle taken, quite retracted in comparison to those of Washington, Jefferson, and Lincoln and is not facing in the right direction. We are in any case being asked to let ourselves be puzzled by what it is we see when we are looking at the results of a movie camera and also by what the Mount Rushmore Memorial betokens. I figure what looks back through the lens not to require eyes, not even images of eyes, but to be whatever it is that a movie camera looks at, which is to say, whatever power it is that is solicited from us in perceiving things on film. I once said that the images of photography are of the world as a whole, and now thinking of what looks back at a director—an image's original audience as reciprocated by these mountainous heads of the presidents, cliffs turned into faces—I would like to say that what looks back, what reveals itself to the viewer's gaze, is the physiognomy of the world, say the face of the earth. To animate, or reanimate, or humanize the world and so achieve a reciprocity with it is a recognizable aspiration of some poetry and some philosophy, as for example when Thoreau writes in the chapter "The Ponds" in *Walden*: "A lake is the landscape's most beautiful and expressive feature. It is earth's eye; looking into which the beholder measures the depth of his own nature." Thornhill's capacity for beholding nature in this way—as unsevered—would be a sign that he is to be saved.

The Mount Rushmore Memorial is a crazy American literalization of this ambition of reciprocity with the world. More specifically it literalizes such an idea as Walt Whitman's that America's mountains and prairies are the greatest of its poems. It is as if the monument proposes a solution to an American ambivalence as old as the pilgrims about the land of America: that it is human, in particular female, a virgin and yet a nourishing mother, but at the same time that we have raped her, blotted nature out by wanting our mark upon her.[5] (I have suggested that the film *North by Northwest*, in the crop-dusting sequence, invokes that ambivalence and calls for a solution to it.) The proposed solution of the monument is that if the mark is big enough and art enough and male enough, the doom of progress may be redeemed. Hardly a saving message to be drawn from the observation and memory of Washington, Jefferson, and Lincoln.

The *Encyclopedia Americana* notes that the faces of the monument measure some sixty feet from chin to forehead and adds, rather proudly I thought, that this is twice as high as the head of the Giza Sphinx. But what else is there to think about but their monumentality, and what more to conclude on their basis than that America has become twice the land of Egypt, twice as enslaving and twice as mysterious? Hitchcock shows that for a projected screen image to encompass the size of these faces is the work of an instant, and thus he at once declares his work in competition with Mount Rushmore as a monument to America, about America, and asks for a meditation on what can now constitute monumentality, on what can be made so as to show the value in commemorating. This is a reason that this film is at pains to anthologize the whole body of Hitchcock's mature, mostly American, work, to throw it all into the balance as a kind of rededication. Rededication is an appropriate mood before a monument, particularly in a moment of self-doubt. And even if this monument exemplifies competition and domination as much as it does commemoration, still it is about founding fathers, a wish, however awkwardly expressed, to get back to origins. Hitchcock has been careful to dissociate his attitude toward the monument from Vandamm's contemptuous dismissal of it with his opening question to Kaplan/Thornhill at the cafeteria: something like, "Now what little drama have you invited me to witness in these gay surroundings?" (This Englishman does not belong to the place but owns a structure mythically close to it, pitched out from the land, less a dwelling than a space station.) And what better rededication than to compete with this monument's way of remembering by showing your fellow inhabitants a better way—a way that does not attempt to petrify and sever the past but to revise the inheritance of it, to reinherit it?

Before giving the answer I have, I pause to note that we could loop back and recount the main topics of *North by Northwest* as topics of seduction—our seduction by one another, by beautiful women and beautiful men and beautiful things, by mothers, strangers, liquor, fame, monuments, politics, America, art, film. The present film asks us to consider our attachments to things less in the light of what things they are than in the light of what mode of attachment we take toward them—for example, fetishistic, scoptophilic, masochistic, narcissistic, or in general, to use a key word of Emerson's, partial. One result of such consideration might be the thought that a healthy suspicion and testing of our attachment to film should extend to our attachment to, say, literature as well and that film and literature are each capable of helping us in this extension.

The mountain-monument seems to have become just another landscape of a cold war, the scene of an escape, as though we had lost the capacity for attachment altogether; but then it is the site of the playing out of one of drama's oldest subjects, the rights of love against the rights, anyway the requirements, of politics. We might come to think that the escape of this pair is seen by Hitchcock to be of national importance. Who are they, and what are they doing on this monument?

I will, as said, assert that they derive from, or from the same source as, the American comedy of remarriage, which I said means to me that their goal is the thing I call the legitimizing of marriage, the declaration that happiness is still to be won there, there or nowhere, and that America is a place, fictional no doubt, in which that happiness can be found. The structure of these comedies, making the goal achievable, takes responsibility over a longish, extendable list of features, two of the principal ones being the achieving of a new innocence and the establishing or reestablishing of an identity. These are pieces of an ancient Hitchcockian problematic. So are the two further features of remarriage comedies that I call the capacities for adventure and for improvisation. I mean by these capacities the virtues that allow you to become at home in the world, to establish the world as a home. The capacities permit, if necessary, living together on the road, as if loving were the finding of a direction, that is, of a directedness, just, as I mentioned, as Hitchcock's title *North by Northwest* names otherwise than a given direction. So important is it to get this capacity for adventurousness straight that in the middle of their escape down the monument the pair pause, comically, surrealistically, to discuss it (as silent comics used to pause, in the middle of chasing one another, to catch their breath). After his proposal to her she asks what happened to his two earlier marriages. He says his wives left him because they found he led too dull a life. For Hitchcock so daringly to mock the suspense he has been building up over this escape, virtually declaring that the two are now standing on a platform in a studio, must mean that he wants to illustrate the significance of this exchange, to enforce the assertion that dullness, taken as the opposite of adventurousness, where these are characteristics of human relationship, spiritual matters, is not something that running around the face of the earth proves or disproves, except allegorically. With those wives even this monumental situation of life and death would have been, spiritually speaking, dull; whereas with Eve the "importance" of the time and place is unimportant for the opposite reason, that anything and everything can be an adventure, however untellable as such from outside. (This is roughly the sentiment of *Bringing Up Baby*.)

The candidates for remarriage must, further, not be virgins, they must have a past together, and they must talk well and wittily about marriage, especially about whether they believe in marriage. The past the pair share in *North by Northwest* is just one night, but it proves ample enough. And one or both of the pair must maintain an openness to childhood, so it turns out to be to Thornhill's spiritual credit that although in the course of the film he becomes big he remains a boy. (The childlike capacity of Grant's temperament on film is stressed, I suppose discovered, in the comedies he made with Howard Hawks.) The man in remarriage comedies is responsible for the education of the woman as part of a process of rescuing or redeeming her from a state in which she keeps herself; this may be characterized as a coldness or an inability to feel, and the education typically takes the form of the man's lecturing or haranguing the woman. In *North by Northwest* Thornhill identifies Eve as a statue and accuses her of having no feelings to hurt, but we are shown by her tears at this moment (at the auction) that what I earlier called the education in his surviving her onslaught has taken effect; to begin her physical rescue, he will later write on his monogrammed match-book a note that contains information no one else in the world is in a position to impart to her. We may also see in this successful delivery his finally getting a message through to a woman, the difficulty doing which began this plot.

This is enough to let me outline what I take as the essential difference in structure between the romantic comedies of remarriage and Hitchcock's romantic thriller. The goal of the comedies requires what I call the creation of the woman, a new creation of a new woman. This takes the form in the comedies of something like the woman's death and revival, and it goes with the camera's insistence on the flesh-and-blood reality of the female actor. When this happens in Hitchcock, as it did in *Vertigo*, the Hitchcock film preceding *North by Northwest*, it is shown to produce catastrophe: the woman's falling to her death, precisely the fate averted in *North by Northwest*. Here, accordingly, it is the man who undergoes death and revival (at least twice, both times at the hands of the woman) and whose physical identity is insisted upon by the camera.[6] Hitchcock is thus investigating the point that the comedies of remarriage are least certain about, namely, what it is about the man that fits him to educate and hence rescue the woman, that is, to be chosen by the woman to educate her and thereby to achieve happiness for them both.

But again, why is the rescue to be achieved from the face of this monument? I have called it the face of the earth, the earth itself become visible, as pure surface. These tiny creatures are crawling between heaven and earth, a metaphysical accomplishment, as if becoming children again. Hamlet, feeling like a child, claims this accomplishment for himself as he decrees that there shall be no more marriages. Thornhill proposes marriage as he and the woman hang from a precipice; a gallant concept, as if marriage were a presence of mind, requiring no assurance of a future. Close-ups of the pair on the surface of the monument faces show them as if on an alien planet. There is no longer nature on the earth; earth is no longer an artifact by analogy, intimating God; it is literally and totally artifact, petrified under the hands of mankind. To place your film in competition with such an achievement is to place it in competition with film's own peculiar power of preserving the world by petrifying it, or anyway fixing it in celluloid. The couple in remarriage comedies are isolated at the end, expected to legitimize marriage without the world, which has no help for pain. The surface of Hitchcock's Mount Rushmore strikes me as a place of absolute spiritual isolation, civilization engulfing even empty space. In one of his first American films, *Saboteur* (to name a final excerpt in this anthology), a man holds a villain from a ledge at the top of the Statue of Liberty, but the villain's sleeve comes loose and he falls to earth. To fall from Mount Rushmore, as I am imagining it, would be to fall off the earth, down the vast edges drear of the world.

Thornhill lifts Eve up directly from the isolation of the monument's ledge to the isolation of the marriage bed, as if identifying both places as the scene of cliffhangers and declaring that they are at home in both. At the lift Leonard is overcome and drops the statue Eve has been identified with, which breaks against the granite monument, opening to produce some film, I take it the present film. I in effect describe *The Philadelphia Story* as a film produced by a rescue which takes the form of the breaking of a statue in favor of a woman. I also claim that the remarriage is, using a repeated phrase of that film, of national importance. My ground is the thought that while America, or any discovered world, can no longer ratify marriage, the achievement of true marriage might ratify something called America as a place in which to seek it. This is a state secret.

Notes

1. Rothman's book was published by Harvard University Press in 1982. I am also indebted to Marian Keane's "The Designs of Authorship: An Essay on *North by Northwest*," *Wide Angle* 4, no. 1 (1980): 44–52.1 should like to mention here Robin Wood's *Hitchcock's Films* (New York, 1970), an intelligent, literate statement about the films of Hitchcock, which, while comparatively early as these things go in English-speaking circles, continues to repay reading. For an account of *North by Northwest* at once more suspicious than mine (about the value of the film) and more gullible (about Hitchcock's remarks about it and about the film's apparently casual evaluation of itself, so to speak), see George M. Wilson's "The Maddest McGuffin: Some Notes on *North by Northwest*," *Modern Language Notes* 94 (1979): 1159–72.

2. A consequent moral equation between these figures is being drawn, another point I took away from a conversation with Rothman and Keane.

3. Subsequent to the original publication of this piece I looked up another document familiar in Hamlet scholarship that Professor Geoffrey Bullough, in volume 7 of his *Narrative and Dramatic Sources of Shakespeare*, describes as "the German prose play *Der Bestrafte Brudermord oder Prinz Hamlet aus Dannemark*, the degenerate version of an English play probably taken over to the Continent by English actors before 1626" (p. 20). Professor Bullough prints the play (among the Sources, Possible Sources, Probable Sources, Probable Historical Allusions, and Analogues; specifically as an Analogue) in an English translation entitled *Fratricide Punished* revised from one made for H. H. Furness's *The New Variorum Edition* of *Hamlet* of 1877. In this play the Laertes character is named Leonhardus.

I mention this not exactly to clinch my suggestion that the name Laertes may be seen to survive in the name Leonard; and not just to indicate a perfectly obvious place in which Hitchcock might have learned this change of name (Furness's famous editions and compilations), a source he may very well have meant to leave a clue for in his own change; but primarily to make explicit the question of when and how a matter of interpretation gets clinched in one's own mind. It might, I think, have happened to me on discovering Leonhardus; but in fact it came with the emphasis on "rot," as read in the paragraph following the one to which this note is appended.

4. Even Raymond Bellour's useful and sophisticated study of *North by Northwest* ("*Le blocage symbolique*," *Communications* 23 [1975]: 235–350), judging from one hurried reading, has not, it seems to me, cleared itself of this question. My remark is directed only to the first half of this monograph-length paper. The second half, devoted to a geometry of the crop-dusting sequence, I have not looked at sufficiently to have a judgment of.

5. Two valuable accounts of the history of American attitudes toward the American land are Edwin Fussell's *Frontier: American Literature and the American West* (Princeton, N.J., 1965), and Annette Kolodny's *The Lay of the Land: Metaphor as Experience and History in American Life and Letters* (Chapel Hill, N.C., 1975).

6. That a given genre yields an adjacent genre by having one of its features "negated" in this way is something I give a little theoretical attention to in the introduction to *Pursuits of Happiness*.

4

The Fact of Television

Again I am indebted to the editor of *Daedalus*, Stephen Graubard, this time for demanding that I say what I could about the phenomenon of television. The occasion was the convening of a study group for which papers were prepared with a view, after discussion, to revising and collecting them for publication as the fall 1982 issue of *Daedalus*, entitled "Print Culture and Video Culture." In addition to the benefit derived from the reactions of the study group, the first version of these remarks was read by William Rothman, who prepared a set of comments that caused changes on every other page as I prepared a second version. This was then read by Norton Batkin, Gus Blaisdell, Jay Cantor, and Arnold Davidson, whose comments I used, as elsewhere, as I prepared the present, here reprinted, version.

O F COURSE THERE ARE interesting facts about television, facts about its technology, about the history of its programs, about the economic structure of the networks that produce it. Most of these facts I do not know, but I think I know what it would be like to learn them, and to start to learn what they add up to. By speaking of the fact of television, I mean to call attention to something else, something I do not, in the same way, think I know how to learn more about, something like the sheer fact that television exists, and that this existence is at once among the most

First published in *Daedalus*, fall 1982; reprinted in *Themes Out of School*.

obvious and the most mysterious facts of contemporary life. Its obviousness is that television has conquered, like the electric light, or the automobile, or the telephone. Its mystery is twofold: first, how it has conquered;
and second, how we (we, for example, who write for and read *Daedalus*)
have apparently remained largely uninterested in accounting for its conquering. (What it has conquered, I wish to leave, or to make, a question,
part of the mystery. Has it conquered as a form of popular, or mass, entertainment? Popular as opposed to what? And what happened to the forms
over which television triumphed?)

The twofold mystery comes to a twofold assumption, with which I
begin, that there is something yet to be understood concerning both the
interest in television and the refusal of interest in it. The latter half of the
assumption is that the absence of critical or intellectual attention to television—both in kind and extent—is not satisfactorily understandable as a
straightforward lack of interest, as if the medium were inherently boring.
Individual intellectuals will, of course, straightforwardly find no interest
there, as they may not in film. But the absence of interest in the medium
seems to me more complete, or studied, than can be accounted for by the
accidents of taste. That the absence is not accidental or straightforward is
epitomized, I think, in the familiar disapproval evinced toward television
in certain educated circles. Members of these circles would apparently prefer not to permit a TV set in the house; but if unable to hold to this pure
line, they sternly limit the amount of time the children may watch, regardless of the content. If this line has in turn been breached, and the choice is
between letting the kids watch at home or at a neighbor's house, they are
apt to speak guiltily—or at any rate awkwardly—about their and their children's knowledge of its programs. As if in reaction, other intellectuals
brazen out a preference for commercial over public television.

Such behavior suggests to my mind a fear of television for which I
have heard no credible explanation. Sometimes people say, loosely I suppose, that television is addictive. And of course it would be a plausible
explanation of both television's attraction and its repulsion if it were credible to attribute addictive powers to it, to believe quite literally that the
tube is not only in the service of boobs, but that it turns otherwise useful
citizens into boobs. (I will cite such a view toward the end of these
remarks.) But I have no acquaintance with anyone who treats television in
all seriousness as if it were the equivalent of, say, heroin. Even if marijua-
na presented a more analogous level of fear, adults worried about its effects
would not make it available to their children, even on a strictly limited
basis, unless perhaps they were already dealing with addiction. Nor does
the disapproval of television seem to me very close to the disapproval of
comic books by an earlier generation of parents, described so well by

Robert Warshow in "Paul, the Horror Comics, and Dr. Wertham."[1] Like any concerned parent who wants to provide his or her children with the pleasures of cultivation, and who does not underestimate how exacting those pleasures are to command, Warshow was worried—having investigated and dismissed as groundless the then fashionable claim that comics incited their readers to violence—about the sheer time comics seem to steal from better things. But he decided that his son's absorption would pass and that less harm would be done by waiting it out than by prohibiting it. The difference I sense from the disapproval of television may be that Warshow was not himself tempted by a craving to absorb himself in comic books, so that he had firsthand evidence that the absorption would die naturally, whereas adults today may have no analogous evidence from their own experience of television, fearing their own addictiveness. Or is there some surmise about the nature of the pleasure television provides that sets off disapproval of it, perhaps like surmises that once caused the disapproval of novel reading or, later, of movie viewing? If this were the case, one might expect the disapproval to vanish when television comes of age, when its programs achieve an artistic maturity to match that of the great novels and movies. Is this a reasonable faith?

Certainly I have been among those who have felt that television cannot have come of age, that the medium must have more in it than what has so far been shown. True, I have felt, at the same time, that so much money and talent have been lavished on it, that if there is anything more in the medium, it could hardly have escaped discovery. From this thought, one of two conclusions may be drawn: that there is indeed nothing more to be discovered and that the medium is accordingly one of poverty and boredom (I once found myself in a discussion of these matters impatiently observing that television is no more a medium of art than the telephone, the telegraph, or the telescope); or, since this is not quite credible, that the poverty lies not in the medium's discoveries, but rather in our understanding of these discoveries, in our failure as yet to grasp what the medium is for, what constitutes its powers and its treasures.

Since I am inclined to the latter of these conclusions, to speculate on what might constitute a better route of understanding is what I conceive my task here to be (together with some speculation about what kind of issue "the understanding of a medium" is). This means that I accept the condition of both conclusions, namely that television has come of age, that this, these programs, more or less as they stand, in what can appear to be their poverty, is what there is to understand. For suppose we agree that television's first major accomplishments can be dated no later than 1953, the time of the coverage of the first Eisenhower inauguration. In that case, it has had thirty years in which to show itself. If Griffith's major films around 1915 are taken to date the birth of film as a medium of art, then it took only ten more years to reach the masterpieces of Chaplin and Keaton; and over the next twenty years, America, to go no further, established a momentum in producing definitive movies—movies that are now among the permanent pleasures of art theaters, of museum programs, of film studies programs, and of late-night television—that was essentially slowed (or so the story goes) only with the help of the rising television industry. One of our questions should be: Did television give back as good as it took away?

The acceptance of television as a mature medium of art further specifies what I mean in calling my subject here the fact of television. A further consequence of this characterization, or limitation of my subject, is that I am not undertaking to discuss the progress and results of experimental video artists. This is not meant to imply that I am uninterested in what might be called "the medium of video." On the contrary, it would be a way of describing my motive here as an interest in what television, as it stands, reveals about this medium. I do not mean to assume that this description captures a topic of assured significance or fruitfulness. I do hope, rather, that it is one way of picking up the subject of this issue of *Daedalus* concerning the supposed general influence of video on our culture at large, on a par with the influence of print. In developing my contribution, I will take my bearings from some thoughts I worked with in speculating about the medium of film in *The World Viewed*.[2] That book also addresses what I am calling the nature of the medium, by asking what the traditional masterpieces, or successes, among movies reveal it to be, not especially what experimental work finds it to be. It is a guiding thesis of that book that major films are those in which the medium is most richly or deeply revealed. (This remains controversial. A reviewer of my recently published *Pursuits of Happiness: The Hollywood Comedy of Remarriage* found that book pretentious and sometimes preposterous, in part because he cannot believe that even the best of Hollywood films are as self-reflective, or intelligent, about their source in the medium of film—if, in a sense, less explicit—as is the work of "modernist self-referential artists" like Godard and Antonioni. Hollywood is a mythical locale, part of whose function is to cause people to imagine that they know it without having taken its works seriously, like America.)

An immediate difference presents itself between television and film. To say that masterpieces among movies reveal the medium of film is to say that this revelation is the business of individual works, and that these works have a status analogous to traditional works of art: they last beyond their immediate occasions; their rewards bear up under repeated viewings; they lend themselves to the same pitch of critical scrutiny as do any of the works we care about most seriously. This seems not to be true of individual works of television. What is memorable, treasurable, criticizable, is not primarily the individual work, but the program, the format, not this or that day of "I Love Lucy," but the program as such. I say this "seems" to me to be so, and what I will have to say here depends on its being so. But my experience of television is much more limited than my experience of movies and of pretelevision radio, so my views about the treasuring of television's works may be especially unreliable. Still, I think that people who have been puzzled by the phenomenon of television as I have been—evidenced by being more grateful, if grudgingly so, to some of it, than familiar aesthetic concepts will explain—must commonly have had the thought, or intuition, that its value is a function of its rule of format. My speculations here are intended as something like experiments to test how far one would have to go to follow this intuition, with reasonable intellectual satisfaction, through the aesthetic range of the phenomenon we know as television.

I have begun by citing grounds on which to deny that the evanescence of the instance, of the individual work, in itself shows that television has not yet come of age aesthetically. (Even were it to prove true that certain television works yet to be made may become treasured instances, as instances, such as the annual running of *The Wizard of Oz*—which serves to prove my case, since this is not an object made by and for television—my topic here remains television as it stands in our lives now.) But movies also, at least some movies, maybe most, used to exist in something that resembles this condition of evanescence, viewable only in certain places at certain times, discussable solely as occasions for sociable exchange, almost never seen more than once, and then more or less forgotten. For many, perhaps still for most people, this is still the fate of film. (It is accordingly also true that some people, perhaps still most, would take it as true of movies that individual works do not bear up under repetition and criticism. That this is a possible way to take film, I was just asserting, and I was implying that it is also partial. I will give a name to this way of taking it presently.) But from the beginning of the art of film, there have been those who have known that there was more to movies, more to think about, to experience, in their ordinary instances, than met the habitual eye. In recent years, this thought is becoming increasingly common (though not at all as common, I believe, as certain people living on the east and west coasts and in certain other enclaves imagine); whereas, as I have indicated, my impression is that comparatively few people maintain an aesthetic interest in the products of network television. A writer like Leslie Fiedler asserts a brazen interest in network television, or perhaps it is a sterling interest. But he insists that the source of his interest lies precisely in television's not producing art, in its providing, so to speak, a relief from art. And then again, it seems to me that he has said the same thing about movies, all movies, anyway all American movies. And if someone did appear to take the different interest, my question would persist: What is it he or she is taking this interest in?

A further caution—as it were, a technological caution—also conditions the remarks to follow. If the increasing distribution of video cassettes and disks goes so far as to make the history of film as much a part of the present experience of film as the history of the other arts is part of their present—hence, in this dimension, brings film into the condition of art—it will make less respectable the assumption of the evanescence of the individual movie, its exhaustion under one viewing, or always casual viewings; or rather, it will make this assumption itself evanescent, evidently the product of historical conditions, not inevitable. At the same time, if the distribution of video cassette recorders and cable television increases, as appears to be happening, to the size of the distribution of television itself, or to a size capable of challenging it, this will make problematic whether television will continue to exist primarily as a medium of broadcasting. I am not so much interested in predicting that such developments will actually come to establish themselves as I am in making conceptual room for understanding the aesthetic possibilities of such developments.

To say that the primary object of aesthetic interest in television is not the individual piece, but the format, is to say that the format is its primary individual of aesthetic interest. This ontological recharacterization is meant to bring out that the relation between format and instance should be of essential aesthetic concern. There are two classical concepts in talking about movies that fit the requirements of the thing I am calling a format, as it were, an artistic kind: the concepts of the serial and of the genre. The units of a serial are familiarly called its episodes; I will call the units of a genre its members. A thesis it seems to be worth exploring is that television, for some reason, works aesthetically according to a serial-episode principle rather than according to a genre-member principle. What are these principles?

In traditional terms, they would not be apt to invoke what I mean by different principles of composition. What is traditionally called a genre film is a movie whose membership in a group of films is no more problematic than the exemplification of a serial in one of its episodes. You can, for example, roughly see that a movie is a western, or gangster film, or horror film, or prison film, or "woman's film," or a screwball comedy. Call this way of thinking about genre, genre-as-cycle. In contrast, in *Pursuits of Happiness,* the way I found I wanted to speak of genre in defining what I call the Hollywood comedy of remarriage, I will call genre-as-medium.

Because I feel rather backed into the necessity of considering the notion of a genre, I feel especially in need of the reader's forbearance over the next half dozen or so paragraphs. It seems that the notion of a genre has lately been receiving renewed attention from literary theorists, but the recent pieces of writing I have started to look at on the subject (so far, I realize, too unsystematically) all begin with a sense of dissatisfaction with other writing on the subject, either with the way the notion has so far been defined, or with the confusion of uses to which it has been put, or both. I am not interested here in joining an argument but rather in sketching the paths of two (related) ideas of a genre; it is an interest in coming to terms with what seem to me to be certain natural confusions in approaching the notion of a genre. In *Pursuits of Happiness* I was letting the discussion of certain individual works, which, so far as I know, had never been put together as a group, lead me, or push me, into sketching a theory of genre, and I went no further with it than the concrete motivations in reading individual works seemed to me to demand. With that in mind, in the present essay I am beginning, on the contrary, with certain intuitions concerning what the general aesthetic powers of video turn upon, and I am hoping to get far enough in abstracting these powers from the similar, hence different, powers of film, to get in a position to test these intuitions in concrete cases. (I may, however, just mention that two of the books I have been most helped by are Northrop Frye's *A Natural Perspective*[3] and Tzvetan Todorov's *The Fantastic*.[4])

Before going on to give my understanding of the contrasting notions of a genre, I should perhaps anticipate two objections to my terminology. First, if there is an established, conventional use of the word "genre," and if this fits what I am calling genre-as-cycle, why not keep the simple word and use some other simple word to name the further kind of kind I am thinking of, the kind I am calling genre-as-medium—why not just call the further kind a set or a group or a pride? Second, since film itself is thought of as a medium (for example, of art), why insist on using the same word to characterize a gathering of works within that medium? As to this second objection, this double range of the concept of a medium is deployed familiarly in the visual arts, in which painting is said to be a medium (of art, in contrast, say, to sculpture or to music—hardly, one would think, the same contrast), and in which gouache is also a medium (of painting, in contrast to watercolor or oil or tempera). I wish to preserve, and make more explicit—or curious—this double range in order to keep open to investigation the relation between work and medium that I call the revelation, or acknowledgment, of the one in the other. In my experience, to keep this open means, above all, resisting (by understanding) the temptation to think of a medium simply as a familiar material (for instance, sound, color, words), as if this were an unprejudicial observation rather than one of a number of ways of taking the material of a medium, and recognizing

instead that only the art can define its media, only painting and composing and movie making can reveal what is required, or possible (what
means, what exploits of material), for something to be a painting, a piece
of music, a movie. As to the first objection—my use of "genre" in naming
both of what I claim are different principles or procedures of composition—my purpose is to release something true in both uses of the word (in
both, there is a process of generating in question), and to leave open to
investigation what the relation between these processes may be. The difference may be consequential. I think, for example, that it is easier to
understand movies as some familiar kind of commodity or as entertainments if you take them as participating not in a genre-as-medium but in
genres-as-cycles, or if you focus on those movies that do participate, without remainder, in genres so conceived. Movies thought of as members of
genres-as-cycles is the name of the way of taking them that I earlier characterized as evanescent. The simplest examples of such cycles used to be
signaled by titles such as *The Son of X, The Curse of X, X Meets Dracula*, and
so on. Our sophistication today requires that we call such sequels *XII, XIII*,
and so on, like Super Bowls. It is part of Hollywood's deviousness that certain sequels may be better than their originals, as perhaps *The Bride of
Frankenstein* is, or Fritz Lang's *The Return of Frank James*.

Still another word about terminology, before going on to consider
the thesis that television works according to a serial-episode rather than a
genre-member principle. In picking up the old movie term "serial" to
mark the contrast in question, I am assuming that what used to be called
serials on film bears some internal relation to what are called series on television. But what I am interested in considering here is the idea of serialization generally, wishing again to leave open what the relations are
between serials and series (as I wish to leave open, hence to recall, the
occurrence of serialization in classical novels, in photographs, in paintings,
in music, in comic strips). One might find that the closest equivalent on
television to the movie serial is the soap opera, since this shares the feature
of more or less endless narration across episodes, linked by crises. But in
going on now to consider a little my thesis about serialization in television,
I am exploring my intuition that the repetitions and recurrences of soap
operas bear a significant relation with those of series, in which the narrative comes to a classical ending each time, and indeed that these repetitions and recurrences are modes of a requirement that the medium of television exacts in all its formats. A program such as "Hill Street Blues"
seems to be questioning the feature of a series that demands a classical
ending for each instance, hence questioning the distinction between soap
opera and series. Similarly, or oppositely, the projected sequence of movies
instanced by *Star Wars* and *The Empire Strikes Back* seems to be question-

ing the distinction between a serial and a cycle by questioning the demand of a serial (a narrative that continues over an indefinite number of episodes) not to come to a classical ending before the final episode. This would bring the sequence closer in structure to literary forms such as (depending on individual taste) the King Arthur legends, the Shakespeare Henry plays (perhaps in a Lamb-like retelling), or Tolkien's *Lord of the Rings* trilogy.

A genre, as I use the notion in *Pursuits of Happiness*, and which I am here calling genre-as-medium, behaves according to two basic "laws" (or "principles"), one internal, the other external. Internally, a genre is constituted by members, about which it can be said that they share what you might picture as every feature in common. In practice, this means that, where a given member diverges, as it must, from the rest, it must "compensate" for this divergence. The genre undergoes continuous definition or redefinition as new members introduce new points of compensation. Externally, a genre is distinguished from other genres, in particular from what I call "adjacent" genres, when one feature shared by its members "negates" a feature shared by the members of another. Here, a feature of a genre will develop new lines of refinement. If genres form a system (which is part of the faith that for me keeps alive an interest in the concept), then in principle it would seem possible to be able to move by negation from one genre through adjacent genres, until all the genres of film are derived. Hitchcock's corpus provides convenient examples: his *North by Northwest* shares an indefinitely long list of features with remarriage comedies, which implies, according to my work on the subject, that it is about the legitimizing of marriage. In this film, as in other adventures, by Hitchcock and by others, legitimacy is conferred by a pair's survival together of a nation-saving adventure.[5] But that film can further be understood as negating the feature of the remarriage genre according to which the woman has to undergo something like death and revival. When this happens in Hitchcock, as in *Vertigo*, the Hitchcock film immediately preceding *North by Northwest*, it causes catastrophe. In *North by Northwest* it is the man who undergoes death and revival (and for a reason, I claim, having to do with the structure of the remarriage form). A dozen years earlier, in *Notorious*, Hitchcock compensates for the feature of the woman's death and revival (hence, maintaining the happiness of a remarriage ending) by emphasizing that her death and revival are not the condition of the man's loving her, but the effect of his failure to acknowledge her (as happens, seminally, according to my discussion of the genre, in *The Winter's Tale*).

The operations of compensation and negation are meant to specify the idea of a genre in *Pursuits of Happiness*, in contrast to what I take to be the structuralist idea of a genre as a form characterized by features, as an

object is characterized by its properties, an idea that seems to me to underlie, for example, Todorov's work on the fantastic tale. I put it this way:

> An alternative idea . . . is that the members of a genre share the
> inheritance of certain conditions, procedures, and subjects and goals
> of composition, and that in primary art each member of such a genre
> represents a study of these conditions, something I think of as bear-
> ing the responsibility of the inheritance. There is, on this picture,
> nothing one is tempted to call the features of a genre which all its
> members have in common. (p. 28)

Such operations as compensation and negation are not invoked either in
genre-as-cycle or in serial-episode procedure. So I am saying that they are
made by serialization as opposed to the generation in genre-as-medium.
But in neither sense of genre are the members of a genre episodes of a continuing story or situation or setting. It is not the same narrative matter for
Frankenstein to get a bride as for Rhoda (in a popular television series of
a few years ago bearing her name) to get a husband. The former is a drama
on its own; the latter serves a history, a before and after.

In speaking of a procedure of serialization, I wish to capture what
seems to me right in the intuition of what are called narrative "formulas."
When theorists of structural or formal matters speak of "formulas" of
composition, they are thinking, I believe, of genre-as-cycle or of serial-
episode construction, in which each instance is a perfect exemplification of
the format, as each solution of an equation, or each step in a mathematical series, is a perfect instance of the formula that "generates" it. The
instances do not compete with one another for depth of participation, nor
comment upon one another for mutual revelation; and whether an
instance "belongs" to the formula is as settled by the formula as is the identity of the instance. (Such remarks are really recipes—most untested—for
what a formula would look like; hence, for what would count as "generation" in this context. I am taking it that no item of plot need be common
to all the episodes of, say, "Rhoda" so that the formula that does the generating is sufficiently specified by designating the continuing characters
and their relations with one another (characters and relations whose recurrent traits are themselves specifiable in definite ways). This is the situation
in the situation comedy. A certain description of the situation would constitute the formula of the comedy. Then the substitution of the unknown
new element to initiate the generation, the element of difference, can be
any event that alters the situation comically—Rhoda develops a rash; her
sister is being followed by the office lothario; her mother's first boyfriend
has just showed up; and so on. A minimum amount of talent is all it takes

to write out the results of the generation competently—which of course does not necessarily mean salably; a much higher order is required to invent the characters and relations, and cast them, in such a way as to allow new generations readily and consistently to be funny.) Whereas in genre-as-medium none of this is so. In what I call the genre of remarriage comedy, the presence or absence of even the title of the genre does not insure that an instance does or does not belong to the genre. Belonging has to be won, earned, as by an argument of the members with one another; as adjacency of genre must be proved, something irrelevant to the existence of multiple series, which, further, raise no issue of the definition and refinement a genre undergoes. ("Belonging has to be won, as by an argument. . . ." Here is an allegory of the relation of the principal pair in such comedies. In their adventures of conversation, the pair are forever taking each other by surprise, forever interesting each other anew. To dream up these surprises and interests demands an exercise of talent that differs not only, or primarily, in its degree of energy from the energies I imagine in connection with developing a series, but differs in its order of deployment: here, the initiating idea is next to nothing compared with the details of the working out, which is what one would expect where the rule of format is, so to speak, overthrown. Here, what you might call the formula, or what in *Pursuits of Happiness* I call the myth, is itself under investigation, or generation, by the instances.)

What difference does any of this make? I expect no simple or direct answer to the question of the difference between generation and serialization. Perhaps they name incompatible ways of looking at human activities generally, or texts. It might be thought, for example, that a series and its formulas specify the construction of the popular arts, whereas genre-as-medium and its arguments specify the construction of the higher arts. John G. Cawehi's *Adventure, Mystery, and Romance: Formula Stories as Art and Popular Culture*[6] perhaps suggests this. Charles Rosen's *The Classical Style*[7] states a related distinction within high art, between the great and the mediocre, or between the original and the academic. Vladimir Propp's classical analysis of the fairy tale virtually declares that you would not expect a sophisticated work of art to obey formulas in that way.[8] But this merely transfers the question What is "that way"? One wants to answer by saying something like, "Mechanically or automatically (or formulaically?)." But maybe this is specific to fairy tales, not to all forms you might call popular. Are black-figure and red-figure vase paintings less formulaic? And are they less than high art? American quilts of the nineteenth century are surely not less formulaic, yet the effect of certain of them is breathtaking, not unlike the directness of certain nonobjective paintings. Like those paintings (I think of certain works of Rothko, Louis, Noland,

Olitski, Stella), these examples exist essentially as items of a series. It would
follow that the concept of existence in a series, of being composed according to a serial-episode principle, does not distinguish popular from high
art, only if, for instance, one accepts such painting as high art, something
not everyone does. And it would follow only if the concept of a series in
painting (or quilts) captures the same thought as the concept of a serial in
film and a series in television. So far as the thought is one of establishing
a formulaic relation between instances, the relation between paintings in a
series certainly seems at least as strong (as, so to speak, mechanical) as the
relation of episodes to one another. In fact, the relation between the paintings seems too strong to yield works of art: here, the instances seem purely generated, or determined, by a format with finite features, each of which
can be specified and varied to yield new items. (I think here of Stella's Z-
forms, or Noland's Chevrons or Ribbons, or Louis's Unfurleds.) The relation between members is exhaustively constituted, one may say, by their
mutual differences, as if to illustrate a linguist's vision, or that of the more
advanced of today's textualists, according to which language, and meaning,
and hence whatever replaces or precedes art, is constituted not by signs
(inherently) possessing or containing meaning, but by the weave of the
relation of difference among them (say their synthesis of distinctive features). But at the same time, the idea of the series can be taken to dispute
the linguistic or textualist appeal to difference, since this appeal generally
accompanies, even grounds, a claim that the sensuous properties of the
signs themselves are arbitrary. What painting in series argues is rather the
absolute nonarbitrariness of format, because the artistic discovery is precisely that this synthesis of features generates instances, each of which
maintains itself as a proposal of beauty. The achievement may be felt as
something like an empirical discovery of the a priori—not unlike a certain
aspiration of philosophy. (The implications of the fact of series for modern painting's disputing of received ideas of craft and style and medium,
and its proposal of surprising consequences for thinking about the relation
of painting and photography, is the subject of a pivotal chapter, "Excursus:
Some Modernist Painting," in *The World Viewed*.)

Another home of the idea of the formulaic is jazz, whose improvisations over most of its history are explicitly made possible by shared formulas, say of riff and progression. But the role of the formulaic in improvisation is familiar in other arenas of performance—in other regions of music
(say, in improvising cadenzas), in other recitations (say, the singing of
epics), and in other theater (say, commedia dell'arte). When people say
they miss television as it was when it was produced live, what they may be
missing is the sense of the improvisatory. And it may be that the diminished role of improvisation on television is an instance of a familiar process

in certain phases of the history of performance, during which the scope of improvisation is progressively diminished in favor, let us say, of the literary; in which, for example, it is no longer open to the performer to fill in the continuo part or to work out his or her own cadenza, for these are instead written out, fixed. Yet room remains for the improvisatory in television's formats, which I will specify after saying something about what those formats are, or are of.

I note here that the idea of improvisation has internal, and opposite, associations with the idea of serialization. In movie serials and in soap operas, the sense of suspense turns on the necessity for improvisation, of manner as well as of plot—humanity as expressed by the power and the readiness to improvise, as much as by the power and the readiness to endure. The issue is how the hero and heroine can survive this, this unprecedented precipice; how the authors can get themselves out. The issue has its comic equivalents, emotional and intellectual. It may be this connection of serialization with improvisation that links serialization with the idea or the fact of the popular. Contrariwise, serialization in music and in painting are as if made to reduce improvisation to a minimum, as if to prove that necessities can be found that are as beautiful in their consequences as contingencies can prove to be.

The point of going into the distinction of two modes of composition was to get at television's way of revealing its medium; it represents an effort to get at something one can see as the aesthetic interest of television. That there is such an interest invited by it, related to, but different from, an interest in what we call its economy, its sociology, and its psychology, and that this interest is still insufficiently understood—which contributes to an insufficiently developed critical tradition concerning television—is the way I am taking the issue of this issue of *Daedalus*. It is the point from which any contribution I may make to it is apt to proceed. If it proves sensible to locate television's aesthetic interest in a serial-episode mode of composition, as contrasted with a genre-member mode, then an investigation of the fact of television ought to contribute to understanding why there should be two principles of aesthetic composition.

What I have said they are principles of is the revelation (I habitually call this the acknowledgment) of an artistic medium. I specify this revelation in *The World Viewed*, by way of articulating what I call there "the material basis" of film. While I propose to continue here to be guided by such an idea, I do not mean just to assume that this idea makes good sense. I claim at most merely that what I am saying here makes sense if the procedures of *The World Viewed* make sense. This is far from certain, but there is more evidence of their working out there than anything I can provide here.

About halfway through *The World Viewed*, I give a provisional, summary characterization of the material basis of movies, apart from which there would be nothing to call a movie, just as without color on a delimited two-dimensional support there would be nothing to call a painting; I call the basis a succession of automatic world projections.[9] To capture my intuition of the comparable material basis of the (aesthetic) medium of television, I begin by recurring to the one remark about television that crops up in *The World Viewed*. The moment is one at which I am at pains to distinguish the fact of movies in relation to the fact of theater, on the blatant ground that in a theater the actors appear in person and in a film they do not. I quote a response André Bazin gives to this blatant ground,[10] one in which he downplays the difference in question, denying that "the screen is incapable of putting us in the presence of the actor": Bazin wishes to say that it relays the actors' presence to us as by mirrors. My response is to note that Bazin's idea here really fits the fact of live television, in which what we are presented with is happening simultaneously with its presentation. This remains reasonably blatant, anyway unsurprising. What surprised me was to find myself going on to object: "But in live television what is present to us while it is happening is not the world, but an event standing out from the world. Its point is not to reveal, but to cover (as with a gun), to keep something on view" (p. 26).

Taking this tip, I will characterize the material basis of television as a *current of simultaneous event reception*. This is how I am conceiving of the aesthetic fact of television that I propose to begin portraying. Why the ideas of a current and of simultaneity fit here in place of the ideas of succession and of the automatic, and why that of event than of world, and why reception than projection, are not matters decidable in advance of the investigation of each of these concepts. The mode of perception that I claim is called upon by film's material basis is what I call viewing. The mode of perception I wish to think about in connection with television's material basis is that of monitoring. The cause for this choice, initially, seems to be that, in characterizing television's material basis, I have not included transmission as essential to it; this would be because I am not regarding broadcasting as essential to the work of television. In that case, the mysterious sets, or visual fields, in our houses, for our private lives, are to be seen not as receivers, but as monitors. My claim about the aesthetic medium of television can now be put this way: its successful formats are to be understood as revelations (acknowledgments) of the conditions of monitoring, and by means of a serial-episode procedure of composition, which is to say, by means of an aesthetic procedure in which the basis of a medium is acknowledged primarily by the format rather than primarily by its instantiations.

What are the formats, or serializations, of television? I mean to be referring to things perfectly, grossly obvious: sitcoms, game shows, sports, cultural coverage (concerts, opera, ballet, etc.), talk shows, speeches and lectures, news, weather reports, movies, specials, and so on.

A notable feature of this list is the amount of talk that runs across the forms. This is an important reason, no doubt, for the frequent description of television as providing "company." But what does this talk signify, how does it in particular signify that one is not alone, or anyway, that being alone is not unbearable? Partly, of course, this is a function of the simultaneity of the medium—or of the fact that at any time it might be live and that there is no sensuous distinction between the live and the repeat, or the replay: the others are there, if not shut in this room, still caught at this time. One is receiving or monitoring them, like callers; and receiving or monitoring, unlike screening and projection, does not come between their presence to the camera and their presentness to us.

I recognize that even in the present sketch of a way to approach matters, this appeal to the idea of "no sensuous distinction" between the live and the repeat, or the replay or the delayed, and the connection of this distinction with a difference in modes of presence and presentness, is going too fast over consequential issues. It doesn't even include the fact that television can work in film as well as in tape. William Rothman has suggested to me that since television can equally adopt a movie mode or a video mode, we might recognize one dimension of television's "company" in the understanding of the act of switching from one mode to another as the thing that is always live, that is, effected simultaneously with our watching. This points to the feature of the current (suggesting the contemporary as well as indicating the continuous) in my articulation of this aesthetic medium's physical basis. It is internal to television formats to be made so as to participate in this continuity, which means that they are formed to admit discontinuities both within themselves and between one and another, and between these and commercials, station breaks, news breaks, emergency signal tests, color charts, program announcements, and so on, which means formed to allow these breaks, hence these recurrences, to be legible. So that switching (and I mean here not primarily switching within a narrative but switching from, say, a narrative to one or another break, for a station or for a sponsor, and back again) is as indicative of life as—in ways to be specified—monitoring is.

(I think in this context of the as yet undefined aesthetic position of commercials. Foreigners to commercial television often find them merely amusing or annoying interruptions (or of course, in addition, marks of a corrupt civilization); native explainers will sometimes affect to find them more interesting than the so-called programs they interrupt. Surely, ordinary people, anyway people without either of these axes to grind, can feel either way on occasion. Nor do I doubt, in all soberness, that some commercials just are more interesting than some programs. What the effort, or claim, to favor commercials over programs suggests to me is that the aesthetic position of commercials, what you might call their possibility—what makes them aesthetically possible rather than merely intolerable—is not their inherent aesthetic interest (one would not sit still, with mild interest, for periodic minute-length transmissions of, say, a passage of Garbo's face or of a Chaplin routine: these glimpses of the masterful would be pointless), but the fact that they are readable, not as interruptions, but as interludes. Of course they can be handled all but intolerably, like late-night used car ads, or offers of recordings "not sold in any store." But even in these cases, the point of tolerability is the requirement of live switching—life, moreover, that is acknowledged by the habitual invitation at these peculiar late hours to "come on down" or to order by writing or by "calling now." Where there's life, there's hope.)

The fact of television's company is expressed not simply by the amount of talk, but by the massive repetitiveness of its formats for talk. Here I am thinking not merely of the shows explicitly of talk, with their repetitious sets and hosts and guests. Broadcasts of sports events are embedded in talk (as sports events are), and I can see the point even of game shows as providing occasions or covers for talk. Of course these shows are reasonably exciting, visually and aurally, with their obligatory jumping and screaming; and even, some of them, mildly educational. But is this excitement and education sufficient to account for the willingness to tune them in endlessly, for the pleasure taken endlessly in them? Nor am I satisfied to cite the reputed attractions, or fantasies, of striking it rich—any more than, in thinking about the attractions of Hollywood thirties comedies, was I satisfied to account for their popularity by the widespread idea that they were fairy tales for the depression. I am struck by the plain fact that on each of the game shows I have watched, new sets of contestants are introduced to us. What strikes me is not that we are interested in identifying with these ordinary people, but simply that we are introduced to them. The hardest part of conversation, or the scariest part, that of improvising the conventional phrases of meeting someone and starting to talk, is all there is time for on these formats; and it is repeated endlessly, and without the scary anticipation of consequences in presenting the self that meetings in reality exact. The one who can get us perennially acquainted, who faces the initiation time and again, who has the power to create the familiar out of strangeness—the host of the show—is heavily rewarded for his abilities; not, indeed, by becoming a star, but by becoming a personality, even a celebrity, famous for nothing but being visible and surviving new encounters.

The appearance just now, or reappearance, of the idea of improvisation indicates the principal room I said was left for the improvisatory in television's persistent formats, its dimension of talk. I would not wish exactly to say that improvisation is localized there, since the dimension of talk is itself all but universally present; but each format for talk will have its own requirements or opportunities for improvisation. The most elaborate of these are, naturally, presented by talk shows themselves, with their monologues, and hence the interruptions and accidents that expert monologues invite, and with their more or less extended interviews. Here, the fact that nothing of consequence is said matters little compared with the fact that something is spoken, that the momentarily famous and the permanently successful are seen, like us, to have to find words for their lives. The gift of the host is to know how, and how far, to put the guests recurrently at ease and on the spot, and to make dramas of overcoming the one with the other, and both with his or her capacity at any time to top what has been said. This is not the same as turning every event into a comic routine, as Jonathan Winters and Robin Williams have the talent and imagination to do. They are too anarchic to entertain guests, or too relentlessly absorbed by their inventions, as if inhabited by them, to invite and prepare for conversation. Johnny Carson is so good at taking conversation near, but not over, the abyss of embarrassment, he has made so good an alliance, not to say conspiracy, with the camera, that he can instruct his audiences' responses with a glance in our direction (i.e., in the direction of the camera)—a power the comedian shares with the lion tamer. Again, it is rather beside the point that the so-called color commentaries for sports events are not particularly colorful, since the point of the role is rather the unpreparedness of response itself. So hungry are we for the unrehearsed, the unscripted, that the persons at news desks feel obliged to please us by exchanging pleasantries with each other (sometimes abbreviated to one of them pleasantly speaking the other's name) as transitions between stories, something that may itself, of course, be scripted—a possibility that epitomizes what it is that causes our hunger here. This provides a primitive version of the complex emotion in having an actor step outside his or her character as part of her or his performance—as, for example, in Bergman's *The Story of Anna*, or Godard's *Two or Three Things I Know about Her,* or as dramatized in the more recent *The French Lieutenant's Woman.* Since the practice of exchanging pleasantries reveals that the delivery of news is a form of acting (it may, I suppose, have been meant to conceal the fact)—hence, that for all television can bring out, the news itself is as likely as not to be fictional, if only because theatricalized—there must be something else television brings out that is as important to us as the distinction between fact and fiction, some matter of life and death. This would be its demonstration that, whether fact or fiction, our news is still something that can humanly be responded to, in particular, responded to by the human power of improvisation. But what news may be so terrible that we will accept such mediocre evidence of this power as reassuring? I will at the end give an answer to this question.

A more immediate question is this. If I am right in taking improvisation to be as apt a sign of human life as we have to go on, and a sign that survives the change from live to taped production, why is it that people who miss the live on television do not recognize where the quality of the live is preserved? It may be that they miss the life primarily of television's old dramatic productions. But it is not television's obligation to provide its audience with the experience of live theater—beyond going out into the world to bring us worthwhile actual performances (live or on tape). Why is the live not seen where it can still be found, and first of all in the improvisations of talk, of exchange? Is this region too tawdry for those who have pictures of something higher? I do not deny a certain paradoxicality in finding life in what is reputedly the dullest, deadest feature of television, namely the omnipresent "talking head." Then the question for us should be: Where did this feature get its deadly reputation?

The remaining category of the material basis of television, after current and simultaneity and reception, the category of the event, is equally to the point here, but to bring out its significance, it will help to look first at the formats that are not made primarily for talk—for example, sports and cultural coverage. These make up the bulk of the television fare ingested by many of my acquaintances (and, except for movies, by me). The characteristic feature of these programs is that they are presented as events, that is to say, as something unique, as occasions, something out of the ordinary. But if the event is something the television screen likes to monitor, so, it appears, is the opposite, the uneventful, the repeated, the repetitive, the utterly familiar. The familiar repetitions of the shows of talk—centrally including here situation comedies—are accordingly company because of their embodiment of the uneventful, the ordinary.

To find comfort or company in the endlessly uneventful has its purest realization, and emblem, in the literal use of television sets as monitors against the suspicious, for example, against unwanted entry. The bank of monitors at which a door guard glances from time to time—one fixed, say, on each of the empty corridors leading from the otherwise unattended points of entry to the building—emblematizes the mode of perception I am taking as the aesthetic access to television.

The multiplicity of monitors, each linked to a more or less fixed camera, encodes the denial of succession as integral to the basis of the medium. In covering a sports event, a network's cameras are, similarly, placed ahead of time. That their views are transmitted to us one at a time for home consumption is merely an accident of economy; in principle, we could all watch a replica of the bank of monitors the producer sees. In that case, we might speak of television's material basis by putting simultaneity into the plural. When there is a switch of the camera whose image is fed into our sole receiver, we might think of this not as a switch of comment from one camera or angle to another camera or angle, but as a switch of attention from one monitor to another monitor. Succession is replaced by switching, which means that the move from one image to another is motivated not, as on film, by requirements of meaning, but by requirements of opportunity and anticipation—as if the meaning is dictated by the event itself. As in monitoring the heart, or the rapid eye movements during periods of dreaming—say, monitoring signs of life—most of what appears is a graph of the normal, or the establishment of some reference or base line, a line, so to speak, of the uneventful, from which events stand out with perfectly anticipatable significance. If classical narrative can be pictured as the progress from the establishing of one stable situation, through an event of difference, to the reestablishing of a stable situation related to the original one, serial procedure can be thought of as the establishing of a stable condition punctuated by repeated crises or events that are not developments of the situation requiring a single resolution, but intrusions or emergencies—of humor, or adventure, or talent, or misery—each of which runs a natural course and thereupon rejoins the realm of the uneventful; which is perhaps to say, serial procedure is undialectical.

As I do not wish to claim that generation and serialization exhaust the field of narration, so I do not wish to claim that they are exclusive. So in saying that television organizes its formats in ways that explore the experience and the concept of the event, and hence of the experience and the concept of the uneventful, I am not saying that film lacks an analogous exploration, only that each medium will work out its stabilities in its own way. The ways will be as close as monitoring is to viewing, and to define such a closeness, and distance, is the sort of task my remarks here are meant to interest us in doing. For example, film and video may occupy themselves with nature, but if the distinction I have pointed to between viewing and monitoring is a valid one, then our experience of nature, its role in this stretch of our lives, should split itself over the different presentations. In *The World Viewed* I suggest a sense in which

> the film frame generally . . . has the opposite significance of the frame in painting. Following Bazin's suggestion that the screen works as much by what it excludes as by what it includes, that it

functions less to frame than to mask (which led me to speak of a photograph as of a segment of the world as a whole), I interpreted the frame of a film as forming its content not the way borders or outlines form, but rather the way looms and molds form. (p. 200)

In such a light, I was led to say, "we are told that people seeing the first moving pictures were amazed to see the motion, as if by the novelty. But what movies did at first they can do at last: spare our attention wholly for that thing now, in the frame of nature, the world moving in the branch. . . . It is not novelty that has worn off, but our interest in our experience" (ibid.). Now, sparing our attention and expending it wholly, which goes into what I mean by viewing, is not a characterization of monitoring, which is rather preparing our attention to be called upon by certain eventualities. The world is not in the monitored branch, whose movement is now either an event (if, say, you are watching for a sign of wind) or a mark of the uneventful (a sign that the change has not yet come). The intimacy of such a difference prompts me to emphasize that by monitoring and viewing, I mean to be calling attention to aspects of human perception generally, so that film and video will not be expected to capture one of these aspects to the exclusion of the other, but rather to stress one at the expense of the other—as each may be stressing different aspects of art; video of its relation to communication, film of its relation to seduction.

My use of the concept of the uneventful is produced by my understanding of the *Annales* historians' interest in getting beyond the events and the dramas of history to the permanencies, or anyway to the longer spans, of common life.[11] This is worth making explicit as a way of emphasizing that the concepts in which I have been speaking of the phenomena of television and movies are as much in need of investigation as are the phenomena themselves. Everything seems to me so doubtful, or intangible, in this area. I would like to have useful words in which to consider why the opera and the ballet I have seen on television in recent years have seemed to me so good, whereas films I recall of opera and of ballet have seemed to me boring. Is it that television can respect the theatricality or the foreign conventionality of those media without trying, as film greedily would, to reinterpret them? And is this well thought of as television's ability to respect the independence of the theatrical event? I did like Bergman's *Magic Flute*, but I also felt that the piece looked like a television production. The question is this easy to beg. And does the idea of respecting the event go into the reason puppets and muppets are at home on television in a way they are not in movies?

Here an answer suggests itself to a question my assumption of the primacy of format might at any time raise: Isn't the television "special" an exception to the rule of this primacy, since, by definition, a special occurs uniquely? The answer is not merely that uniqueness proposes a television format (like farewells, awards, roasts) that any number of stars and celebrities can occupy, and occupy again and again, so long as not regularly, that is, serially. The answer has also to specify what the format is that can occur outside a series. Take the fact that the entertainment special, designed to showcase a star or celebrity, familiarly takes the form of a variety show. The fittingness of the variety show format for television I can now attribute to the fact that a variety show just is a sequence of events, where events are interpreted as autonomous acts or routines constituted by incidents of excitement that are understandable as essentially repeatable, in another show and in another town. The concept of event here captures the sense of the variety and the discreteness—that is, the integrity—of the items of such shows, as it does in naming the items of track and field meets, and of bouts on a fight card.

The broadcasts of cultural events may also seem another set of exceptions to the rule of format, other instances of unique occurrences. But what is unique here, and what is above all memorable, is the performance itself, say of Balanchine's ballet on Stravinsky's *Agon*, the performance at which the pair of dancers of the difficult canon passage got off to a false start and had to begin again. Beyond the performance, the television presentation itself may be of interest, perhaps because of its novel camera installations, which make for a greater fidelity to the details of the performance, or because it was the first to use subtitles in a particular way. But these features of the presentation form an essentially repeatable format, usable and refinable in future broadcasts of ballet performances. If, however, the television presentation becomes so integral to the performance, the performance itself having been designed to incorporate the possibilities of presentation into its own integrity, that the ideas of "repeating" the format or of refining such things as camera "installations" no longer make clear sense, then the television format would have been led to the condition of genre-as-medium. I have seen too little in the way of such works to have any useful response to them. They must in any case be part of the realm of experimental video art, which, as said, I am here leaving out of account.

I note that the variety format also fit the requirements of radio in its network days. It is, I think, commonly said that in its beginning, television "took over" many programs, or ideas for programs, from radio. Empirically or legally, no one could deny this, but ontologically, so to speak, or aesthetically, it should be wondered why radio was so ready a source for television. The better thought may be that television took its formats from many of the same places radio had taken them, for example, from vaudeville, and that the reason they could share these sources is that

both are forms of broadcasting and monitoring, that is, currents of simultaneous event reception. Since one of these currents is made for the ear
and the other also for the eye, it may be wondered what ratio of these senses is called upon by various events. Why, for example, is the weather given
its own little dramatic slot on news programs, whereas the performance of
the stock market is simply announced? Does this have to do with the
weather's providing more visual interest than the market, or with its natural involvement in drama, or with its perennial role as a topic of conversation between strangers, or with its being an allegory of our gathering
frame of mind, or simply with the fact of interest in predicting it (as if
retaining some control over the future)? If the interest in predicting it
were exhausted by its practical bearing on our plans for the days ahead,
announcing it would serve as well as dramatizing it or making a little lecture about it. Prediction is of interest with respect to the stock market
only, on the whole, to those who have a specialized connection with it,
those, for example, who play it, for whom not just a day's outcome, but a
day's events of fluctuation or stability, matter.

Of more fateful interest concerning the format of news is its invitation
of the television item I have perhaps most notably omitted in my more or
less informal itemizing of formats, namely, that of the event shaped expressly for the possibilities of television coverage itself, something that came
upon most viewers' consciousnesses most memorably with the civil rights
and antiwar demonstrations of the sixties, and subsequently with the staging
of terrorist actions. In citing the theatricality of scripted news recitation, and
in emphasizing television's tropism toward the event, I am indicating what
the possibilities of the medium are that shaped events seek to attract; but the
fact of television no more explains the occurrence of such events than it
explains the effects of weather on our consciousness. For what would have
to be explained, as my reference to the *Annales* historians is intended to register, is exactly our continued attraction by events, our will to understand our
lives, or to take interest in them, from their dramas rather than from their
stabilities, from the incident and the accident rather than from the resident,
from their themes rather than from their structures—to theatricalize ourselves. But this is something that Thoreau, for one, held against the interest
in reading newspapers a century and a half ago, an interest he described as
amounting virtually to an addiction.

The *Annales* historians' idea of the long time span oddly applies to
the altogether extraordinary spans of narrative time commanded by serialization. The ultimate span is that commanded by successful soap operas,
in which the following of its yarns can go on and on for years. I said a while
ago that serial procedure is undialectical. Here I might add that the span
of soap operas can allow them to escape history, or rather to require

modification of the concept of history, of history as drama, history as related to the yarns of traditional novels. The lapse of fictional time in a soap
world can be immeasurably shorter (or slower) than that of the span of
time over which one may watch them. (Forty or so years ago my mother
frequently tuned the radio to a fifteen-minute serial called "Helen Trent,"
as she and I were getting ready to go off, respectively, to work and to
school. The idea of the serial was announced each morning by asking
whether a woman can find romance after thirty-five, or maybe it was forty.
I can imagine that this serial still persists. But if so, Helen Trent must still
be something like thirty-five or forty years old.) However dire their events,
they are of the interminable, everyday, passages and abysses of the routine,
which may help explain the ease with which members of their audience
take their characters (so it seems) as "real." Without attempting to account
for the specialized features of the stories and audiences that make soap
operas possible, I call attention to the fact that the most prestigious, even
sensational efforts originating on television in recent years have been serials—either the snobby sort the BBC has patented ("Upstairs/Downstairs,"
"The Forsyte Saga," "Tinker, Tailor," "Brideshead Revisited"), or the anti-
snobby American sort ("Roots," "Dallas"). Here I am merely assuming,
without argument, that eleven weekly hour-length episodes of, say,
"Brideshead Revisited" command an order of time incommensurate with
film time. It is equivalent in its effect neither to something on film that
would last eleven hours, nor to something that would last eleven weeks
(whatever such things would be), nor, I think, to eleven films of an hour
each. Not only does an hour signify something in television time that has
no bearing on film time, but it is internal to the establishment of its formats that television obeys the rhythm, perhaps even celebrates the articulations, the recurrences, of the order of the week, as does Genesis. The
way in which it celebrates this, by further dividing and repeating the day
in terms of minutes and seconds, would be a function of television's establishment in industrialized societies, with their regimentation of time.

It may be thought that one of the formats I listed earlier itself proves
that one should make much less of the differences between film and video
than I am inclined to make, or rather proves the emptiness of the differences: I mean the perfectly common format of running movies on television. Of course, no one would claim that the experience of a movie is just
the same run on television as projected on a screen, and everyone will have
some informal theory or other about what the difference consists in—that
the television image is smaller, that the room is not otherwise dark, that
there is no proper audience, hence that the image is inherently less gripping, and so on. But how much difference do such differences make? It
seems to me that subtleties here can be bypassed or postponed, because a

difference, sufficient to give us to think, between the medium of film and that of video is that, in running a film on television, the television set is (interpretable as) a moviola, though unlike a moviola, a monitor may be thought of as a device for checking a film without projecting it. A way to begin characterizing the difference, accordingly, is that the experience of a film on television is as of something over whose running you have in principle a control; you are not subjected to it, as you are by film itself or television itself.

But to go further with this line of difference would require a theory of the moviola, or editing viewer; I mean a theory of the relation between the experience of this way of screening a film and that of its full or public screening. The moviola may be thought of as providing a reproduction of the original, or as effecting a reduction of it. In the latter case, we need to think, for example, that a piano reduction of a symphonic score is not merely a reduction of physical scale; perhaps it should be thought of as an extreme case of reorchestration. Equally, a piece for piano can be transcribed for orchestra, and so on. Are there analogous intermediate and reciprocal operations lending comprehensibility, or perspicuousness, to the relation between small and large screens? (Naturally, it may seem that the relation between small and large screens, being merely mechanical, should be clearer than the relation between transcriptions and their originals. My point is that as a matter of fact, of the fact of experience, this is not so.) In the former case, that of reproduction, we need a theory of the reproduction, which can cover everything from a black-and-white half-page photograph in an art book of a fresco a hundred times its size, to a duplicate cast of a statue.

It is a contrary of the long time span that applies to individual episodes, whose events are, however dramatic, transient. So the aesthetics of serial-episode construction comes to a suggestion that what is under construction is an argument between time as repetition and time as transience. Without considering that this is a way of characterizing the thinking of Nietzsche's *Zarathustra*, and following that, of Heidegger's *What Is Called Thinking?*, I surmise that something had better be said, in conclusion, about what these speculations seem to add up to.

I go back to the fear or repulsion or anxiety that I have found television to inspire in what I called educated circles, and I ask whether the considerations we have been assembling provide a realistic level of explanation for this fact of television. To indicate the depth of the level required, I mention a book recommended to me by several sources as I was casting about for touchstones in starting notes for my present remarks, *Four Arguments for the Elimination of Television* by Jerry Mander.[12] The book wishes to convince its readers that television, like "tobacco, saccharin, some food dyes, certain uses of polychlorinated biphenyls, aerosols, fluoroscopes and X rays to name a few" may cause cancer and for that reason alone ought to be banned. And there are plenty of other reasons: it is addictive, and "qualifies more as an instrument of brainwashing, sleep induction and/or hypnosis than anything that stimulates conscious learning processes"; it is a form of sense deprivation, causing disorientation and confusion; it suppresses and replaces creative human imagery; it is an instrument of transmutation, turning people into their TV images; it contributes to hyperactivity; "it accelerates our alienation from nature and therefore accelerates the destruction of nature." Is this a disturbance merely of style? Perhaps the most astonishing stretch of what I have been able to read of this book is its section in praise of Victor Tausk's description of the "Influencing Machine." Mander is convinced that television is the realization of the ultimate influencing machine. But the point of Tausk's extraordinary paper is that to think there are in reality such machines is symptomatic of schizophrenia.[13] I cannot tell whether Mander knows this, and whether, if he does, he is declaring that he is schizophrenic, and if he is, whether he is claiming that television has driven him so, even as it is so driving the rest of us, and perhaps claiming that it is a state in which the truth of our condition has become particularly lucid to him. Without telling these things, I am still prepared to regard this book, the very fact that numbers of reasonable people apparently take it seriously, as symptomatic of the depth of anxiety television can inspire.

The depth of it seems to me also expressed in the various more or less casual hypotheses one hears about, for example, the role of television in determining reactions to the Vietnam War. Some say it helped end this war, others (understandably) that it made the war seem unreal. One of the most haunting images I know from television is the footage of the Vietnamese priest immolating himself in protest against the war. Bergman considers this image in *Persona*, as if considering at once the refuge there is in madness and its silence, and the refuge there is in television. The maddened, speechless heroine stares at the burning priest both as if she has been given an image of her pain, even a kind of explanation of it, and as if she is the cause of such pain in the world, as of its infection by her.

But the role of television in explanations of catastrophe was in preparation before the war in Vietnam. Consider that the conquering of television began just after World War II, which means, for the purposes of the hypothesis I wish to offer here, after the discovery of concentration camps and of the atomic bomb; of, I take it, the discovery of the literal possibility that human life will destroy itself; that is to say, that it is willing to destroy itself. (This, too, had been in sufficient preparation; it was realistically described by Nietzsche. In my taking this as a lesson of World War II, the lesson there seems no way for us to learn realistically, I detect the lingering effect, for all its excess, of a once well-known essay of Norman Mailer's, "The White Negro.") And the conquering continued with the decline of our cities and the increasing fear of walking out at night, producing the present world of shut-ins. Not to postpone saying it any longer, my hypothesis is that the fear of television—the fear large or pervasive enough to account for the fear of television—is the fear that what it monitors is the growing uninhabitability of the world, the irreversible pollution of the earth, a fear displaced from the world onto its monitor (as we convert the fear of what we see, and wish to see, into a fear of being seen). The loss of this inhabitability would mean, in Heidegger's view, the loss of our humanity, whether or not we remain alive. Of course children may not have contracted the fear; and the child in us is capable of repressing the fear, ambivalently. My hypothesis is meant to respond to the mind's demand of itself to take up the slack of mismatch between the fact of television and the fact of our indifference to its significance—as though this slack were itself an expression of the fact that a commodity has conquered, an appliance that is a monitor, and yet that what it monitors, apart from events whose existence preceded its own (cultural coverage, sports, movies), are so often settings of the shut-in, a reference line of normality or banality so insistent as to suggest that what is shut out, that suspicion whose entry we would at all costs guard against, must be as monstrous as, let me say, the death of the normal, of the familiar as such.

I am not unaware that the charge of psychosis may well now be shifted in my direction. If so, it should have been leveled at me at least a decade ago, when *The World Viewed* appeared, since the concluding paragraph of that book prepares such a hypothesis:

> A world complete without me which is present to me is the world of my immortality. This is an importance of film—and a danger. It takes my life as my haunting of the world, either because I left it unloved or because I left unfinished business. So there is reason for me to want the camera to deny the coherence of the world, its coherence as past: to deny that the world is complete without me. But there is equal reason to want it affirmed that the world is coherent without me. That is essential to what I want of immortality: nature's survival of me. It will mean that the present judgment upon me is not yet the last.

The development I have introduced here lies in the thought that the medium of television makes intuitive the failure of nature's survival of me.

I suppose it is a tall order for the repetitions and transiences of television, the company of its talk and its events, to overcome the anxiety of the intuition the medium embodies. But if I am right, this is the order it more or less already fulfills, proving again the power of familiarity, for good and ill, in human affairs; call it our adaptability. That this anxiety has a fitting object, in the possible disappearance of nature, does not, for me, rule out a psychological etiology for it, say in guilt, toward that same object. And—who knows?—if the monitor picked up on better talk, and probed for intelligible connections and for beauty among its events, it might alleviate our paralysis, our pride in adaptation, our addiction to a solemn destiny, sufficiently to help us allow ourselves to do something intelligent about its cause.

Notes

1. In *The Immediate Experience* (New York, 1964).

2. Enlarged Edition, Cambridge, Mass., 1979. Cambridge, 1981.

3. New York, 1965.

4. Translated by Richard Howard (Ithaca, N.Y., 1975).

5. I spell this out in *"North by Northwest,"* reprinted in this book.

6. Chicago, 1976.

7. New York, 1971.

8. *Morphologie du conte*, trans. Marguerite Derrida (Paris, 1970).

9. P. 72; this is taken further and modified to characterize cartoons in "More of *The World Viewed,*" pp. 167ff.

10. *"What Is Cinema?* trans. Hugh Gray (Berkeley, 1967), p. 97.

11. See Stanley Cavell, "The Ordinary as the Uneventful (A Note on the *Annales* Historians)," *Themes Out of School*: 184–94, and also *On History*, essays by Fernand Braudel translated by Sarah Matthews (Chicago, 1980).

12. New York, 1978, pp. 348, 394.

13. An English translation of Tausk's paper, "On the Origin of the 'Influencing Machine' in Schizophrenia," originally published in 1919, is included in *The Psychoanalytic Reader*, ed. Robert Fliess (New York, 1948), pp. 31–64.

5

The Thought of Movies

What follows appeared in the winter 1983 issue of the *Yale Review*. It was delivered on May 20, 1982, at the Kennedy Center in Washington, D.C., under the sponsorship of the American Film Institute, as the Second Annual Patricia Wise Lecture. I was told, in my invitation to prepare the lecture, that the idea of the series was to provide an occasion for writers and scholars not centered within the film community to describe the importance to their work, or to contemporary culture, of the existence of movies. I found I wanted to use the occasion to respond with fair consecutiveness to the repeated quizzing I have been subjected to over the years about my interest in film, especially on the publications of my books about film, *The World Viewed* (1971) and *Pursuits of Happiness: The Hollywood Comedy of Remarriage* (1981), the publications which, I assumed, had produced the invitation to me to give the Wise Lecture. So I am glad for the opportunity to have the lecture printed, essentially as it was delivered, with no effort to remove what I had been careful to include within it—my sense of its occasion.

IT MUST BE THE NATURE OF American academic philosophy (or of its reputation), together with the nature of American movies (or of their notoriety), that makes someone who writes about both, in the same breath, subject to questions, not to say suspicions. The invitation to deliver

First published *The Yale Review*, winter 1983; reprinted in *Themes Out of School* and in Cynthia Freeland and Thomas Wartenberg, editors, *Philosophy and Film* (Routledge, 1995).

this year's Patricia Wise Lecture is the first time I have been questioned about this combination of concerns, or obsessions, by a group of people committed to sitting quietly for the better part of an hour while I search for an answer.

The question has, I think without fail, come my way with philosophy put first: How is it that a professor of philosophy gets to thinking about Hollywood films?—as though becoming a professor of philosophy were easier to accept than thinking and writing about movies. So defensive have I grown that it took me a while to recognize that for most of my life the opposite direction of the question would have been more natural: How is it that someone whose education was as formed by going to the movies as by reading books, gets to thinking about philosophy professionally?

For a long time I believed the connection to be a private crossroads of my own. It became explicit for me during that period in my life I learned later, in a calmer time, to call my identity crisis. After college, in the late 1940s, I was accepted by the extension program of the Juilliard Conservatory as a composition major, following some two years of increasing doubts that music was my life. Almost as soon as I arrived in New York and established myself in school, I began avoiding my composition lessons. I spent my days reading and my nights in a theater, typically standing for the opera or a play, and then afterwards going to a film revival on 42nd Street, which in the late forties was a rich arena within which to learn the range and randomness of the American talkie. What I was reading all day I privately called philosophy, though I knew no more about what other people meant by the word than I knew why it was in philosophy that I was looking for the answer to the question my life had become.

Since I had spent my undergraduate years torn between the wish to be a writer and the fact of composing music for the student theater—for anything ranging from numbers for our annual musical revues to incidental music for nothing less than *King Lear*—what I learned in college would scarcely, I mean by European standards, have added up to an education at all. But I was encouraged to go on learning from the odd places, and the odd people, that it pleased my immigrant, unlettered father and my accomplished mother to take me to—he who was in love with the learning he never would have, and she who while I was growing up made a living playing the piano for silent movies and for vaudeville. The commonest place we went together was to movies. So while before I entered college I would not have heard a performance of, say, the Beethoven Ninth, and lacked any obvious preparation for it in the history of music and of German culture, I had known enough to attend carefully, for example, to the moves of Fred Astaire and Ginger Rogers and Jerome Kern, so that when the chorus in the last movement of the Ninth sings the two principal themes in counterpoint, the ecstasy this caused me had been prepared by my response to the closing of *Swing Time*, in which one of the pair is singing again "A Fine Romance" while the other is singing again "The Way You Look Tonight." This would not have constituted the preparation I claim for high art unless it had gone beyond cleverness. It is essential that each of the Kern songs is as good individually as it is, so that when the pair modify and cast them together in the reprise, each can be seen capable, so to speak, of meaning the separate song he and she have on their minds.

In the same way the lyrics of such songs were preparation for the high poetry I had yet to discover. In my early adolescence lines such as

> Heaven, I'm in heaven
> And the cares that hung around me through the week
> Seem to vanish like a gambler's lucky streak,
> When we're out together dancing cheek to cheek.

were what I thought of as poetry—nothing else will be poetry for me that cannot compete with the experience of concentration and lift in such words. It seems to me that I knew this then to be an experience not alone of the behavior and the intelligence of the words with one another, nor only, in addition, of the wit and beauty of invoking the gambler's run of luck, but that it was an experience of these (though I would have lacked as yet words of my own in which to say so) together with the drama of using the vanishing of the streak, which is a bad thing, as a simile for the vanishing of cares and the access to heaven, which is a good thing—as if beyond bad and good there were a region of chance and risk within which alone the intimacy emblematized or mythologized in the dancing of Astaire and Rogers is realizable. Eventually I would be able to note that happiness and happenstance spring from the same root, that the pursuit of happiness—whether this is an occasion for a step into selfhood or into nationhood—requires the bravery to recognize and seize the occasion, or as Emerson had put it, "the courage to be what you are." I am not claiming that I, then, on 42nd Street, had already planned my book on the Hollywood comedy of remarriage; but rather that that book is in part written in loyalty to younger versions of myself, some of whom were, or are, there. Certainly I can sympathize with Steve Martin's half-crazed hero in the recent *Pennies from Heaven* when he says, crying from the heart about the songs he peddles and believes, "Listen to the words!" And I am, I guess, claiming that that younger version of myself, playing hooky from Juilliard and in the poverty of his formal education reading all day and spending half the night in theaters, was already taking to heart Henry James's most memorable advice to aspiring writers. In "The Art of Fiction" James says:

The power to guess the unseen from the seen, to trace the implications of things, to judge the whole piece by the pattern, the condition of feeling life in general so completely that you are well on your way to knowing any particular corner of it—this cluster of gifts may almost be said to constitute experience. . . . Therefore, if I should certainly say to a novice "Write from experience and experience only," I should feel that this was rather a tantalizing monition if I were not careful immediately to add, "Try to be one of the people on whom nothing is lost."

By the time the time came for me to write my book about a set of Hollywood romances [*Pursuits of Happiness*], I had come to count on myself as one of the people willing not to be lost to his or to her experience, hence to count on being able to survive the indignities of sometimes guessing unconvincingly and of sometimes tracing things in thin air. So, for instance, in my book I build a sense of the shared structure of the comedies of remarriage out of an understanding of Shakespearean romance; and I discuss the blanket in *It Happened One Night* in terms of the censoring of human knowledge and aspiration in the philosophy of Kant; and I see the speculation of Heidegger exemplified or explained in the countenance of Buster Keaton; and I find in *The Awful Truth* that when the camera moves away from an imminent embrace between Cary Grant and Irene Dunne to discover a pair of human figurines marking the passage of time by skipping together into a clock that has the form of a house, that in that image something metaphysical is being said about what marriage is, that it is a new way of inhabiting time, and moreover that that is a way of summarizing the philosophy, among others, of Thoreau and of Nietzsche.

Figure 5.1

So I suppose I should not be surprised that this book of mine has met with some resistance from its reviewers. More than once it has been called pretentious. Put aside for the present the possibility that its ideas are poorly executed or voiced in the writing—there is nothing I can do about that now. If that is not the whole story, then the charge of pretension must have to do with the connections I make between film and philosophy; at any rate, the charge leveled against either separately would hardly be worth responding to. But what in the connections may strike one as pretentious? It is important to me to bring out what I find to be a harmless way of issuing the charge, and a harmful way.

The harmless way takes the connections as a matter of preference, and on this basis I can see that one who is not familiar with the texts I mention may prefer that I not drop their names. I have two excuses for doing so. First, since I find in movies food for thought, I go for help in thinking about what I understand them to be thinking about where I go for help in thinking about anything, to the thinkers I know best and trust most. Second, as is typical of a certain kind of American, I find what I do to be pertinent to any and all of my fellow citizens, and I secretly believe that if they saw it as I do, they would all immediately devote themselves to doing it too.

This accounts in part for an American's readiness to lecture his fellows, a practice that made an impression on de Tocqueville during his visit to us in the 1830s, the decade before Thoreau moved out to Walden to prepare his kind of lecturing, or dressing down. It is a practice some will find insufferable and others generous. The practice raises for me the issue whether Americans have anything to their name to call a common cultural inheritance, whether you can name three works of high culture that you can be sure all the people you care about have read or seen or heard. This lack of assured commonality would be another part of the cause for our tendency to lecture rather than to converse with one another.

The harmful way of charging my book with pretension takes it for granted that philosophy and Hollywood movies occupy separate cultural intentions, with nothing to say across their border, indeed with not so much as a border between them. The immediate harm ithis view lies in its closing off an exploration of what those Americans to whom it matters may be said to have instead of a common inheritance of high culture, namely an ability to move between high and low, caring about each also from the vantage of the other. This has its liabilities, naturally; for example, of indiscriminateness and of moments of incomprehensibility to the outside learned world. But it also, to my mind, accounts for what is best, or special, in our work; for example, for the reach in Thoreau's prose from the highest sublimity to the lowest pun. I am reminded that de Tocqueville also remarked a liveliness among the populace of our democracy that he missed in his populace at home and which he attributed to the fact that in America there is genuinely public business which requires learning and intelligence to take part in. This seems to me the condition for the kind of mutual respect called upon in putting together the high and the low.

For someone, or most people, to take for granted that there is no border between philosophy and movies, for this to carry its apparent conviction, there must be available fairly definite, if unconscious, interpretations both of what philosophy is and of what the Hollywood movie is. Philosophy would have to be thought of as a more or less technical discipline reserved for specialists. But this would just interpret what it is that makes philosophy professional; and however internal that state is to philosophy and indeed to the growing professionalization of the world, it does not say what makes philosophy philosophy.

I understand it as a willingness to think not about something other than what ordinary human beings think about, but rather to learn to think undistractedly about things that ordinary human beings cannot help thinking about, or anyway cannot help having occur to them, sometimes in fantasy, sometimes as a flash across a landscape; such things, for example, as whether we can know the world as it is in itself, or whether others really know the nature of one's own experiences, or whether good and bad are relative, or whether we might not now be dreaming that we are awake, or whether modern tyrannies and weapons and spaces and speeds and art are continuous with the past of the human race or discontinuous, and hence whether the learning of the human race is not irrelevant to the problems it has brought before itself. Such thoughts are instances of that characteristic human willingness to allow questions for itself which it cannot answer with satisfaction. Cynics about philosophy, and perhaps about humanity, will find that questions without answers are empty; dogmatists will claim to have arrived at answers; philosophers after my heart will rather wish to convey the thought that while there may be no satisfying answers to such questions in certain forms, there are, so to speak, directions to answers, ways to think, that are worth the time of your life to discover. (It is a further question for me whether directions of this kind are teachable, in ways suited to what we think of as schools.)

It would not become me to proceed, in speaking on this occasion of my interest in movies, other than by way of faithfulness to the impulse to philosophy as I conceive it. Apart from the best I can do in this attempt, I would not have approached the question whether the same sensibility that is drawn to and perplexed about philosophy is drawn to and perplexed about movies.

There is, I suggested, an interpretation of Hollywood movies that is the companion of the interpretation of philosophy as a specialized profession. This interpretation takes movies as specialized commodities manufactured by an industry designed to satisfy the tastes of a mass audience. Conventional capitalists as well as conventional Marxists can equally take such a view. It is no more false than is the interpretation of philosophy as a profession, but it is no less partial, or prejudicial. Just as it would be possible to select films carefully with an idea of proving that film can attain to art (people interested in such selections will on the whole not include Hollywood talkies in this selection), so one could heap together abysses of bad and meretricious movies with an idea of proving one's bleakest view of Hollywood. These are not my interests, and have nothing special to do with assessing the life of movies.

What interests me much more in these terms about Hollywood is that for around fifteen years, say from the middle thirties to the early fifties, it provided an environment in which a group of people, as a matter of its routine practice, turned out work as good, say, as that represented by the seven movies forming the basis of my book on remarriage comedies—work, that is to say, as good, or something like as good, as *It Happened One Night* (1934), *The Awful Truth* (1937), *Bringing Up Baby* (1938), *His Girl Friday* (1940), *The Philadelphia Story* (1940), *The Lady Eve* (1941), and *Adam's Rib* (1949)—work that must participate in any history of film as an art that I would find credible. I am not, perhaps I should say, claiming that this work is the best work in the history of world cinema, nor that these films are better than the experimental or nonfiction films contemporary with them. I am, I guess, claiming that they are good, worthy companions of the best; and also that we have as yet no way of knowing, no sufficient terms in which to say, how good they are.

So it is no part of my argument to insist that major work can only come from such an environment or to deny that significant movies continue to be made in Hollywood. But I expect that no one still finds that they come almost exclusively from there, and routinely, say every other week, something like twenty or twenty-five times a year. Over a period of fifteen golden years, that comes to between three hundred and four hundred works, which is a larger body of first-rate or nearly first-rate work than the entire corpus of Elizabethan and Jacobean drama can show.

How could we show that it is equally, or anyway, sufficiently, worth studying? Now we are at the heart of the aesthetic matter. Nothing can show this value to you unless it is discovered in your own experience, in the persistent exercise of your own taste, and hence the willingness to challenge your taste as it stands, to form your own artistic conscience, hence nowhere but in the details of your encounter with specific works.

It is time for some more extended examples. I choose two principally, one beginning from a question I have about a moment in *The Philadelphia Story*, the second from a question I have about the mood of *Pennies from Heaven*.

The Philadelphia Story is in some ways the central member of the remarriage comedies brought together in *Pursuits of Happiness*, but beyond allowing me the pleasure of saying something consecutive about my commitment to these comedies, the example here is meant to isolate for attention one of those apparently insignificant moments in whose power a part of the power of film rests. If it is part of the grain of film to magnify the feeling and meaning of a moment, it is equally part of it to counter this tendency, and instead to acknowledge the fateful fact of a human life that the significance of its moments is ordinarily not given with the moments as they are lived, so that to determine the significant crossroads of a life may be the work of a lifetime. It is as if an inherent concealment of significance, as much as its revelation, were part of the governing force of what we mean by film acting and film directing and film viewing.

We need always to be returning to the fact of how mysterious these objects called movies are, unlike anything else on earth. They have the evanescence of performances and the permanence of recordings, but they are not recordings (because there is nothing independent of them to which they owe fidelity); and they are not performances (because they are perfectly repeatable).

If what I might call the historical evanescence of film will be overcome when the new technologies of video cassettes and discs complete the work of late-night television and revival theaters, and the history of movies becomes part of the experience of viewing new movies—a relation to history that we take for granted in the rest of the arts—this should serve to steady our awareness of the natural evanescence of film, the fact that its events exist only in motion, in passing.[1] This natural fact makes all the more extraordinary the historical fact that films are still on the whole viewed just once and reviewed on the basis of just one viewing, hence that the bulk of the prose even dedicated moviegoers read about movies is the prose of reviewing, not the demanding criticism and the readings and appreciations one takes for granted as being devoted to other arts. It will compensate my having to choose examples that I cannot be assured we have in common if doing so serves to bring this contingency of film viewing and reading into question.

The moment in *The Philadelphia Story* occurs late, when Katharine Hepburn, hearing from Jimmy Stewart that he did not take advantage of her drunken state the previous night, turns from the assembled audience and says, in a sudden, quiet access of admiration, "I think men are wonderful." Nothing further comes of the line; its moment passes with its saying, like a shadow passing. Struck with the strangeness of this moment, I found in composing *Pursuits of Happiness*—and it is something that one of my reviewers, and on the whole a sympathetic and learned one, found more hysterically inappropriate than any other of my perceptions—that to my ear this line alludes to the moment in *The Tempest* at which Miranda exclaims, "How beauteous mankind is!" Evidently I had not, for that reader, made sufficiently clear my general need for the Shakespearean connection in relation to remarriage comedy; nor had I gained sufficient credit with him to get him to put his sense of appropriateness in abeyance for the moment and specifically to try out what I called an allusion amounting almost to an echo. This is something I am going to ask you to consider doing. Let me go over what I am basing myself on in such cases.

The point of the title "remarriage" is to register the grouping of a set of comedies which differ from classical comedy in various respects, but most notably in this, that in classical comedy the narrative shows a young pair overcoming obstacles to their love and at the end achieving marriage, whereas comedies of remarriage begin or climax with a pair less young, getting or threatening their divorce, so that the drive of the narrative is to get them back together, together again. The central idea I follow out along various paths, but roughly the idea is that the validity or bond of marriage is assured, even legitimized, not by church or state or sexual compatibility (these bonds, it is implied, are no deeper than those of marriage), but by something I call the willingness for remarriage, a way of continuing to affirm the happiness of one's initial leap. As if the chance of happiness exists only when it seconds itself. In classical comedy people made for one another find one another; in remarriage comedy people who have found one another find that they are made for each other. The greatest of the structures of remarriage is *The Winter's Tale*, which is, together with *The Tempest*, the greatest of the Shakespearean romances.

But I want the Shakespearean connection with remarriage comedy also for less stupendous structural reasons. Shakespearean romantic comedy lost out, so a way of telling the history goes, to the newer Jonsonian comedy of manners as setting the standard for the future of the English stage. Now I claim that the emergence of film, especially of the talkie, discovered another theater, several centuries later, for that older, Shakespearean structure. Some features of the older comedy that found new life on film are, for example, that it is the woman rather than the man who holds the key to the plot and who undergoes something like death and transformation; that there is some special understanding she has with her father, who does not oppose (as in conventional comedy) but endorses the object of her desire; that the central pair are not young, so that the issue of chastity or innocence, while present, cannot be settled by determinations of literal virginity; that the plot begins and complicates itself in a city but gets resolved in a move to a world of nature—in Shakespeare this is called the green world or the golden world; in four of the seven major Hollywood comedies of remarriage this world is called Connecticut.

But such structural connections are in service of a further reason for the Shakespearean connection, namely to locate the mode of perception called upon in movies, anyway in movies of this kind. The connection in effect implies that what allows film to rediscover, for its own purposes, Shakespearean romance, is that unlike the prose of comic theatrical dialogue after Shakespeare, film has a natural equivalent for the medium of Shakespeare's dramatic poetry. I think of it as the poetry of film itself, what it is that happens to figures and objects and places as they are variously molded and displaced by a motion-picture camera and then projected and screened. Every art, every worthwhile human enterprise, has its poetry, ways of doing things that perfect the possibilities of the enterprise itself, make it the one it is; each of the arts has its own poetry, of course, so has each sport, and so I am sure have banking and baking and surgery and government. You may think of it as the unteachable point in any worthwhile enterprise.

I understand it to be, let me say, a natural vision of film that every motion and station, in particular every human posture and gesture, however glancing, has its poetry, or you may say its lucidity. Charlie Chaplin and Buster Keaton live on this knowledge, and perhaps bring it to its purest expression; it is my claim in *Pursuits of Happiness* that the Hollywood talkie finds an equivalent for this expressiveness, this expression of lucidity, in the way certain pairs of human beings are in conversation. (An implied threat to their happiness is that they are, somehow because of this fortune, incomprehensible to everyone else in the world they inhabit.) Any of the arts will be drawn to this knowledge, this perception of the poetry of the ordinary, but film, I would like to say, democratizes the knowledge, hence at once blesses and curses us with it. It says that the perception of poetry is as open to all, regardless as it were of birth or talent, as the ability is to hold a camera on a subject, so that a failure so to perceive, to persist in missing the subject, which may amount to missing the evanescence of the subject, is ascribable only to ourselves, to failures of our character; as if to fail to guess the unseen from the seen, to fail to trace the implications of things—that is, to fail the perception that there is something to be guessed and traced, right or wrong—requires that we persistently coarsen and stupefy ourselves.

Business people would not run a business this way; this was something Emerson admired about American business; it is why Thoreau asks for what he calls "a little more Yankee shrewdness" in our lives. And

Emerson and Thoreau are the writers I know best who most incessantly express this sense of life as missed possibility, of its passing as in a dream, hence the sense of our leading lives of what they call quiet desperation. The movies I name comedies of remarriage find happiness in proposing that there is relief from just that Emersonian loss, that there are conditions under which opportunities may be discovered again and retaken, that somewhere there is a locale in which a second chance is something one may give oneself. (It is my argument about *The Philadelphia Story* in *Pursuits of Happiness*—which I won't try to go into here—that the Philadelphia in its title is the site of the signing of the Declaration of Independence and of the Constitution of the United States, so that America is the name of the locale of the second chance, or it was meant to be. Remarriage is the central of the second chances.)

Now I'm taking that apparently insignificant moment of *The Philadelphia Story*, the evanescence of the seven syllables "I think men are wonderful," as one in which a character is taking such an opportunity, and the movie proposing one to us. It may help to note that the companion line from *The Tempest*—"How beauteous mankind is!"—is also seven syllables long and that both lines occur at the late moment in their dramas at which the principal female is about to undergo a metaphysical transformation. The Hepburn character is to move from the state of chaste goddess (a state each of the four men in her life either accuses her of or praises her for) into what she calls feeling like a human being; and in *The Tempest*, in response to Miranda's exclamation, Ferdinand's father asks whether she is a goddess, to which Ferdinand replies

> Sir she is mortal,
> But by immortal providence she's mine.

By the way, while the line of Miranda's I am measuring Hepburn's with does not contain the word "wonderful," its more familiar, wider context runs this way:

> O wonder!
> How many goodly creatures are there here!
> How beauteous mankind is! O brave new world
> That has such people in it!

Remember that we are what has become of the new world, the idea and the fact of which so fascinated Shakespeare and his age. If one is interested enough to go this far with the conjunction of Hollywood comedy and Shakespearean romance, one will be bound to ask what the point of such a moment is, I mean why this crossroads of wonder is marked so carefully in these dramatic structures. My answer for the comedies of remarriage would run in something like the following way. I think of them, as a group, to be dedicated to the pursuit of what you might call equality between men and women (and of this as emblematic of the search for human community as such—but I am letting this pass for the present), the pursuit of their correct independence of, and dependence upon, one another. What the comedies of remarriage show is that, as the world goes, there is an unfairness or asymmetry in this pursuit, because women require an education for their assumption of equality, and this must be managed with the help of men. The first task for her, accordingly, is to choose the best man for this work. Because of the history between them—both their private history and the history of their culture—they are struggling with one another, they have justified grievances against one another; hence I sometimes characterize these movies as revenge comedies. If their relationship is to go forward the pair must get around to forgiving one another, and, continuing the asymmetry, it must primarily be the woman who forgives the man, not just because she has more to forgive but because she has more power to forgive. And yet in these movies it may be hard to see what the particular man in question needs such radical forgiveness for. He has done nothing obvious to harm the woman, and the specific charges the women bring against the men—Clark Gable's disdainfulness in *It Happened One Night*; Cary Grant's craziness in *The Awful Truth*, and his deviousness in *His Girl Friday*, and his gorgeous thirst in *The Philadelphia Story*; Henry Fonda's sappiness in *The Lady Eve*; Spencer Tracy's forcefulness, even brutishness, in *Adam's Rib*—these are features the woman honors as well as hates the man for, which is doubtless why she can forgive him. It is not fully explicit until the last of the definitive remarriage comedies, *Adam's Rib* in 1949, that what the woman has against the man is fundamentally the simple villainy of his being a man; hence that is what her happiness with him depends on her getting around to forgiving him for. The form this takes in the line from *The Philadelphia Story* about men being wonderful, I take, accordingly, as an expression of admiration at the sheer fact of their separateness, wonder as it were that there should be two sexes, and that the opposite one is as such admirable.

This is hardly the end of anger between them; there are always their differences. But it is a kind of promise to spend as long as it takes—say till death them do part—to work out what those differences are, what they come to.

At some point—always supposing that one can believe that a conjunction of Shakespeare and Hollywood comedies is not hysterically inappropriate—a more sympathetic doubt about the conjunction may seem called for, prompting one to want to know how serious I am about it, whether when I say, for example, that film has a natural power of poetry equivalent to the power of Shakespeare's dramatic poetry, I really mean poetry in the same sense. Here I might just respond by saying that that is not a question to which I have an answer apart from the thinking and the writing I do and have done, about movies among other matters. But I want to pause, before turning to my concluding example, to sketch an answer more openly philosophical, in particular one that accounts more openly for the periodic appearance of Emerson and Thoreau in my thoughts, those here tonight and those in *Pursuits of Happiness*. Because while my insistence on writing about philosophy and movies in the same breath, insisting on both of them, but especially on their conjunction, as part of my American intellectual and cultural inheritance—while this has caused me a certain amount of professional tension, it has caused no more than my insistence on inheriting Emerson and Thoreau as philosophers.

Do I really mean philosophers? In the same sense that Plato and Descartes and Kant are philosophers? While this is not a moment to argue the point, I take the moment to ask you to conceive the following possibility: that Emerson and Thoreau are the central founding thinkers of American culture but that this knowledge, though possessed by shifting bands of individuals, is not culturally possessed. It would be an expression of this possibility that no profession is responsible for them as thinkers. Mostly they do not exist for the American profession of philosophy; and the literary professions are mostly not in a position to preserve them in these terms. They are unknown to the culture they express in a way it would not be thinkable for Kant and Schiller and Goethe to be unknown to the culture of Germany, or Descartes and Rousseau to France, or Locke and Hume and John Stuart Mill to England. I do not think it is clear how we are to understand and assess this fact about our cultural lives, but you can see that someone with my interests might wish not to miss the occasion for noting the fact out loud in the nation's capital.

(Here I am seeing our reception of our best writers, like our reception of the best Hollywood movies, as part of America's tendency to overpraise and undervalue its best work, as though the circus ballyhoo advertising of Hollywood movies were covering doubts we have that they are really any good at all. I guess this is a preachy thing to say; and maybe that is what's meant sometimes when I'm called pretentious. But preachiness is equally part of the American grain in me, a risk you run in hanging around Emerson and Thoreau as much as I have lately. It is a tone associated in remarriage comedies especially with Katharine Hepburn's high-mindedness. She gets lectured about it by the men in her life, repeatedly dressed down. And once, in *Adam's Rib*, Spencer Tracy allows himself to say to her, "You get cute when you get causey." Of course this makes her sore. And I think I know just how she feels.)

But now if our central thinkers are unpossessed, unshared by us, it will not be expected that we can readily come to intellectual terms on the issues that matter most to us, as say the fundamental issues of art and of philosophy can matter to us. Emerson and Thoreau fully knew this difficulty in getting themselves understood. I have taken as a parable of Emerson's dedication of himself as a writer the following sentences from one of his early, most famous essays, "Self-Reliance":

> I shun father and mother and wife and brother when my genius calls me. I would write on the lintels of the door-post, Whim. I hope it is somewhat better than whim at last, but we cannot spend the day in explanation.

Two remarks about this. First, shunning father and mother and wife and brother is, according to the New Testament, required of you when the Lord calls you and you seek the kingdom of heaven. And according to the Old Testament, writing on the lintels of the door is something you do on Passover, to avoid the angel of death, and it is also where writings from Deuteronomy are placed, in mezuzahs, to signify that Jews live within and that they are obedient to the injunction of the Lord to bear his words and at all times to acknowledge them. So Emerson is putting the *calling* and the *act* of his writing in the public place reserved in both of the founding testaments of our culture for the word of God. Is he being serious?

My second remark about Emerson's passage is that it acknowledges his writing to be posing exactly the question of its own seriousness. In the parable I just cited, he both declares his writing to be a matter of life and death, the path of his faith and redemption, and also declares that everything he writes is Whim. I understand this to mean that it is his mission to create the language in which to explain himself, and accordingly to imply both that there is no such standing discourse between him and his culture, and that he is to that extent without justification before himself. The course open to him is to stake the seriousness of his life, his conviction, on what, before his life's work, we will have no words for: call it whim. So if I answer that my insistence on, for example, aligning movies and Shakespeare and philosophy is based on whim, you will know how to take me.

Now I'm ready to offer as my concluding example, to challenge our convictions in the worth of movies as subjects of thought, *Pennies from Heaven*, a much less lucky movie than, say, the seven thirties comedies I listed in the original genre of remarriage. Those movies are likeable and comprehensible enough to be worth taking and treasuring as light comedies, without working to consciousness any more of the material in *Pursuits of Happiness* than occurs to you casually. Whereas if the brilliance of *Pennies from Heaven* doesn't strike you right off, if you don't become convinced at any rate fairly swiftly that the shocking juxtaposition of attitudes it presents is part of a study, among other things, of the unsettling power of movies, it is likely to seem too unpleasant and confused to think about at all. It is bound to be somewhat hard to think about since it is a Hollywood musical that apparently seeks to undermine the conventions that made possible the Hollywood musical. The subsequent paradox is that its success depends on its undermining itself. If it absorbs the power of conviction of the Hollywood musical then it has not undermined that power. If on the other hand it does not absorb the power of the Hollywood musical then it lacks the power of conviction altogether. It would answer this paradox to say: This movie has the conviction of a work that undermines the conventional sources of conviction in its medium, precisely by reconceiving the sources of that conviction. This sounds like something that might be said of the course of modernism in the other major arts; it is a reason I have sometimes said that art now exists in the condition of philosophy, since it has always been the condition of philosophy to attempt to escape itself, which for several centuries has taken the form of each new major philosopher wishing to repudiate the past of the subject—I mean repudiate it philosophically. As famous, and successful, as any such effort in the arts is Bertolt Brecht's repudiation of theatricality by means of theater itself; theater, hence, reconceived.

But in thinking about movies this is so far merely words; it is an idea that has no commonly appreciated and acknowledged realization in film itself. It tells us nothing about whether, for example, *Pennies from Heaven* succeeds or fails in the new terms we allow for it. The moral remains that nothing but the details of the individual work can tell.

Take the two most obvious details in which this film calls into question the conventions of classical Hollywood musicals, the fact that they employ the dubbing of voices, and the fact that they go to any fictional lengths in order to motivate realistically their fantastic songs and dances. When the small-time hero, refused financing by the banker, breaks into a happy duet with him, his voice dubbed by a woman's; or when the crippled, mumbling beggar takes on an athletic, dazzlingly mounted performance of the title song; the violence of emotion I felt as I stared at the conventions of the Hollywood musical brought to trial was only increased by the fact that I found the numbers expert and gripping. So if *Pennies from Heaven* is parody, it is at the same time tribute, homage: it acknowledges that the reputedly naive musicals on which it lives were as artful and as mysterious as anything it can claim for itself. It shows that conventions of the Hollywood musical are deeper than we may have thought, that their discovery of human desires and satisfactions cannot be undone or outpaced merely by exaggerating them, and indeed in no obvious way at all. And if this is true of the Hollywood musical, where in successful film, or in art generally, is it not true?

Yet this film fails its own knowledge at the end and strikes, to my ear, so false a note as to help ensure its lack of consideration. What happens is this. The hero is arrested for a terrible crime we know has been committed by the crippled beggar, and the film's examination of the human voice and the sentiments of popular song climaxes with the hero's finding his own voice not in song but in plain speech as, on the gallows, he speaks the words of what may be recognized as the verse to the song "Pennies from Heaven." To ask a writer's words to be so sound that they can be said on the gallows is an ambitious test of writing; I find that these words, said by Steve Martin, passed well enough. If so, then nothing should stand in the way of the fiction's happy ending. The governor might have driven up in a limousine, his way cleared by screaming motorcycles, and sung a song of pardon to our hero. Instead the movie slinks to a conclusion by having the hero reappear to his sweetheart for no reason within the fiction, mouthing something like, "We've worked too hard not to get a happy ending." This is roughly to suppose that the conventions that lend the movie its power are disposable at will.

How wrong this is, is reinforced if we notice that the climax of the movie alludes to a more famous dramatic work with pennies in its title, the Brecht-Weill *Threepenny Opera*, which concludes with its bourgeois criminal hero singing on the gallows and being brought a reprieve by a messenger on horseback. So in failing to find out how to say that its hero deserves a pardon, perhaps in the form of an ironic consolation, *Pennies from Heaven* is faithless at once to its Hollywood medium and to its source in the Brechtian theater of estrangement.[2]

Let us end on this movie's other and most dangerous moment of imitation and homage, the reenactment by Steve Martin and Bernadette Peters of the Astaire-Rogers routine on Irving Berlin's "Let's Face the Music and Dance." What the movie is studying here most extravagantly is the nature of what is called our identification with the figures of drama. This reenactment, along with the voices that take over the characters as they go into song, reveals the identification with figures on film not as a process of imitating them but as a product of being possessed by them. Now of all the impersonations one might have tried of the distinctive stars in the history of Hollywood, from Chaplin to Gable and Hepburn, the one no normal person in his right mind would have tried to translate from the realm of fantasy into the public realm is the sense of himself in an Astaire routine: no one else could perfectly enough lend his body to the demands of that spirit. So one must ask how good the Martin-Peters enactment is of this impossible possession. And I find the answer to be that it is convincing enough to make me ask how convincing the original is, whether it fulfills its own dramatic invitation to face the music and dance.

I note that it is perhaps the most weirdly motivated of all the memorable Astaire productions. He prefaces the dance with a little drama in which he loses his money at a casino and then, wandering outside with a pistol to use on himself, sees a woman in an evening gown mount a parapet; he grabs her before she can leap, throws away the pistol, and begins the song and dance. Described in this way, apart from its experience, it may be wondered how they get through all this without laughing.[3] But within the experience, or in remembering such experiences, we know that Astaire has thought about what motivates dancing, about what provides its occasions, as well as anyone who ever lived; so we had perhaps better think further about it in the present case.

The little opening drama, in which the actions set in music are neither spoken nor sung nor danced, invokes the condition of mime, of what the Elizabethans called a dumb show, of the sort used in *Hamlet* by the players of the play-within-the-play who act out their drama silently before they speak their parts. If you take this undanced prelude or invitation to dance in this way, as a kind of prophecy or parable of Astaire's understanding of his dancing, then he can be taken to be declaring that it is meant as a removal not from life but from death. Though the idea of escaping life is a more common view of dance and of comedy, and I guess of art in general, than Astaire's idea of redeeming death, it is no less metaphysical. Astaire's view of dancing as facing the music, as a response to the life of inexorable consequences, which turn out to be the consequences of desperate pleasures, would then be a concrete translation of what such a thinker as Nietzsche meant by dancing (as when Zarathustra speaks, urging: "Raise up your hearts, my brothers, high, higher! And don't forget your legs! Raise up your legs, too, good dancers!")—something I guess he would have learned, among other things, from Emerson, from such a passage in another of Emerson's early essays as this: "All that we reckoned settled shakes and rattles; and literatures, cities, climates, religions, leave their foundations and dance before our eyes." Can an Astaire-Rogers dance, projected on a screen, be this good? How good would this good have to be?—This is serious business.

Postscript

It was pointed out to me by a student at Yale, on my return for other matters some months after I had given a version of this lecture there, that the ending of *Pennies from Heaven*, which I criticize as faithless to its sources in the Hollywood musical and in Brechtian theater in its avoidance of a stance toward the hero's threatened execution, is readable as a further reflection of the hero's fantasy life, hence as his last moments on the gallows. We hadn't more than a few minutes in which to pursue the idea, so I may have misunderstood what he said. My response is this.

Dennis Potter's novelized version of the material to *Pennies from Heaven* fairly obviously does not know what its own end should be, whether part of the hero's fantasy life, or a further appeal on its behalf, or some final regret that there is no use in such an appeal, or a complaint against society for not listening more carefully, or a complaint against the songs for being dismissable. Regarded as the prospectus for a movie, these alternatives may well have seemed undecidable, for the movie must work its own way into such matters. The possibility that the movie takes the option of adopting the hero's fantasy is one that crossed my mind, but it makes matters worse, I think, than I said, worse than making some cheap fun of itself.

The hero's prior bursts into song and dance have the effect of authenticating his inner life, convincing us not only of its existence but of the justice, however mad in imagery (in, some might say, the Utopianism), of its demands. An accomplishment worthy of any art. After these outbursts, it followed (as a kind of price of their elations) that the film's return to grim reality was a return to something no less indebted to the Hollywood past than its treatment of the musical is. A way to tell the structure of *Pennies from Heaven* is as one that alternates musical absorptions of Hollywood (of the thirties and early forties) with counterabsorptions of that same Hollywood; the counterabsorptions work as a kind of negative Utopianism to match the mad positive Utopianism of its music and its music's words. An obvious source for the returns, the counterabsorptions, is such a "woman's film" or "tearjerker" (as if we knew what these are) as George Stevens's *Penny Serenade* of 1941, with Irene Dunne and Cary Grant. I suppose this is deliberate, not only because of the connection in name, but because one of the married pair in the earlier film (in this case the woman) is a hawker of popular music (of records, not sheet music), and a spinning record recurrently punctuates the narration as the film works its way through the death of an innocent and the death of innocence. A less specific source of the counterattitude to reality, to reality as consisting of a planet without music, seems to me something like a Fritz Lang *film noir* early in his American career, for example, *You Only Live Once* of 1937, also about a loser condemned to die for a crime of which he is innocent, which also ends (almost) in a prison yard, with a succeeding ironic fantasy of freedom.

The sources of negative or dashed Utopianism will be harder to recognize than those of the musical numbers, but the alternation of genres provides at once an interpretation of the hero's sensibility, of the common-ness of his craziness, and an insight of significance into the Hollywood of its golden age, namely that it depicted a unified world, a universe. The "fugitive couple" of certain of its melodramas are negations of just those pairs in certain Hollywood comedies who are hardly less isolated from society, hardly less incomprehensible to it, but whose isolation and incom-prehensibility work themselves out with fortune more willing to smile. (The happier pairs have easier access to money. It remains to be deter-mined how far this is the difference that matters, and how far it is the sym-bol of the difference.)

It is up to each of us to find our participation in these high-hat highs and low-down lows. Now if the conclusion of *Pennies from Heaven* is to be identified as the hero's fantasy, and it is to be taken on the model of his ear-lier bursts into song, then, since it has no follow-up, it forces us to read his fantasy as merely some apparently well-understood, ironic escape from some well-understood reality.

And this seems to me faithless at once to the hero's inner life, refus-ing the just appeal in its tawdriness; and to the freedom it seemed to assign us in determining our relation to these events; and to the power of film itself, whose dangers and values of seduction it had honored, if feared, in its own production, but now seems, in an act of self-disrespect, to claim to transcend—to claim some privileged position from which to assess the value of movies, of fantasy, of art, of such freedom as we can find the means to express and hence to claim. Far be it from me to deny the connection between high and low tawdriness, or escape; but to discount them is not something we need art for, high or low.

I take this moment to avert a related ambiguity in what I was saying in my lecture. When I note the extraordinary persistence of the conven-tions in viewing movies just once (interspersed with the odd cult-object viewed countless times), and reviewing them on the basis of one viewing, I am objecting not to the practices in themselves but to their dominance, and lack of assessment, in general movie culture. Certainly I am not recommending repetitive viewing to no particular point, as the better alternative. On the contrary, the casual, or surprised, appeal to memorable passages has a value that studiedness may sacrifice, a value not merely of spontaneity (whatever that is), but of a depth that only a certain immedia-cy will capture, as by surprise. The sacrifice of literary immediacy to stud-iedness is more familiar ground, and I can imagine that the practical difficulties in the way of checking one's reactions to the events of film (for all the technology of cassettes, etc.), or one's recall of them, may at some time have a leavening effect on our literary culture, remembering the value there was (however practically necessitated by its own economy) in citing common literary works from memory, a time when a smaller literary world had works in common, a time (except for such things) not to be envied. It resulted in some misquotation (of a particular kind), but its outcome was of contexts in which one recognized the point of having a memory, a public memory. This is something I want from an eventual film culture as much as I want film's rigorous, orderly study. Such is my justification for continuing to explore *Pennies from Heaven* on the basis of one viewing. My excuse is not having had it available since needing to see it again. (How hard did I look for it? A new question for one's intellectual conscience.)

Notes

1. Norton Batkin took me back to this idea. His work, represented by *Photography and Philosophy*, the doctoral dissertation he submitted to the Department of Philosophy at Harvard in May 1981, goes far with it, into the nature of photography's stillness.

2. I have added a postscript that amplifies this claim.

3. Arlene Croce testifies to such a feeling in her elegant and useful *The Fred Astaire and Ginger Rogers Book* (New York, 1972), p. 88.

6

What (Good) Is a Film Museum?
What Is a Film Culture?

HOPES FOR MY CONTRIBUTION to a discussion of movies and the humanities were described to me in more than one way. (1) I was asked to speak to the issue of the relevance of film to my own teaching and writing; and (2) I was asked to speak about what the projected museum of film at Astoria should take as its specific mission, in our academic as well as in our more public life. I will try to keep these questions in sight, but not to approach them directly. About (2), concerning the museum's specific mission, since that must be tied to the museum's resources, to what it can most effectively, within the bounds of the law, connive to acquire and preserve and exhibit, it is a matter about which I need to receive, not one about which I can provide, instruction. About (1), concerning my own interests, while film is as pertinent to what I think about as any art is, or as America is, or my past, and while I write more and more explicitly about each of these regions, my thoughts do not summarize very usefully. I may begin by saying that a question that is becoming increasingly urgent and puzzling for me is rather one that reverses the usual direction of film's burden of proof. My question is not why film should or could be of interest and service to humanists or to intellectuals at large, but how it comes to pass that it is *not* generally found inescapably interesting, a necessary subject of speculation, to any humanist writer and scholar to whom art and America and his or her past is of interest.

Remarks from the Astoria Foundation Meeting: The Humanities and the Moving Image Media, October 1983.

In responding to a request last year from the journal *Daedalus* to write something about the aesthetics of television for its projected number entitled *Print Culture and Video Culture*, I found myself starting with a question of fear, with the question why (as it seemed to me) television is feared, why intellectuals who seem willing to think about just about anything seem unable even to admit that they so much as know what there is to watch on television, beyond of course news and sports. My answer had to do with a speculation about some fear of what it is that television as a medium may naturally seem to monitor, some unnerving message about the state of the world, as if in watching the tube we became metaphysical entrance guards, or intensive care technicians, looking mostly at an unchanging scene of reassuring evenness and repetitiveness, but prepared in principle for events of emergency and invasion. I wonder if something analogous isn't true of our relation to film.

After movies conquered as a mode of popular entertainment in the thirties and forties, few would still hold out against them, as few would hold out against reading novels, as an inherent waste or corruption of the human sensibility. Yet it seems to me that for all the development of professional or preprofessional programs in film study over the past ten or fifteen years, there remains a prohibition concerning them, not against attending movies nor against talking and expressing judgments about them, but against thinking about them, abandoning oneself to them, including them in one's deliberations and conversation, as one would include the novels and poetry one cares most about.

This will not seem a problem to those who are convinced that most movies essentially constitute some well-recognized form of entertainment and/or that the most valuable movies are (as perhaps the most valuable novels and poems are) esoteric to the culture at large, fit for the thoughts and conversation only of experts, sensibilities equal to them. For someone like myself, impressed rather by the common coincidence in film of familiarity and profundity (something common to film in comparison with the rarity of the combination in literature) the intellectual neglect of movies—their unshared thoughts—seems mysterious. (Large numbers of paintings, and much larger numbers of pieces of music, possess the combination of familiarity and profundity, but then we do not, for some reason, expect ourselves to be able to, or to want to, put our experiences of them into words.) Our lack of shared intellectual seriousness toward movies (of course I do not deny individual exceptions to this) suggests our relation to our sexuality: we are now free to talk the subject to death in general terms, and to judge instances of it, perhaps in the form of denying judgment to others; but we are no freer than we ever were in noting our specific interests and investments in this fact of our lives (with the great exception of gender preference, where the massiveness of the support that has had to be mobilized rather proves the rule). You may well claim that more specific matters here are private. But is this what we think about our relation to movies?

If your experience does not match my suggestion that film lacks a place for serious public discussion, I would not seek to contest the matter further. But if it does match, I can pick, almost out of the blue, two issues I have taken up about movies that may relate their failure, or resistance, in founding serious public conversation to a fear of what they reveal about our lives.

One issue is something I have claimed to share with writers so different from one another in other respects as Robert Warshow and Walter Benjamin, the sense that if film is accepted as the basis of art then the concept of art will suffer change. The fear in this is not alone that the concept of one of our most prized enterprises will become foreign to us. (This is true and important enough. It oddly parallels in my work my insistence on receiving Emerson and Thoreau as philosophers, something that pressures the concept of philosophy as this is shaped in the profession of philosophy.) The consequent fear I see is that movies would then have to be accepted as speaking to our common lives with a depth, as well as an immediacy, no different in principle from the depth of Shakespeare or Dickens or Verdi or Manet; which means acknowledging their revelations of our involvements in the commonest fantasies of romance and of melodrama, and say of the long history of our puzzlements about the legitimacy in what is called marriage. Accepted, I mean, as speaking in terms that we may not elsewhere go beyond, that may reach the limits of our imaginations and intellects, and from which we are accordingly not exempt. As if movies may publicly manifest exactly what we publicly do not discuss.

The other issue I recall here bearing on a fear of film is my questioning of the popular theory expressed, roughly, by saying that film has "changed the way we see." My challenge to this is not exactly to its truth, and certainly not to its sense that movies are sufficiently significant to go with a radical change of nothing less than human perception as such. My challenge comes from a sense that this theory explains the wrong thing about the importance of film, or misses a prior condition that needs explanation, namely how it is that film assumed this kind of power in our lives. My thought is that it could not have achieved it unless human perception had *already* changed, so that the dominance of the moving image (where and when it is dominant) drawn by this change is an indispensable place in which to diagnose it.

The condition of human perception I claim film reveals is our modern fate to live in the world primarily by viewing it, taking views of it. As if something has increasingly been happening to us over the past two or three centuries that has produced a sense of *distance* from the world. (A familiar name for this is our alienation. Kierkegaard simply speaks of it as our being "away.") I have found help in thinking my way into this sense from the philosophical speculations of Heidegger and of Wittgenstein, but I find the issue already full blown in the writings of Emerson and Thoreau, whose dedication to what they call the common, the low, the *near*, is as to something that others feel as threatening the world but that they feel is being lost to the world. I might express the fear of film, along these lines, as one of a sense that we may perish from a nostalgia for the world, from what I have called a nostalgia for the present. It is as an extension of this idea that I have characterized film as a moving image of skepticism, a manifestation of our capacity to doubt the existence of the world.

I hack out these bits and pieces of words and preoccupations of mine in order to suggest their pertinence to what I can say about what I would like to see a museum of film do. I would like it to challenge our amnesia of film in our serious conversation by combating our fears in reconceiving the nature of art, and hence to help us to see what the art of film itself may have to say about our common subjection to distance, nostalgia, and skepticism.

How can a museum of film do such things? My answer is principally: by existing.

The force of this answer should come out in considering how remarkable a fact it is that there should exist such a thing as a museum of film, that the youngest of the major arts should be old enough, or fragile enough, that fundamental instances or modes of it will be lost unless they are systematically collected, preserved, and exhibited. And lost not as the objects in museums of natural history or of technology would be lost, the way past cultures can be lost; but the way objects in museums of high art would be lost, a part of present culture.

During the time I was pondering my possibilities for saying something useful on the present occasion, I came across articles on the idea of a museum in the two most recent issues of *The New Criterion* that underlined for me how remarkable I was finding, and was hoping others would find, the idea of a museum of film. In the most recent issue my emeritus colleague Nelson Goodman in a piece entitled "The End of the Museum?" begins by providing a witty assessment of an impression he says "one gets from some museums and some writing about museums . . . that a museum functions much like such other institutions as a house of detention, a house of rehabilitation, or a house of pleasure." His own serious comparison is of a museum with a library, since both "are fundamentally educational rather than recreational institutions" and since both collect and preserve works and make them publicly available, with two differences: "First, while most users of a library know how to read the books there, many visitors to the museum do not know how to see, or how to see in terms of, the works there; and second, the works in a museum must be viewed under severe and stultifying restraints." Goodman seeks to get his museums to see that to teach their visitors how to see and, as part of that enterprise, to lessen the restraints of viewing, is internal to their mission of making their works available; for "the museum's major mission" is "to make works work."

In the preceding issue of the same magazine, in a moving autobiographical piece entitled "Museums," Hortense Calisher finds that in her experience the social ambitions of museums and the cultural aspirations of those who attend them have made them into something that strikes her as mortuaries, preparing things for the grave. She relates this to the possibility that she has, so to speak, graduated from the instruction of museums, an instruction that worked powerfully in its very indifference to her presence and attention. It is as if Goodman is saying to her: You see museums as mortuaries because in fact most of them are just that; but they *needn't* be. And as if she had replied to him in advance: You see museums as continuing to be educational institutions because, as philosophers will, you would rather press a vacant possibility than consult the crowded fact. I believe Goodman and Calisher may have something to learn from one another here. My response to the issue on which I have joined them is that while I hope museums will do (whatever else they may have to take on) their proper work of collecting, preserving, and exhibiting as efficiently and effectively as they can, there is no one thing that all their visitors will or can or even should get out of them, and that whether a museum's works work depends incomparably more on what else happens in an individual visitor's life, on its other chances for education, or cultivation, for companionship, and for fantasy, than anything a museum can do with its works. The question comes back to what the peculiar good is of a museum, what it does that no other institution does as well in a given cultural system, does for its public and does for its objects and for the specific cultivation of the art from which those objects take their lives.

I said that the Goodman and Calisher statements underlined for me, in effect, how different a museum of film is from the museums their various characterizations remind us of. Nothing you could do in conceiving of a museum and its arrangements could be more radical, or press harder on the concept of the museum, than the very fact of turning the proper activities of museums onto *these* objects, call them movies.

To begin with, the very fact that a museum intervenes in the life of a movie, that it treats it as something to be valued, may as such be a revelation to its viewers. That museums have such a sanctifying effect, and that it may be abused, say by those whose aspirations are less to high art than to higher society, was something the surrealists were pleased, among other things, to demonstrate, for example by exhibiting, notoriously, a urinal. But what surrealism went rather out of the way to do movies do naturally, namely make us question what "exhibition" is, and does.

A remarkable fact about movies is that while they are among the last visual objects to reach museums they are in some ways more at home there than more traditional objects of art are, because nothing counts as removing them from a more natural, or original, or intended, setting. One setting is equal to any other, is as original as any other, that has an adequate print, decent equipment, and a favorable environment. One may, accordingly, think of "rerun" movie houses, a relatively new element of our cultural system, as constituting protomuseums of film. Similarly, consider that many of those, perhaps most, who visit museums of art do not habitually visit galleries showing contemporary work, whereas all of those who will attend a museum of film will be expected to attend film's equivalent of the gallery of contemporary work, that is to say, the ordinary first-run movie house, and even some film festivals. Which means that a museum of film potentially has the luxurious obligation of introducing its visitors not only to major works of the art it treasures, but beyond this of providing a focus of exchange in which the live experience of its art can achieve the coherence and articulation we expect of a shared cultivation, in which it can actually, through its choices and its presentations, go to create the culture it celebrates.

Finally, the authenticating of a film's value by a museum's acceptance of it implies that this object not only is worth seeing (which you might have learned from your acquaintances or from the journalism which still constitutes most writing about film) but that it is worth seeing again. Most films (certain cult objects aside) are still viewed, as people from the beginning have mostly viewed films, just once; and most writing about a film is still done on the basis of one viewing. (Of course I do not deny that regular reviewers of film have in the past ten or fifteen years served the cause of film well, much better in my experience than regular book reviewers have served the cause of books.) Hence the sheer existence of a film museum, drawing every day the implication that objects of film are to be pondered, that they bear up under, and reward, repeated viewing, and our best conversation, rebukes our culture of film as it stands. It is a standing challenge to the idea that film is fully understandable as a mode of popular art, indeed it challenges the idea that we so much as know what constitutes the concept of the popular in this context.

How can the good of a film museum be maximized, its significance put to the clearest use? In the light of what I have been saying, this question becomes such questions as: How can the museum best contribute to the work of defining and establishing its culture? How can it manifest film's survival of the transient, its natural demand for, and reward of, writing (or say thinking) that goes beyond the stage of reviewing? Such questions, against the framework I have tried to indicate, should give a certain edge to the proper practical questions of any museum: What should it wish to acquire, or to trade for, and along what priorities? How should it arrange to exhibit the things it begs and borrows?

Any museum will constitute a concrete answer to such questions. My hope for this museum is that it may keep such questions alive in its practice. Because the museum will have—after a certain success in acquisition—less control over what it acquires than over which of its acquisitions it exhibits and over how it exhibits them, my initial and most urgent proposal (in ignorance, to repeat, of the museum's current resources) is, I guess predictably, that its exhibitions be thought of in partnership with writers and scholars, in some kind of adjunct relation to the museum, who are prepared to compose the texts that should accompany each exhibition. The meanest effort of any film series, or of the smallest archive of film, or of what I called protomuseums of film, will have to have *some* texts of words to go with its screenings. In my experience these are generally slapdash collections of longish quotes, more or less unassessed, from whatever reviews or other writings happen to be at the disposal of the overworked organizers of the screenings, who will regard, and should regard, their primary tasks as lying elsewhere. This not only does as much harm as good, in perpetuating the intellectual and emotional coarseness, or anyway casualness, toward movies that the screenings themselves are meant to challenge, but it misses the beautiful opportunity in the very irresistibility of the call for words.

The museum should at once seek to beg and borrow, on some regular basis, a body of writers and scholars of film who can draw on the growing body of writing and scholarship concerning film that exists now, and who will commit themselves to substantial essays accompanying each exhibition. A program of serious publication by the museum (serious intellectually and visually) stands to make a greater difference to the definition of film culture, to the possibilities for conversation about film, to the specification of what one should hope to know in order to have a culture of film, than the analogous difference a set of monographs and catalogues, which remain a recognized obligation of the comparatively ancient cultures of museums of painting and sculpture, can normally still aspire to make to those cultures.

Given an effective commitment to such a program of writing and publication, the question put to me, inquiring after the desirable effects of a film museum on humanistic scholarship and writing, would have been, as it ought to be, preempted. The museum would have already, and unignorably, taken its effect.

7

What Photography Calls Thinking

This chapter was prepared initially at the invitation of the Graz (Austria) Photography Symposium, held in October 1984, and was delivered there in a somewhat different version. Participants in the symposium were asked to speak about their personal approaches to the medium of photography under the title and with the typography: *THE POWER (and the glory) OF PHOTOGRAPHY*. Hence the echoing of the words in that title in the course of my remarks.

WHAT I HAVE SO FAR published on the subject of photography (in *The World Viewed*, 1971, reprinted 1979, *Pursuits of Happiness*, 1981, and *Themes Out of School*, 1984) approaches it mostly through motion, through the photographic basis of cinema, and I will mostly continue that approach here. I begin with certain ideas I have recurrently explored concerning the relation of photography and reality. It is around something like a relation to reality—as of the mind to the world—that certain fashionable mottoes concerning the power of photography form themselves. Some notable and, I find, oddly empty examples are mottoes to the effect that "Photographs always lie," or that "Photography has changed the way we see."

First published in *Raritan*, spring 1985; reprinted in Richard Poirier, editor, *Raritan Reading* (Rutgers University Press, 1990). Portions of Chapter 10 of *Cities of Words* are adapted from this essay.

To say that photographs lie implies that they might tell the truth; but the beauty of their nature is exactly to say nothing, neither to lie nor not to. Then what purposes may be served, or disguised, in attempting to deny so obvious a fact, in attempting instead to mean that emptiness? If the purpose is to counter those, real or imagined, who bluntly claim that photographs never lie, then the counter only replaces the Village Idiot by the Village Explainer. There must be some more attractive purpose. I believe the motto serves to cover an impressive range of anxieties centered on, or symptomatized by, our sense of how little we know about what the photographic reveals: that we do not know what our relation to reality is, our complicity in it; that we do not know how or what to feel about those events; that we do not understand the specific transformative powers of the camera, what I have called its original violence; that we cannot anticipate what it will know of us—or show of us. These matters will be touched on as we proceed.

People who say that photography has changed the way we see, typically, in my experience, find this a good thing, something for us moderns to get excited by, to speculate from. Susan Sontag's *On Photography* stands out within this line of thought in finding the changes introduced by photography to be a bad thing, something to deplore, whatever praises may be due it. But to say that photography has changed the way we see strikes me as something like the reverse of the truth. The remark does not explain the power of photography but assumes it. Photography could not have impressed itself so immediately and pervasively on the European (including the American) mind unless that mind had at once recognized in photography a manifestation of something that had already happened to itself. What happened to this mind, as the events are registered in philosophy, is its fall into skepticism, together with its efforts to recover itself, events recorded variously in Descartes and Hume and Kant and Emerson and Nietzsche and Heidegger and Wittgenstein.

The name skepticism speaks, as I use it, of some new, or new realization of, human distance from the world, or some withdrawal of the world, which philosophy interprets as a limitation in our capacity for knowing the world; it is what Romantics perceive as our deadness to the world, which they understand philosophy to help sustain, and hence to be in no position to help cure. Why skepticism broke upon the mind when and as it did, what succession of guises it assumes, what the roles may be of, for example, the New Science, of the displacement of kings, of the dying of God, are questions I suppose open to historical answer. I find the issues of skepticism fully at play in Shakespearean tragedy and romance. It is perhaps the principal theme of *The World Viewed* that the advent of photography expresses this distance as the modern fate to relate to the world by viewing it, taking views of it, as from behind the self. It is Heidegger who calls it distance; Thoreau rather thinks of it as the oblivion of what he calls our nextness to the world; Emerson preceded Thoreau and Heidegger in calling nextness to the world nearness to it; Kierkegaard and Wittgenstein say, in different contexts, that we are "away"; others speak of alienation.

Since for me philosophy is still—as the names Heidegger and Wittgenstein are meant to suggest—finding its way in this question of skepticism, and since for me the question of photography is bound up with the question of skepticism, I am not likely to regard any proposal as illuminating the one that does not illuminate the other.

Hence I take mottoes about photography's lying, and its changing the way we see, as so many fragments of some pre-Cartesian or pre-Kantian or pre-Heideggerian moment of philosophical surprise or titillation at human vulnerability or, say, finitude. They may be valuable in pointing to the recesses of the question of photography, but in their empty seriousness, they seem to me efforts to evade the question of what a photograph is. I am likely to characterize this question as asking what a photograph is thinking about—as I have asked, concerning literary and cinematic texts, what the text knows of itself. I am not unaware that these ways of speaking have been found offensive or provocative beyond consideration. Such matters are nowadays sometimes referred to as the text's textuality, or its self-reference. I sometimes speak of the text's self-acknowledgment, and sometimes of its knowledge of others, of me. I will not try to provide here any basis for choosing among these descriptions.

It may help to say that by wording my intuition in the form "what the text knows of me" I do not first of all suppose this to denote anything personal. For example, the photograph tells me that I am subject, inherently but impersonally, to some version of hallucination. In writing in *The World Viewed* of the photographic basis of movies, I said that film proposes an artistically unheard of relation between the presence and absence of its objects. In a photograph we see things that are not, in actuality, before us. You may feel that I am missing the plain fact that what we are seeing is a photograph, which *is* before us. But I am not denying that. I am on the contrary asking that we ask what that means, what a photograph is, and I feel you are missing its strangeness, failing to recognize, for example, that the relation between photograph and subject does not fit our concept of representation, one thing standing for another, disconnected thing, or one forming a likeness of another. When I see that child there in the photograph of the group of school children posing outside the country schoolhouse, the one standing just in front of their teacher Wittgenstein, I know that the child is not here, where I am; yet there he stands, his right arm slightly bent, his collar somewhat disarranged. So, of course, can you point

to a figure, perhaps that very child, in a painting, but I think everyone will
sense that the words are said in a different spirit about a visual representation than they are about what can be called a visual transcription, a difference registering the fact that in the taking of the photograph the object has
played a causal role altogether different from its role in the making of the
painting. A representation emphasizes the identity of its subject, hence it
may be called a likeness; a photograph emphasizes the existence of its subject, recording it; hence it is that it may be called a transcription. One may
also think of it as a transfiguration. Here is one sense of the glory of photography, perhaps due to its power, perhaps to its impotence. It is because I see
what is not before me, because our senses are satisfied with reality, while that
reality does not exist, that in *The World Viewed* I call film "a moving image
of skepticism." This version of hallucination is not exactly mad, but it suggests, as skepticism does, my capacity for madness. (Roland Barthes
acknowledges an intuition of derangement as a normal possibility of the
experience of the photographic in the closing pages of *Camera Lucida*.)

I said I would proceed to raise the question of the photographic primarily by way of the moving picture, not by way of the still (so it has come
to be called) photograph. The principal movie I will interrogate as to its
thoughtfulness about itself is Frank Capra's *Mr. Deeds Goes to Town* (1936,
with Gary Cooper and Jean Arthur). I choose this example for two general reasons. First, because it is just the sort of popular American film about
which it seems most paradoxical to speak of artistic self-reflexiveness, and
it may therefore serve to make us wonder whether we know what the concept of the popular means when applied to the art of film. Second, since
Capra's own writings about his films are as gullible, sentimental, and, let
me say, unintellectual, as he perhaps wishes his audiences to be, this apparently gullible, sentimental, and unintellectual film may serve to emphasize
that I am speaking not of the man Capra but of the power and glory of a
medium, of what it knows of itself. (That this man Capra turns out to be
a master in letting this medium show itself may eventually force us to
revise our idea of who or what "the man Capra" is.) I will work toward the
Capra film by first illustrating briefly, with two pairs of related films, the
kinds of revelation of the medium I expect to find in any significant film—
a significant film being one precisely on the basis of which such revelations
of the medium are most significantly made. Of course this process of
mutual revelation, between a work and the work's medium, being
hermeneutic, is circular, global.

The first pair of films are the earliest and the latest of the seven films that, in *Pursuits of Happiness*, define the genre I call "the comedy of remarriage." In the latest, *Adam's Rib* (directed by George Cukor, 1949, with Katharine Hepburn and Spencer Tracy), an early sequence consists of the depicted screening of a home movie. The enclosing, sophisticated film relates itself to the enclosed, primitive home movie (primitive but complete, like a Wittgensteinian language game) in such a way as to demonstrate the near but not full coincidence of the two films: their framing edges, on reframing, move closer to one another without quite coinciding, creating an effect as complex and illuminating as similar moments in Vertov's *Man with a Movie Camera* (1929), they share the same principal actors and characters and one minor actor and character; they end in the same setting and with the same conclusion (a house in Connecticut for which they have just finished paying off the mortgage). The differences between the enclosing and the enclosed movie—apart from that relation itself, which remains incompletely assessed, and apart from the fact that the enclosed is silent and the enclosing has sound, another incompletely assessed matter—seem to go little beyond a matter of style (which is not to suggest that style is itself a clear matter, but merely that it is not everything). The similarities and differences between the larger and the smaller movies generate a long philosophical story, but in the end I draw a short, multipart moral from that story: the event of film itself is the fundamental cinematic event, not what the filmmaker does to the event, not, for example, whether it was composed in continuity or in discontinuities, which once seemed the fundamental aesthetic question of film; the aesthetic significance of a given film is a function of the way in which and degree to which it reveals or acknowledges this fact of its origin in the medium of film; the full discovery of the significance of an artistic medium, in the revelations and acknowledgments of its significant works, would be accomplished only by the complete history of an art, I mean by an exhausted art, supposing there is such a thing.

The earliest of the comedies of remarriage, *It Happened One Night* (directed by Capra, 1934, with Clark Gable and Claudette Colbert) specifies "the event of film itself" as an event of censoring. This is how I read the film's most famous prop, the blanket hung across a rope strung between two beds in a motel room to divide the space between the man and the woman. The specification of this division of masculine from feminine space depends on two ideas: first, the idea of taking the blanket as an allegory of the working of a movie screen—it conceals the woman's presence from the man while continuously registering her presence causally by her voice and by the dents and ripples her motions impart to the vertical rectangle of fabric; second, the specification depends on accepting the pertinence, in connection with the ensuing limitation and transgression of knowledge, of invoking Kant's idea of the limitations and transgressions necessitated by human reason in establishing the presence and absence of the world. Again there is a long philosophical story generated by these claims, but the short double moral I draw from this story is that the effect of censoring (as elsewhere) is not to banish but to displace and magnify the sense of the erotic; and that the narrative of remarriage is an account, or rather recounting, of what in the English tradition of philosophy is called the problem of other minds, as studied for example in the final part of my *The Claim of Reason*.

This double moral emphasizes the following points of method in the way I approach the study of film. What you may call the aesthetic importance of such a film as *It Happened One Night*—a certain cultural importance may be measured by its having received more Academy Awards than any previous film—is not secured by its position within the genre of the comedy of remarriage, nor by its containing an element that can be understood to allegorize the work of the movie screen, nor by its bearing up under a comparison with the project of the *Critique of Pure Reason*. The conditions of the aesthetic power of film, as with the exercise of any human power, cannot be known in advance of a certain criticism, or say critique, of that power, and a conviction in the architectonic of the critique—a satisfaction in the placement of concepts within the structure of importance—is not had apart from its application in individual cases. Sciences call such application experimentation; humanities call it criticism. If we say that what organizes or animates the results of experimentation is mathematical discourse, then we might say that what organizes or animates the results of criticism is philosophical discourse, and perhaps go on to consider the following: a physicist can allow himself/herself to rely on the soundness of a piece of mathematics once for all, and independently of his/her own ability to derive the mathematics; such is the nature of mathematical conviction, or proof. Whereas a critical reader cannot leave it to others to derive the philosophy he/she invokes, because that philosophy is either derived by such a critic in each act of criticism, new each day, or else it is intellectually unanimated, dead, at the disposal of fashion. (Here as elsewhere, one of the best uses of philosophical acumen is to spot and turn aside useless, invasive philosophy.)

The second pair of films I mention in specifying a work's revelation of the photographic medium begins with perhaps the central member of the genre of remarriage comedy, *The Philadelphia Story* (directed by George Cukor, 1940, with Cary Grant, Katharine Hepburn, and James Stewart). The surface narrative of the film has to do with a reporter and photographer who, through blackmail by the unscrupulous publisher of a sensationalist weekly magazine (one that makes news of gossip and gossip of news—it is modeled on *Time* magazine), are insinuated into an upper-class household to do a feature story about a wedding behind this household's commonly impenetrable doors. The film ends with the wedding ceremony about to begin; as it happens, all three principals are standing before the minister. From nowhere the unscrupulous publisher appears at their side and interrupts the ceremony by himself taking the wedding photos. The film then comes to an end with the following events. At the click of the publisher's camera the trio instinctively snap their heads toward it and their startled looks freeze.

Figure 7.1   Figure 7.2

It is as if that is what the still camera captured, a gesture suggesting that no photograph can be candid, that any camera necessarily imposes on its subject its own conditions of capture, and that identifies the publisher's camera and its motives with the camera of this film. Then that still photograph becomes a page which, when turned, reveals a second still photograph in which Cary Grant and Katharine Hepburn appear alone, embracing, beyond the reach of James Stewart.

Figure 7.3   Figure 7.4

In *Pursuits of Happiness* I read the significance of the turn to stillness in this way: However we understand the provenance of these wedding photos—whether as magazine pages, or perhaps as moments of a wedding album, even perhaps as production stills—the fact of their photographic stillness, after the context of motion pictures, is shocking. It feels as if "we are seeing something after the fact, whereas didn't we just now take ourselves to be, as it were, present at the wedding? . . . What is the difference [between motion and stillness]?"

The fundamental question of the relation between photographic motion and stillness was not one I was prepared to think about very deeply. I let it go once I had located its function in this film, namely that it makes us question the illusion of our presence at these events, and asks us to question the nature of dramatic illusion. I related this, in turn, as I relate other moments in my book, to a problematic in Shakespearean romance, in this instance to Shakespeare's pervasive study of audience.

To take the thought a step further, I want now to pair *The Philadelphia Story* with Dusan Makavejev's 1971 film *Sweet Movie*. As good a way as any of summarizing this immensely complex work, which combines documentary and fictional materials and methods, is to say that it is a psychological-political-philosophical meditation on two themes: first, on a progressive mutual destruction of claims to truth and claims to fantasy which leaves us helpless to believe the one and to take guidance from the other—as if the confusion of news and gossip, depicted in *The Philadelphia Story* as a matter of distaste to a cultivated sensibility, had now become a global matter of intellectual and emotional poison; second, it is a meditation on the title of the song that underscores the film's opening sequence, "Is there life after birth?" The film is punctuated by, or rather organized around, images and thoughts of birth, and of rebirth, as of exhumation from premature burials—it may be a suffocation in the beds of sugar or the vats of chocolate with which the American and the Russian halves of the globe cloak the failures of their revolutions; or it may be the digging up of the mass graves of the massacred Polish officers in the Katyn Forest; or it may be ceremonies of the radical Muehl commune from Vienna, providing a new and bouncing infancy for the bloated grown-up body of one of its group. It is as if the film is asking: Are there ways of thinking, is there a language, in which to speak of such things usefully, nonpoisonously? Is there a form of life, that is, in which such a language may be used? (I have in mind, of course, in this gloss, Wittgenstein's formulation, "To imagine a language is to imagine a form of life"—implying that philosophy needs to take instruction here, that it tends to imagine language as dead, no longer spoken.) Makavejev ponders these questions by subjecting his film to them, getting it to ask of itself whether it creates life or death.

This self-questioning is epitomized and confronted in the final sequence of *Sweet Movie*, as lucid and beautiful an acknowledgment as I have seen of the power and glory of film. The final sequence opens, tinted a monochrome blue, with five corpses wrapped in plastic shrouds and laid neatly on a river bank. They got there through astounding paths of circumstance which cannot now be retraced. The wrapped bodies begin to stir, and the human beings we knew to be inside, call them the actors, begin removing themselves from these cerements or cocoons, exhuming or metamorphosing themselves. The figure nearest us proves to be the boy who had been the main object of a dance of seduction by a woman who in Makavejev's depiction allegorizes phases of the imagination of the Russian revolution. The boy turns his face toward us, looking past us, as at the invisible camera, whereupon the frame freezes and his looking is thus preserved. Gradually the blue tint gives way, and color returns to the frame, upon which the film ends. Formally this ending is a meditation on film's properties of color or its absence, of motion or its absence, and of sound or its absence. The fruit of the meditation is produced through the interpretation of the plastic shrouds or cerements as visual figures for strips of film. Then, the boy's looking out from the screen, half exhumed from his cocoon of film, becomes Makavejev allowing his own youth to confront the grown-up he has become—touched by the horror of the world he now works within and to that extent consents to—and to pose the question as to whether his film creates life or death. The return of color declares that he takes himself as on the side of life, but the stillness and silence of the frame threaten that answer.

The pair of still and silent frames that end *The Philadelphia Story* are from a different world, and yet the hint of death is also present even there, in arcadia. *Pursuits of Happiness* does not insist on this but it does ask if there is not "some lingering suspicion that the picture of the trio was already a kind of wedding photo?"—that somehow, as Edmund madly says in the final moments of *King Lear*, "I was contracted to them both. Now all three marry in an instant.' " What Edmund means by the three marrying is that he is in an instant going to join them in death. The violence and range of Shakespeare's problematic of marriage, which continues throughout his tragedies and romances, the violence of its creation and its decreation, applies also to the comedy of remarriage, because marriage is there legitimized, authorized, not by state, church, sexuality, or children, but only through the pair's unsponsored willingness to choose one another again, so that the plot will contain the fact or threat of divorce. The ground of this willingness for repetition turns out to be the woman's feeling that she is still in need of creation (as in different ways Nora feels in Ibsen's *A Doll House* and Hermione feels in Shakespeare's *A Winter's Tale)* and that for some reason she has chosen this man to provide the necessary midwifery of this new birth (unlike Nora's case; like Hermione's, but without the full mystery of her choice). "The creation of the woman" alludes in my book to a simultaneity of projects: to the institution of marriage by God in Genesis, creating the woman from the man; to the progress of the feminist movement; to the transfiguration given to or imposed upon particular women of flesh and blood by the camera's power of photogenesis.

The violence of the camera's creation I understand to be declared in another Cukor film, *A Woman's Face* (1941, with Joan Crawford, Melvyn Douglas, and Conrad Veidt), where the power of the photographic may be taken as allegorized by the power of plastic surgery. A related idea is taken up in the recent *Gorky Park* (1983), where the medical reconstruction of a head without a face is an emblem for the reconstructability of a murder, perhaps of history as such, and, at the same time, of the process by which the camera preserves the human figure. Horror films will necessarily hint at the camera's transfigurative power, in their disfigurations, recreations, or decreations, of the human being. In my book this shows the genre of horror film to be adjacent to the genre of remarriage comedy.

After one more introductory word I will propose an application of film's participation in creation and annihilation to the frivolously obvious, I mean the apparently frivolous, *Mr. Deeds Goes To Town*.

Photography's participation in death—as if in preserving its subject a photograph removes it from life, mounts it, like a trophy—is an idea that kept surfacing in *The World Viewed*, where I would have been prompted to it by what I had read of André Bazin, with his recurrent sense of the photographic as a kind of life mask of the world, the twin of a death mask. It occurs centrally as I note that the photograph speaks of its human subjects as distracted from the future awaiting them, hence as blindly facing death, a condition displaced with particular lucidity in shots of candid happiness, where the metaphysical transience of such instants marks their subjects with mortal vulnerability; and I close that book with a vision of the world viewed—the world as photographed—as the world of my immortality, the world without me, reassuring in the promise that it will survive me, but unsettling in the suggestion that as I stand now the world is already for me a thing of the past, like a dead star. Romantic writers such as Coleridge and Wordsworth and Emerson and Thoreau mean to awaken us to our harboring of such a vision, and to free us from it. Yet our nostalgia deepens. Memory, which should preserve us, is devouring us. We must, as Thoreau put the matter, look another way. (I should like to cite, in this connection,

Garrett Stewart's "Thresholds of the Visible: The Death Scene of Film" in *Mosaic* XVI/1–2, which studies film's presentation of death in connection with recent studies of the presentation of death in written narrative. The idea of the death of the world occurs as a frisson within the vulgar ironies of such settings as those of the *Planet of the Apes* movie series and the television serial *Buck Rogers in the Twenty-Fifth Century*.)

Leaving the issues of stillness and motion so undeveloped, the moments I have described from *The Philadelphia Story* and from *Sweet Movie* suggest that stillness emphasizes the death in mortal existence while motion emphasizes the life of it. So long as these emphases do not deny that both speak of both, in their particular ways, no theoretical harm is done, if not much good. In turning to *Mr. Deeds* I focus on a feature of human mortality that the *motion of* motion picture photography cannot fail to capture. It may seem about the most trivial feature of human beings there could be, the fact that they are more or less nervous, that their behavior is fidgety.

This fact of human life becomes the climactic evidence cited by Mr. Deeds (Gary Cooper) while defending himself in a law court against the charge of insanity. His successful interpretation of this evidence causes general social happiness and wins him the ecstatic embraces of his estranged beloved, whereupon the film concludes. That propositions of such ludicrousness can be seen to illustrate, even to explore, philosophical sublimities is surely part of my fascination with so-called popular movies. About the film's plot, all I will say before looking at a few moments of that trial is that Deeds was arrested for trying to give away his sudden inheritance of $20,000,000, on the complaint of lawyers—who have their designs on the money—that his behavior shows him mentally incompetent. He has also just found out that the woman he has fallen in love with is a reporter who, using his feelings for her to extract a sensational series of newspaper features, has held his escapades up to ridicule, naming him "The Cinderella Man." In a detention hospital room he has withdrawn into silence.

The trial occupies the last twenty minutes or so of the film, and starts out with Gary Cooper maintaining his silence, refusing to plead further with a world that has erotically and politically ridiculed and jailed him for his Utopian fantasies. What causes him to speak again, which means, narratively, what prompts him to defend himself, is an obvious critical question. A less obvious question concerns the participation of Capra's film in the genre of melodrama, in which muteness is a signal feature, and in which the breaking of silence is a climactic declaration of personal identity and the confrontation of villainy. It is an image of ecstasy or exaltation expressed in this instance as the power and the willingness to communicate one's presence, to have one's existence matter, one's own terms taken seriously. (Emphasis on muteness and self-revelation is among the many discoveries in Peter Brooks's valuable study *The Melodramatic Imagination*, 1976.) Less obvious still is what the camera's evidence of fidgetiness has to do with these matters.

Mr. Deeds appeals to fidgetiness as a universal human attribute, if not exactly a normal one, in defense of his playing the tuba at odd hours, a practice taken by the prosecution and its witnesses as a major piece of evidence of madness. Deeds's defense is that his tuba playing is his version of something every human being does under certain universally recurrent conditions. The other versions he cites of such behavior are tics (a man's compulsive nose twitching, a woman's knuckle cracking) and doodling (drawing aimless designs, filling in *O*s). I say he "cites" these instances, but in fact his speech becomes a kind of voice-over narrative as the camera illustrates each of these involuntary movements in closeup, as if it is setting up exhibits of evidence for Mr. Deeds's case. The evidence is, accordingly, not for the depicted judges and spectators, for whom the closeups are invisible, but for us. He does cite two such practices without photographic illustration—ear pulling and nail biting—as if to declare that the act of photographing is deliberate. This underscores Deeds's alliance with the camera. It is his acknowledgment that to provide such illustration or evidence is a power and possible glory natural to the moving picture camera, that the most apparently insignificant repetitions, turnings, pauses, and yieldings of human beings are as interesting to it as is the beauty or the science of movement.

Think of this interest or power as the camera's knowledge of the metaphysical restlessness of the live body at rest, something internal to what Walter Benjamin calls cinema's optics of the unconscious. Under examination by the camera, a human body becomes for its inhabitant a field of betrayal more than a ground of communication, and the camera's further power is manifested as it documents the individual's self-conscious efforts to control the body each time it is conscious of the camera's attention to it. I might call these recordings *somatograms* (cf. cardiograms, electroencephalograms), to register the essential linking of the pattern of a body's motions with the movements of the machine that records them. We seem to have no standing word for what somatograms record. "Mannerisms" is partial in its noting of characteristically recurrent behavior; "manners" is partial in its attention to social modification. Freud uses the word *Fehlleistimg* (usually translated as parapraxis) to gather together something like the stage of behavior I have in mind, but his examples are more selective than mine must be. The plain word "behavior" has the right generality, but in a time still unpredictably marked by the psychological and philosophical sensibility of behaviorism—in which behavior is reduced to something outer, from which something inner (call it mind) has been scooped out—the expressiveness of the range of the restless is more or less incomprehensible.

Emerson's essay entitled "Behavior," from *The Conduct of Life*, is an effort to rehabilitate this concept of behavior, along with that of manners, to return the mind to the living body. Here is a sample:

> Nature tells every secret once. Yes, but in man she tells it all the time, by form, attitude, gesture, mien, face and parts of the face, and by the whole action of the machine. The visible carriage or action of the individual, as resulting from his organization and his will combined, we call manners. What are they but thought entering the hands and feet, controlling the movements of the body, the speech and behavior? . . . The power of manners is incessant,—an element as unconcealable as fire.

Emerson's effort of conceptual rehabilitation constitutes this marvelous essay as a major contribution to the aesthetics of cinema (as well as to the aesthetics of acting, a coincidence hardly merely coincidental). Mr. Deeds has a particular name for the condition that causes universal fidgetiness. His name for it is *thinking*. "Everyone does silly things when they think," he declares. He uses the word "think" or "thinking" repeatedly, and each time emphasizes that each individual does something idiosyncratic when he or she is in the condition of thinking. Why he includes playing the tuba as part of his particular somatogram—not, say, as an item in his profile as an aspiring American musician and artist—is, of course, a further question. I want to stay with the question at hand: how has Deeds been brought to break his silence in order to speak of the connection between thinking and silliness? Why is it now that he is willing to claim his identity and his contribution to the polity and his personal happiness against the villainous incomprehension of the world?

My answer depends on taking his appeal to the concept of thinking with greater philosophical seriousness than others may be prepared, right off, to grant it. I have taken Deeds's perception of fidgetiness as disclosing an essential feature of the human, not simply of the animal, body; it marks a creature in whom the body and its soul do not everywhere fit. (I wish to leave open the question whether this is true of the human creature as such, or whether it may be true only of the human creatures in our epoch, and especially true of those creatures in the period of capitalism that Deeds's social program of redistribution defines, one in which a large number of evidently hardworking, unenvious, independent people are needlessly being deprived of what they need in order to make a living. "Need" is another recurrent term of Deeds's discourse. His word for those who do not wish to work is "moochers"; he is shown to be indiscriminate in his application of this term.) And I have taken the idea that fidgetiness always accompanies thinking to mean that it proves thinking, or the *desire* to think, which, as Heidegger asserts, is essential to the possibility of thinking. It is the connection of thinking with the human desire of the possible, of realization, that prompts me to see in Deeds's words, and the way he uses them, a recapturing in the everyday of Descartes's perception of what thinking itself proves, namely the existence of the human. So that when Deeds begins to speak, defending his sanity, he is performing, as the climax to be expected in a melodramatic structure, a version of Descartes's cogito, taking on the proof of his own existence, as if against its denial by the world.

Some will be unwilling to grant this degree of seriousness to Mr. Deeds's courtroom lecture on silliness and thinking, and they may wish to protect their sense of the serious by suggesting that Deeds's words are at best a parody of philosophy, not the thing of philosophy itself. I am sympathetic to this. But I have shown cause elsewhere to suppose that at some stage serious philosophy may come to manifest itself as—one could say, to exist most immediately as—a parody of philosophy. I have based this idea on Emerson's and Edgar Allan Poe's apparently parodistic adoptions, or adaptations, of the cogito argument. Because Emerson's adaptation will play a direct role in my conclusion about the movie *Mr. Deeds Goes to Town*, I pause here simply to state his observation that we are no longer able to announce the cogito for ourselves, no longer able, as he puts it, to say "I think" and "I am," on our own, for ourselves. I take this to imply that we are without proof of our existence, that we are, accordingly, in a state of preexistence, as if metaphysically missing persons. Emerson's famous word for lacking words of our own is "conformity." It obviously has precursors in Romantic perceptions of the human as dead, or deadened, and it is a specific conceptual precursor of Nietzsche's "last man," hence of Heidegger's *Das Man.*

Before we dismiss Deeds as lacking the authority or the circumstances in which to assume the cogito (matters essential to Descartes's broaching of the issue), we had better be sure that we know who this man is and what his circumstances are, know them as well as we must know, for example, who and where one of Poe's narrators is in order to know the spirit in which to take his tales. We have to make up our minds whether we grant Deeds the authority to mean the line from Thoreau that he identifies when he says early in the film: "They built palaces but they forgot to build the people to live in them"; or whether, alternatively, we withhold this grant and thereby rebuke his pretension in voicing it. He says it in his first conversation with the woman, alone at night on a park bench, as part of establishing an initial intimacy with her; a few moments later he seizes an occasion to run from her and jump on a screaming fire engine. Is this what philosophical authority looks like? I note that the line preceding the one about building palaces is also from Thoreau, but not identified as such in Capra's script: "People here seem to have the St. Vitus Dance." (Capra's limitation as a reader of Thoreau and Emerson may show in the circumstances of this line. Deeds says it about New York, with the implication that in small towns such as the one he comes from behavior is radically different. Even I would find it hard to believe that Capra invites this interpretation to show the limitation only of his character Deeds, implying that he has himself a yet more transcendental perspective.) St. Vitus's Dance is the more familiar name for the disorder called chorea, found mostly in children and associated with temporary brain dysfunction. In Deeds's phantasm (and for that matter in Thoreau's) there is no radical distinction to be made between St. Vitus's Dance and human behavior as such (as it has become), as if human behavior is now in general the result of brain damage. When the two comically dotty old maid sisters testify in the court room that not only Deeds but everyone except themselves is "pixilated" (controlled by pixies), they discredit their earlier testimony that Deeds is thus affected. Everyone thereupon agrees that this shows the sisters to be mentally incompetent. But the only difference between their expressed view of the world and Deeds's view is that he does not clearly exempt himself, any more than Thoreau exempts himself, from the madness of the world. Perhaps this is what philosophical authority sounds like.

To dismiss Deeds as too silly for philosophical thought is to deny him a voice in defining what is silly, one of his characteristic words. And if we deny him this voice, how are we different from the corrupt prosecution, who would exercise an analogous denial by having him declared insane? And how do we understand the muteness that prepares the condition, you may say the seriousness, of his cogito? The woman who loves him screams that he is being crucified. (Frank Capra, like other American artists, finds the figure of Christ near at hand for identifying the posture of his heroes. Some will find this an irredeemably coarse habit, perhaps in the way Nietzsche found Luther's intellectual habits to be coarse.) Without going that far, the question remains how far we credit the grief, the sense of rejection, that this hero's extended muteness bespeaks. Our answer to that question determines how seriously we take this man's intellectual seriousness. If our philosophical sensibility fails us here it may be failing us at any and all times, so that it is we whose perceptions and powers of sympathy will prove to be coarsened and muted.

Evidently, my questions concerning the seriousness with which we grant the intellectual seriousness of *Mr. Deeds* is some kind of allegory of a more extensive question about whether we will grant to Frank Capra the capacity to undertake a significant artistic response to Emerson and Thoreau. My anxiety about communicating such a thought with due seriousness has waxed and waned since the time, in preparing the chapter on Capra's *It Happened One Night* for *Pursuits of Happiness*, I broached the idea of Capra's filmmaking as incorporating a mode of vision inherited from American transcendentalism, even to the point of sharing American transcendentalism's inheritance, in turn, of German culture (specifically, in Capra's work, of German expressionist cinema). The anxiety tracks my knowledge that lovers of American movies have taken such remarks of mine to be needless and pretentious, together with my sense that professional students of film are often not prepared to credit such company for American movies, colored by my observation of American professional philosophers, for whom, with perhaps a growing number of exceptions, such speculation is fit, at best, for an intellectually frivolous hour. It has been urged upon me that such dismissals should not matter to me so much. But I think one can see in the work of Emerson and of Thoreau and of Capra that, in their various American ways, analogous dismissals have mattered as much to them.

To provide a fair test of this question of Deeds's intellectual seriousness, we would need to *place* Deeds in that courtroom, arrive at him, derive him, exactly as he comes to be derived from paths of narrative and cinematic development most of whose contours cannot possibly be accounted for here. I will accordingly end these remarks by returning specifically to the path of the power and glory of photography, asking after the role the camera plays in Deeds's willingness to speak and to claim his happiness with the woman.

I pick up from two ideas already discussed. First, that Deeds will show his awareness that the motion picture camera bears an affinity with metaphysical restlessness, that it has its own imperative to keep moving, and second, that this awareness is, in effect, an acceptance of Descartes's perception that the human stands in need of proof in each case, by each case, together with Emerson's perception that we are mostly incapable any longer of taking on our existence by ourselves. And I take it that Deeds's insight is that a reverse field of proof is available by way of the motion picture camera, so that while thinking is no longer secured by the mind's declaration of its presence to itself, it is now to be secured by the presence of the live human body to the camera, in particular by the presence of the body's apparently least intelligent property, its fidgetiness, its metaphysical restlessness. In Descartes the proof of thinking was that it cannot doubt itself; after Emerson the proof of thinking is that it cannot be concealed.

Am I saying that the camera is necessary to this knowledge? Descartes says that my existence is proved "each time I say 'I think,' or conceive it in my mind." Must I commit myself to saying that my existence is proved (only) each time the camera rolls my way? I ask a little license here. My idea is that the invention of the motion picture camera reveals something that has already happened to us, hence something, when we fail to acknowledge it, that is knowledge of something fundamental about our existence which we resist. And the camera also reveals and records that resistance—recall that, in the course of Deeds's lecture to the court, each time the camera follows his attention to a person's body's motion, that person's reflex is shown to be to attempt to hide the motion. We can think of what the camera revelas as a new strain either in our obliviousness to our existence, or in a new mode of certainty of it.

If the price of Descartes's proof of his existence was a perpetual recession of the body (a kind of philosophical counter-Renaissance), the price of an Emersonian proof of my existence is a perpetual visibility of the self, a theatricality in my presence to others, hence to myself. The camera is an emblem of perpetual visibility. Descartes's self-consciousness thus takes the form of embarrassment.

Deeds is accordingly the name of one who sees the stakes in this altered condition and who submits himself to the camera's judgment, permits its interrogation—its victimization—of him. It is an unlooked-for species of bravery. Psychologically, submission to a somatogram—to the synchronization between body and camera—demands passiveness, you may say demands the visibility of the feminine side of one's character. Capra's mastery of the medium of film, or his obedience to it, guides him to make certain that we are aware of the beauty of Gary Cooper's face, and in one instance he photographs him posed as in a glamour shot of a female star, lying on his back across a bed (playing the tuba it happens, as if that mattered), capturing his full length from a vantage just above his head.

Figure 7.5

Cinematically his submission declares what I have called the natural ascendancy on film of the actor over the character, so that the rightness of its being specifically Gary Cooper who plays Deeds comes here to the fore, as if Capra is interpreting the embarrassment (say the self-consciousness) of the Emersonian proof—that thinking cannot be concealed—in terms of Cooper's world-historical capacity for shyness, and vice versa, giving a metaphysical interpretation of this American mode of shyness.

Narratively the condition of Deeds's happy ending is that his victimization be interpreted, or redeemed, as his willingness to reverse roles with the woman. We know of his boyish wish for romance, his wish "to rescue a damsel in distress." Jean Arthur asserts once and for all her superiority over him in the realm of action, call it the male realm, by pretending to him to be such a damsel. She has ridiculed exactly that wish of his by naming him The Cinderella Man—he is more in need of being rescued than in a position to provide rescue. But this, in turn, is the expression of her own condition of romance: her wish to discover a man for whom she could make it all right that he has been badly frightened by desire and lost a slipper. At the end he shows her this loss, this desire.

He has twice run from her, each time at a moment when his desire was importunate. Early, as mentioned, when he runs to the fire engine from the park; then later, elaborately, when, as she completes reading aloud to him the love poem he has composed for her, he races down the night streets, stumbling noisily over visible and invisible garbage cans, in a solo of awkwardness that cinematically registers the falling of an American male in love. In the courtroom his starting to speak is the sign that he has stopped running. He claims the woman's love by acknowledging that the shoe fits, that he was, so to speak, at the ball, that he has desires and can ask her to rescue him from his fear of expression.

Narratively the man's willingness to speak, to express desire, comes in response to the woman's courtroom declaration, under cross-examination, that she loves him (a familiar Hollywood topos). I think we are entitled here, further, to understand the man's reading of this woman's declaration of love as a signal of her own distress. Thus, after all, she grants him his wish to rescue, to be active, to take deeds upon himself, earning his name; as he grants her wish to her. So this film participates, with comedies of remarriage, in what I have called the comedy of equality and reciprocity.

The words with which the man had broken his silence were: "I'd like to put in my two cents"—which is still useable American slang for expressing an opinion. Our next step should be to consider why this man, whose adventure recounts the inheriting and attempted bequeathing of one of the richest fortunes in the country, initiates his willingness to quit his silence and to claim the inheritance of his existence, his right to desire, by speaking of speaking as an issue of "two cents." Of course one can bring any number of ideological suspicions to bear here. I think the film deserves also the following line of consideration.

The right to speak not only takes precedence over social power, it takes precedence over any particular form of accomplishment; no amount of contribution is more valuable to the formation and preservation of community than the willingness to contribute and the occasion to be heard. Further, unlike $20,000,000, the contribution of two cents is one that can be responded to equally by others; it leaves your voice your own and allows your opinion to matter to others only because it matters to you. It is not a voice that will be heard by villains. This means that to discover our community a few will have to be punched out, made speechless—one interpretation of Deeds's repeated violence, punching men on the jaw. It is a fantasy of a reasonably well-ordered participatory democracy. It has its dangers; democracy has; speech has. If the motion picture camera contributes its uniqueness to help keep this Utopian idea alive, that is power and glory enough to justify its existence, a contribution somewhere between two cents and the largest fortune in the world.

8

A Capra Moment

Because the widespread presence of film studies in higher education is still in its first generation, the overwhelming majority of those who presently teach the subject cannot have acquired their teaching degrees within the field.

Each college or university that has wished to teach film systematically has had to find its own home for film—often in the English department, sometimes distributed among various departments of modern and/or comparative literature, sometimes as part of the theater or visual arts, sometimes as a newly created department, occasionally even one that is authorized to grant the Ph.D.

For me, all this chaos has been worthwhile, not merely because I love film and wish to see it lovingly studied under any reasonable circumstances, but because film study has profited me in the rest of my humanistic work. When, for example, a Shakespearean structure is found to underlie a genre of Hollywood comedy, that structure is freshly illuminated along with the genre.

But the chaos and the new raw degrees have meant that film, especially in these intellectually volatile years, will sometimes be taught less responsibly than, or in poor isolation from, established humanistic subjects with their long history in certifying competence. These difficulties will help to justify the refusal of many of my academic colleagues to grant the study of film a place in a serious university curriculum.

First published in *Humanities*, August 1985. This essay is incorporated into Chapter 8 of *Cities of Words.*

A N INDISCRIMINATE SCORN OF film study strikes me as a continuation
of America's contempt, or ambivalence, toward its best contributions to world happiness, like jazz and public friendliness. I take
the present opportunity not as one for further preaching on the text of
film's worthiness despite its sinfulness, but for presenting a specific
instance of how I think about film. It is only in one's concrete feeling for
particular films that genuine conviction of its value for study can, or
should, develop.

To exemplify this conviction here I take as my example a moment
from Frank Capra's *It Happened One Night* (1934, starring Clark Gable and
Claudette Colbert), a moment whose apparent commonplaces or evanescence found no place in my long and difficult chapter on the film in
Pursuits of Happiness: The Hollywood Comedy of Remarriage (Harvard
University Press, 1981). A man and a woman are walking away from us
down an empty country road.

Figure 8.1

I knew afresh each time I viewed the film that this moment played something like an epitomizing role in the film's effect upon me, but I remained
unable to find words for it sufficient to include in my critical account of
the effect. I have now found some that begin to satisfy me, and to air them
is my present happiness.

It will help prepare the way to explain that *It Happened One Night* is
one of the seven talkies made in Hollywood between 1934 and 1949
definitive of a genre I name remarriage comedy. The title "remarriage"
registers the grouping of a set of comedies which differ from classical comedy in various respects, but most notably in this: In classical comedy the
narrative shows a young pair overcoming obstacles to their love and at the
end achieving marriage, whereas comedies of remarriage begin or climax
with a pair less young, getting or threatening their divorce, so that the
drive of the narrative is to get them back together, together again. The
central idea is that the validity or bond of marriage is no longer assured or
legitimized by church or state or sexual compatibility or children but by

something I call the willingness for remarriage, a way of continuing to affirm the happiness of one's initial leap, as if the chance of happiness exists only when it seconds itself. In classical comedy people made for one another find one another; in remarriage comedy people who have found one another find that they are made for each other. The greatest of the structures of remarriage is *The Winter's Tale*, which is, together with *The Tempest*, the greatest of the Shakespearean romances.

In accounting for the effect upon me of the moment preceding the one in focus here (of the pair on the road), I was led to speak of the "American transcendentalism of Capra's exteriors." In thus aligning Capra's work with the thought of Emerson and of Thoreau I was trying to locate one of Capra's signature emotions—the experience of an ecstatic possibility, as of a better world just adjacent to this one, one that this one speaks of in homely symbol, one that we could (in romance, in social justice) as it were, reach out and touch; if only. . . . My alignment was formed by a series of shots of Claudette Colbert responding to a meditative description by Clark Gable in which he has invoked "those nights when you and the moon and the water all become one and you feel you're part of something big and marvelous." The description felt to me (and I imagined, to the character played by Colbert) to be an expression at once of an old fantasy of the man's, and of his fresh memory of the previous night which the two of them had spent together, ended by their sleeping in separate regions of a haystack. The description, taken in itself, is not much more than newspaper filler. But set to Gable's entranced recitation, and authorized both by Colbert's entranced responsiveness to it and by our own memory of their night in the moon-bright open field (and of their arriving there by fording a stream filled with reflected stars), the words take on the weight of a passage from *Walden*. (Even seen in motion, in the crossing of the stream it is somewhat hard to make out that Gable is carrying Colbert slung over his left shoulder, holding a suitcase in his right hand, her high heels pointing in the direction of their progress. But the point of the shot for my purposes is clear: The stream is shattered by stars. It is an image of something Thoreau calls "sky water.")

Figure 8.2

Capra's transcendental moments derive in part from German expressionist cinema (as Emerson's transcendental thought derives in part from German philosophy); they display the mood of a character stretched across that character's setting. But the German settings tend toward the closed and their mood toward the haunted; the Capra tend toward the expanded and their mood toward a tortured yearning. If one does not find or will not permit the mood, the Capra moment is apt to produce titters, as from emotion with no visible means of support.

The moment I concentrate on here occurs the morning following the night in the open field. The shot lasts under thirty seconds, during which the pair have this exchange (the woman speaking first):

—What did you say we're supposed to be doing?
—Hitchhiking.
—Oh. Well. You've given me a very good example of the hiking. Where does the hitching come in?
—Uh, a little early yet. No cars out.
—If it's just the same to you I'm going to sit right here and wait 'til they come.

Despite what I started thinking of as the "nothingness" of this shot—remarking the spareness of imagery, the conventionality of the words, the apparent off-handedness of the characters' manners—the transcendental mood seemed to me continued in this early grey morning. But then I felt: Certainly it continues. This just means that the powerful, expressionistically enforced mood of the night before persists, for us and for them. It is only natural, given that the sequence had climaxed with an extreme close-up of the pair resisting an embrace; they are unreleased.

Figure 8.3

Then again I felt: No. I mean the mood persists not just as in memory but as present, continued by the new setting at dawn. The spareness, the conventionality, the off-handedness are somehow to be understood with the same expressionist fervor of the moonlit night scene. Of course in the new setting the cosmos will not be concurrent with the words that are said, but rather the words will have to be heard as covering, barely, the attraction of the mood. Even the variance of the pair's individual manners suggests the covering—the man somewhat depressed, the woman somewhat manic. So I imagine them as moving together but each keeping to himself and herself, filled with thoughts of one another, trying to accommodate to what has passed between them and to their knowledge that they each know what the other is going through, including an unreadiness to become explicit.

My critical claim is that this understanding is not a guess on my part as to how a couple of other people must be, or ought to be, feeling, based on what I know of their time together; but that it is a reading, a perception, of what I am calling the transcendental mood of this utterly specific shot now before us, a reading of its very nothingness. To substantiate this claim, I must provide this reading. I begin by repeating the recasting of the title description I suggested in introducing the shot, and I divide it into four segments: On the road/walking/together/away from us. I take up the segments in reverse order.

Away from us. It is my general impression that the motion picture camera held on a human figure squarely from behind has tended to inflect some significance of human privacy and vulnerability, of self-reflection, of the capacity or necessity to keep one's counsel. I expect everyone can recall analogous shots of Charlie Chaplin's Little Tramp walking away down a road. Beyond noting this as providing one of the sublime groups of images on film to capture human isolation, vulnerability, yet hopefulness, I note that such a shot naturally constitutes the ending of a film. What is one of them doing at something like the center of the present film? This is in effect to begin asking: How does this specific shot inflect the range of associated shots that invoke the sense of privacy, vulnerability, thoughtfulness, and so on?

Together. The pivot of inflection is that while they still keep their individual counsels they are joined by moving in concert exactly away from us. It is an essential feature of the genre of remarriage comedy that the films defining it each close with some indication that the principal pair, in reentering the state of matrimony, are crossing some border that leaves us out, behind, with no embrace of their own, with nothing meant to insure or to signal that they will find, or rather refind, their happiness. In *The Awful Truth*, the pair at the close are metamorphosed into figurines on a Swiss clock; in *His Girl Friday* they run away from us down a flight of stairs; in *The Lady Eve* a door closes in our faces; in *Adam's Rib*, curtains close; in *The Philadelphia Story* the pair freeze into still photos; in the present film the ending consists of a mostly empty, darkened frame in which we see a mythical blanket barrier tumbling down. But the centered walk away down the road we are considering here does also feel like something is ending, hence like something is beginning, some border being crossed. It is this undefined openness, as if leaving the past behind them, that marks this particular inflection of vulnerability, of thoughtful anticipation.

Here is a place to pause for an instant to see whether the words of this sequence are as unremarkable as we have assumed. What becomes of words on film can prove to be as significant a matter as what becomes of people and things on film. Take the line, "Oh. Well. You've given me a good example of the hiking. Where does the hitching come in?" I hope you can come to the place—it will not happen on a first viewing—of wondering whether "hitching" here pertains to getting hitched, and even to what Katharine Hepburn refers to in *The Philadelphia Story*—having to explain to her assembled wedding guests about the successful failure of her wedding plans—in saying that "There's been a hitch in the proceedings." Not only was this man on this road with the woman supposed to be helping her return to her so-called husband, but generally hitches in hitching are the study both of classical comedy and (oddly reshaped in significance) of remarriage comedy. I find the thought reinforced by the surprisingly touching fact that the woman is limping; she has a hitch. So Capra's shot immediately, ironically, informs us that hitching has already come in, more or less before our eyes, that the tying of the (hitch) knot, the entanglement of lives, is on the way and will not, for some happy reason, come undone. (This sketches the moral of the remarriage structure.)

Walking. What they are doing is walking together on a road, hiking until hitching. This fact began to take on thematic importance for me some time after a colleague inquired whether I had thought about the range of vehicles in the film, suggesting that they form a little system of significance as striking as the system I had found in the various food consumed in it. Thinking this over (there is a yacht, a bus, a roadster, one or two limousines, a flight of motorcycles, a freight train, a private passenger plane, a helicopter) it seemed to me that the vehicles mostly emblematize or differentiate matters whose disposition in this film we know independently—power, isolation, vacuity, the capacity for community; whereas, the system of foods and their modes of preparation or gathering provides the basis of relationships that serve to establish and measure acceptance and rejection. Even so, the intuition of significance in the system of vehicles still seemed to me just. I have come to understand it in its contrast as a whole with—hence its emphasis upon—the human fact of walking; just as I had taken the system of foods as a whole to emphasize the human fact of hunger. Being hungry and being on the road are familiar scenes of the depression. Hollywood comedies of the period are often chastised as fairy-tale distractions from the terrible realities of those times. I do not deny that some were, maybe most. But the best among them were tales that continue the extreme outbursts of hope in human possibility that were also part of the realities of those times; otherwise their persistent popularity and instructiveness would seem to me inexplicable. Hunger in *It Happened One Night* stands for the reality of imagination, the imagination of a better world, a better way than we have found. Now I wish to make explicit a companion representativeness in its idea of walking together. Accordingly let us consider where it is they are walking.

On the road. In four of the seven definitive remarriage comedies the denouement of mutual acknowledgment is achieved by a removal of the pair to a place of perspective that, following Shakespeare's psychic geography, I call "the green world." I find that *It Happened One Night* compensates for its lack of this more or less explicitly mythical location by its presentation of perspective acquired on the road, which is the classical and no less mythical location of picaresque quest and adventure. Its interpretation of the green world as the location of successfully achieved romantic marriage is, hence, an interpretation of successfully achieved romantic marriage as itself the process of quest and adventure.

There is another declaration of this road as a mythical or psychical locale. After Gable's lecture to the woman about the three modes of thumbing a ride and then his proving to be impotent to stop the first three cars by any item in the sequence of his means, the road suddenly produces, as from nowhere, an unending stream of cars rushing past his abashed thumb and disappearing around the bend into nowhere, as if the proper rebuke to this male expansiveness is to show the man failing to stop each and every car on earth. This cosmic rebuke, as by the medium of film itself, sets up the succeeding rebuke by the woman, who famously stops a car by showing some leg, thus proving once for all, as she says happily to the gloomy man, "that the limb is mightier than the thumb."

It was in connecting, more or less consciously, the ideas of the road as the equivalent of a spiritual realm of perspective and adventure, with the persistence of a transcendental sense of dawning landscape as calling out a moment of openness and beginning, and with the specific cosmic rebuke of male assertiveness, that I turned, for the first time in years, to Walt Whitman's "Song of the Open Road." I remind you of what there is to be found there. The thirteenth section opens:

Allons! To that which is endless as it was beginningless,
To undergo much, tramps of days, rests of nights,
To merge all in the travel they tend to, and the days and the nights
   they tend to,
Again to merge them in the start of superior journeys. . . .

The fifteenth and final section concludes:

Camerado, I give you my hand!
I give you my love more precious than money,
I give you myself before preaching or law;
With you give me yourself: will you come travel with me?
Shall we stick by each other as long as we live?

The mood is of course different from that of the shot of our pair on
the empty dawning road. But if you will take Whitman's closing questions as
lines for the invention of a new wedding ceremony, they match as perfectly
as any I know the questions and the tasks proposed by the genre of the comedy of remarriage. (By "the invention of marriage" I mean a task of these
comedies that they share with Shakespearean theater, as in *Antony and
Cleopatra* and in *The Winter's Tale*.) It follows that I am proposing the shot of
this pair on the road walking together away from us as a wedding photo.
      Even if you will take it so for this moment, you may not for the next.
Not every moment will yield to, or require, the mood of Whitman's
ecstasies and exhortations, any more than every moment can tolerate, or
use, the sentiments and elations of Capra. But I imagine that these artists
themselves composed knowing this, even that they meant to declare it,
respectively, of the nature of poetry and of film, to acknowledge their
intermittence, our evanescent readiness for them. Or in Emerson's words
from "Experience": "Since our office is with moments, let us husband
them." Or as Wittgenstein will put a similar thought: "What dawns here
lasts only as long as I am occupied with the object in a particular way." We
have perhaps most poignantly in film, something we have in any art, the
opportunity to find, but always the freedom to miss, the significance of
the nothing and the nowhere.
      Am I claiming that Capra is as good as Whitman and Emerson? Am I
saying that he intended the matters I have invoked to account for my mood
with a moment he has provided? These are reasonable questions, deserving
reasoned answers. Until then I may put my approach to them this way.
Capra shares certain of the ambitions and the specific visions of Whitman
and Emerson, and he knows about working with film roughly what they
know about working with words. If your fixed view is, however, that no film

(anyway none produced in the Hollywood sound era) could in principle bear up under any serious comparison with major writing, then our conversation is, if it has begun, at an end; for I would take the fixed view, or attitude, as representative of a philistine intellectuality fully worthy of the philistine anti-intellectuality from which we more famously suffer.

9

The Fantastic of Philosophy

I T IS WONDERFUL TO BE HERE—here in this house that Wittgenstein designed, and in this city that fashioned Wittgenstein. It is almost seven years since I began visiting the Philosophical Institute at the University of Vienna and first met the young philosophers whose conception and publication we are celebrating today. Our intellectual companionship over the years has been an inspiration to me. It cheers me to think that our exchanges have played some part in the story that leads to today's event, and I take the event as a promise of continued and growing exchanges between Austrian and American philosophers.

This companionship has, of course, allowed me a perspective on my own temperament and tendencies in philosophizing; but beyond this, it has encouraged my sense that the task of cultural perspective is not only privately useful but philosophically creative. The interests among philosophers here in the richness of specifically Austrian thought has helped my own preoccupation with the richness, and the poverty, of specifically American thought, above all with the extraordinary fact that those I regard as the founders of American thinking—Ralph Waldo Emerson and Henry David Thoreau—are philosophically repressed in the culture they founded. My efforts to release this repression are not interested, perhaps I should say explicitly, any more than I understand the attention to Austrian thought here to be interested, in ridding itself of foreign influence and participation. On the contrary, my wish to inherit Emerson and Thoreau

First published in *The American Poetry Review* 15.3, May–June 1986; reprinted in Stanley Cavell, *In Quest of the Ordinary* (University of Chicago Press, 1988).

as philosophers, my claim for them as founding American thinking, is a claim both that America contains an unacknowledged current of thinking, *and* that this thinking accomplishes itself by teaching the inheritance of European philosophy—an inheritance that should make me not the master of this European philosophy, but also not its slave.

Something apparently common to philosophy among the cultures of the West is, in recent centuries, philosophy's attention to the claims of science as the highest, or sole, access to knowledge. A way to attend to the distinctness of a culture's thinking is to meditate on the relation between its institutions of philosophy and literature. It is imaginable that a philosopher inspired by the German-speaking tradition of philosophy would not be content with results that failed to encompass, or say release, the knowledge embodied in his or her history of literature; whereas for a philosopher inspired by the English-speaking tradition, the invocation of Shakespeare or Milton or Wordsworth or Dickens was always apt at best to be a matter of occasional personal taste or embellishment, of essentially no professional interest. American thought, in my view, runs between these inspirations. To claim Emerson and Thoreau as of the origin in America, not alone of what is called literature but of what may be called philosophy, is to claim that literature is neither the arbitrary embellishment nor the necessary other of philosophy. You can either say that in the New World, distinctive philosophy and literature do not exist in separation, or you can say that the American task is to create them from one another, as if the New World is still to remember, if not exactly to recapitulate, the cultural labors of the Old World.

As an emblem of such issues of exchange within cultures, and between cultures, and between generations, I have chosen, for this day of celebration, to report my intervention upon being invited twelve months ago by the graduate student association of a literary-philosophical culture as foreign to American as to Austrian culture—namely by the Ph. D. students of the Japan Institute of Harvard University—invited to participate in one of the panels in a day-long symposium they were organizing on the topic of the fantastic in Japanese literature, and specifically to comment on two scholarly papers by members of their association.[1] The fact that the association was of the young, at the beginning of their scholarly careers, helped to reassure me that the invitation was meant not to verify my ignorance of Japanese literature but extended in hopes that I might like to learn something about it and to respond, if I had a response, from my corner of the American world—even perhaps to learn something more about how I got into that corner.

Our panel of the symposium was entitled "We Are Not Alone," and reading over the papers I was to comment on created in me something like the haunted experience of the fantastic, call it the uncanny, since the literature they describe is completely unfamiliar to me but the descriptions they give of that literature seem so familiar that I feel I have known what they speak of forever. The papers invoked such ideas as that of the imaginary journey, especially in quest of the self; and such ideas as that of being on some boundary or threshold, as between the impossible and the possible; and ideas of the confrontation of otherness; and of some adverse relation to the modern scientific sensibility.

My sense of the familiar here is not, I think, sufficiently accounted for by noting that our Western literature contains its own vein of the fantastic in literature, a vein represented, say, in the works that Tzvetan Todorov adduces as evidence for his theory of the fantastic, exemplified by the tales of E. T. A. Hoffmann. My feeling seems more particularly to do with the sense that American literature as such is eccentric in relation to the European, a deviation familiarly expressed by saying (almost inevitably with a certain prejudice) that where Europeans have written novels the Americans have composed something else, call them romances. If we consider that Nathaniel Hawthorne himself uses this distinction to permit himself an appeal to "the Marvelous" and remember that Anthony Trollope, in reviewing Hawthorne's *The Marble Faun*, speaks of Hawthorne's "weird imagination" and compares him with Monk Lewis; and further consider the imagination of Poe, and then the uncanniness of a white whale, it suggests itself that in contrast to Europe's definite but marginal interest in the fantastic, America has been centrally preoccupied with it. Accepting accordingly a point insisted upon by both the papers I was commenting on, that the literature of the fantastic has generally either in fact or in principle found it hard to be accepted and lifted out of the realm of the unserious or twilight zone into the central day of literature, I was led to pose the following supplementary question for consideration: What might it betoken about a culture's literature that its *founding* works are works of the fantastic?

Let me begin to specify this question by placing within our circle of concern a founding text of American writing that I do not imagine has been proposed before as an instance of the fantastic, Thoreau's *Walden*. That work obviously exhibits two of the principal characteristics of the fantastic I just listed, since *Walden* may accurately and well be characterized as an imaginary journey, and along lines that present themselves as boundaries or thresholds. That it situates itself in terms of a range of dualities has I believe struck many of its readers—between civilization and wilderness, between the future and the past, between human and animal, between heaven and earth, between dream and waking life, and, I would like to say, between philosophy and literature. That it is a book of imaginary travel is perhaps less remarked, but the fact is declared in the book's third paragraph:

I have traveled a good deal in Concord; and everywhere, in ships, and offices, and fields, the inhabitants have appeared to me to be doing penance in a thousand remarkable ways. What I have heard of Bramins sitting exposed to four fires and looking in the face of the sun; or hanging suspended, with their heads downward, over flames; . . . or dwelling, chained for life, at the foot of a tree; or measuring with their bodies, like caterpillars, the breadth of vast empires; or standing on one leg on the tops of pillars—even these forms of conscious penance are hardly more incredible and astonishing than the scenes which I daily witness.

People may call such a description literary as a way of dismissing it, but it is no more or less literary than, say, Rousseau's vision of the human with which he opens his *Social Contract*, as born free and everywhere in chains. That is a vision, as Thoreau's is, essential to the theorizing that follows it, one that identifies the audience of the writing (as well as its author) and that defines the harm it means to undo. Thoreau's sense of what he sees as "incredible and astonishing" more openly identifies his work as partaking of the fantastic, the implication being that what is fantastic is our ordinary lives and that nothing more persistently, you may say uncannily, proves this than his readers' finding *him*—who is the soul of practicality— to be fantastic. Of all the writers who have suggested something like this idea, that the reader of the book, not the exceptional figures within it, is (the other that inhabits the realm of) the fantastic, none can go beyond Thoreau's systematic notation of the idea, nor (what is most pertinent for me) beyond his seriousness in claiming the uncanny vision as essential to philosophy—to the extent that philosophy is what attacks false necessities and false ideas of the necessary, as in Rousseau, but no less in Plato and Descartes and Hume and Kant and Marx and Nietzsche and Heidegger and Wittgenstein. But this claim of philosophy to the uncanny (and vice versa) requires a further inflection of what it means to see the reader as fantastic, a matter we will come to.

To prepare for it, let us ask if *Walden's* vision really fits a further essential characteristic of the fantastic, the confrontation of otherness (hence of selfhood), emphasized by Todorov. Surely the point of Thoreau's depicted journey is to depart from others, not to confront them; he knows from the beginning that others are the curse of human existence. This is humanly, surely, his greatest limitation. And surely no supernatural creature or enchanted habitat suddenly comes upon him in his woods. Or is this true?

Now we have to guard against taking the encounter with otherness or strangeness too narrowly. If this encounter is a wish both to find and to escape solitude, to escape the unnecessary isolations of selfhood, call this narcissism; and if the fantastic (as again Todorov suggests) is in some adverse relation to the modern scientific sensibility; then look what happens to Freud's famous observation (in "A Difficulty in the Path of Psycho-Analysis") that "the universal narcissism of men, their self-love, has up to the present suffered three severe blows from the researches of science." Freud lists Copernicus's cosmological blow, recognizing that mankind is not the center and lord of the world; Darwin's biological blow, putting an end to the presumption that man is different from and superior to animals; and that blow of psychoanalysis, which discovered that "the ego is not master in its own house," its own mind. These blows are each understandable as discoveries of otherness or estrangement: cosmologically, estrangement from the universe as our home; biologically, from the idea of ourselves as superior to our origins; psychologically, estrangement from our own soul. But exactly these sad estrangements are for Thoreau ecstatic or fantastic opportunities: the sun is but a *morning* star (there is room for hope); we are indeed animals, and moreover we are still in a larval state, awaiting metamorphosis; we are each of us double and each must learn "to be beside oneself in a sane sense" (as opposed to our present madness). (In another context we would have to cite a fourth dimension of otherness in *Walden*, one more in focus these days, concerning the so-called discovery of America and *its* others. Thoreau's book is dominated by his sense of America's accursed, fantastic failure to recognize that native otherness; it amounts for him to the failure yet to discover America.)

Now Freud would have had his reasons for not mentioning the blow delivered by *philosophy*, within the scientific era, to human narcissism—philosophy's discovery of the limitation of human knowledge, as it were *despite* the advent of modern science and its own narcissism; limitation especially in its radical form as the threat of skepticism, the threat that the world, and the others in it, may, for all I can know, not exist. This is the traumatic thought that Descartes's *Meditations* undertakes to recover from, and it is pertinent for us that at one point Descartes declares his philosophical purpose to be to check the possibility that he is alone in the world, thus anticipating the title of the symposium panel my participation in which I am reporting on here. The proof that he is not alone demands for Descartes no less than the ontological proof for God's existence, a proof that God's existence is necessary. It follows that if that proof is not, or is no longer, credible to us as it has not been credible in respectable philosophy since its apparent annihilation in Hume's *Dialogues on Natural Religion* and in Kant's *Critique of Pure Reason*—then the question of metaphysical isolation is in principle again torn open, and the literature of the fantastic appears as a philosophical underworld of attempted answers to skepticism. (Here I have to say that I cannot imagine for myself having come upon this perception of the material of this literature apart from my understanding of Wittgenstein's *Philosophical Investigations* as a project to allow skepticism its permanent role in the human mind, one not to be denied but to be placed (within different historical guises and economies). What this requires, as I read Wittgenstein, is learning to bear up under, and to take back home, the inevitable cracks or leaps of madness that haunt the act of philosophizing and haunt the construction of the world—to take the madness back to our shared home of language, and take it back not once and for all (for there is no once and for all within life) but each day, in each specific, everyday site of its eruption.)

This points to a good place for me to begin, hence a proper place for me to stop in a moment, in thinking about the experience of the fantastic: namely, to Freud's study of a major instance of the literature of the fantastic in his essay "The Uncanny." A good place for me because (as I go into at more length in "The Uncanniness of the Ordinary")[2] in taking up E. T. A. Hoffmann's romantic tale "The Sandman," Freud begins by denying that the uncanniness of the tale is traceable to the point in the story of "uncertainty whether an object is living or inanimate," which is to say, to a point precisely recognizable as an issue of philosophical skepticism—skepticism with respect to the experience of others like myself, things philosophy in its English-speaking manifestation calls other minds. Freud insists that instead the uncanny in Hoffmann's tale is directly attached to the idea of being robbed of one's eyes, and hence, given his earlier finding, to the castration complex. But since no denial is called for (the castration complex may precisely constitute a new explanation or interpretation of the particular uncertainty in question), Freud's denial that the acknowledgment of the existence of others is at stake reads to me suspiciously like a Freudian confession that philosophy and its constitution of otherness (in its existence and as its topic) is as fearful to him as castration is. It should give us to think.

This issue of skepticism toward and acknowledgment of the existence of others, the question whether we see their humanity, turns out to be the guiding issue of *Walden's* fantastic language, hence of its own existence. In its thirteenth paragraph we find:

> What distant and different beings in the various mansions of the universe are contemplating the same one at the same moment! . . . Who shall say what prospect life offers to another? Could a greater miracle take place than for us to look through each other's eyes for an instant?

Looking through each other's eyes would be a way of putting a solution to the skeptical problem of others, a way past looking at others through our unkind eyes, alone, before which their existence cannot be proven, whether in Descartes's world, or in Hoffmann's, or in Freud's, or in Wittgenstein's. But the miracle of looking through each other's eyes is also a Thoreauvian description of what the writer of *Walden* means writing to be—his anticipating his reader's eyes, and his offering them his. So that the fact of writing, of the possibility of language as such, is the miracle, the fantastic. Accordingly the brunt of proving that others exist falls upon writing and reading (whatever these are), or say on the literary, on the fact of its existence between us, constituting us—so long, that is to say, as the genuinely literary, the conversation, exchange, of genuine words, lasts.

The inflection of the idea of the reader as fantastic, required in Thoreau's claim of the uncanny for philosophy, is thus an idea of the reader's willingness to subject himself or herself to taking the eyes of the writer, which is in effect yielding his or her own, an exchange interpretable as a sacrifice of one another, of what we think we know of one another, which may present itself as mutual castration, in service either of our mutual victimization or else our liberation. That to imagine the forgoing of a primary narcissism requires so primary an image of violence as the threat of castration—or: that to take one another's eyes is an image whose terror has to be faced in seizing its beauty; call this the sublimity of otherness—warns us not to sentimentalize our interventions. (One sentimentality is to say that writing, art generally, is meant for entertainment—as though entertainment were itself less violent and greedy than, say, instruction.) Taking one another's eyes is the chance outside science to learn something new; which is to say, outside science, to learn something. This seems to me a decent answer to my opening question concerning the task betokened by a culture's literature (and philosophy) that takes the fantastic as not less than central. It is perhaps what you would expect of a literature attempting to invent itself, to convince itself that it exists; as it is surely something you would expect of a literature attempting to preserve the literary as such from perishing, which is a way of defining romanticism's uncanny task.

It would not become a philosopher with my interests to quit my contribution to this symposium without mentioning a realm of the fantastic in which the distinction and issue of low versus high art, or marginal versus central art, precisely disappear, I mean the realm of cinema. What I have in mind here is not especially films of explicit magic or fantasy, the sort of thing special effects are perfectly suited to. I have in mind rather film's unaided perfect power to juxtapose fantasy and reality, to show their lacing as precisely not special. I once had occasion to put together a number of films constructed on the fantastic principle that the world of unyielding fact and the world of satisfied wish look the same, become juxtaposed without cinematic marking to set one world off from the other, creating in their viewers moments, I think one may say, of uncanny disorientation. (This is in my "What Becomes of Things on Film?") The principal films I began with were Bergman's *Persona*, Buñuel's *Belle de Jour*, Godard's *Two or Three Things I Know about Her*, and Hitchcock's *Vertigo*. To these I added Mizoguchi's *Ugetsu*, whose closing image is of a husband returned from a marvelous journey of the erotic to find his poor old house as he had left it, but empty. He lies down on the floor, curled like a child, and in the grey light his wife circles the room. We ache with the man for her to be real, for the beautifully familiar to succeed, or resucceed, the beautiful unfamiliar; but the stern, intermittent tap of a wood block wedges itself between time and eternity, and she vanishes. It is as great an image of the uncanny as I know on film. The experience of it scatters our always regrouping doubts whether we are any longer capable of that hesitation between the empirical and the supernatural on which the experience of the fantastic depends (or, having invoked Thoreau, let me say, instead of the supernatural, the transcendental). And we are reminded that the capacity to let fact and fantasy interpret one another is the basis at once of the soul's sickness and of its health.

Notes

1. "Some Contours of the Fantastic in Modern Japanese Fiction," by Joel Cohn; "Fantastic Voyage: Refractions of the Real, Re Visions of the Imagined," by Regine Johnson.

2. "The Uncanniness of the Ordinary," in *In Quest of the Ordinary*: 153–80.

10

Two Cheers for Romance

B Y THE TITLE OF THESE remarks I mean to indicate both that romance is of more value than is assigned it in the recent assessments of it I have looked at, but also, of course, that it is not worth a full-hearted three cheers. And at the same time I was glad to hark back across decades to E. M. Forster's *Two Cheers for Democracy*, remembering still its concrete humane efforts—the likes of which seemed to me rare and valuable even where I did not share its specific intuitions—to balance (that is, to live) in our everyday returns of cares and obligations, the claims of the best available manners and politics together with the various claims of the most valued personal relationships. The way I speak of romantic marriage in the pages that follow is meant at all times to register—if inadequately, then as if for future reference—the out-turned public and the in-turned private faces implicit in the concept of marriage; faces that, could they but see one another, would betray one another's secrets.

The brochure announcing the symposium for which the present essay was composed contains a melancholy list of problems about love—conceptual problems tumbling on top of biological and social issues—for which nothing in the way of solutions seem to be hoped for. And its text includes a pair of what it calls "historical facts" from which I would like to take some bearings in broaching what I have to say on this occasion. These facts are "the lack of a universal cultural identification between love and marriage and, in our own culture, the relatively recent preference, even

First published in Willard Gaylin and Ethel Person, editors, *Passionate Attachments: Thinking about Love* (New York: Free Press, 1988).

153

yearning, for a marital relationship based on romantic love." A specification of this line of thought, and a claim arising from it, are to be found in a recent collection of essays entitled *Women: The Longest Revolution* by Juliet Mitchell, whose other writings include the influential *Psychoanalysis and Feminism*. In the section entitled "Romantic Love" she undertakes to "reformulate the whole conception of the shift in romantic love from medieval to modern times." I will quote from this chapter at some length both for its own interest and because I will be taking exception to some of its formulations.

Mitchell cites two feminist writers as precursors of her view. From Shulamith Firestone's *The Dialectic of Sex* she quotes these lines among others:

> As civilization advances and the biological bases of sex class crumble, male supremacy must shore itself up with artificial institutions . . . where formerly women have been held openly in contempt, now they are elevated to states of mock worship. Romanticism is a cultural tool of male power to keep women from knowing their condition.

And the thesis of Germaine Greer's *The Female Eunuch*, summarized by Mitchell, joins the rise of Protestantism with

> a new ideology of marriage. . . . Marriage would no longer be an arranged business deal between powerful lineages . . . ; it had to be seemingly free and equal. Because of this, from having been the sort of fantasy province of a small nobility, romantic love came to replace parental coercion as that which forced one into marriage. From being excitingly adulterous and oppositional to the status quo in the Middle Ages, romantic love became a prelude to Establishment marriage of modern times.

Mitchell's own feminist account is that the new ideology of marriage, as a contract between equals, left equality merely "notional" (say, verbal) and that "romantic love shifted from being the male subject's search for his lost feminine self to being a consolation for a woman's future confinement in domesticity." Mitchell's more ambitious formulation takes into account what happens to the man as well as what happens to the woman in the shifting of romantic love. Beyond the feminist writers, she bases her own view also on Denis de Rougement's *Love in the Western World* (published in 1940), which she regards as "still the classical book on the subject of love." De Rougement proposes a more fundamental, less historically specific characterization of romantic love as something inherently in contradiction with marriage because inherently it is not about sexuality; it is opposed to the propagation of the species; it is, this romantic love, essentially about a mystical quest for union with lost regions of the self. Mitchell summarizes de Rougement's "central thesis" by saying: "What seems to go together is not love and marriage, but love and death." (You get a feel for de Rougement's perception here if you think of a region of works Mitchell does not mention, such as *Romeo and Juliet, Antony and Cleopatra, Tristan and Isolde, Madame Bovary, Anna Karenina*.) Mitchell counters de Rougement's refusal to translate what he describes as a religion of romantic love into sexual terms, and she goes on to interpret his descriptions of romantic love's narcissism and bisexualism as fitting what we understand as pre-Oedipal, pregenital sexuality. This allows her to ask us, surely sensibly, to realize that "if the women cannot be romantic lovers as subjects of their own search for self, men cannot be so either," and that the "false sexual equality" in later romantic novels produces endings that, as they imagine "the confinement and the submission of the woman," usually find "some form of emasculation of the man."

All this seems to me worth pondering, but certain aspects trouble me from the start. Are these criticisms of marriage that is based on romance directed at what marriage of necessity has become under the pressure of romance, or are they directed at the changing historical forms romantic marriage has so far discovered for itself? Consider that government by consent (the modern liberal state) has arisen in the Western world within the period following the supposedly romantic shift. It too has bad things to answer for. And you can say, analogously, of government by consent that the consent is merely notional and that such government has become merely a consolation for the private citizen's future confinement to domesticity, or say to privacy; that is, to a life essentially without his or her own political voice. But in what spirit are such criticisms made? They are criticisms that democracy has made of itself, and which it forever tries to keep itself open to. But are we to take it that we know now of some better aspiration in favor of which the idea of government by consent is to be abandoned? Or are we—as I think—bound to be faithful to such government because only within it can truer consent be hoped for and achieved?

The critics of romantic marriage that I was citing, however, do not describe a form of marriage they could want, or give a sense of what good may be hoped for and achieved in marriage initiated by romance. They seem rather to concede fully that whatever good can be said of the institution has been said by its own ideologues; for example, by writers of popular romances, the sort of thing Henry Fonda, in Preston Sturges's film *The Lady Eve*, says he must sound like as he declares his eternal love to Barbara Stanwyck; he calls what he sounds like "a drugstore novel."

Juliet Mitchell takes her literary evidence for the views she gives of romance and marriage importantly from drugstore novels ("The popular romantic novels by Barbara Cartland or Denise Robbins, or stories in women's magazines"), and it is on this basis that she claims that "we no longer have a dominant strain of romantic literature in which the man is the subject of the passion." Essential as the evidence of drugstore literature may be, what causes this extraordinary reliance on its all-but-exclusive authority for what our culture tells itself about love and marriage? I propose to go on (in the space allotted me) to take the testimony of another dominant source of romantic fable that Mitchell has either forgotten about or has not experienced, that of the classical Hollywood film at its best. And I will introduce my discussion of two such films by noting the pertinence to our subject of a play of Shakespeare's, an item which can also be found in our finer drugstores. If it can sensibly be claimed of any work central to our high culture that it represents, even schematizes, the shift from marriage as political (or social or economic) arrangement to marriage as romantic alliance, it can so be claimed of *Antony and Cleopatra.* Now if we go to that work for instruction about this shift, do we find that the woman is not the subject of her own story but merely its object, say its victim? This is what the men of the play may like to believe, and try to achieve, Octavius Caesar most consistently, whose fond desire is to keep Cleopatra from suicide so that he may trail her behind his triumphant chariot in Rome as his chief trophy. And are we prepared to say that Marc Antony forgoes his quest for his lost feminine self? There are indeed invitations at the end of his story to take him as emasculated. But what has caused this? I guess at least half of its readers would like to say, again with the Romans of the play, that Cleopatra is the cause, which more or less means that the cause is the conquering of marriage by romance. But there are major reasons also for denying that this is what Shakespeare's play takes the cause to be, from among which I pick two: (1) what Cleopatra wants from Antony is what she calls marriage; she wants him as in her word a husband; (2) Antony leaves Cleopatra in the first act on hearing that his wife Fulvia is dead, and returns to Cleopatra only when he is again safely and legally married at Rome. I do not know of any critic of this play who records this second pair of facts, but recording them helps me to propose as follows: the first half of the play gives a portrait of a man whose type Freud characterized in the famous sentence (from "The Tendency to Debasement in Love") "Where they love they do not desire and where they desire they cannot love"; but the play then takes this man to a state in which he is defeated not by the hopeless attempt to maintain this split but in the hopeful attempt to overcome it.

What I think of as the moral of the play is that no one any longer knows what marriage is, what constitutes this central, specific bond of union, as if it is up to each individual pair to invent this for themselves.

Society can no longer ratify it, say after Luther denied that marriage is a sacrament and after Henry the Eighth showed that the political arrangements of marriage are themselves subject to the dictates of romance. Society is itself in need of ratification, perhaps by way of individuals consenting to it as a place within which to plight their troth. When, for example, Spencer Tracy harangues Katharine Hepburn in *Adam's Rib* (where they play a married pair of lawyers who take opposite sides in a courtroom case concerning a wife and mother of three who has shot her husband); harangues her, chastising her for forgetting that what marriage is, is a contract, as defined by the law; one feels that this is his anger speaking, that he is denying half of the truth, leaving out the heart of the matter.

I draw the moral of *Antony and Cleopatra* directly from the fact of its last act, which I interpret as the effort—on the part of Cleopatra and Shakespeare—to invent a new form of marriage ceremony, one in which the woman presents herself as a queen, a mother, a nurse, an actress, and a lover, and in which the enormity of her narcissism and bisexuality is broken into by nothing less than a marriage with or in heaven itself. Among her dying words, the astoundingly daring cry, "Husband, I come," which transforms the idea of death that de Rougement associates with romance into an orgasm that mystically creates their marriage in eternity. I am not asking anyone—any more than I assume Shakespeare was—simply to adopt this as one's preferred wedding ceremony. But I do assume that the play's working asks us to consider what our fantasies are of the way in which, as in the classical formulation of marriage, two become one. That these fantasies may invoke the discharge of earth into heaven suggests that de Rougement's insistence on the dimension of the mystical in romance should not so hastily be reduced.

That no one any longer knows what creates the bond, the union, of marriage, is also the moral I have derived (in *Pursuits of Happiness*) in studying a group of the best Hollywood romantic comedies of the 1930s and 1940s, a group I name comedies of remarriage. It is from these and related movies that I would like now to suggest a working formulation of what I referred to a few minutes ago as an imagined new good of romantic marriage, of something that might suggest what hope there is in it, why certain versions of it (perhaps not those pictured in the "dominant strain of romantic literature" that Juliet Mitchell focuses on) might be worth struggling with from within. I assume that the new good to be hoped for from romantic marriage has something to do with the discovery of, or the need of, some new dimension of the *personal* in relations between the sexes, a mutuality not quite political and an intimacy not exclusively sexual. If I call it a new discovery of privacy, this may serve to align this quest with the risks of the new idea of government by consent. Marriage looked at from this perspective would be the name of some new way in which men and women require of one another that they bear the brunt of one another's subjectivity, in relative insulation from the larger world of politics and religion, which (for now at the least) has rejected this subjectivity, or let it loose.

Had I kept to an economy for these remarks that would have preserved my original title "Romanticism and Skepticism," my claims for a new imagination of, or pressure on, romantic marriage over the past few centuries would have been even more extreme. I would have interpreted the idea of bearing the brunt of one another's subjectivity as providing (or sustaining the) proof of one another's existence, and would have gone on to argue as follows: When Descartes came upon modern philosophical skepticism in the seventeenth century (the problem of the human capacity to know anything at all, beginning with the existence of the world, the problem that produced his famous pivotal conclusion: "I think, therefore I am"), one of his goals was to establish that he was, as he puts it, not alone in the universe. To establish this, nothing less than a proof of God's existence (on the basis of the indubitability of that "I am") was required of his philosophical powers. As philosophy—say in Hume and in Kant—knew itself no longer possessed of such powers, major romantic writers (in America, Emerson and Thoreau, and Hawthorne and Poe, for example) proposed an idea of marriage, call it daily mutual devotedness, as the only path left us for walking away from exactly that skeptical doubt of cosmic isolation. In Emerson and Thoreau this devotedness is first of all due the universe itself, or say nature; to be faithful there one might have to leave what we mostly call marriage. One should feel that this shows a certain bravery of imagination in Emerson and Thoreau; but then one had better also consider the extent to which it shows their cowardice of imagination. In Hawthorne and in Poe, domesticity is more literally pictured as the marriage of human beings. The horror in their writings is accordingly a function of the idea that marriage cannot bear up under its metaphysical burden of ensuring the existence of one's other, hence of partaking of the other's securing of one's own existence. In one of Hawthorne's many tales of marriage ("Wakefield"), the narrator—I leave open the question of his tone—describes a man who has abandoned his marriage, for no comprehensible reason, as an "Outcast of the Universe."

In *Pursuits of Happiness*, the name I give to the new requirement upon romantic marriage, as reflected in the Hollywood comedy of remarriage, is the requirement of conversation. I take up the idea of conversation from John Milton's great tract on divorce (written roughly in the period in which Descartes was meditating his doubt and its overcoming), in which Milton defines marriage as "a meet and happy conversation" (and by "conversation" he does not mean just talk, but he does definitely also mean talk). Milton's tract, written as a theological defense of divorce, is at the same time a defense of the Puritan Revolution, and in claiming that sacred bonds may be dissolved when the meet and cheerful conversation for which they were entered into falls into a melancholy and intractable silence, it is clear that he is referring to the consent that creates legitimate government as much as to the agreement that constitutes marriage. (As if legitimacy altogether is now to be decided in the freedom of individual consciousness. No wonder marriage would be looked to as a way to share this terrible burden of individual authority. John Locke's more famous justification of consent, in his *Second Treatise of Government*, with its subdued description of the terrible cost of withdrawing consent—as it were of seeking to divorce society—was being written a dozen years after *Paradise Lost* appeared.)

The pair of films I will invoke here are from the era of the great remarriage comedies, but unlike those comedies they do not show us what a marriage may look and sound like that can bear the new exchange of subjectivity, the modern brunt of intimacy. They virtually do not show marriage at all (as if declaring our inability to recognize it any longer), and as if to emphasize this fact they contain a full complement of widows, widowers, bachelors, old maids, divorcees, and derelict or isolated husbands. I take them as showing, instead, how a newly conceived marriage may be pursued, or how, failing that possibility, marriage may rationally be rejected in favor of a life that promises something better than the old possibility.

The first of the pair is *Mr. Deeds Goes to Town* (directed by Frank Capra in 1936, starring Gary Cooper and Jean Arthur), one of the central so-called screwball comedies; and the second of the pair is a melodrama, or what used to be called a "woman's film"—*Now, Voyager* (1942, starring Bette Davis, Paul Henreid, and Claude Rains). Both films show the therapy of love in the form of the therapy of romance, of passion not as the goal of love but as the awakening of love, to the very possibility of accepting mutuality with another. I mean the phrase "therapy of love" in allusion especially to Freud's fullest piece of literary interpretation, lavished on Wilhelm Jensen's romantic fable *Gradiva*, in which the woman Gradiva's procedure in leading her rightful but perplexed lover to marriage with her is dwelt on by Freud to bring out its similarity to the procedure of psychoanalytic psychotherapy, viewed as what Freud there calls a love-cure. I regard these films as, at the very least, the artistic equal of Jensen's tale, fully worth the attention Freud gave the tale. And these are films of worldwide fame and popularity; in principle we could here have them in common, or three hundred others like them, at our disposal for our mutual instruction. I say "in principle" because of course I know that in fact we do not have them in common. And I do not just mean that some of you will not in fact have seen these particular films. Some of you will not have read, or may not well remember, *Antony and Cleopatra* either, but you will not think it odd for someone to speak of it seriously. (Perhaps you should.) I do not believe we know why it seems odd to discuss such films with the same seriousness. Given my conviction in the value of these films, I think one should find their popularity remarkable. Since commonly their popularity is taken as given, the claim that they are intellectually rich is commonly found to be incredible. Such is the uncreative position to which our culture so often in such cases confines itself.

In *Mr. Deeds Goes to Town*, a country boy who plays the tuba and composes popular verses for greeting cards (a reasonable emblem of popular movies) inherits $20 million from a remote uncle, goes to New York to collect, shows he is naturally smarter than the city slickers but not smart enough to overcome their political power. He is arrested on the complaint of his uncle's lawyers, who claim that his attempt to give away his fortune shows him to be mentally incompetent; at the same time he learns that the woman he has fallen in love with is a devious reporter who, using his feelings for her to extract a sensational series of newspaper features, has held his escapades up to ridicule, naming him "The Cinderella Man." At his sanity hearing he at first refuses to speak in his own defense, even against further testimony that he is, in the words of a comic expert Viennese psychiatrist, "obviously *verruckt*," and in the word of old maid sisters from his home town, "pixilated." After the woman reporter declares in open court that she loves the young man he successfully rises to his defense—not exactly by proving that he is not mad, but just that he is no madder than the common run of humanity—causes general social ecstasy, and wins the embraces of his beloved.

Mr. Deeds, like certain other romantic comedies, spends half of its energy ridiculing romantic love, the principal spokesperson of this ridicule being the principal woman of the plot who, of course, will eventually herself succumb to it. Her subjection to passion becomes a lesson in humility, in humanity you might call it, teaching her the defensiveness of her previous pride in her cleverness and autonomy. Since the man speaks several times about his wish to rescue a damsel in distress, you may join the woman in ridiculing his fantasy of marriage as a fairy tale romance, and then go beyond this by ridiculing the woman in turn for succumbing to this fantasy. And you may cap your superiority to the film by repeating the most frequent view of such movies that finds its way into words—namely, that they are fairy tales for the depression, made to help distract the populace from its economic misery. In this view such movies ask little more of us, in addition to a willingness to be pleased (no small matter), than to believe that their ending may be formulated in words such as, "They lived happily ever after." What we are shown in *Mr. Deeds*, for example, is something I find to be distinctly different. The woman can be said to become a damsel in distress, but just in a sense in which the man can equally be said to have discovered himself as another damsel in distress. Distress turns out on this showing to be the access and confession of desire. The mutuality of desire confuses and frightens the pair, for all their separate, shrewd strengths, but they at last commit themselves to pursue it together. In the closing image of the film the man lifts the woman in the middle of a now mostly empty courtroom, as if to carry her over a threshold, and they stand there kissing repeatedly as the music swells. (I guess not just the music.)

Figure 10.1

Of course you can say that this is Hollywood code for their living happily ever after. But you can alternatively appropriate this image in terms that to my mind it more accurately invites, interpret it to say that no one, including the pair, knows how to arrive at the threshold to which they are drawn, that the threshold is of some inner place they have to discover together, and that marriage is the name of this adventure or quest that they are committing themselves to, with no assurance of success.

In Deeds's defeat of the Viennese psychiatrist (one of his feats of overcoming that elicits the world's acceptance of him and the woman's consent to love for him), we again have before us a choice of interpretations. You may take Deeds's victory over the foreign thinker to be a sign of Capra's American anti-intellectualism; or you may take it, as I do, that we are shown a contest between approaches to psychological understanding, and that Deeds's victory is of psychological awareness—or aliveness in principle open to ordinary human beings, and inevitably open to those who are open to it—over certain claims to a privileged expertise that is closed to that openness.

Now, Voyager also features a psychiatrist, but as in other Hollywood melodramas—as opposed to its comedies (a matter for critical speculation)—the role is positive and it is instrumental in achieving the therapeutic success of the film. I must sketch this film a little less briefly.

The good psychiatrist, Dr. Jaquith (Claude Rains), tells the tyrannical mother of Charlotte Vale (Bette Davis) that Charlotte is having a nervous breakdown and he recommends residential therapy at his clinic in the country, called Cascades. Residence at Cascades produces in Charlotte the most dramatic metamorphosis that I know of in film, as she goes from aggressive plainness to dazzling attractiveness. (A subtext of the movie is given when Charlotte's mother refers to her as "my ugly duckling.") Charlotte, transformed, is sent on a cruise to try out her new wings, and that is where she meets Jerry (Paul Henreid), traveling alone because his wife is too sickly to share any fun. Jerry is worried about his daughter Tina, who Charlotte at once divines was not wanted by the wife. Henreid performs his world-historical romantic trick of lighting two cigarettes at the same time and then handing one to Bette Davis. What I am calling the therapy of romance in this film is epitomized by an inspired sequence in which, while the two of them are at dinner on shipboard, Charlotte is overcome by what strikes her as the fraudulence of her situation. She shows Jerry a family photograph of the Boston Vales, about which he asks: "Who is the funny fat lady with all the hair?" and the now slender, impeccably dressed and groomed, ravishing Bette Davis replies: "I am the funny fat lady with all the hair." One feels that this extraordinary revelation of her inner identity is meant to defend herself from further facing her desire, released toward this dashing yet kind stranger; at the same time the strength to make the revelation is essentially a function of the very metamorphosis of desire which he has helped to establish. He is not put off by the dark side of the fantasy of the ugly duckling (namely, what it was from which metamorphosis was called for, hence the stain of doubt that the metamorphosis really happened); and accepts her identity in her suffering while at the same time accepting her identity as she is. She knows that she will be grateful to him for this forever. Her return to Boston is a sequence of triumphs—over her mother, over her wider family, over her social circle. She attracts the love of a handsome, socially perfect widower her mother is desperate for her to marry, but she breaks her engagement to him in the knowledge that her life remains elsewhere. (So it is not true of Charlotte that she is coerced into marriage either by a formidable parental wish for alliance of family fortunes or by the promise of romance.) On returning for respite to Cascades she encounters Jerry's daughter Tina, who has become a patient there and with whom she forms a therapeutic alliance, something none of the professional staff has been able to do. Charlotte thus becomes the good mother to her lover's child as well as to herself. After her own mother's death she transforms the mausoleum of the Vale mansion into a life-enhancing haven for young and old, recognizes that Jerry is stuck in his guilty marriage, convinces him and Dr. Jaquith to let her continue to mother Tina, and devotes her fortune to expanding Cascades, where Dr. Jaquith appoints her to the board of directors.

I give this somewhat mocking summary of the film (it is of critical interest that summary inherently tends toward mockery), which I hope at the same time suggests my great admiration for it, in order to go on to pose a question which we cannot answer in the absence of the film itself. Granted that some asymmetry is proposed between this man and this woman (that is, equality and reciprocity between them is ruled impossible) in whose favor is the asymmetry cast? I gather that a certain feminist reading of such a film would run as follows: Marriage under those social conditions, as under present conditions, would have been confining enough, but this hopeless romance, this prohibition of marriage, is even worse. Here the woman is relegated to child rearing and house managing and man serving with no compensating social role whatever and with no real private—that is, erotic—compensation either. Her value is assessed as merely a function of social nobleness earned through self-sacrifice. This view is obviously consistent with the various ideologies of marriage cited and extended by the accounts of Juliet Mitchell, to the effect that women have to be made to want marriage (as still conceived).

The trouble with this view of the film is that it is essentially Jerry's view of what Charlotte is doing. It is he who says to her: "No self-respecting man would allow such self-sacrifice as yours to go on indefinitely." And I find that my response to this sentiment is well represented by Charlotte's response to Jerry's statement: "That's the most conventional, pretentious, pious speech I ever heard in my life." And when a moment later he tells her: "You should be trying to find some man who'll make you happy," her reply is withering (and remember that it is Bette Davis saying the words, slowly, as if seeking to fathom the origin of each of them): "Some man who'll make me happy? I've been laboring under the delusion that you and I were so in sympathy, so one, that you'd know without being asked what would make me happy." This turns out to be something she describes as their sharing a "fancy" of making a place for his unwanted child to achieve metamorphosis. After a few more words, and with a last pair of cigarettes lit, Jerry asks: "And will you be happy, Charlotte?" to which Charlotte replies with the famous closing lines of this film: "Oh Jerry, let's not ask for the moon; we have the stars."

Granted that you can appropriate this ending in Jerry's guilty way, I close by sketching another way of appropriating it. Charlotte's closing speeches are about the two of them "being one," which I noted as our classical conceit for being married. She says in effect that the condition of this state is the sharing of fantasy, which she believed was satisfied in their case; which is to say, she took them to be in a state of marriage. Doubtless it is not all a marriage might be, but what marriage is? How much it may be is recorded in her saying to the man, "We have the stars." I take this to imply that they have had a share of the moon, it is in place, the metamorphosis was achieved. If we now take the image of stars against the image from Hawthorne about finding oneself an Outcast of the Universe when we abandon the thing we are rightfully wedded to, she is saying: We are not such outcasts, that much salvation is ours. I think it is clear that Jerry does not get the idea and that he is, and so to speak prefers being, cast out, wedded to that remove. Charlotte's discovery that she and Jerry are not, as it were, married is evidently for her harder to bear than her earlier discovery that something is more important to her than bed with Jerry. In both discoveries Charlotte has—forever with Jerry's help—quite transcended his orbit of comprehension. Accordingly, I cannot doubt that this is a romantic quest whose subject is the woman, with the principal man of the romance a self-appointed object or victim.

Now, finally, I will suggest that one possibility of constituting marriage is presented by this film as something more mysterious yet, in a way that the readers of this volume should find suspicious, but one that I hope we could in principle leave open. Jerry was brought to Charlotte's house, for that final interview with her, by Dr. Jaquith. (We will hear from Charlotte that the interview is Dr. Jaquith's test of Charlotte and Jerry's resolve not to pursue their private romance; to have the child together they must not do together what causes children. This still leaves open a question: is Dr. Jaquith's "test" meant to see whether the couple is capable of obeying his prohibition, or is it to provide Charlotte with an occasion for seeing that her economy of desire has shifted? Or rather her economies—she is involved in more than one household.) Before that interview we are given a moment in which Dr. Jaquith and Charlotte are seated together on the floor of her remodeled (metamorphosed) drawing room studying the architectural plans for the addition she is proposing for Cascades, the habitation they share.

Figure 10.2

This image, colored by the feeling of the moment, I read as registering that these two are also married. Now before you jump to the conclusion that she has not resolved her transference in her relation with her therapist—a matter surely to be considered—I hope you will be willing to think of these words and images in terms of Freud's 1915 essay, "Observations on Transference Love," in which he insists in all honesty on the point that "the state of being in love which makes its appearance in the course of analytic treatment (i.e., the transference love) has the characteristics of a 'genuine love.' " The analyst does not act to fulfill this love in its own terms because it is exactly his or her peculiar task not to act on it, but instead to teach an attitude that allows freedom from the dictation of action by desire. One might say that it is only because transference love is a version of real love that this learning can take place. The question for me is whether Charlotte Vale's modification and satisfaction of the various strands of her desire (and of the concept of marriage) may be imagined as achieving a credible and creditable degree of psychic freedom. She had written to Dr. Jaquith to inform him of breaking her engagement to the eligible widower, expressing her confusion over her action. This man, she said, offered everything a woman is supposed to want: a man of her own, a home of her own, a child of her own. Now in these terms my question about this film becomes: Do we see at its conclusion the life of a woman who has found the way to her version of these things, including work of her own? Or do we feel, on the contrary, that she has merely fallen into the grip of an ideology which forces her to find substitute compensations for the actual or literal possession of such things, as those things are themselves now only substitute compensations for the genuine autonomous quest for a woman's own existence?

We cannot sensibly begin now to respond to these issues, by screening the film and working through our experience of it together. That is a pity, but just a contingent fact. What is a thousand pities is something I noted earlier: that we do not ask such questions of such films even when the occasion for the asking might present itself, that is, even when we possess the film in common. And that is not just a contingent fact but a systematic work of self-deprivation. Our participation in this deprivation is eased by a pair of assumptions, one about the culture at large, one about its major films: according to the one assumption, our culture's romantic ideology of marriage, serving to depress a woman's quest for her own existence, goes essentially unchallenged by the culture at large; according to the other assumption, Hollywood movies are popular commodities whose possibilities are unproblematic and which, in particular, simply serve to support that ideology of marriage, since certainly they would not themselves help to challenge it. Both feminists and antifeminists seem to have conflicting uses for this pair of assumptions. And the fear must be massive that keeps us unaware that movies at their best powerfully reflect back the culture's knowledge to itself of its own doubts and ambivalences concerning these very assumptions. Had I time to say why I initially put the idea of skepticism into the title of these remarks—the idea that we privately doubt that the world exists and ourselves and others in it—I might guess that the fear such movies divine in us is the fear of daily, repetitive, ordinary, domestic existence; the fear of finding it and the fear of not finding it, "it" being what you might call the marriage of romance with marriage.

11

The Advent of Videos

Recently I was asked—given various remarks of mine about our changing relations to the viewing of film, as in "The Fact of Television" in a collection of mine called *Themes Out of School*—whether I could say something about the effect on movie viewing of the explosive increases in the circulation of movies on video cassettes, through renting and purchasing and recording (and, it should be added, through duplicating and trading). The following speculations are some initial responses to this query.

SUPPOSE THAT NO EVENT SINCE the conquering of film by television as the dominant form of, let us say, popular art has been so fateful for the idea of seeing movies as the commercial establishment of video cassettes and their home players. Can the sheer convenience of circulating movies as videos account for this effect? Had seeing movies been, or become, inconvenient?

Movies on videos perfect the challenge—begun in broadcast television, intensified in cable—to movie-going as an institution established when half the population of the nation went to the movies (the new movies) every week. The extent of experience shared, as food for thought, or talk, was something good; the limiting of the experience was not good, requiring a choice from a small set of offerings to be seen, on the whole,

First published in *Artspace*, May–June 1988.

just once. Worse still was its intellectual consequence, the assumption that a movie is on the whole made, and meant, to be viewed just once, as if its value (say as food shared for thought) is used up by each viewer on coming across it, after which it ceases to exist, to matter to anyone. The effect of such an idea is to deny that movies have a history, that they warrant the efforts of criticism, analysis, and interpretation lavished on the major arts. Of course movies would not have flourished as they did unless they *worked* for an audience on one viewing. But something analogous could be said of the work of Shakespeare or Dickens or Verdi, and we seem not to have used up their stores of pleasure and instruction.

The institution of single viewing encouraged an institution of movie reviewing and criticism that bases itself on what can be recalled (or what cannot fail to be remembered) on one viewing, jauntily recorded, stamped with a grade, never, or hardly ever, to be checked. So resilient and voracious is this intellectual paradigm of clips and grades that, even though there are now television shows consisting of movie reviews, so that a moment or sequence could in principle be shown and then considered, the format of these shows reproduces visually the old critical paradigm of clips and grades—but now enlivened by disagreements over the grades. It gives one to think that the institution of single, unchecked viewing is as if designed to repress the significance of movies, as if that were the price of the delight we take in them. In that case the coming of the video, challenging the institution—making seeing a movie *again*, or on call, in principle at least as convenient as seeing it for the first time—is as a return of the repressed. The paradoxical result of even the titles so far available at video stores is something like a general recognition of film as an art.

But what about movies would we repress? Surely it is something both about what it is that movies characteristically express, their content, and something about the medium in which they express it, the medium of film "itself."

As an illustration of content, take one of the moments from Hollywood classical film that survived (or exploited) the condition of single viewing, becoming unforgettable for masses of people: the ending lines of *Now, Voyager* (the 1942 Bette Davis film in which Paul Henreid is forever placing a pair of cigarettes between his lips to light with one flame, then presenting one to Davis), as this woman says to this former lover: "Oh, Jerry, let's not ask for the moon. We have the stars." Along with this shared memory, however, goes a shared mismemory, or misinterpretation, or unnecessary interpretation of the moment, according to which the woman is nobly sacrificing herself to the man's interests (call this preserving his guilty marriage). But this nobleness of sacrifice is explicitly the interpretation of her behavior insisted on by this particular man, this Jerry;

and however one judges his character, one cannot in all seriousness take him to represent the authoritative voice of this film. I find the ending to show, rather, that the woman has transcended the (his) invitation to a role of self-sacrifice, at any rate as such a role is conventionally pictured; that she accepts the man's "noble" interpretation of her precisely to reveal his impotence to pursue their relationship together; and that she is helping him (nobly helping, or gallantly; he is, or was, a friend) to save face in his defeat. I do not say that seeing the film again, perhaps on a video, will of itself establish my counterinterpretation (my interpretation of the film's counterintelligence); it requires argument. I say only that the "argument," which is about the major direction of the film's force, is apt to be worthless apart from such re-seeing.

An instance of what I mean in speaking of the repression of the significance of the medium of film itself comes up in projecting a good print of *Now, Voyager*, from which it is obvious that an establishing shot of Rio de Janeiro is made with a piece of stock footage. An audience now may be prompted to laugh at the clumsiness. But might it be guided to consider that the clumsiness is itself meant, that the power of film (here, to make anything or any place follow or coincide with any other, in the world of the mind) is being used to comment on the power of stock sentiment, perhaps to mock it, perhaps to pay a certain homage to it, since the medium of film trades in the value of sentiment? If a video fails to pick up this clumsiness it will not so much as supply backing for an argument on this point, much less settle one. But then the value of videos goes immeasurably farther than their ability to settle things.

Not only should a video raise—as often as not for the first time—issues raised by a film itself (say by its original, of which it is accordingly a reproduction) but the video should raise the issue of what the relation is between original and reproduction: in various ways a video is like a slide projection of a painting, in others like a piano reduction of a symphony, in others like a scale model of a town. Any of us is apt to have some pet thought about what the relation is between viewing a film in public and watching a video in private. But since the question of the relation of these formats is to raise the questions of what each of these formats is, why settle for a pet thought? Since at home the image is smaller and its running is under one's control; and since the space for viewing is close, lit, and familiar; and since the audience is of one's choice—that is not a public—and of no more than conversational size, if that; the effect of the image is . . . what? Less? Not much of a thought.

Both admirers and detractors of Hollywood films have cause to confine their delights, and to constrict their tears. To allow this repression as well as to invite the challenge are both essential to the art of this golden

cinema. The small but stubborn and clear voice of the video—making subsequent playing as convenient as initial—may join either the effort to
repress or the effort to challenge the repression, but it alters the odds in
favor of challenge. It can tell us, or remind us, for example, that in *Old
Acquaintance*, the year after *Now, Voyager*, Bette Davis is dressed, on her
entrance, in obviously male-derived clothes, laying the suggestion of the
film that she is the active rival of her friend's husband for the friend's love
(the friend played by Miriam Hopkins). This is more explicit in George
Cukor's remake of *Old Acquaintance* over forty years later as *Rich and
Famous*, with Jacqueline Bisset and Candice Bergen, which guides this pair
to a concluding embrace in Connecticut, thus invoking this film's relation
to a genre of Hollywood film of which Cukor was a master, the comedy of
remarriage, for which his *The Philadelphia Story* and *Adam's Rib* are
defining examples. The invocation shows (to the extent that *Rich and
Famous* does its work) that the questions posed in the genre of remarriage
comedy—whether we know what the role is of romance in marriage, what
the role of gender is in romance, what the bond or meld is of devotion and
intimacy that constitutes what we call marriage—remain in question.
In the beauty and intelligence of their handling of these questions, remarriage comedies earn a late relation to their central discussions in
Shakespearean theater and in opera. Of the marvelous connections
Moonstruck sets up with remarriage comedy, I note its reasonably explicit
declaration that film seeks the expressive power of music, here in the form
of opera. The mutually telling, educative exchanges between the characters played by Cher and Nicolas Cage on the subjects of fate, suffering,
brothers, of the misery of love—are authorized by the credibility to the
woman of the man's passion for opera, that is, by whatever it is about the
man that causes his passion for opera. These exchanges declare that film's
power to transfigure the words of a script inherits music's power to
transfigure the words of a libretto. (It should go without saying that the
art of writing good film scripts and good librettos is the art of eliciting
those powers.)

I think of this feature of *Moonstruck*, in turn, as a response to a
moment just over fifty years ago in Frank Capra's *Mr. Deeds Goes to Town*,
when the surprised young heir (Gary Cooper) of a famous fortune balks at,
among other things, the expectation that he continue his rich uncle's sub-
sidy of opera, observing to the opera committee that if the institution loses
that much money every year "they must be putting on the wrong kind of
shows." To dismiss Mr. Deeds as an American provincial, laughably ignorant of cultural peaks, is an impulse that cannot fully establish itself in us,
since that response to him is exactly the response of the ignorant cultural
snobs on the committee. Then is Capra accepting Deeds's apparent dis-

missal of opera? I find Capra's film's answer to suggest that the shows "they" ought to be putting on are movies, such as this one called *Mr. Deeds Goes to Town*, which will not lose money and will provide for its culture what opera provides, or used to; nothing less.

This suggestion is in effect an homage film is paying opera. The debt is recounted in Cukor's *Gaslight* in 1944, for example, in which a woman whose voice is violated in marriage identifies a further voice for herself through an idea and memory of opera. And to invoke the debts of film to opera is a way of looking at *A Night at the Opera* of 1935, in which the Marx Brothers' efforts to interrupt the performance of *Il Trovatore* should be read not as a burlesque of opera (on a par with their burlesques in this film of manners and legalities) but as an acknowledgment of opera as a worthy competitor or companion of their challenges to authority (most blatantly a recognition of Harpo's refusal to trust to words).

Does this understanding of a span reaching from *Moonstruck* to *Mr. Deeds* really engage the fact of the video format? Shouldn't we rather consider that opera has in recent years been circulating, and looks good, on television—that opera itself exists on video—hence that certain opera stars are now recognizable as specific human beings bearing a particular relation to their roles, in something like the way Cher bears a particular relation to her roles? I would like to take the fact of the video (circulating like the plastic-covered book of old rental libraries) as an emblem of the enigmatic intersection of film and television, that crucial, star-crossed territory of our lives consecrated to, constituted in, the moving image.

Take further from this territory certain invasions of the movie screen by the television monitor. The issue of this ontological relation is raised in films such as *The Terminator* and *Predator*, where in each case the screen is recurrently occupied by—so as to be identified with, to a certain undefined extent—a view-finding device on a weapon system: an infrared image in the latter, a computerized target image in the former. The general identification on film of a deadly weapon with a camera is hardly new. But in *The Terminator* the monitored visual field is identified as that of the "man himself," hence this human figure, or guise, is marked as itself the deadly weapon. The obviousness of this conceit is meant, I gather, to undergo complication in pondering why it is Arnold Schwarzenegger's bodybuilder's body that "has" this visual apparatus. The idea that our several "senses" are each some species of monitoring apparatus which serves, as it were, to enhance (or diminish) our access to the material world seems a realization of the skeptic's peculiar fears or fantasies (the senses as converters of an unknowable source, receivers over an unsayable distance). In Wittgenstein's arresting figure: "The human body is the best picture of the human soul" (*Investigations*, p. 178). But how about the bodybuilder's (enhanced) body? And ponder further that when the Terminator's body is burned or stripped away what appears is not a system of "remains" or "insides," but another functioning (if quite diminished) body. Or do we conceive it (it is a sort of schematic, golden skeleton) as a body frame? What conception have we of our own skeleton? Is it hidden, at the moment? Has this camera revealed it? Comparable questions are raised in the revelations of James Whales's *The Invisible Man* (1933), where the camera acknowledges both that it makes something invisible to us (for example, the existence now of the persons it captures) and makes something visible to us that may otherwise be invisible (the distance and mystery of the existence of persons).

The pressure put on the film screen image by the television monitor image can be no simpler than the untold extended relations between film and television as such will determine. Take the final episode of the five years of the critically admired television series *St. Elsewhere*, which concludes with an autistic child looking into a snow globe (the child's toy) at what proves to contain a model, or set, of the St. Elsewhere hospital. The moment reads (in the frame of the setting in which the boy's father, chief of medicine in the hospital narrative, is depicted as a blue-collar worker whose working-class father in turn is [was], in the hospital narrative, the director of the hospital) as if the series has been the imaginings of a disturbed boy. (Or just lonely? I cannot swear now whether in the snow globe revelation [as in a reverse crystal ball] the boy is depicted as normal or remains autistic. Nor can I swear that this matters.) The idea surely has its brilliance. But a danger is that it makes one feel stupid for having from time to time followed the series, or explains why one felt that way from time to time. What is the attitude of this show of brilliance?

Suppose we take the snow globe as a figure for a television tube (with its own convexity, and its own "snow"). Were this a film, I would feel confident in supposing the film to explore its figuration through some such connection with an object—as with the child's merry-go-round music box in *Blonde Venus*, or with the woman's hand mirror in *The Lady Eve*, or Hitchcock's telescope in *North by Northwest*, or the screening blanket in *It Happened One Night*, and so on. But with a moment at the end of a five-year television series, I have no such confidence in the identification, I cannot assess the seriousness, as it were, of its wit. Are the writers (somehow I know that there may well be more than one, and that the relations between writer and director, and between writer and producer, are aesthetically different from these relations in filmmaking) declaring their superiority to the networks, representing the television screen as providing amusement for the autistic (or as turning us into autistic children), as the front of a boob tube; or to the audience, whom they may expect not to get the joke played on them (now? over the past five years?); or to the ancient narrative device itself of a framing in which a character at the end awakens from a painful impasse? My lack of confidence here, or of a way of understanding the lack, is a reason I do not know how to situate my thoughts on television, whether to claim, say, that "The Fact of Television" does or does not discover (or continue the discovery of) television as a subject for philosophy.

Take another conclusion in the territory of screen and monitor intersection. In *No Way Out* a television image is demonstrated to have the capacity for enhancement (by way of the computer) to the power of recovering otherwise unreadable traces of a photograph—instanced as the returning portrait of a now-identifiable person (Kevin Costner) with hands raised toward his face as if warding off this capture: as if the world that interests us is no longer surely to be captured on unaided film; as if the events of our world now may pass film by. (The distinction between filming the world and monitoring an event is a decisive one for "The Fact of Television.") The further irony is that the unshakably incriminating evidence provided by the enhanced image (that from which there is no way out) is of the wrong thing (the man is not exactly guilty of a killing, but of spying and loving—a knowledge of the equivalence of these actions is perhaps what the man is warding off). So perhaps the suggestion is that we ponder yet again the fact that the photographic image is from the beginning an enhancement of its subjects, call this the work of photogenesis—a condition whose significance can only be determined in the life of the arts of the photographic.

A concluding thought on a more consciously vexed question. I assume that the process of colorization of old black and white movies for television airing will not disappear when its novelty wears off, that the success of colorizing a film in attracting larger audiences than its "original" now attracts is a state of things that will persist—in short, that the process will remain economically rational. On that assumption, and without now raising the question whether the virtue of this attraction (that more people do see and enjoy something of great works) outweighs the vices of it (for example, that these people do not see and do not enjoy something of these works, that they are deprived, without their knowledge, of something essential to their greatness), a prior question presents itself: Why is colorization so attractive (to those to whom it is not repellent)? My obvious answer is that it gives to movies the look of color television. So the question becomes: Why is *that* attractive? But that is a question "The Fact of Television" goes to rather surprisingly painful lengths to answer, in conjunction with the question why television is (also) repellent.

12

Prénom: Marie

They say miracles are past; and we have our philosophical persons to make modern and familiar, things supernatural and causeless. Hence is it that we make trifles of terrors, ensconcing ourselves into seeming knowledge when we should submit ourselves, to an unknown fear.

—Shakespeare, *All's Well That Ends Well*

AT THAT TIME I WAS GLAD FOR the invitation to prepare an introductory note for the volume Maryel Locke and Charles Warren were proposing to put together on Godard's *Hail Mary*, the idea of which, and now the materialization of which, are both so excellent. But I can only use the occasion of its appearance to congratulate them publicly, together with their coauthors, on the condition that now, in a time not essentially different, however broken it seems, from that in which I agreed to write, I find something worth saying beyond the private salute. I will not date my search beyond noting that today is Friday. Let's see what the weekend brings.

First published as the foreword to Maryel Locke and Charles Warren, editors, *Jean-Luc Godard's* Hail Mary: *Women and the Sacred in Film* (Southern Illinois University Press, 1993).

175

Of course I am at once attracted to the idea of the ordinary, we may say the banal, as scandalous, hence to the fact that *Hail Mary*, in its ordinariness, its smallness, caused a version of the scandal it depicts. (I am thinking of the scandal as tripping up settled ideas of importance, hence of interest and of destruction. Christianity has been a way to this unsettling. Philosophy has had its ways, as in Wittgenstein's *Philosophical Investigations* [sec. 118]: "Where does our investigation get its importance from since it seems only to destroy everything interesting, that is, all that is great and important.") And I am of course attracted at the same time to the interpretation of Mary and of touching Joseph as simultaneously a story of psychic trauma and of skepticism.

I begin by recalling that at the late birth of film into the shared intellectual life, such as it was, of the American 1950s, and then into its unshared political life, such as it may have been, in the second half of the 1960s and the early 1970s, Godard, I suppose more than any other filmmaker, was throughout in attendance. How far from that time was the appearance of the dual films *Prénom: Carmen (First Name: Carmen)* and *Je vous salue, Marie (Hail Mary)* in, respectively, 1983 and 1984? If you were inclined to side with the earlier Godard's politics, so with his apparent enlisting of art in the service of politics, then you are apt to sense a falling off, or backing off, in the later work, and become disappointed or disaffected with its apparent avoidance or evasion of politics. If, contrariwise, you were inclined against Godard's earlier politics, and perhaps sensed his hatred of hateful, exploitative society as a cover for his spiritual coldness and isolation, then you are more apt to feel, and welcome, a redemptive move in the later work, a search for perspective on the individualities of his work that signals an affecting effort to take responsibility for it, for its irresponsibilities that are as necessitated artistically as they ever were politically. But in that case *Hail Mary* will have traveled the familiar route from a totalizing politics to a totalizing religion, and from an apparent quest for a transcendence of the self (if just from one circle or stance to the next) to a self-indulgent transcendentalizing (or philosophizing) of nature or retheologizing of science.

Suppose, though, that *Hail Mary* is not an evasion of politics but a critique of it, of what Godard had at some time named politics. (Can we bear to hear those words of Marx again: "The critique of religion is the beginning of all critique." But shouldn't the ending, in principle, have been the critique of critique itself, of the claim to have found a position from which to measure the cost of accounting for the costs of other people's ideas, of all but your own? This ending is so easy to postpone.) And suppose that Godard's criticism of his irresponsibilities is a continuation of a mode of criticism there in his work from the beginning—since the later films are recognizably continuous with the earlier, bearing no different signature. Then from what perspective is such an effort at truth to be assessed? Does philosophy provide one?—call it thinking. (We were duly warned in *First Name: Carmen* that something basic, banal, is amiss with our registration of our experience into, for example, a division of politics and poetry. In that film, the line "Beauty is but the beginning of terror," remembered from the *Duino Elegies,* is dangerously tossed into a context invoking terrorism.)

If Godard is thinking, and his thinking is to provoke thought, then he must be thinking about film and about films; about, let's say, the conditions of their possibility. Wasn't he always? But in *Hail Mary* his thinking is not expressed by more or less routine showings of his hand, self-reflections on the fact of a film's making, of the sheer fact that what he has produced is a film. Because the question he is raising at that time is precisely whether this that appears is, or what it means to say that it is, a film—it is unlike other things so called. The question raises others—whether it is comprehensible that those responsible with him for it can want it, as it is; whether it is something to be proud or ashamed of, encouraged or disheartened by, an opening or a closing of further work, of others' work, scandalous or glib.

In this film Godard is thinking whether thinking, say spirit, is representable on film, and in which ways film represents body, say flesh. Is a quick young woman (with organized help, but against opposition), shooting the moon through a basketball hoop, thinking? Are a man called Gabriel and a young girl, having just landed on earth, stopping to retie a shoe using one hand offered by each of them, thinking—stopping to remind themselves, awkwardly—that "one mightier than I cometh, the lachet of whose shoes I am not worthy to unloose" (Luke 3.16)? When a woman asks a man called a professor what's on his mind and he answers, as the woman shows she knows, by quoting late Heidegger, and the man goes on to say, "I think politics today must be the voice of horror," is he in a state of physical revulsion? The woman, called Eva, probes the authenticity of the man's reaction by asking, "The voice, but the way or the word!" This echoes Mary's probing (or postponing) of the earlier, annunciatory "Follow Thy way" by asking, "My Way! But the voice or the word?" Does Eva's invocation of Mary's words receive them as underwriting her voice (as of all women), or as undermining Mary's? Leaving the question open, the man's revulsion from politics is hardly to be understood as an avoidance of it. It is much rather a claim that the victory (in fact and in theory) of what is at that time called politics over religion, over philosophy, over art, was (is) a voiding, unassessed, inexpressibly so, since it leaves nothing to assess itself with. Or does the matter reduce itself to showing that the exciting linking of politics to philosophy and horror was a matter of a sublimated turn of seduction, since the professor goes on to propose, and the woman concedes, that time and space have conjoined for them to expect the advent of sex?

If Godard is observing, in this man and woman, difficulties of thinking politically, the end of the film finds him observing in Gabriel and Mary difficulties of thinking religiously. Gabriel—which man not?—standing beside his car with something on his mind to say to a woman in the street, calls to her and then says, "Nothing. Hail Mary." But now, with her child taken over by the world, having nothing at this interval to do with her ("Jesus sayeth unto her, Woman, what have I to do with thee? mine hour is not yet come" [John 2.4]), she seems to take Gabriel's salute as a sublimated turn of seduction. Is it that she is free now to respond this way, hence free not to? Or is it that she is bound, if despite all she is responsive to a man, to make herself comprehensible to men, hence to renounce, or to rename, the man's way of comprehending her? Either way, her invitation of lipstick poses the question of who is called Gabriel, who assumes, or arrogates, the right to hail Mary, to voice an opening word.

In my imaginary of Godard as touchingly, awkwardly, addressing this question to himself, to his own right of hailing, I accept it as a turn I had missed in his work at that time, a couple of hundred full moons ago, when I wrote of him, with stuffy admiration: "I do not wish to deny Godard's inventiveness, and no one can ignore his facility. But the forms of culture he wishes to hold in contempt are no less inventive and facile. . . . An artist, because a human being, does have a position and does have his reasons for calling his events to our attention. What entitles him to our attention is precisely his responsibility to this condition. . . . One reads the distance from and between his characters [not, as has been claimed, as a Brechtian discovery but] as one does in reality, as the inability to feel; and we attribute our distance from the filmed events, because of their force upon us, to Godard's position toward them" (*The World Viewed*, pp. 99, 98, 97). Now I would like to imagine the maker of *Hail Mary* as genuinely surprised by the scandal his film occasioned, both because, as implied, the Christian project understands itself as scandalous beyond any further complications, and because Godard's film seems to me understandable as before all scandalous to himself: it would no doubt, if it could, constitute a stumbling block to all the dances of death, say to the world's inability to stop and think; but surely before that to his own terrible facility in explaining this inability.

Then what is called Joseph? When he says to Mary that he'll go jump in the lake, she instructs him that he is in effect calling himself by the wrong name: "Ophelia's no role for you." She would have learned this philosophy of naming—that we are called by the names we give ourselves—from Carmen, even Godard's Carmen, who had asked her own Joseph what comes before a name. He had given her the answer *"Prénom,"* what we call a Christian name, or now more usually I expect a given name; in any case, another name. This also smacks of theory, this time of names as radically arbitrary. (That on a certain picture of exiting there is no exit from the store of names does not mean that we have not had to break into the store. Hence perhaps the sense of ourselves as extraterrestrials. Since I and language precede one another, there is no beginning to us.) Carmen rejects this theory, demanding to be called on her own terms. To me this seems a welcome rejection of the current notion according to which (if I understand its implications) declaring one's subject-position is supposed to exhaust one's subjectivity.

How has Mary so called herself? Is she going on her willingness to trust—and not to trust—her own innocence, to be possessed by no man but by an idea, say a word? Does she put before all her willingness to let something matter, to happen to her unforgettably? But these attributes resemble those Godard's Carmen assigns herself in taking Carmen on. They seem attributes of philosophy. Here the question whether Mary skirts skepticism may come to the fore. Unlike Kleist's Marquise of O——, Godard's Mary seems never to be driven in her unfathomable position to the shore of madness. Yet we see her thrashing on her bed, sheets twisted more or less around her, as if eventually and equally to swaddle or to shroud—as if soul should become body, or abandon body, hence yield the desire to know beyond itself. The Marquise of O—— is drawn to madness by her questioning how this pregnancy has happened. Godard's Mary is kept sane by the acknowledgment that it has happened, while shaken by the question why something so disproportionate has happened to her. It may become anybody's question.

The idea of a body "having" a soul is apparently so banal from Mary's perspective that she turns the words into the question of a soul having a body. Her doctor is impatient with her for this confusion, even though he has just verified that she is bodily both virginal and pregnant, which could be explained as her being immersed in the spirit, a state describable not as a spirit possessing the body but perhaps as spirit enveloping the body, so in this way having it—whether as a plan has risks, or a person has premonitions, or as a pond has fish, or the hand has fingers, or as the mind has mountains. Perhaps what the obstetrician lacks is the concept of being born again. Death and departure are as different in the case of the soul as in the case of God. What prevents the announcing of the death of the soul? Or was this Nietzsche's question?

Isn't Mary serious in her speculations? Doesn't her life depend upon them? That Wittgenstein takes the idea of the soul as "having" a body to be philosophically arousing *(Investigations,* sec. 283) is encouraging but not decisive. The body's having a soul suggests that in the array of bodies we encounter, certain among them may not have souls, an idea of the presence of humanoids or other aliens of some other species, zombies, golems, automatons, an inhabitation of eternal death. We do not, not even a Mary among us at this time, I assume, have an analogous idea of our familiarity with an array of souls some of which are fated to be encountered in the presence of bodies. Accordingly, the idea of the soul having a body seems rather my idea of what makes my body mine, and of the change it will suffer at my death, should it survive me. Then, in a word, it would be I who have a soul—or not—something else besides an ego, so to speak. Then self-intimacy seems, paradoxically, to ease my imagination of others, to reach them without attempting to overcome their distance or separation from me—as if knowing others, whatever men think, is not entering them but bearing them, bearing their annunciations of us, so renunciations.

I used Mary's invocation of Shakespeare to justify my calling, in my epigraph, upon Shakespeare's words on miracles—all but beaten into banality by fame—from another play of and about the mystery and magic and trick of marriage, and of the irony of human identity, especially of the identity of husbands and sons and kings, and of the defiling of a woman that is no defiling. We would ask, were there time at this time for philosophical patience, what idea of miracles Godard's Mary's Joseph has that backs him in claiming, "Miracles don't exist." To retrieve the picture would take the patience Kierkegaard exercises, in his book on Adler, in claiming that the church has lost or forgotten the concept of revelation, so that it is religiously in the position, awkward for this church, of knowing that it necessarily cannot recognize anything that happens—however interesting or important or destructive—as a revelation. Yet in a time and place closer perhaps to Kierkegaard's than ours, Ibsen's *A Doll's House* calls marriage "the miracle of miracles," and its heroine's justification for walking away from her sacred duties as wife and mother depends on acknowledging that under that concept she has not been taken in marriage.

If we may still, barely, take Ibsen seriously on such a matter, with or against what grain can we take the moment in Cukor's smallish film *Adam's Rib* in which Eve, I mean Amanda, the wife-attorney (Katharine Hepburn), amazedly asks of a dainty hat given her by her husband-attorney (Spencer Tracy), "Isn't that a miracle?" The seriousness or banality of that description (of the hat and of its gift) doesn't really come into question until the ending sequence, where the husband and the wife, about to disappear into bed, are both wearing hats, so that a miracle and the echo or contest of a miracle are associated with the possibility of marriage. If, further, we remember Freud's listing the hat, in his *Interpretation of*

Dreams, typically a woman's hat, as a symbol for the male genitals, then we may pose for ourselves the following question about our experience of this pair's disappearance into their marriage. Do we experience their joining the struggle between the sexes as a contest over who wears the hat? Or do we instead understand them as joining to contest this concept of the struggle? The scandal in such a (Hollywood) film's accepting marriage as a struggle against so-called marriage took some four decades after the making of such films to recognize, and they still hardly constitute big news. That Godard's small, thoughtful film, with its plain events and its reconceptualizing, or say recalling, of a popular set of names, caused its scandal almost at once, as part of its reception, is, to my mind, glad news.

A parting memory. Of the pieces of Bach called upon for the sound in *Hail Mary,* the choice underscoring the early basketball sequence is the opening Prelude of the first volume of *The Well-Tempered Clavier.* It is—how may we forget it?—the piece appropriated by Gounod to which, on which, to set his *"Ave Maria."* Godard's charming identification here of his work with Gounod's asks us to think of the exploitation of Bach but also of the insight in Gounod's seeing that that piece of Bach's is interpretable as an accompaniment (an accompaniment to *that,* to hailing Mary, which Godard accepts as imperishable, but contests). And, I suppose, asks us to think further that these small insights may blur Bach's insight into smallness, or plainness—that this minimal figuration of C major in the opening Prelude is not fragmentary, not lacking; it is intact and open, virginal and pregnant. (Mary said, "Being a virgin should mean being available, or free. Not being hurt.") Blank of signature, and its dozen accidentals heard to be movingly necessary, the Prelude's indestructibility as a field for generations of child's play (each learning to position herself or himself at that initial, unprotected, middle C) confirms its right to continue into a pair of volumes whose demands and possibilities circle, and again circle, inexhaustibly, the universe of the major and minor keys. Men's insights seem in general not to contain such patience.

13

Nothing Goes without Saying

Reading the Marx Brothers

OVIES MAGNIFY, SO WHEN pictures began talking they magnified words. Somehow, as in the case of opera's magnification of words, this made their words mostly ignorable, like the ground, as if the industrialized human species had been looking for a good excuse to get away from its words, or looking for an explanation of the fact that we do get away, even must. The attractive publication, briefly and informatively introduced, of the scripts[1] of several Marx Brothers films— *Monkey Business* (1931), *Duck Soup* (1933), and *A Day at the Races* (1937)— is a sublime invitation to stop and think about our swings of convulsiveness and weariness in the face of these films; to sense that it is essential to the Brothers' sublimity that they are thinking about words, to the end of words, in every word—or, in Harpo's emphatic case, in every absence of words.[2]

Marx Brothers films, as unmistakably revealed in these scripts, are extensively explicit about their intentions. Their pun-crammed air, well recognized as a medium of social subversion, also presses a standing demand to reach some understanding—which is incomparably better avoided than faked. Someone is always barking sentiments at the Brothers such as "Keep out of this loft!" to which Chico once replies, "Well, it's

First published in *London Review of Books*, January 6, 1994.

183

better to have loft and lost, than never to have loft at all," upon which Groucho pats him on the shoulder and says, "Nice work!" (*Monkey Business*). (When is to speak to do something? When is to bark to say something?) Groucho's positive evaluation is an instance of the recurrent reflexiveness in the Brothers' craft, letting us know that they know that we may fall to imagining that they do not know what they are doing. A repeated example, as if to wake us from this stupor, is Chico's turning to Groucho with pride, asking: "Ats-a some joke, eh Boss?" Groucho is complimenting Chico not only on countering a dour threat with a serene wipe-out, but on maintaining his responsiveness to a world deadened with banal and unreasoned prohibitions. (Occasionally, as in *Duck Soup*, Groucho specifically probes to see whether the compliment is warranted, as when he feeds Chico a straight line and says in an aside: "Let's see you get out of that one.") To me it is a philosophical compliment. So I have been aggrieved to hear Groucho called a cynic. He is merely without illusion, and it is an exact retribution for our time of illusory knowingness that we mistake his clarity for cynicism and sophisticated unfeelingness.

Intention, or the desperate demand for interpretation, is gaudily acknowledged in such turns as Chico's selling Groucho a tip on a horse by selling him a code book, then a master code book to explain the code book, then a guide required by the master code, then a subguide supplementary to the guide—a scrupulous union, or onion, of semantic and monetary exchanges and deferrals to warm the coldest contemporary theorist of signs; or as acted out in Chico's chain of guesses when Harpo, with mounting urgency, charades his message that a woman is going to frame Groucho (both turns in *A Day at the Races)*. But Groucho's interpretive powers achieve distinct heights of their own.

The famous packed cabin sequence from *A Night at the Opera* is simultaneously an image of the squalor of immigrant crowding and of the immigrant imagination of luxury. Groucho is outside, as befits him, ordering exhaustively from a steward (getting food is one of the Brothers' standing objectives). After each item is ordered, Chico's voice from within the cabin appends, "And two hard-boiled eggs," which, after Groucho dutifully repeats it, is punctuated by a honk from within, which Groucho effortlessly responds to by adding, "Make that three hard-boiled eggs." That Harpo evidently accedes to Groucho's understanding of his honk is variously interpretable. You can imagine that Groucho has some private knowledge of Harpo's language; or you can see that Harpo's insatiability, or unsocialization, signals that he has no language (that is, that he is unable to speak in the etymological sense of being in the state of infancy). In the latter case, Harpo trusts Groucho implicitly to know his wants and to have them at heart, a trust well placed. That Harpo is shown to be asleep during Groucho's exchange with the steward suggests that Harpo is honking, wishing, in his dreams, and so with the directness of infants, preceding the detours of human desire, a possibility of dreams separately noted by Freud. Originality in speech is the rediscovery of speech. (It is, by the way, not true, as it is said, that Chico can trick Groucho. Groucho has nothing to lose and is not out to win anything for himself. He follows Chico's elaborate cons out of pure interest, to see, as if to satisfy his professional curiosity about the human situation, how they will come out. One outcome is as interesting as another. Of the other thinkers I know fairly well, I believe only Thoreau is Groucho's equal in this capacity for disinterested interest, or unattachment.)

The familiar, or familial, relation between Groucho and Harpo in the arena of food suggests a relation in their sharing of certain gestures of lechery. If they were really lecherous they would no longer be funny. (Adam Gopnik was making such a point about Woody Allen a couple of months ago in the *New Yorker*.) Being parodies of lechery, they enact claims on the part of each human creature ("All God's chillun" is how they name them in *A Day at the Races*) to be loved, for no reason. Harpo would not know what to do if one of the women he chases stopped running; for him the instincts of hunger, of sex, and of the destruction of whatever can be snipped or chopped, seem equal in imaginary satisfaction. Groucho, the opposite of innocent, is a lover, but one who thinks it just as hilarious as anyone else might think it that he should be found lovable. It does both him and Margaret Dumont an injustice not to see that he wins her love and is a faithful husband to it; he courts her as fervently as, and much more persistently than, he does any other woman—he amuses her, shocks her, tells her the truth, expresses contempt for the boring and brutish flatterers in her second-rate world who would deceive her for their private purposes, and with good spirits survives her doubts about him and her faiths in him. How much can one ask for?

I see no good sense in being reasonable in my admiration for these achievements. Thinking recently about the conditions of opera, as mysterious and as initially contrived as the conditions of film, I asked myself why it was, when the Marx Brothers' thoughts turned to opera, that they proposed (or inspired others to propose to them) in *A Night at the Opera, Il Trovatore* as their example. In their realm, nothing goes without saying. It turns out, in this juxtaposition, that Leonora's initial mistaking, as it were, of her love of one brother for that of the other, becomes a fundamental issue: it is to the villainous brother, in the early shadows of the drama, that she declares: "My love." Perhaps she was not wrong about herself that initial time. Then one remembers that the Marx Brothers are brothers, and declare their family resemblance in one of their greatest turns, in *Duck Soup*, when Groucho and Harpo all but become mirror images of each other.

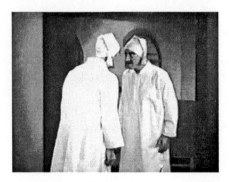

Figure 13.1

And then one considers that these brothers, famous for their absurdities, may be taking on, as a grand enemy, the famously dark fixations of *Trovatore* that just about anyone regards as exemplary of the supposed absurdities of grand opera; and so consider that their competition with that darkness, absurd only in its terrible lack of necessity, is to use the power of film to achieve the happy ending in which the right tenor gets the part, the film concluding triumphantly with the opera's most famous, ecstatically melancholy duet.

Other speculations about their choices of routine keep finding confirmation—these brothers are dashing way ahead of us. Thinking more or less blankly one time of the ships on which they approach America, quite early in *Monkey Business* and quite late in *A Night at the Opera*, I think further: of course! The films present America as requiring discovery and as providing a home for immigrants. Then not only am I swiftly embarrassed at having forgotten that the elaborate finale of the first half of *Monkey Business* is just about the anxiety of needing a passport to enter upon the American streets of gold, but I am soon rewarded by finding Groucho conclude an exasperatingly contentious exchange with Chico by looking at the camera and declaring "There's my argument! Restrict immigration!"; and rewarded again, or piqued, when—in response to Chico's and Harpo's attempt to thwart the woman's plan to frame Groucho (to compromise him in Margaret Dumont's eyes) by hanging, so to speak, new sheets of wallpaper over Groucho and the woman seated cozily on a couch—thus concealing them from the entering suspicious one—Groucho pokes his head out of the sticky sheets to observe, "I must be a citizen. I've just got my second papers," that is, the final documents in an alien's naturalization process (as if any process could naturalize this alien).

Until my father died, seventy years after arriving on America's shores as a young man, and not many fewer than that after naturalization, he never fully shook the feeling that something might be discovered to be wrong with his "papers." Perhaps helped by this knowledge, I go further into the sequence with Chico that leads to Groucho's momentary wish never to have been cast together with him. It opens in the captain's cabin, where Groucho is so to speak impersonating the captain.

GROUCHO: A fine sailor you are.

CHICO: You bet I'm a fine sailor. . . . My father was-a partners with Columbus.

GROUCHO: Columbus has been dead for four hundred years.

CHICO: Well, they told me it was my father . . .

GROUCHO: I'll show you a few things you don't know about history. Now look . . . *[Drawing a circle on a globe]* Now, there's Columbus.

CHICO: That's-a Columbus Circle . . .

GROUCHO: Now, Columbus sailed from Spain to India looking for a short cut.

CHICO: Oh, you mean strawberry short cut.

And it gets still further afield. It is some mimesis of the shattered tiles of facts and interpretations, the urgent emplacement of which had to prepare masses of arrivals for citizenship, learning who their new fathers are, the fathers of their new country, and searching to put new and old names to unheard-of objectives. And when Groucho lets out in disgust, "Do you suppose I could buy back my introduction to you?" I again find myself speculating: the comedy is that of outrage, of exhaustion, of the last straw. And again I feel rewarded. I'll come back to say how in a moment.

The sense of culture as something overheard, and probably as tales or plots of incomprehensible manias, comes out also in those asides of Groucho's that fill the space of responses to impossible situations and incomprehensible demands.

WOMAN: But I haven't any children.

GROUCHO: That's just the trouble with this country. You haven't any chil-
              dren, and as for me . . . *[Dramatically]* I'm going back to the
              closet, where men are empty overcoats.

Or again, also from *Monkey Business:*

SAME WOMAN: What brought you here?

GROUCHO *[Dramatically]:* Ah, 'tis midsummer, madness, the music in my
                          temples . . .
Or again:

SAME WOMAN: You can't stay in that closet.

GROUCHO: Oh, I can't, can I? That's what they said to Thomas
              Edison, mighty inventor, Thomas Lindbergh, mighty
              flyer, and Thomas Shefsky, mighty like a rose. Just
              remember, my little cabbage, that if there weren't any
              closets, there wouldn't be any hooks, and if there weren't
              any hooks, there wouldn't be any fish, and that would suit
              me fine.

To speak, as I believe is still common, of Groucho's "one-liners," as if this
were his characteristic genre of response, is not helpful, not just because it
is so incomplete, even inaccurate, but because what it omits reaches from
the closeness to madness, or hysteria, of so much of what he has to say, to
the sheer range of reference of his uncontrollable thoughts—from some
memory of Russian or Cartesian melancholy about overcoats and empty
men, through wisps of operetta, to a string of heroes that the natives seem
to name Thomas, for the moment missing a Jefferson but including a
figure from the Yiddish theater otherwise known as Boris Thomashefsky,
associated, compulsively if not altogether surprisingly, with some association of Abie's Irish Rose with the teary mother's song "Mighty Like a
Rose," all sometimes addressed to imaginary characters, here one called
"Kapellmeister," later one called "Your honor." This delirium is to be
compared, not identified, with Harpo's closeness to madness, as when, in
his frantic search for the frog who has jumped away from his place in
Harpo's hat, Harpo hears a man confess that he has a frog in his throat,
grabs the man and pries open his jaws to retrieve his companion. It touches the madness of childhood. And it enacts an unexpected understanding

of Wittgenstein's perception, in *Philosophical Investigations*, that Augustine, as characteristic of philosophers, "describes the learning of language as if the child came into a strange country and did not understand the language of the country; that is, as if it already had a language, only not this one." This is illuminatingly implausible if taken as about the condition of infancy, with no language yet in the picture; but illuminatingly plausible if taken as about an older child, with a certain budget of words; all due for unforeseen futures, hence against an idea of the condition of immigrancy, between languages.

What is this humor? If we take Bergson's theory of comedy as bespeaking a form of madness, of men behaving like machines, and vice versa, then we can say that the Marx Brothers turn this theory on the world, showing themselves to remain improvisatory, original, in a setting of absolutely mechanical reactions to them ("This is an outrage"; "I've never been so insulted in all my life"; "Beat it!"; "Oh!"; "Just what do you mean?"; "Hey. Hey. Hey"; "Are you crazy or something?"). Their madness is a defense against madness, and neither is something over which they claim control; it is a struggle to the finish, in which the question is Which side will create the last word, or destroy it?

Let's accordingly go back to the idea of a comedy of the last straw, or rather of a comedy about the last straw, about the sometimes fatal whimsicality with which people announce the judgment that a straw is the last. In *Duck Soup*, Ambassador Trentino (played by the Caesaresque Louis Calhern) says to Margaret Dumont: "Mrs. Teasdale this is the last straw! There's no turning back now. This means war!"—words Groucho may well be imagined somewhere to dispose of in his own person, if perhaps he decides to take an imaginary slight as directed to his entire regiment. When later in *Duck Soup* Groucho uses the words "Gentlemen, this is the last straw," it is in response to picking up a straw boater with its crown flapping, from among the rubble of war. Then what, if anything, do we make of Harpo, in *A Day at the Races*, attacking a mattress with a knife, pulling out the straw, and then feeding it to a horse he discloses in a closet? I would like to take this in conjunction with the line of Groucho's that closes *Monkey Business*, when after events in an old barn in which a wagon wheel becomes an imaginary wheel of fortune, a cow bell becomes a time bell in a brawl and a watering can and then a buggy lamp are talked into as microphones, Groucho turns to a pile of hay and starts pitching strands into the air. Asked what he's doing he replies: "I'm looking for a needle in a haystack." Now some moments earlier we had seen Groucho rise from under this hay and ask: "Where's all those farmers' daughters I've been hearing about for years?" and then disappear under the hay again. It strikes me that Groucho's self-interpretation of looking for a needle in a haystack undertakes to transfigure the coarse genre of farmer's daughter gags into a search—almost hopeless, with just room for good spirits to operate—for a heart's needle of pleasure somewhere within the dry medium of this world (like the bereft husband in *L'Atalante* diving into the river, eyes open for his vanished love).

For Groucho, throwing last straws to the wind, the world as it stands has placed its last straw, suffered its last judgment, a long time ago; yet the world as it may yet be, attested in any event in which genuine interest is shown—like a Harpo craving, a Chico scam, a young woman in love and trouble, the scandalized, ecstatic devotion of Margaret Dumont—exists beyond counts of straw.

Evidently I take the value of the published scripts of these films not to be solely or primarily that of sending us back to the films (the films themselves must do that), but also that of releasing these words and deeds from a confinement to film, or to what we think of as film, or think of as a Marx Brothers film. Released to themselves, these observations are free to join the observations of, say, Bergson; or Brecht, whose *Three Penny Opera* is no more valid a development of *The Beggar's Opera* than *Duck Soup* is (it needn't be as good as *The Three Penny Opera* still to be very, very good); or Beckett whose two barrels housing the married pair in *Endgame* make excellent sense, even of the idea of the stowaway, of the four barrels in which the stowaway brothers have set up house below decks at the opening of *Monkey Business*. And then we are free to think about one of Groucho's responses to the recurrent idea that a situation he's created, this time involving his medical practice, is "absolutely insane." Groucho: "Yes, that's what they said about Pasteur." No doubt the direct reference is to the celebrated Paul Muni film *The Story of Louis Pasteur* made the year before *A Day at the Races*, but must one deny that Groucho is claiming his own discovery of a germ theory, this time about the disease of language, about its corruption by communications of a corrupt world? He puts it differently, but not much differently.

I was talking about Groucho's searching for pleasure, another topic about which these films are, if asked, fully explicit. In *Duck Soup*, after Firefly (Groucho), in song, promulgates the laws of his administration as not allowing smoking, telling dirty jokes, whistling, or chewing gum, he sums it up, still singing:

> If any form of pleasure is exhibited
> Report to me and it will be prohibited.

From which it does not follow that the Brothers trust any given form of pleasure, any more than they trust any other fixation, any more than they trust; they test. Nor are their films as films exactly or purely pleasurable, any more than compulsive punning is exactly or simply funny. The unpolished air of the filmmaking, and Groucho's Brechtian objectivity, are not meant to be winning, any more (if no less) than Groucho's crawling and meowing on a balustrade.

The broad groan in response to a broad pun is a criterion of real, if a little sublimated, pain. "This is no time for puns" says Groucho, gasping with them, almost at the end of *Monkey Business*. Had someone the presence of mind to say this to Groucho, he might have answered: "Yes, that's what they said about Shakespeare." No time is the time for puns, since puns stop time, stop the forward motion of assertion, peel back the protective self-ignorance of words; is this the pain of puns? Their pain is that of, let us say, incessant thinking—thinking among the endless things there are to say, which of them we shall have forever said, and not said, now. Their pleasure is the illusion that nothing is going unsaid.

And what is the cultural economy, say the relation between high and low thinking, in a society whose as it were popular culture has such as the Marx Brothers in store—what is its art, its philosophy, its politics, its entertainment, its seriousness?

Let us before ending linger once more over an invitation into whose depths of implication I cannot deny Groucho perception, and, as always, without presumption, he is nothing if not tactful. It comes as part of the packed cabin sequence, cited earlier, that royal levee of services, when a woman appears to Groucho with a portable beauty tray hung before her and asks, "Do you want a manicure?" Groucho replies: "No. Come on in." I take for granted that some will be satisfied to suppose that he means, fixatedly: "No, but I want something else you could provide." Let us suppose, however, that he has the poise with meaning, whatever command of it accrues from obedience to it, to mean or imply at least also the following: "No, but there are lots of others here; perhaps they want what you suggest"; and "Nobody really wants a manicure, but if that's all you're offering, I'll take it"; and "No, but come in since you're here and we'll see what happens." All this is quite in character for Groucho. An array of implication, like the disarray of puns, will threaten anarchy, against a demand for autarchy; but both work to make what sense is to be made of a world whose sense is stolen, in which it is to be stolen back. Both show aspects of our victimization by words, fools of them, but thereby show that there are, still, ordinary words, beyond and between us, whose lives we might imagine, which might share lives we can imagine—not simply signs and signals hovering over a destroyed landscape.

A few years ago, on a walk during a conference break, a French philosopher and I exchanged friendly regrets that we were not, as it were, culturally better prepared to do the promise of each other's work more explicit justice in our own. He reported that American friends of his had been urging him to read Emerson and Thoreau, which seemed to both of us an unlikely eventuality. I took the implication quite kindly, anyway impersonally, that no one would, or could easily, without insult, urge an American intellectual to read Montaigne and Descartes and Rousseau and Kant and Hegel . . . Culture is—is it not?—European culture. Besides, Emerson and Thoreau had read them. Had I then been fresh from reading the film scripts before me now, I might have replied—whether hopefully or not is uncertain—that to the extent he was wondering what was on my mind, hence in that tangle of American culture, an equally accurate access, and one in a sense more efficiently acquired, could be had by a few days of immersion in half a dozen Marx Brothers films. But that would have been, to borrow a self-description of Thoreau's and of Walt Whitman's, bragging.

Notes

1. "Film script" is not an unambiguous designation. In the present edition, on which my remarks here are based, it designates a record of dialogue and action faithful to the finished film (supposing there is a canonical version of that). This is a sound choice and I have no quarrel with it. Other choices would have been to publish the scripts as they stood before filming, but there is apparently no surviving such text for *Duck Soup*, whose script here is therefore wholly reconstituted from the film, and in any case such a collection would serve quite specialized purposes; or to publish original scripts together with their respective reconstitutions as filmed. This dual publication was followed by Viking some twenty years ago for *A Day at the Races* and for *A Night at the Opera*. In obvious ways this is desirable— such documentation underscores the collaboration, or mutual inspiration, of the Brothers with some of the most gifted writers, and teams of writers, of comic observation and plot, of gags, and of songs during the golden period of interchange between Hollywood and Broadway. But the mere credits included in the present scripts should themselves suggest this. Anyway, what is mutual inspiration?

2. *The Marx Brothers:* Monkey Business, Duck Soup *and* A Day at the Races (London: Faber and Faber, 1993).

14

Seasons of Love

Bergman's *Smiles of a Summer Night* and *The Winter's Tale*

I WAGERED THAT WHEN THE time came to produce a contribution to the
Cahiers jubilee of film's invention I would find myself happy to remember and to speak personally, as the invitation urged us to do, about
Ingmar Bergman's *Smiles of a Summer Night* (1955). The time is here and
the wager of sentiment has been magically won. Several weeks ago a conjunction of omen-happy events placed me in Stockholm's Royal Dramatic
Theater at a performance of Bergman's production of *The Winter's Tale*.
Because I found it from beginning to end to take its place with memories
of the most inspired times I have experienced in the theater, it was bound
to enter into these present thoughts.

Thematically, at least, this late play in the Shakespeare corpus bears
intricately on *Smiles of a Summer Night*. But ontologically, its direct value
will lie in emphasizing theater's most obvious and absolute difference from
film, that each one who comes within range of, for example, the present
volume can view the same film, and it may present itself everywhere such
a one is to be found; whereas the experience of the event of theater
demands one's presenting oneself there and then. So the pleasure I feel in

Originally written for "Jubilee" issue of *Cahiers du cinéma* commemorating the one hundredth anniversary of the first film screening, 1994. (The issue never appeared.)

193

the possibility of saying something useful about an object of which we are quite likely to share the experience exists in a certain tension with the pressure I feel toward the necessity of saying something memorable about a related event of which we are very unlikely, and because we are very unlikely, to share the experience.

Smiles of a Summer Night was not the first film I loved, but it was the first in which I came away from the experience of a film with the sense or revelation that, as in instances of the great arts, everything means something, and took that experience home to spend, it turned out, all night inviting my journal to continue telling what everything came to in this particular case, or whether there is a something that an everything could come to, and whether we should desire such a thing. (I had already had sufficient evidence that the soul is not a unity.) Since *Smiles* declares itself as depicting, hence smiling upon ("hence"?), at least three distinguishable kinds of love, it rather commits me to say something by way of locating the kind of love it has inspired in me, hence the kind that film is apt to inspire. It represented to me, put otherwise, some new standard to which an articulation of the response to film had to rise.

This is attested to by my apparently random impulse to select *Smiles of a Summer Night* as one of the two films—I have forgotten the other—that I took along to screen and lecture about during the civil rights summer of 1964 in Mississippi. I joined for a couple of weeks a small group of Harvard students whose contribution to that summer was to offer a set of courses meant to constitute that year's summer school of Tougaloo College, a small, ambitious black institution outside Jackson, Mississippi. Having the previous year tried my hand at Harvard, more eagerly than successfully, at teaching a graduate seminar in aesthetics concentrated on film, I wanted, in addition to philosophy lectures, to introduce film into our Tougaloo offerings, and my first pedagogical goal was to convey my sense that film proposed a serious project of thinking. I had no idea then how to convey this with a popular American film, without at any rate changing the subject to one of general aesthetics. So although virtually any film in that context would have carried a pedagogically usable transgressiveness, I went to the extreme of choosing one that still seemed to me foreign. While my confusion communicated itself, so did my wish to acknowledge my own sense of film's foreignness as an academic subject, and so, it seems, did my sincere commitment to the film and my sense through it of intellectual liberation. So my naive sophistication was not pedagogically useless after all.

The opening encounter with this film that I refer to occurred on the night of April 27, 1960, a piece of knowledge earned from having just now uncovered the journal of mine containing that night's reflections. I was thirty-four years old, precisely half my lifetime ago, evidently lost in the middle of life's journey within the bright parks of Berkeley, where I was completing my fourth year as an assistant professor in the philosophy department—separated from a marriage with a friend, jointly responsible for a three-year-old daughter, unable or unwilling to complete my belated Ph. D. thesis, under notice from my department that unless it was submitted within the coming academic year my promotion to tenure would not be recommended and my position would terminate, and pretty securely wrapped in general sentiments of guilt and failure. In short, I shared elements of an economy of discredit with various of the characters in *Smiles of a Summer Night*—with the isolated father (Fredrik, played by Gunnar Björnstrand), with his unoriented, unclaimed wife (Anne, played by Ulla Jacobsson), with his turbulent, seminarian son (Henrik, played by Bjorn Bjelfvenstam), with his former and future love (the aging, skeptical actress Desiree, tending to a child alone, played by Eva Dahlbeck).

Reading through the pertinent twenty or so pages of that journal, I seem to recall pretty well the treasures of romantic excess with which I wished to greet each discriminable motion, each change of light, each posture and juxtaposition taken by my old, or rather new, love—with each pool or lake of water lights; with each word of Desiree's bracing, deflationary humor in response to Fredrik's insufficiently serious seriousness; thrilled to remember the titles, and noting their pertinence, of each romantic piece Henrik melodramatically flings himself at the piano to invoke; taking to heart the casual richness of symbolism at a European artist's disposal, as in the gargoyle figures of a public clock, whose procession at one hour shows a hunchback followed by a bride and the next hour shows the bride followed by death; awed by such narrative finesse as presenting two women (Anne and her "friend" Charlotte) gossiping about Desiree's power over and independence of men, with particular reference to each of their husbands, and thus imitating, by similarity hence by difference, the French comedy in which we had seen Desiree perform, exploring both the content of such comedy and the mechanism of it in relation to the comedy and mechanism of the film now before us; and moved to the depths at the civilized violence of one soul's intelligence of another, desperate to ponder the roll of dice between a liberating and a stifling understanding, or between sincerity and cynicism.

These excesses—I assume they are pieces of the normal overevaluation conferred by infatuation—are reflected in the film's depicted excesses, for example, of the forest-framed racing carriage carrying off the young lovers; of the repeated crash of music, as of a broken fanfare, that both marks the young man's shadowed face as he shelters the young woman in one arm and with the other gives rein to the horses, and that then marks his father's face as he witnesses this scene; of the flowing, sheer scarf the young woman flings free as they gallop away, which wafts onto the roadbed for the crumpled father-husband to pick up, the veil he could never lift from his virgin bride. And then we might adduce the excess of meaning in the film's handling of the scarf-veil-shroud itself, picking up the tainted purities of Pyramus's Thisby's bloodied mantle and of Desdemona's handkerchief, so invoking for its summer night both Shakespeare's midsummer dream and the Shakespearean romance of jealousy in *The Winter's Tale* that, as it were, reroutes Othello's occupation. We had seen that sheer fabric in two earlier versions, at length when, after Anne closely questions her experienced soubrette Petra about the demands of men and confesses that she remains inexperienced, and Petra replies that she can tell that from her skin, the two young women tumble down cascades of laughter into one another's arms and onto a bed, covered and caught together by folds of this sheer cloth; and briefly when, in the sequence immediately preceding that of the elopement, Henrik buries his face into a window curtain made of such a fabric and utters a prayer that accepts and transcends the prohibitions of the passages from Luther on virtue that he had read aloud as some simulacrum of sexual advance—using, as inexperience well may, the censoring of love as love talk—to uncomprehending, all-too-comprehending Petra. Then he had fervently read out Luther's words against temptation and unsteady claims to virtue; but now, within the feel and the imagination of sheer fabric, he prays further: "O Lord, if your world is sinful, then I want to sin. Take my miserable virtue away from me." The prayer is answered when, as if to tempt heaven, Henrik tries suicide, and his bungling of it produces Anne on a magic bed, an undisguised realization of the romantic replacement of religion by the excess of love (essentially Kant's definition of fanaticism).

But am I really remembering the excesses of my experience that first night, I mean participating again in their illuminations or illusions, or am I simply remembering that one night a long time ago I participated in what *I* now knowingly or historically read as excesses? Since I grant film the power of art to keep such experiences in store, retaining them with treadable traces of feeling, not toward the past but into the present, the question of memory is at once eased and increased. I must persist beyond those early journal notations, whose very formulations of consciousness will have dissipated experience and its traces (those notations are rarely art, they rarely conserve the locus of experience). Put otherwise, I must find a fresh moment, one remaining outside the "everything" that I have said means something in the film. It is essential to what I take the work of art to be that there are always such fresh moments of entry, even fresh everythings. Hence I know that I must have already encountered what I seek to reencounter, so it must occur in the form of remembering. But since I cannot systematically search for the significant memory trace—even if I review the film's events on a video, as of course I did the last thing before beginning this writing—what I seek evidently falls under Proust's notion of involuntary memory. (I am responding here to Walter Benjamin's study of Baudelaire in which he goes over some familiar ground in Freud and in Bergson, but freshly contextualizes it against his interest in Baudelaire's perception of the modern as the period in which human experience becomes lost to itself, or exhausted, we might say stolen. Emerson anticipates the question of the experience of the loss of experience, or say explores the loss of experience in terms of the experience of loss, or rather of the failure of that express experience, ten years before, as it were, the Second Empire, in his essay "Experience.")

Mightn't I, however, find some promising field on which to await this (re)encounter with *Smiles of a Summer Night*? I might think about Bergman's other films; or track the connection of *Smiles* with Renoir's *The Rules of the Game* and with *The Marriage of Figaro*, narratives of other distressed marriages, in settings of entertainment and accident, where married love is tested by romantic love; or figure further the allusions to theater, fairly explicitly to Marivaux; or to photography, in the contrast proposed between Fredrik's early visit to a photographer's studio to collect portraits of his wife, portraits he revisits at the middle and toward the end of the film, where the photographer modestly protests, to balance his praise of his own work, "It's the subject that's important of course," a remark which, taken as an observation about these fixated, fetishistic images, is a banality, but taken as about motion pictures is illuminating, implying that the subject of the camera is primarily the actor and not primarily the character, as if the actor may learn from the camera of his or her freedom to find his character.

It is here, in staking a field on which to await fresh impressions, inner or outer, that my memory of Bergman's production of *The Winter's Tale* comes a bit systematically into play. To begin with, it matches *Smiles of a Summer Night*'s study of or competition with theater by taking up a comparable study of film by theater (or what I think may be understood as such a study).

While I felt that Bergman's production was quoting images from his films, I am too out of touch at the moment with these films to be able to prove this one way or the other, and it is in any case not what I mean in speaking of this production's study of film. I mean something more elusive, as in the way Leontes and Hermione are given to caress and kiss on momentarily parting in their opening scene with Polixenes, a quickness of erotic shock you expect rather from cinematic closeness. Or more massive, as in the full promenade of the cast that Bergman imports to open the play, an event which both unifies as it were the frame and depth of the stage and takes its course as if for all the world made in slow motion. The effect of this painstakingly and gorgeously articulated gesture is manifold, and I want to take bearings from it, however brief, meant to lead back to *Smiles of a Summer Night*.

The promenade serves, hence joins, various strata of interests, from the history of Shakespearean reception and specifically of Swedish national inheritance, to the ontology of theater and ritual, to the acceptance of this particular play's presentation of famous dramaturgical cruxes. The literary or historical trace for its nineteenth-century setting is a printed nineteenth-century program (photographed for inclusion in the present production's program) announcing a production of *The Winter's Tale* in a country chateau staged soon after the belated translation of Shakespeare into Swedish, in Sweden, as elsewhere, an event within Romanticism. The promenade unites the population of the cast with that of the chateau, actors with audience, and began somewhere from within the space of the contemporary audience of which I was for an evening a member, as gradually made itself felt some seven or eight minutes before the scheduled time of the performance. (My friend Marian Keane, with whom I attended the performance, had seen the production also several nights earlier and made sure, without hinting why, that we were in our seats a good twenty minutes early. It is from her report of conversations with Swedish students and friends of hers that I have the tip about the provenance of the photographed program and the pertinent Swedish translation.) I began noticing that some people, at a glance dressed more formally than others in our audience, continued their entrance into the theater down the side aisles and then up several stage-wide risers into the set of a chateau's ballroom; while other people, similarly dressed, took their places along the front row of the auditorium, which I then recognized, from half-a-dozen rows back, was replaced by or supplemented with chairs of the same painted wood as that of the sparse furniture on the stage.

Whatever context this setting prepares for the sound of romantic poetry (I suppose continued in the Swedish folk tunes used in the play's places for songs); and beyond the running proof this establishes that in theater, unlike film, the space of actors and of audience is empirically continuous, and that in religion or ritual, where empirically continuous space is metaphysically divided, what divides it must be established by references essentially outside those boundaries; the gathering, enveloping, circling promenade invokes *The Winter's Tale*'s subject of the expanse of time (in creation and in destruction) by sending the sense of the play's time reeling backward to well before Polixenes's words that open Act I identify the present moment of representation as some "Nine changes of the wat'ry star" since his arrival in Sicilia. Bergman's treatment reveals Shakespeare's Prologue (characteristically a conceptually dense and fateful exchange between courtiers) to have been indefinitely placed in time, so we are free to imagine that it epitomizes the first days of Polixenes's visit, indeed we are asked to imagine it so, since Hermione in the opening scene appears here, shockingly, unpregnant (raising the question from whose perspective this fact would be denied). And when the lines justify having Leontes silently called away, Bergman finds a further moment in which to allow Hermione and Polixenes to be caught in a charge of mutual desire which works, in a production so clearly layering the history of Shakespeare production, both to recognize a basis for Leontes's mad suspicions (he correctly associates the satisfaction of Hermione's desire for another child with the beginning of Polixenes's visit), and at the same time, magnifying a common desire for the same woman, to heighten the homosexual plane between the two men.

The expansion of time before the emergence of the events which we know from Shakespeare's text about these characters provides, further, an inspired preparation for Bergman's meeting of a famous crux in the play's dramaturgy—the suddenness of Leontes's outburst of jealousy. In the present context it occurs after a measure of time that is neither short nor long. The expansion of time, and the unpredictable leaps of the erotic, are both functions of the texture of the promenade, which, mostly proceeding two by two, establishes in pantomime countless points of shared consciousness, new conversations, excited hopes, as may be expected at a sumptuous gathering of friends and strangers, establishing a field, while it maintains decorum, of erotic electricity. (I report another happy omen in preparing this text. A day or two after giving this description, I spent an evening reading, for not unrelated purposes, Baudelaire's impassioned account in 1861 of the uncomprehending reception, or rejection, of *Tannhäuser* and of *Lohengrin* in Paris. The electricity and propriety of Wagner's choruses is specifically noted and elaborated by Baudelaire as a point widely misperceived. I mention this also, knowing that Bergman also stages opera, to leave open, something beyond my knowledge, how far Bergman, in his production of *The Winter's Tale*, may be arriving at summations of his extraordinary range of work.)

The other comparably notorious dramaturgical crux, at the far end of the play, is the stone likeness of Hermione coming to life. Bergman treats this also with frightening lucidity and originality and it also profits

from the energies of the promenade, especially from its ritualistic binding
of this social concentration. Hermione again appears, shockingly, in the
wrong shape, or rather in the wrong inflection—not vertical but horizontal (I assume this is unprecedented)—not as a freestanding statue but perhaps as the figure carved on the length of a sarcophagus. This maintains
the level of magic explicitly in the scene but takes its place in greatly ampli-
fying the scene's dimension of religion. I don't know who first remarked
that Paulina—particularly, I imagine, in view of her declaration, "It is
required / You do awake your faith"—figures St. Paul; I add the feature of
her undertaking the role of ratifier of marriage. Luther is equally to be
characterized as a theorist of faith and of marriage, but where St. Paul had
said, "It is better to marry than to burn," Luther is open to its possible
counter, "And what if you marry and freeze?" The religious amplification
I had in mind is installed in Bergman's placing of the opening of Act V (in
which Leontes, his counsellors, and Paulina discuss his remarrying and the
issue of succession) in a chapel dominated by a painted, startlingly lifelike
statue of a virgin figure, which one vaguely and wildly imagines to be the
one destined to come to life. And in this chapel Leontes's confession of his
continued sense of the wrong he has done is manifested by his appearance
in the robes and stains of a flagellant. This vision of Bergman's raises the
question of what Paulina will call "unlawful business" as strongly as does
the possibility of her assistance through "wicked powers," an irresolution
concerning the heretical that befits a region in which, as in Uppsala, an
intact and striking Gothic cathedral houses Lutheran services.

We are here barely a step away from returning to *Smiles of a Summer
Night*, where irresolutions of the struggle between sincerity and ceremony
(power and form, Emerson says; but every romantic or preromantic will
have some such say) are portrayed as matters both causing the sound of its
depicted Marivaux-like declamations about love, as well as inspiring
Henrik's Luther text about refusing to invite the birds of temptation to
nest in your hair. As transition to the step to summer, I take into consideration another of Bergman's strokes of theater, this time from his *Winter's
Tale*'s portrayal of spring.

Autolycus bursts into the business of the sheep-shearing festival
riding, complete with helmet and goggles, a raucously motorized three-
wheeled, double head-lighted cart. From the cart he produces his lovingly itemized wares to peddle ("Gloves as sweet as damask roses, / Masks for
faces and for noses; / Bugle-bracelet, necklace amber, / . . . Pins and poking-
sticks of steel; / What maids lack from head to heel"). For a while this
seemed to me a brilliant but false distraction, designed to cover an inability or unwillingness to orchestrate each measure of pastoral mood and
method, as had been achieved throughout the winter plunge into madness,

and will prove to be achieved for the enigmatic redemption to come. Instead of the ballroom finding an opening onto a country scene, or being flown to reveal one, dark screens faintly painted with tree shapes were brought on to wall off the back half of the stage, leaving a shallow front field in which costumes supplemented with occasional garlands are what signs there are to back the words of nature's rebirth.

But then a reading occurred to me of Autolycus's anachronistic motor cart that unfolded the scene to further thought, or to faith. Since out of the cart Autolycus plucks his stuffs and gifts and jewelry and new ballads and, in brief, his endless improvisation of fantasms, and since this vehicle carries its lights and has an autonomy through its participation in a realm elsewhere (Autolycus claiming as his own the figure of the messenger—Hermes was his ancestor), I find in it a reasonable representative, or presentiment, of a motion picture projector—as if what historically called for the completion of the invention of the moving picture, with its quite unprecedented knack for transformations of the world, was the cultural conjunction of the dominance of the machine together with the problematizing of the imagination of nature. Film thus takes on, in its way, a defining task of romantic poetry. (There is also in *Smiles* a unique appearance of a machine, also bursting threateningly into a pastoral setting, Count Malcolm's raucous automobile, perhaps the first horseless carriage in his town.) Bibi Andersson, from *The Seventh Seal* (1957), *Wild Strawberries* (1957), and *The Magician* (1958)—the period of *Smiles of a Summer Night*— is cast as Paulina. She has an opposite number in Petra from *Smiles*, who is forced to listen to the Luther that Paulina virtually quotes. Petra also takes on, with another servant, the arranging and ratifying of a marriage, and also in a context of magic and unlawfulness, transgressions that in the film take the form of more or less familiar and interlocking oedipal triangles (but with two ancient woman unaccounted for, both associated with Desiree, her maid and her mother). This marriage, or elopement of young lovers, shows true marriage to require the destruction of false marriage—a reckless dash into the unknown. And the consequent transfigurations in both works are marked by the special attention given to the bride's skin, in Paulina's case to a public testing, almost taunting her onlookers, of Hermione's stone-still body, noting, for example, its still-wet lips, to determine whether it has awakened from death; in Petra's case to a private brush of Anne's cheek, to determine whether it has bequeathed its virginity.

No wonder, I say to myself again, that I found both *Smiles of a Summer Night* and *The Winter's Tale* to bear upon the Hollywood comedy of remarriage (as defined in my *Pursuits of Happiness*). Both feature an estranged pair finding one another again, and both undertake disquisitions on faithfulness; *Smiles* marks the alternation of day and fateful night, and it opens in a town and moves to a country site in which perspective is found (the pastoral of *The Winter's Tale* is a version of this place of perspective). All this is definitive of remarriage comedy. As is the question of how (mythically, or psychically) you get from town to country. Malcolm's vehicle, in its opposition to Charlotte's galloping horse, worthily contributes to this problematic.

But unlike remarriage comedy, both show the principal woman as a mother and as having a mother, or attended by a mother figure (I assume Paulina counts this way too). This difference puts a particular pressure, as it were, on the principal man of remarriage comedy: he may never quite recover from the stupefaction to which the narrative commits him, but he must express a present, responsive desire for the woman, not alone a need of her and gratitude for her. I earlier expressed my relatively early provincial thrill that the intelligence going into such a work as *Smiles of a Summer Night* can permit its manifestation in terms of high culture—beyond the references to Marivaux and Luther, there is Henrik's pertinently playing Liszt and Schumann; Malcolm's whistling Mozart's, or rather Don Giovanni's, "*La ci darem la mano*"; Malcolm's kneeling before his wife beside a chateau's pavilion, mocking the promise of faithfulness, as if challenging Mozart's authorization of the sincerity of Count Almavira's contrition at the end of *The Marriage of Figaro*. And in permitting genuine exchanges of feeling in, for example, such words as Fredrik's question, as he stares at his ludicrous image in Desiree's mirror, dressed in another man's robe and slippers, "How can a woman ever love a man?" answered by Desiree's matter-of-fact response, "A woman's point of view is seldom aesthetic," I found passages that by themselves seemed, to that persistently culturally starved teacher of philosophy that I had become, in one stroke to redeem academic discourse for human sociability.

Such things encouraged me to imagine, in response to the evident domination in the film of the field of love by women (Desiree's plan for the dinner, her mother's entrancing tale of her wine as a love potion, Charlotte's and Petra's conspiratorial presences), that Bergman was referring to Rilke's Portuguese Nun, who reveals an economy of love between men and women in lines, as I recalled them, such as "My love for you no longer depends upon your recognition of it," and of whom Rilke says that she outwore her love like a glove. I did not need such expressions or thoughts to come to my appreciation of the smartness of Hollywood remarriage comedies, but I know that I banked on them for, let's say, moral support in expressing my conviction in the depth of the American films' own, differently manifested, intelligence.

Reciprocally, the economy of love in those American comedies, measured in a pair's discovery of a mutual language and in their claiming one way or another to have known one another forever, or to have grown up together, raises the question of how strictly, or in what way, *Smiles of a Summer Night*, in participating, at some unknown distance, in the remarriage genre, authorizes the separation of different kinds of love: the American pair are not young, yet the feature of knowing one another forever is essential, if variously interpretable, to the imagination of these films, and it is shown to be all that the young lovers of *Smiles* take time to say to each other before escaping: "I loved you all the time."

The linking of the love of young lovers and the love of clowns—the first and second smiles in *Smiles*—seems to be remarriage comedy's way of heading off the third smile, the love of the depressed, the confused, the lonely, the sleepless, represented by Count Malcolm and Charlotte in *Smiles* and represented in remarriage comedy by conventional marriage, precisely the state that the women of these textures are seeking an alternative to.

In denying the status of the sacramental to the institution of marriage, Luther, and after him Kierkegaard, seem only to have increased its psychic significance, or say mystery, for modern times, attested in film's acknowledgment, hence bearability, of the privacy of the human face. It is a power that, in turn, some theory or practice of filmmaking may seek to deny. But is its attestation a genuine articulation of a trace in my encounter with film, or is it a fond memory (as Katharine Hepburn says of herself in a bleak moment before the denouement of *The Philadelphia Story*) of some prior formulation? That will depend on whether the tracks were fresh which took me from Bergman's presentation of summer and Shakespeare's of winter and spring to my reencounter with the tumbling falls of acknowledgment ("You've had a great fall, Lawyer Egerman," Desiree says to him, "but you're landing softly") in remarriage comedy.

15

Words of Welcome

W HO WOULD DOUBT, IN 1995—the hundredth anniversary of the invention of the moving picture—that this technological event, and then the event of film's emergence no more than two decades later as the newest of the great arts, imply leaps within the history of the arts, and in human consciousness generally, whose consequences we are still just beginning to measure? Nor do I doubt that film has barely begun, with certain revelatory exceptions, to inspire a degree and continuity of critical or philosophical response worthy of itself. It seems to me a cause of wonder that universities at large remain unpuzzled by this lag. Say that the art of film occurs in two main branches or states, call them fictional and factual film (setting aside animated film—allowing that not all moving pictures are animated). Since the branch of the factual or documentary film has captured no general audience for itself (it exists generally in connection, for example, with museum programs or as part of popular science education on public television), the community of those seriously interested in making and viewing documentaries tend to find one another in regions of the modern university. But the university is mostly silent about them; which is to say, it does not behave like a university with regard to them.

Such is the problem of film that even these few opening words will, and should, seem prejudicial. Some will continue to feel that film is

First published as the foreword to Charles Warren, editor, *Beyond Document* (Wesleyan University Press, 1996). The essays introduced in this chapter appear in *Beyond Document* and not in this volume.

receiving at least as much academic attention as a popular art deserves. This is perhaps no longer as common a sentiment as it was, but the false-ness or philistinism of this sentiment always masked a more troubling con-cern that, even among those who know the marvels of the heights and depths of film, not many have allowed themselves to bring film into their classrooms and writings, at least not as something more than a kind of exotic intruder. Is this out of institutional or intellectual intimidation? Or is it out of a still-unrecognized fact that film presents a standing challenge to the received distinction between popular and serious art and shows that we do not know what these words are good for? (I do not take our intel-lectual or academic position to have exactly improved by the introduction of courses on film that take it as a popular art, true as in some sense that is.) Some may object that the distinction between fictional and factual film is not a pure one, that fact and fiction spill into one another, that these concepts mark not separate genres of film but linked dimensions of all film. However correct this is, it leaves the contrast unarticulated, and leaves untouched the difference along these lines between dimensions of film and analogous dimensions of any representative art. Some will still feel that the real distinction is not between the fictional and the factual within the art of film but between film as art and film as document. But it is not easy to understand how one who has experienced even a small set of the great documentary films discussed in the essays that follow could go on with a clear mind insisting that the documentary film, whatever else it is, is not a medium of art.

It is against such a background of issues that I imagine Robert Gardner to have been led to the idea of sponsoring a lecture series, out of Harvard's Carpenter Center for the Visual Arts, under the title *Beyond Document*. The idea was to invite a set of interesting writers, not necessar-ily or even preferably writers who had previously published thoughts about film, to deliver a lecture designed to help form the basis of an accompanying symposium, and to later take its place in a volume collect-ing the texts together. Vlada Petric, curator of the Harvard Film Archive, began putting the idea into practice, and I was enlisted to sound whatever connecting notes might prove useful in the course of introducing each of the invited lecturers. The charge to the speakers was to take up any issues of the documentary film and to concentrate on any film or set of films that genuinely engaged them. Five such lectures and symposia were held over the five semesters from the spring of 1989 to the spring of 1991. The result was a satisfyingly intense and varied sequence of texts, but at its con-clusion those of us involved in turning the lectures into a volume found that some supplementation was in order—even considering the originally envisioned additions to the volume: a contribution by Robert Gardner meditating on his experience of his work as a maker of films; one by Vlada Petric epitomizing his scholarly knowledge of Dziga Vertov's significance in the history of the documentary; and two by Charles Warren, the editor of the volume, one on Dusan Makaveyev's *WR: Mysteries of the Organism*— surely among the richest films ever made on the very subject of the incorporation of fiction and fact by one another, in film and in history—and a second contribution sketching enough of a history of the documentary to allow readers new to the subject to place the names and titles invoked in the essays to follow.

Three people were approached to help further fill the frame we seemed to have in mind. Patricia Hampl and Susan Howe, superb writers who had not before written about film, were invited to think whether accepting an assignment to do so might not prompt a direction they wanted to explore. They thought, and the estimable results are here. Hampl elegantly takes on in her prose the signature moral problem of documentary film, that of exposing the lives of others, or rather causal imprints of fragments of those lives, to serve one's own story. Her discovery of her townsman Jerome Hill's remarkable work should find further friends for it. Howe's discovery of already acclaimed—and always underknown—masterpieces of Vertov and of Chris Marker incorporates the thrill of meeting artists who uncannily confirm strains of her ecstatic ways with writing, picking up the pieces in mourning. And Helene Keyssar was asked to look for a way of constructing an account of nonfiction filmmaking by women—the single instance here of an essay in which a massive case in the history of the documentary was meant to be covered. She proved able to turn an awkward, not to say impossible, task into a beautifully practical one by reflecting a sea of work through a pool of resounding examples.

The resulting book is thus meant to document a period of time, and a place, in which certain strangers and friends have undertaken to chart ways of addressing the documentary in film so as to prompt others to notice their own involvement in this hemisphere of the newest of the great arts, and therewith, with encouraged attention, in the world of film as such. To preserve the formative event of the original five public lectures, they are printed here in the order in which they were delivered, as essays 1, 3, 5, 7, and 9. The justifications for the dispersal of the seven further contributions went through a succession of phases in which thematic connections and contrasts, stylistic consonances or dissonances, large and small diameters of reference, were juxtaposed differently. In the end the decisions manifest the intuitive sense of balance and movement that was ascendant when time for further experiment was called.

It is further to preserve or recapture some sense of the five double occasions of lecture and symposium, which my introductory words of

welcome for those occasions were meant to facilitate, that they are reprinted essentially as they were given, but collected in this one prefatory space,
less most of the professional facts about each speaker that are now collected more handily at the end of the volume. I had contemplated composing
new introductions to each of the additional texts, but the misguidedness of
such an idea swiftly revealed itself: the public lectures variously honor a
commitment to immediate discussion that was not part of the mission of
the later texts. Indeed, a reason for inviting additional texts was to allow
certain dimensions of the experience of film to come to the fore that the
format of the accompanying symposia would in some cases have kept back.
I note that since Robert Gardner's contribution differs from the others, as
befits that of the only filmmaker whose words are presented here, I further
extend the modes of discourse exemplified in this volume by including
here my introductory appreciation of his film, *Forest of Bliss*, written for its
premiere in 1985.

Jay Cantor

The opposition between documentary and fictional film signifies two great
branches of the art of film, each with its own history, its own audience, and
on the whole its own directors in obedience to their own imperatives of art
and politics and culture and morality and perhaps religion; and at the same
time it signifies two dimensions or directions of all film, no more to be kept
from touching or pervading one another than are fantasy and reality, or
myth and ritual, or language and the world. The mutual attraction between
the documentary and the fictional has become a great subject of each
branch, as, say, in the narrative of Robert Gardner's filming, which inevitably
intrudes upon, and bears consequences of, the narrative of the ritual that
inspires it; the use of documentary procedures to compose what are for all
the world, or for some of it, feature (autobiographical) films in the form of
Ross McElwee's *Sherman's March* and *Time Indefinite*; or in the excavations
faced and effected in Dusan Makaveyev's *WR: Mysteries of the Organism* and
Sweet Movie, which may be articulated as a struggle against the invasion of
fact by fiction conducted by an articulation of fiction by fact.

   The films Jay Cantor asks us to think about—*Night and Fog*, *Shoah*,
and *Hotel Terminus*—have taken upon themselves, in the topic of the extermination of the Jews of Europe, some ultimate site of the suffocation of
fact and fantasy in one another. Such films create, by means of our surviving intelligence, and of the complicitous, violent, redemptive camera, a
refusal of this process of the ridding of the human voice, and the coordi-
nation of human choice.

Cantor calls his most recent fiction *Krazy Kat*, "a novel in five panels." One way to describe its work is to say that it undertakes to depict
the conditions—psychological, political, economic, cultural, historical,
critical, philosophical—under which a cartoon is possible, for the moment
this particular one, that with the simplicity of figures and the repetitiveness
of situations of the Krazy Kat cartoon strip afforded pleasure and instruction for the crazy quilt of American immigrant society in the
decades before World War II; the novel goes so far as to depict the failures
of those conditions after the invention of nuclear destruction that closes
that war.

An immediate extension or guise of this investigation, in the novel's
third or center panel, is to depict the conditions under which the pleasure
and instruction of film is possible—that is, of talking, moving pictures, or
talking, moving panels. Allow me to read a passage from that region, since
Cantor has left himself in his present essay no time for comedy. It is a
scene in which the Producer is talking to Krazy about the idea of her making a comeback in the, for her, drastically new medium of film; to get her,
as Cantor puts it, to work again. The panel takes Krazy and her companions over the novel's landscape of the concepts of character and star, of
producer and audience, of seduction and writing and death; and through
topics of dream and skepticism and of the relation of the popular and the
serious in the arts. At a certain point it gives us what is—or becomes, in
the Producer's mouth—an American explanation of the successful occupation of American literary studies (hence film studies) over the past two
decades or so by the forces of European critical theory:

> "Look, Kat," the Producer said, "anyone tells you that they know
> what they're doing in this business, they're lying. Because I want to
> tell you something: Nobody knows nothing about this business!" He
> shook his head, muttering sadly, "Crazy business. Crazy business."
> He smiled at her. "OK, Kitty. Get up off your knees. You don't have
> to beg anymore. I'll tell you how I learned the secret of picking b.o.
> smashes. Come backstage with me, darling, and I'll show you the
> wires and gizmos. You'll like that! You'll be in on the secret, see—
> American audiences love to be in the know. They love to go back-
> stage. They want to see the machinery that fools them, the back pro-
> jections, the special effects. Right? Right! They don't realize that
> showing them the machinery is the show, and while they're hypno-
> tized by the gears going round, the microchips blinking on/off, while
> you let them see the marketing surveys that reveal their kinky emo-
> tional ratchets and levers, you can really get your hands deep down

into their pockets. They get hypnotized thinking they're learning
how the rubes get hypnotized.

On the next page the panel takes a further leap:

> "Audiences are children, Krazy." He smiled sadly. He straightened
> up and put his hand to his forehead in salute: "They're geniuses," he
> concluded. "You're a woman, right, Krazy? I mean it's hard to tell.
> My research people tell me that sometimes the others call you her,
> sometimes him. That's depraved. It's decadent. It's disgusting. Very
> Now, right? I like it."

A great question of the novel is whether we can wish for happiness
in a world in which we are faced so continuously with our apparently lim-
itless taste for cynicism and destruction. It raises from an unexpected angle
Kant's frightening question whether we may act so as to deserve happiness.
Forced by Cantor's choice, in the essay he has prepared for this occasion,
to think back to three documentary interrogations of the extermination of
European Jewry, I turned from his text, for the moment adrift in a sense
of my helplessness, to further writing that his writing may at any moment
call upon (as if to keep open the circles in which we may be shocked at ourselves)—to, among others, a haunting remark in Wittgenstein's notebooks
during the last year of World War II: "The whole planet can suffer no
greater torment than a single soul." (Is this echoing Kierkegaard somewhere, or a predecessor of his?) This makes it imaginable, it seems, for
another to help bear the greatest torment, contain it. Then this is a promise that, one to one, link by link, we may bury the helplessness of our past.
Then art—for us the art arising from the fact of film—may be measured
by its readiness for such a move. It is the measure I grant to such writing
as Jay Cantor offers us.

William Rothman

At one point in William Rothman's intricate text, as he is unraveling certain of the overlapping conceptual strands in the relation between film and
literature, and between a classical fiction film and a screenplay for that
film, and between imagining or envisioning a film and interpreting or
transcribing a film, he turns aside and says: "I find myself feeling homesick
for the field of philosophy." Not everyone is in a position to feel and say
quite that, but I trust everyone who cares for film knows an analogous
longing and perhaps a counterpart metaphysical surprise verging on fear

at an instant when the sheer *fact* of film seems remarkable—that it is at once the most obvious and the most mysterious of the arts, and that its advent into human culture raises afresh every question philosophy has ever raised about the arts, from the endless question about what art is, and what its origin and history and its makers and its audiences are; to whether the arts are a unity, and what the gains and losses are of their interactions; to the roles of technology and representation in the various arts, and their various relations to reality and dream and illusion and nature and politics; to the distinction between the high and the low in human culture.

The statement announcing the *Beyond Document* lecture series orients itself toward the denial—and with an understandable impatience that the denial remains necessary—that the nonfictional camera is a simple instrument of recording; and it enters a call for further consideration of what that camera's instrumentality or agency is, what it is that the documentary inflection creates a medium for. William Rothman's extraordinary first book on film—*Hitchcock: The Murderous Gaze* (1982)—may be taken as a study of the camera's agency, its tracking and magnification of the lucidities and obscurities, and the subtleties and banalities, of human agency, hence of human passion. His essay here takes it as given that the cameras of nonfictional and fictional film are each inextricable from human activity and passivity. He takes it as a fact of our experience that the best of the films called documentaries contain the intelligence (hence the power of questioning intelligence), and the poetry and drama (hence the heart for questioning poetry and drama), that one expects of the best of the films called features. Starting from this commonality, Rothman in effect asks on what grounds, if any, these different regions of film are interestingly different.

He finds ground between specific territories within these regions of the world of film—between a territory of fictional film he calls the classical system and a territory of nonfictional film he (with reservations) persists in calling cinema verité—sufficiently common to allow an orderly consideration of differences. One of the ways Rothman marks a commonness between these specified regions is to say that in both of them the photographic grounding assures that the world has made its impression. The invitation is unmistakable, since philosophy has been invoked, to think of this grounding in terms of the classical Empiricists' picture, as in Locke and Hume, of impressions as the basis of human understanding, scoring the tabula rasa of the mind. In Rothman's view impressions enter the mind's camera obscura, which is evidently the last place to take impressions for granted, since the mind will have its designs upon them. The common ground of the world's impression stands out against the yet different region of the world of film called animation, where instead of impressions of the world—say of its oscillation between the theatrical and the private—we are presented with drafts of the world's animism, perhaps of its circulation or metamorphosis out of and into the human organism, made explicit, within the precincts of the Carpenter Center, in the work of Suzan Pitt.

In Rothman's cover letter accompanying the distribution of his paper to participants in the symposia, he notes that his text turned out to be more abstract than he had expected. I am for my part happy about this surprise. He and I have long shared the sense that something about film makes the fact of its making, of the choices it represents, peculiarly invisible to its audience; and I have experienced over many years Rothman's combating of this invisibility in the particular way he takes his classes through the shot-by-shot events of a sequence of film—a practice whose range is reflected in his collection of essays entitled *The "I" of the Camera.* But just because of my admiration for his pedagogy, I greedily wanted him also to devote that kind of attention to theorizing his practice. And because I knew his talent for providing the pleasures of abstract thought, as well as for respecting those of concrete objects, I would recurrently try to encourage in him a homesickness for philosophy.

Perhaps I had been thinking about Novalis's remark that philosophy is essentially homesickness (sick of it, sick for it). I know I had been thinking about what film is.

Eliot Weinberger

Eliot Weinberger reports that after attending the most recent Margaret Mead Film Festival, he found himself generally in agreement with "nearly all ethnographic filmmakers [who], in interviews, have remarked that the genre of ethnographic film is still in its infancy." Only generally in agreement, however, since he emphatically recognizes, as in his passages that read moments of Robert Gardner's *Deep Hearts* and *Forest of Bliss,* that "there are certain films [categorizable as ethnographic, or at any rate, ethnopoetic] which contradict this notion." It follows that it is not exactly ethnographic film as a genre that remains in an undeveloped state, but a general run of ethnographic filmmakers, as if their relation to the camera remains what it is generally for tourists—amateurish, obvious, repetitive, imitative.

Allowing that this is true, what could account for it? We might ask; If the ethnographic film remains generally in its infancy, in what state does the writing about ethnographic film find itself? What is the state of the genre's critical community? It is my impression that Eliot Weinberger writes—as in certain ways others in this book write—out of a sense of an absence of such a critical community or communities. Some such sense is

indeed one of the motivations in establishing this whole series of contributions, to create a momentum of discussion of nonfictional film that gets
beyond undeveloped, repetitive quarrels over what the concept of the documentary implies—quarrels over whether it obviously asserts an epistemo-
logical claim to have found the royal road to cultural reality, or whether
any such claim instantly betrays its ignorance in the face of the mechanism
of the camera, with its innocence or decadence in the face of the unrolling
of politics.

But again—supposing this sense of absence of a critical community
is accurate—what would account for the implied ignorance and innocence,
and for the reactive arrogance that must claim to reveal it? Weinberger
explores an answer in a quarrel between science and art, epitomized
among other places in what he calls a "scary comment" that he quotes
from Timothy Asch: "The camera can be to the anthropologist what the
telescope is to the astronomer or what the microscope is to the biologist."
Weinberger notes the apparently false assumption here that "the matter
on the other side of the ethnographic lens is as imperturbable as galaxies
or amoebas." But couldn't one go on to develop some theory about the
perturbations the camera causes? It takes considerable theory, after all, to
understand what the telescope or microscope tells us. Is it Weinberger's
point that Asch is not aware, or denies, that this place of theory is required
also in anthropological understanding? Another apparent assumption that
may be taken in Asch's comment—not a necessary one, but easily
recruitable in advancing the claims of science over those of art—is that the
training and experience that goes into making a film is closely analogous
to the training for making and reading microscopic slides or telescopic
photographs. That all are practices related to theory, and that their results
may all be beautiful and useful, seems obvious enough. But it should be no
less obvious that variations in the quality of the evidence that microscopes
or telescopes provide and discrepancies in the interpretation of this evidence are communally resolvable (except in a stage of scientific crisis),
whereas the quality and interpretation of a film—as with any artifact showing the work art does—is inherently, permanently contestable (which is
perhaps to say that the arts are always in a state of crisis). From which it
does not follow (a point Weinberger emphasizes) that the evidence provided by film regarded ethnographically is less rich or necessarily less objective than that provided by more elaborate scientific instrumentation. What
follows is that there is no standing set of procedures—no unargumentative
paradigm—to help articulate the camera's ethnographic significance.
Which in turn is to say: a practice of criticism is required.

Weinberger begins by telling of a peculiar tribe of people he calls
Ethnographic Filmmakers. Among many other fascinating characteristics

Weinberger has discovered, they worship a deity known as Reality, whose chief enemy is Art. It is irresistible to summarize what I have said in giving an initial response to Weinberger's text by adding to Weinberger's myth: these filmmakers have an unhealthy relation with a tribe called Critics, with whom they speak solely in a language of conflict, called Philosophy, which no one knows very well but no one knows so much less well than everyone else that arguments cannot begin. They merely cannot end. And these filmmakers tend to spend most of their days in corners of places called Universities, which do not really seem to want them, any more than they really want philosophy past a certain point. So that instead of trying to turn their intimate but unfruitful exchanges to better use, filmmakers and philosophers may each exert themselves to prove that they belong precisely in the University, and the direct route to such conviction is to appear as part of or as adjunct to Science.

Maureen Howard

When Robert Gardner and Vlada Petric first asked me to introduce the progress of lecturers in the envisioned *Beyond Document* series, I recognized a pair of guiding ideas in their initial description of the series: there was, first, the plain wish to call attention to the massive fact, and comparatively neglected dimension, culturally and theoretically, of the documentary in the world of film; and a wish, second, to invite writers from outside the dominance of academic film studies, whose ways of addressing issues of film as document—epistemological and political and artistic issues— could not be confined to the conventions and discourses of the professional study of film. Every academic field has, and needs, such conventions— it is what establishes the field as (in the European, not quite American sense) "scientific," fit for orderly presentation in a university. But every healthy field also has, and needs, a sense of itself as intelligibly related to some social good not defined by its professional necessities.

Maureen Howard has picked for her subject the treacherous and popular form—treacherous emotionally as well as intellectually—called the docudrama, in which fact is more or less knowingly fictionalized and fiction more or less unknowingly treated as ponderous fact. Among writers and readers there is common agreement that—in the words of one of our celebrated short-story writers—"Maureen Howard belongs in any list of the best American novelists practicing today." The statements on the cover of her fifth novel, entitled *Expensive Habits*, stress its intelligence, elegance, and complexity. Having just finished reading that work I can testify to the clear presence throughout it of those admirable qualities; but they do not capture the particular sense, reading it, of something harrowing the moments we are shown—not alone because the events depicted are, openly and hiddenly, hard to bear, in their violence and their pathos, but because the text's responsiveness to the events it depicts is as relentless as the events themselves are, so that you sometimes feel, remembering it, as you do with writing at its best, frightened by your ignorance of the significance of your everyday hours, that their richness and their deadliness are passing unnoticed before and behind you. This is something the documentary is meant to document.

Science and art can both be said to check experience, habitually to overthrow it. Science accomplishes this by beginning from, and maintaining, its perspectives of lucidity, seeing where to discount irrelevance; art accomplishes it, taking itself unawares, continuously, beginning with its opacities, not placed to discount irrelevance, searching for perspective.

In *Expensive Habits*, Howard further anticipates our subject of the documentary in obvious and unobvious matters of its content. Its principal character is a novelist who also writes for movies, and it contains a couple of scenes with an old lover of hers, a movie producer and his new young wife, a heavy-metal singer, making bravura fun of the pair's preparations for filming an authentic docudrama about Nazis. How Howard's novel takes up the cost of its own fun is essential to its business—relating in plot and prose the antics of this pair who are contending for the fables and images of our public lives, to the psychic dangers of clapping individual lives into the space of a serious book, such as the one happening before us.

Howard's complex awareness is always at work in the tactfully straightforward manner of the essay she has prepared for us. In *Expensive Habits*, its central woman implicitly relates her writing, hence herself, to the profession of her first husband, a surgeon, as well as to astronomy, the intellectual passion of her adolescent son: writing as opening the heart and as scanning the heavens. In her essay on docudrama, Howard identifies herself with two further characters from that novel: in her superstitious invoking of Christ she invokes the superstitions with which she endows the writer's Central American housekeeper, fatefully connected with the docudrama under construction in that book—mockudrama she calls it; again, in naming herself, in her essay, "a back number," she identifies herself for the moment with the writer's present husband in *Expensive Habits*, to whom that writer assigns the epithet "former," meaning particularly an aristocratically derived former radical of the 1960s, an emissary to the present, sent from no one.

In her essay she invokes the grief, along with the rage, out of which her novel is written, almost always within earshot of a sociable tone (as if not to make the all-but-unbearable world more irrelevantly unbearable); she even repeats the novel's occasional trick of casting a strategic sentence, in whole or in part, in iambic pentameter. A full sentence about her father reads: "We fell apart, no setting that aside." The idea is not to write poetry. It serves, rather, to demonstrate the truth of Nietzsche's remark that writing good prose is a constant battle against writing poetry—call this a battle against the (always dangerous, sometimes essential) unwillingness to make yourself sociable, here and now, to friends and strangers.

To deal with the modern interpenetration of fact and fiction, of document and drama—or, as Nietzsche more or less puts it in *The Use and Abuse of History*, the twisting of one's culture with the history of one's culture—is not the work of a moment or of a known theory (since part of the struggle is precisely against the expensive habit of substituting theory for experience); it is rather the long task of modern life, in which grief and rage, or love and hate, are to distinguish themselves as best they can from one another, and both from the intolerance of irony that rests itself in cynicism.

Phillip Lopate

Philosophy has announced for two and a half millennia that the mind, or a language, or any image, does not merely, or not at all, mirror what we may call reality, or may call the world, or nature; yet in each generation there are individuals, even crowds, who discover some idea of language's prejudices with a sense that they alone realize the idea's validity or its power, as if each is discovering philosophy itself. I think there is good reason why this banal discovery—or discovery of banality—should take this enthusiastic form: philosophy exists only in discovering for oneself the power of such a thought.

Phillip Lopate is a helpful voice to have join our explorations beyond the document. One of his recent books, *Against Joie de Vivre* (1989), is a collection of what Lopate calls personal essays. In one of these essays, with the title "What Happened to the Personal Essay?", he characterizes "informal, personal essays [as tending] to seize on the parade and minutiae of daily life: vanities, fashions, oddballs, seasonal rituals, love and disappointment, the pleasure of solitude, reading, going to plays, walking in the street"—the banalities of life, as most of life is, one may think. And yet Lopate, invoking Montaigne, declares that "in an essay, the track of a person's thoughts struggling to achieve some understanding of a problem is the plot." The strength to come to an understanding of one's banal plots and repetitive tricks (call them one's melodrama) is not banal; but neither need it be as rare as it seems to be. To put this strength into our hands is a precious gift of the essayist, as that figure is described in Lopate's essay; it is the gift not to fear the finality of the banal, a perspective philosophy endlessly fails, for all its perspectives, to possess for itself, something it endlessly seeks and almost always disparages.

Phillip Lopate invokes another, perhaps companion, fear dogging these still early years of academic film study: the fear, and fact, of ignorance—the fact not only that no one knows everything required to know what film is and has been, but that no one knows the dimensions of our ignorance. Suppose we may assume a certain working knowledge, if sketchy, of the chronologies of film in two or three cultures. Which is more important for our purposes in the neighborhood of film studies: the philosophy or the history of art, or of theater, or of art criticism; the sociology of institutions or the economics of entrepreneurship; or the history or philosophy of technology or of perception and cognition? Lopate, as a writer and a teacher of writing, and with the contrariness he values in the essayist, in the long, disturbing essay that ends *Against Joie de Vivre*, "Suicide of a Teacher," asks: "What else was being a teacher but trying to respond as humanly as possible to problems that would not wait for an expert?"

He also (despite, or as a way of qualifying, his professional writing about film and his official participation in such institutions as the New York Film Festival) identifies himself as a film buff, in the complex and evocative essay "Anticipation of *La Notte:* The 'Heroic' Age of Moviegoing." A certain sense of paradox arises in putting this direct claim of a buff's enthusiasm together with the book's title that questions our grounds for joyfulness. But this sense of paradox conveys a spiritual or human crisis that runs through the book: its title essay epitomizes the crisis by invoking a great passage from a text of Simone Weil's that ends: "So much for joie de vivre. . . . I don't really know what I'm waiting for. But I think it hypocritical to pretend satisfaction while I am still hungry." This testing of the claim of pleasure, or enthusiasm, is painfully pertinent at this moment of film studies, or generally in what mostly administrators still call the humanities—when the ancient question, cyclically repressed, of the nature of the pleasure of works of art, or of enthusiasm in works of the mind, is newly under investigation or suspicion. Surely it calls for a renewed investigation of the equally ancient question of the nature—of the dangers, and of the necessities, you may say of the politics—of pleasure as such.

In his essay here Phillip Lopate specifies his hunger in the special case of film—despite, as it were, the joys he evidently also encounters there. He calls for more or better or clearer work in a genre of film his essay strives to define, and that several times he suggests may not quite even—or yet—exist. I predict that many of you will search your memories for instances of film that ought to satisfy his hunger; and I expect he means you to—if you first recognize the hunger in yourself.

Robert Gardner

Forest of Bliss is the latest in Robert Gardner's body of films—joining among others *Dead Birds* and *Rivers of Sand*—which is increasingly recognized as among the most significant accomplishments in the world community of nonfiction filmmaking, call it anthropological or documentary filmmaking. But these titles, or any others that seek to limit in advance the achievement of work such as Gardner's, will be overcome by the very power, the poetry, of that achievement. As creative work may in any genre or form of art, *Forest of Bliss* acts to burst its form, as if its maker is challenging its origins, taking his work into its own exploration of the conditions of art and of life that make it possible, as if becoming answerable for, and to, the medium of film itself. It is to Gardner's engagement of this answerability—the questioning of the limits of his art—that I call your attention.

You do not need words of mine to help you recognize that you are confronted by images of extreme beauty in *Forest of Bliss*; that in it some ritual of the dead, hence of the living, is being approached (never as a whole, as if one might be finished with it); that the approach is at every turn forwarded and threatened by the commercial traffic in ritual, where flies tramp across warm coins; and that the absence of Western words among the film's eloquent tracks of sound is one sign of the film's respect for difference, for otherness, respect both for the other's mystery and for its own power to communicate what it wishes known. It is a version of that respect for his or her subject or material that every true artist manifests. Genuine filmmakers, documentary or nondocumentary, will, for example, take it as part of their artistic mission to locate and account for their presence at lives and deaths, at tears and cries and laughter not their own. The absence of voiced narration in *Forest of Bliss* accepts this issue as a standing one—the issue of intrusion or of false domination—an issue accepted as well by the explicit virtual absence of awareness on the part of the living subjects of the film that they are under surveillance by a camera.

How, then, does *Forest of Bliss* achieve its account of itself, its declaration of its subjects' independence of its camera's capture, its answerability to the condition of film by its questioning of its own existence? The answer I ask you to consider as you view this film is that it allows its making, its presence to its world, not just here and there to be noticed by that world, not just there and here to comment on our uncanny sense of familiarity with and of difference from that world, but to let that world as a whole interrogate every moment of the film's presence, of its life, hence of our own viewing of it—as if the cremation ritual in the holy city of Benares asks us to account for the rituals of our lives that so essentially absorb, among other things, cameras—that is, our lives that feed on our views of the lives of others, as if the reality of our own lives is no longer authorizable by themselves. The rhetorical texture of the film, that moment to moment reflects our viewing as our being viewed—our being discovered by what we discover—is woven by the sequence of identifications to which Gardner's camera declares or exposes itself.

You will see, for example, breathtaking shots of wild dogs; of enchanted sails; of a river in which things and steps and days begin and end; of children's tiny red kites drawing in a red sky; of structures that are and are not ladders; of marching handprints and histories of marigolds; of clumps of logs balanced for honest sale and then balanced on a human back for trotting to their part in the endless transmission of fire. And in each case an allegory is proposed of this camera's (perhaps not just this one's) life—of what it hungers for and would be eaten by, of its roving and floating and flowing and standing, and its aspiration to ascend to heaven while it is bound to the hands of a human child, of its readiness to adorn the world that lends itself to its traffic, of its labors of measuring and carrying that at every moment threaten to overtake the quest of transcendence. Perhaps above all one will consider the camera's self-exposure in subjecting itself to the fact and the idea of a ritual of cremation, of a ritual figured as transfiguration itself: film is the medium of transfiguration— as painting is the medium of representation, or its denial; as theater is the medium of impersonation, or its denial; as music is the medium of transformation, or its denial—blessed or cursed with the fate, in the same gestures, to destroy and recreate everything it touches. So that I see *Forest of Bliss* as staking itself on its strength to participate in the fact and the idea of life and death as cycles of metamorphosis, hence in the human effort to redeem the violence of death and the violence by which life sustains itself—that they may not be stupid and inconsequential reparations, but fruitful, faithful, and memorable, as in the perpetuations of ritual, and as in the transfiguring provocations of such a film as this one.

16

Groundhog Day

From: Stanley Cavell
Sent: Thursday, September 09, 1999 7:31 PM
Subject: *Groundhog Day*

Dear Bill,

Sometime in the late summer of 1996 an editor of the *New York Times Magazine* wrote to me concerning a feature they wanted to run as part of the celebration of the one hundredth anniversary of that periodical. They were asking people, as what they called experts in various fields, to respond to the relevant version of the following assignment: pick a work (in my case a film made since 1971) that will still be discussed, viewed, and cherished one hundred years from now, and write fifty words about it. They gave, as I recall, if one wished to participate, two or three days in which to respond.

I could not offhand find the mood in which such a task seemed to promise the right sort of amusement or instruction, but I brought it up with the family that night at dinner. We confined ourselves to American films, to keep the assignment from being sunk in judiciousness, and fished around for an intelligent, moving film, good enough to be worth thinking about but unobtrusive and enjoyable enough to kid a seriously unanswerable question;

This chapter reprints an e-mail sent to William Rothman containing a fifty-word piece written for the one hundredth anniversary of *The New York Times Magazine*, September 29, 1996.

221

moreover, and, critically important, one about which I could find fifty words I wanted to say about it. *Groundhog Day* (1993) came up later that evening when I saw that the meaning of the recurring day invited something from Emerson, and an implication, accordingly, toward Nietzsche's eternal recurrence, which those who care about such things would catch.

My words, printed in the *Times Magazine* for September 29, 1996, were these:

> A small film that lives off its wits and tells a deeply wonderful story of love. It creates a version of the question I ask here—of what will endure. Its version is to ask how, surrounded by conventions we do not exactly believe in, we sometimes find it in ourselves to enter into what Emerson thought of as a new day.

My choice of film (I don't know about the effect of the words) has had two sorts of response.

One sort is represented in the letter to the editor printed in the October 20, 1996 number of the *Magazine*, in full as follows: "It is unfortunate that some of the experts invited to speculate on the late-twentieth-century canon chose to be flippant or cynical and suggest works that are banal, trivial or inconsequential, at best. 'Cats'? 'Ground-Hog Day'? Come on."

The other sort of response is more rewarding, but evidently doesn't move people to make it public. I am sure that no other four dozen words of mine has earned me a greater number of appreciative responses. One was from a young man who is starting a fan club around the film, and I suppose, related films, whatever these will be, and asked me to join. Another, sure enough, came from a philosopher who told me he was inspired by my choice to write his first paper ever to deal with a film. Another exemplifies not so much the content of the episode as the power of the *New York Times*. It was reported to me by a friend passing through town with whom I was to have lunch, that as he was leaving his preceding appointment, saying he must leave because he was going to meet Stanley Cavell at noon, one of those present asked: "Isn't he the one who likes *Groundhog Day*?" So my choice has affected my identity. And since that happened just this past summer, some three years after the event, my choice has proven itself prophetic: memory of the film, and discussion about it, gives every sign of making it into the next century.

Yours,

Stanley

17

Something Out of the Ordinary

IT HAPPENS THAT I LIVED FOR the first seven years of my life in a house placed three or four miles from the site of this hotel, in a neighborhood intermittently still recognizable from my childhood images of Atlanta. I realized, in choosing the material to present in response to the honor of delivering this year's presidential address to our division of the American Philosophical Association, that I was fantasizing it as representing some fragment of a map by which to figure how that distance and direction into the city and to this room can have been traveled. I want such a map, since I keep discovering that I have to go back to collect belongings that others may not have come to care for as I have.

A conjunction of quotations, from texts that were I think among the earliest I recognized as belonging to some body of work called philosophy, may give an idea of what it is I want to talk about today, in important part to reminisce about. The first is from John Dewey's *Construction and Criticism*, dating from 1929:

> As Emerson says in his essay on "Self-Reliance": "A man should learn to detect and watch that gleam of light which flashes across his mind from within, . . . else to-morrow a stranger will say with masterly good sense precisely what we have thought and felt all the time, and we shall be forced to take with shame our own opinion from another." . . . Language does not help us at this point; rather the

Presidential Address delivered before the Ninety-Third Annual Eastern Division Meeting of the American Philosophical Association in Atlanta, Georgia, December 29, 1996.

habits of our vocabulary betray us. . . . To know what the words mean we have to forget the words and become aware of the occasions when some idea truly our own is stirring within us and striving to come to birth.

No wonder—to do a little initial ax grinding—it is commonly said, in the recent valuable rediscoveries or reconstructions of Dewey's achievements, that pragmatism is an intimate continuation of Emersonianism. And no wonder I keep finding that what is called pragmatism so often strikes me as an intimate negation of Emersonianism. For while Dewey takes up the Emersonian theme of our suffocation by conformity and the accretion of unexamined habit, Dewey discards the power that Emerson precisely directs against fixated form, the power of turning our words against our words, to make them ours (ours again, we might say, as if things had ever been otherwise). How Emerson's manner in what he calls his essays accomplishes this task, and why, in the face of my knowledge of how grating his manner can be to contemporary philosophical sensibilities, I take it to be a mode of thinking lost without taking it up as philosophy, has been an insistent theme of mine for a decade and a half now.

The quotation I conjoin with that from Dewey is from Nietzsche's *Birth of Tragedy*, published about sixty years earlier, when Dewey was thirteen years old and Nietzsche roughly twice thirteen. Nietzsche wrote then:

Art has never been so much talked about [by critics, journalists, in schools, in society] and so little esteemed. . . . On the other hand, many a being more nobly and delicately endowed by nature, though he may have gradually become a critical barbarian in the manner described, might have something to say about the unexpected as well as totally unintelligible effect that a successful performance of *Lohengrin*, for example, has on him—except that perhaps there was no helpful interpreting hand to guide him; so the incomprehensibly different and altogether incomparable sensation that thrilled him remained isolated and, like a mysterious star, became extinct after a short period of brilliance. But it was then that he had an inkling of what an aesthetic listener is. (Chapter 22, closing)

Nietzsche's portrait of the unexpected and vanishing existence of the aesthetic listener recalls me to an early essay in the collection that makes up my first book, *Must We Mean What We Say?*—so much of which is engaged by my need to justify an interest in what J. L. Austin and the later Wittgenstein name the ordinary—an essay called "Aesthetic Problems of Modern Philosophy," in which I propose that Kant's characterization of the aesthetic judgment models the relevant philosophical claim to voice what we should ordinarily say when, and what we should mean in saying it. The moral is that while general agreement with these claims can be "imputed" or "demanded" by philosophers, they cannot, as in the case of more straightforward empirical judgments, "postulate" this agreement (using Kant's terms).

I was not able then to press this intuitive connection very far, for example to surmise why there should be this connection between the arrogation of the right to speak for others about the language we share *and* about works of art we cannot bear not to share. I gestured at comparing the risk of aesthetic isolation with that of moral or political isolation, but what I could not get at, I think now, was the feature of the aesthetic claim, as suggested by Kant's description, as a kind of compulsion to share a pleasure, hence as tinged with an anxiety that the claim stands to be rebuked. It is a condition of, or threat to, that relation to things called aesthetic, that something I know and cannot make intelligible stands to be lost to me.

Experience lost or missed is what the conjunction of my opening quotations speak about (Dewey's of missing an original idea striving to get formed; Nietzsche's of losing the world opened in art, instanced in opera), and they are parts of what is for each writer a fundamental criticism of his present culture. This fact or fantasy of experience passing me by is also explicitly a way in which I have wished to word my interest in Austin and in the later Wittgenstein, especially I think when their procedures present themselves as *returning* us to the ordinary, a place we have never been. It seems that the more I might find their instances trivial, the more puzzled I could become that I had not realized, or could not retain the realization of, their discoveries—such as, in Wittgenstein, what it is we go on in calling something a chair, or saying that someone is expecting someone, or is walking, or why I sometimes imagine a difficulty over pointing to the color of an object (as opposed to pointing to the object). To know how to tell such things, it seems, is just to know how to speak. My oblivion of them came to strike me, intermittently, not exactly as revealing my life to be unexamined, but as missed by me, lost on me.

Experience missed, in certain of the forms philosophy has interested itself in this condition, is a theme developing itself through various of my intellectual turns in recent years, ones I would be most unhappy to exclude from this occasion, ones that have exacted their costs to justify as part of a prose that claims an inheritance of philosophy; yet ones that have afforded me rare pleasure and instruction and companionship—I mean for instance my interests in Shakespeare and in Emerson and Thoreau and in film and, most recently in an extended way, in opera.

To epitomize the surprising extensions of the theme, and as an experiment highlighting the difficulties in the way of showing and sharing the pleasures in its discoveries, I am going, toward the end of my remarks, to screen a brief film sequence, chosen also so as to allow some chance, on a very small scale, of showing a difference in my approach to aesthetic matters from that of most, of course not all, work in aesthetics in the Anglo-American ways of philosophy, or for that matter in the practice of Kant (though not from passages to be found in Hegel and in Nietzsche and, for better or worse, in Heidegger), I mean the sort of emphasis I place on the criticism, or reading, of individual works of art. I think of this emphasis as letting a work of art have a voice in what philosophy says about it, and I regard that attention as a way of testing whether the time is past in which taking seriously the philosophical bearing of a particular work of art can be a measure of the seriousness of philosophy.

The fragment of film I have chosen readily allows itself to be dismissed as inconsequential; but to my mind it proves to be a memorable enactment of the ordinary as what is missable. It is a routine from a Hollywood musical comedy of the early 1950s, consisting essentially of a man walking along a train platform, singing a not evidently demanding song to himself. The man, it happens, is Fred Astaire, by now all but incontestably recognized throughout the world as one of the greatest American dancers of the twentieth century. He is also incontestably not, or not exactly, much of a singer, so the fragment contains an open invitation to judge the routine and its apparently uneventful cinematic presentation, to be trivial. It is a task—one I welcome—to try to make such a conclusion a matter of judgment rather than one simply of taste; as it were to challenge taste.

To give this task a decent chance of success I need to do a bit more philosophical table setting, and then go on to give some details of my interest in the voice in opera along with a related interest in Austin's sense of the powers of speech.

I have rather assumed, more or less without argument, since that early paper of mine cited earlier, that Kant's location of the aesthetic judgment, as claiming to record the presence of pleasure without a concept, makes room for a particular form of criticism, one that supplies the concepts that, after the fact of pleasure, articulate the grounds of that experience in particular objects. The implication of such criticism is that its object has yet to have its due effect, that something there, fully opened to the senses, has despite that been missed. I shall claim that while it is not a fact that the Astaire routine is trivial, the sequence can be seen to be about triviality; and to show that will require showing how its pleasure derives from its location of formal conditions of its art.

A further variation in the relation of the ordinary to what may be seen as the aesthetic is taken up in a later essay in *Must We Mean What We Say?* which goes back to my having responded to Wittgenstein's *Investigations* as written, however else, in recurrent response to skepticism but not as a refutation of it; rather on the contrary, as a task to discover the causes of philosophy's disparagement of, or its disappointment with, the ordinary, something I have called the truth of skepticism. In that essay, "Knowing and Acknowledging," the ordinary is discovered not as what is perceptually missable but as what is intellectually dismissable, not what may be but what must be set aside if philosophy's aspirations to knowledge are to be satisfied. There I articulate my sense of what happens to philosophy's aspirations by saying that skepticism is not the discovery of an incapacity in human knowing but of an insufficiency in acknowledging what in my world I think of as beyond me, or my senses; so that when I found, in a following essay on *King Lear*, that Shakespearean tragedy enacts the failure to acknowledge an other, hence forms a lethal set of attempts to deny the existence of an other as essential to one's own, I came to wonder whether Shakespeare's tragedies can be understood as studies of (what philosophy identifies as) skepticism.

If in being drawn to the skeptical surmise Descartes reaches a point of astonishment that opens him to a fear of madness, and the young Hume a point that presents itself to him as his suffering an incurable malady from the knowledge of which he seeks to protect his (nonphilosophical) acquaintances, a point that to Kant represents a scandal to philosophy's quest for reason, then can the great literature of the West not have responded to whatever in history has caused this convulsion in the conditions of human existence? Or were the philosophers not to have been taken quite seriously in their airs of melodramatic crisis? Yet might it not well haunt us, as philosophers, that in *King Lear* doubt as to a loving daughter's expressions of love, or in *Othello* doubt cast as jealousy and terror of a wife's satisfaction, or in *Macbeth* doubt manifested as a question about the stability of a wife's humanity (in connection with witches), leads to a man's repudiation or annihilation of the world that is linked with a loss of the power of or the conviction in speech?

Or, again, should we consider rather that philosophy has indeed properly drawn the moral of tragedy, namely that since we all already know that skepticism is some species of intellectual tragedy, or folly, we are advised that the rational response to it is not to revel in it or cultivate its allure, but to seek to avoid it. To take a celebrated instance, when Quine implicitly blocks skepticism out of the court of epistemology—that is, naturalized epistemology—by (as in *Pursuit of Truth*) "repudiating the Cartesian dream" and enrolling philosophy "as a chapter of the science of an antecedently acknowledged world," he cites as a normative point of philosophy's self-inclusion in science that it "[warns] us against telepaths and soothsayers" (p. 19). I discover that the year that book of Quine's was published I was giving a lecture about *Macbeth* in which I articulate the terror Macbeth seeks refuge from as an interaction of telepathy and soothsaying. I spell them differently, namely as mind reading and prophecy. Take them as terms of criticism naming enemies of reason, and link them with the list of philosophy's irrational competitors identified in Kant's *Religion within the Limits of Reason Alone*, which he names fanaticism, superstition, delusion, and sorcery. This budget of favorite enemies of the Enlightenment also constitutes a fair set of dimensions of the events in *Macbeth*, and indeed, in different economies, of those in the other great tragedies of Shakespeare. So I have also in effect suggested that Shakespeare's tragedies are themselves something like warnings against the craving for telepathy and soothsaying, and I do not know that they and their kin have been less effective in their warnings than scientific philosophy has in its, nor that to choose one against the other is safe.

In Quine's construal of philosophy's ambitions for empirical knowledge—what he calls the construction of "a unified system of the world"—the only, but indispensable, role of experience is to provide for such a system its "checkpoints in sensory prediction." It is, I suppose, in response to such an idea that, for example, William James and John Dewey complain of other empiricisms that they have a poor view of experience. The richer experience Dewey champions he tends to call aesthetic; James most famously documents varieties of the religious. Even if you disagree with Quine's view of epistemology you can enjoy the demonstration of the power, even the beauty, of science in showing how far a little experience can go. Whereas you have to agree with James and Dewey farther than I do—and I mean to grant all honor to their efforts to save experience from its stifling by unresponsive institutions—in order not to feel sometimes that they demonstrate how a mass of experience can go philosophically almost nowhere (for Dewey into a hundred abstract rejections of some patently unintelligent thesis together with its obviously undesirable antithesis; for James into a mere surmise of transcendence).

May we think as follows? If philosophy of science can be taken to be what philosophy is, that is because philosophy is, and is content to be, recognizable, or practicable, as (a chapter of) science; whereas were philosophy of art to make of itself a chapter of one or more of the arts, it would no longer be recognizable as philosophy. Without challenging this now, what I am proposing is something rather else, following what I construe Kant's examples of the transgressions of reason, in their intersection with

Shakespearean drama, to suggest (perhaps it is Hegel's suggestion) that the arts, beginning with tragedy (or, in Hegel's aesthetics, ending with tragedy), may variously be seen, or claimed, as chapters of the history, or development, of philosophy, hence perhaps of certain of its present manifestations. I am going in a little while to extend the thought to a polar relation of tragedy, to a Hollywood musical. It is a suggestion based on two contentions that I have argued for in various contexts over the years. First, that in the modern period of the arts—marked variously by splits in the audience (and conception) of art between the academic and the advanced—the great arts together with their criticism increasingly take on the self-reflective condition of philosophy (teaching us, let us say, to see that *King Lear* is about theater as catharsis, that *Macbeth* is about theater as apparition, *Othello* about the treacherous theater of ocular proofs, *Hamlet* about what surpasses theatrical show). The second contention is that the medium of film is such that—from the time of its first masterpieces in the second decade of its technological establishment—it could take on the seriousness of the modern without splitting its audience between high and low or between advanced and philistine.

To prepare more specifically for proposing an Astaire routine as a checkpoint, or touchstone, of experience, I want to summarize the way it figured in the introduction to a course on the aesthetics of film and opera I gave for the first time two years ago. The idea of the course is that words and actions suffer transfiguration in opera (the art which replaces speaking by singing) that bears comparison with their transformation on film (the art which replaces living human beings by photographic shadows of themselves). So my summary must begin to specify in which philosophical formation film and opera form chapters that measure some particular conditions of these arts, or call them media.

Here I should simply confess that my interest in opera is tied to a conviction that matches yet one further way I have formulated an interest in the work of Austin and the later Wittgenstein. Their sense of returning words from their metaphysical to their everyday use is driven by a sense of a human dissatisfaction with words (not as it were solely a philosophical dissatisfaction) in which an effort to transcend or to purify speech ends by depriving the human speaker of a voice in what becomes his (or, differently, her) fantasy of knowledge, a characterization I have given of what happens in skepticism. In Wittgenstein's case of a man striking himself on the breast and insisting "Only I can have THIS sensation!", we are to witness a speaker abandoned by his words, or abandoned to mere words. Now opera is the Western institution in which—beginning in the same decade as the composition of the great tragedies of Shakespeare—the human voice is given its fullest acknowledgment, generally by showing that its highest forms of expression are apt not to be expressive enough to avoid catastrophe, especially for women.

If we provisionally characterize the medium of opera as music's exploration of its affinities with expressive or passionate utterance, then one specific response it invites from the recent present of philosophy as represented in Austin's work, is to determine how his theory of speech as action may be extended, in a sense re-begun, in order to articulate a theory of speech as passion that can propose an orderly study of the effects of the voice raised in opera; but this must in return allow the study of opera to inspire philosophy's interest in passionate speech. To sketch the progress of my thoughts in this project will still not exactly prepare for the use to which I wish to put the Astaire sequence, but it will share the burden of significance I load it with, and help to specify why I press it into service.

The examples which initially I ask a theory of passionate speech to illuminate are in part from the operas I assigned in my course. It is important for my purposes that all are war horses of the medium and that they still, or again, inspire new productions: *The Marriage of Figaro, Don Giovanni, Carmen, Tannhäuser, Otello, La Bohème*, and scenes from *Idomeneo, The Magic Flute*, and *Lucia di Lammermoor*. I want also to be guided by the war horse examples from emotive or expressive utterance that were the rage in moral philosophy, and so-called value theory more generally, in the years I was in graduate school. I recall the list from A. J. Ayer's *Language, Truth, and Logic*: "You acted wrongly in stealing that money," "Tolerance is a virtue," "You ought to tell the truth," and, most delightfully, "I am bored." Ayer characterizes the expression of moral judgment, famously, by denying that they say anything but "are rather pure expressions of feeling, and are calculated to provoke different responses, and as such do not come under the category of truth and falsehood" (p. 108), "they are not in the literal sense significant" (p. 103). Now the claim that certain familiar human utterances are compromised in their meaningfulness on the ground that "they do not come under the category of truth and falsehood" is precisely the thesis to which Austin, in his theory of speech acts, provides massive classes of counterexamples. Austin opens with the examples "I do" (take this woman, etc.), "I bet you . . ." "I name this ship . . ." "I give and bequeath . . . ," and says of them: "It seems clear that to utter the sentence (in, of course, the appropriate circumstances) is not to *describe* my doing of what I should be said in so uttering to be doing . . . : it is to do it. None of the utterances cited is either true or false: I assert this as obvious and do not argue it" (p. 6). But the philosophical kick of the examples rests on two earlier of Austin's introductory remarks about which he is prepared to say that he asserts them as obvious: "the type of utterance we are to consider is not, of course, in general a type of non-sense," and that "they fall into no hitherto recognized *grammatical* category save that of 'statements' " (p. 4).

Notably absent, it appears, from the types of utterances Austin goes on to investigate are those war horse examples of Ayer's, or their descendants, that Austin's theory is designed to challenge. This may have been a tactical decision, meant to shift a new argument on to philosophically fresh ground ("a new site for field work," Austin would call it). But there is reason to think that Austin's experience had been fixated by the way he re-begins his theory to include the perlocutionary in distinction from the illocutionary force of speech acts. When he is led to say, "[C]learly *any* or almost any perlocutionary act is liable to be brought off, in sufficiently special circumstances, by the issuing, with or without calculation, of any utterance whatsoever . . ." (p. 110), he is evidently in the territory in which Ayer was tying ethical words both to "the different feelings they are ordinarily taken to express, and also [to] the different responses which they are calculated to provoke": here Austin distinguishes between ordering someone to stop (illocutionary) and getting them to stop by saying or doing something alarming or intimidating (perlocutionary), but Austin is able to do next to nothing with the field of the perlocutionary comparable to his mapping of that of the illocutionary. It is from here that I am suggesting Austin's theory must re-begin again—going back again to the fact of speaking itself, or I might say, to the fact of the expressiveness and responsiveness of speech as such. How?

Let's reformulate slightly and say that in a passionate utterance the feelings and actions I wish to provoke (Ayer) or bring off (Austin) are ones I can acknowledge, or specifically refuse to acknowledge, as appropriate responses to my expressions of feeling. This is presumably true even of Ayer's "I am bored," which, if it is said to you by a child, is perhaps an appeal for an interesting suggestion or offer of amusement, and if by a friend (romantic or not) is apt still to be an appeal and still to set a stake on some piece of our future together. You had in either case better answer, and carefully. Again, Ayer observes that "if I say to someone, 'You acted wrongly in stealing that money,' I am stating no more than if I had simply said, 'You stole that money' . . . [and] evincing my moral disapproval of it" (p. 107). So presumably I could equally have said, "Why did you take that money?" which specifies that I am questioning your conduct, and I suppose more drastically staking our future. This would be clearer if Ayer had observed, more explicitly to the moral point, that saying to someone "You acted wrongly in stealing" is saying (not no *more* than but) no *less* than that you stole it and is (not just *simply* but) *distinctly* expressing disapproval. Ayer's suggestion that that is all I am stating suggests there might be more. But having confronted you, questioned you, faced you with your conduct, what more is there, except in the same vein—prepared as I may be to reason, depending upon your response—for me to *say?*

I propose that something corresponding to what Austin lists as the six necessary conditions (he sometimes calls them rules) for the felicity of performative utterance holds for passionate utterance. Austin's are (1) there must exist a conventional procedure for uttering certain words in certain contexts, (2) the particular persons and circumstances must be appropriate for the invocation of the procedure, (3) the procedure must be executed correctly and (4) completely, (5) where the procedure requires certain thoughts or feelings or intentions for the inauguration of consequential conduct, the parties must have those feelings or thoughts and intend so to conduct themselves, and further (6) actually so conduct themselves subsequently. Now in the case of passionate speech, in questioning or confronting you with your conduct, all this is upended, but specifically and in detail.

There is (as Austin notes) no conventional procedure for appealing to you to act in response to my expression of passion (of outrage at your treachery or callousness, of jealousy over your attentions, of hurt over your slights of recognition). Call this absence of convention the first condition of a passionate utterance; and let's go further. Whether, then, I have the standing to appeal to or to question you—to single you out as the object of my passion—is part of the argument to ensue. Call standing and singling out the compound second condition of passionate utterance. This compound condition for felicity, or say appropriateness, is not given a priori but is to be discovered or refined, or else the effort to articulate it is to be denied. There is no question therefore of executing a procedure correctly and completely, but there are the further unshiftable demands, or rules, (third) that the one uttering a passion must have the passion, and (fourth) the one singled out must respond now and here, and (fifth) respond in kind—that is to say, be *moved* to respond—or else resist the demand.

Austin observes that "The I who is doing the action [while not always explicit] does . . . come essentially into the picture" (p. 61). In the case of performative utterance failures to identify the correct procedures are characteristically reparable: the purser should not have undertaken to marry us, but here is the captain; you can refuse understandably and without hard feelings the offer of a bet beyond your means, or refuse a gift as premature or excessive; but failure to have singled you out appropriately in passionate utterance characteristically puts the future of our relationship, as part of my sense of my existence, on the line. One can say: the "you" singled out does come essentially into the picture. A performative utterance is an offer of participation in the order of law. And perhaps we can say: A passionate utterance is an invitation to improvisation in the disorders of desire.

Here a certain relation to opera, using the representative examples I mentioned, should become manifest. Let's begin with Carmen since her singling out of Don Jose notably produces his Flower Song as his most articulated response to her. This in effect acknowledges opera as the scene of passionate utterance since here a set aria is directed to Carmen as to an audience, one with the freedom to resist it, judge it, as inappropriate or ineffective (which she does). Then there is Donna Elvira, a perfect type of the abandoned woman, who receives a perfectly conventional response from the man, Don Giovanni, as she charges him with being a monster, a felon, and a deceiver: he asks her to be reasonable and to give him a chance to speak, and then contrives to slip away, leaving Leporello to cover his tracks. There is here no being *moved* to respond, only a move to avoid response. Tannhäuser is singled out by each of two women, or by each of two moods of one woman, each time because of what it is they avow that his voice has done to them. His response to Venus is three times to declare his love and each time to ask for his freedom; his response to Elizabeth is to respond as if to Venus and thus to cause his expulsion from the place he has imagined was the field for his freedom. Lucia's aria of madness is the recognition, or absence of recognition, that the one she has singled out has been silenced. The extremity of demand of The Queen of the Night for vengeance is in a sense matched—that is turned aside—by the metaphysical claim to spiritual purity by Sarastro. Almaviva's Countess is answered by Almaviva at the denouement of *Figaro* in a two-word plea for forgiveness, attracting Mozart to provide him with a Shakespearean height of understatement, one whose appropriateness, or sincerity, it is also for us to divine. For Ilia, in *Idomeneo*, there is no acceptable or appropriate response possible from the man her love has singled out, since she is at the same time committed to hate him as the captor of her and her people; only the Gods can—and do—respond. With *Otello* the man takes on the position of the abandoned one, as if to deny that his isolation has been lifted, and suffocates the possibility of response, no form of which is bearable for him. By the time of Puccini and *La Bohème*, there is no singling out by passion, no specific response to what has become a general emotionality, as if the power of specific expression is as such becoming a thing of memory.

I have shared the sense that the idea of language as expression is unlikely to get very far as a theory of language in part because human beings have so few natural expressions. But this seems to me to underestimate what happens when creatures of a certain species fall into the possession of language and become humans. As I read Wittgenstein, as well as

Freud, what happens is that they become victims of expression—readable—their every word and gesture ready to betray their meaning.

In the conjunction of Austin's appeal to the ordinary, and specifically its power to reveal the action of speech, together with the passion of abandonment in the raised speech of opera, I can provisionally locate the pertinence I attach to the Astaire sequence we are about to screen. Each of my claims of singling out and of response in the operas requires a judgment of the music with which they are elicited. With what confidence do I place such judgments, especially since, for all the fact that I was trained as a musician, my dominating musical experience is of a culture that does not compete with the operatic cultures of Italy and Germany and France. (I claim, for example, that when Carmen rejects Jose's Flower Song as a response to her singling him out, saying, in triple piano, "No, you do not love me," she is responding truly, as it were objectively, to something she hears in his music, or say his tone. But every other description I know of that moment takes her to be continuing to taunt the man and to seduce him into coming away into her life.) My confidence lies in recognizing that the traditions of jazz and of American musical comedy represent, for some of us, comparable contributions to world art, and if these can be taken as bearing on the experience of opera (and indeed, as I will wish to note, on the issue of the ordinary) then I will have what aesthetic reassurance I can claim, since I ought to be able to know and to experience just about everything there is in such a ninety-second sequence as we are about to witness.

It is the opening number from one of the last, not perhaps the best known, but among the most critically admired, of the classical Hollywood musicals adapted from a Broadway original, called *The Band Wagon*, directed by Vincente Minnelli, with Cyd Charisse as Astaire's partner. The judgment I make in asking you to view the sequence expresses my pleasure in it and awaits your agreement upon this.

Now of course this particular experiment stands to be compromised (beyond questions of my tact in choosing the particular object) by the remarkably persistent air of exoticism in presenting a piece of film in service of serious intellectual intentions, especially a popular film. But I do not see that the initial mild indecorousness this risks should be more disturbing, come to think of it, than holding a philosophical lecture in a hotel ballroom.

Let me set the scene. The occasion of the number is that the character played by Astaire—a song-and-dance man whose star has faded in Hollywood and who is returning nervously to New York to try a comeback on Broadway—exits from the train that has returned him, takes the awaiting reporters and photographers to have come to interview him, and is rudely awakened to reality as a still-vivid star steps out of the adjacent car and the newshounds flock to her (Ava Gardner in a cameo appearance). As our hero walks away ruefully, a porter offers a remark to him on the rigors of publicity to which stardom subjects a person, and upon answering, "Yes, I don't know how they stand it," Astaire arrives at his song, entitled "By Myself."

Let's begin uncontroversially. From the beginning of the song at a baggage cart to the conclusion of the song at a gate, the camera has led the man in one continuous shot; at the end of the singing it stops as he does and then, as it were, watches him leave through the gate; we then cut to a view from within the station and see the man continue his walk toward us, humming the same tune, then pause, and shift nervously, as if expecting someone. If this were theater, the routine would clearly end with the exit out of the gate. Being a film, the entrance into the station may count as part of the song. Overall it seems as nearly uneventful as a photographed song can be. Astaire had begun singing with a little self-conscious laugh, magnified by its producing a palpable cloud of cigarette smoke. It is a self-reflexive response to the fact that in him thinking (manifest here, classically, as melancholy) is about to become singing. I report that when I recall Astaire's delivery of "By Myself," it brings with it a sense of emotional hovering, not so much a feeling of suspense as one of being in suspension, a spiritual bracketing.

I cite two pairs of facts to begin a sketch of an account of this touchstone of experience, one pair concerning the song, the other concerning the presentation, or representation, of the person Astaire.

About the song. Here I merely assert two features that it would be impractical to try to verify now, though I would love to. First, I was led to it, or confirmed in its suitability, by an essay of the great Italian composer Luigi Dallapicolla in which he announces his discovery of a tradition of arias in classical Italian melodrama (meaning the tradition of opera exemplified at its highest by Verdi), one that uses five-three quatrain form—the phrases occurring in the pattern AABA, with the emotional crescendo peaking in the third, or B phrase. Now an AABA form is the basic form of song in the so-called Golden Age of the American musical theater, from the 1920s through the 1940s, when the major works of Gershwin, Irving Berlin, Jerome Kern, Rodgers and Hart, Cole Porter, and others, were originally produced. The song in the Astaire sequence is from the Broadway production of the 1930s and exhibits an ingeniously modified AABA form in which, moreover, it satisfies the observation that the emotional climax is reached in the third phrase. The second feature I mention about the song is that its melodic and harmonic organization contributes to the experience to which I assigned the concept of hovering. Here I simply note that harmonically its opening chord progression analyzes as a certain form of cadential preparation that can be said also to fit precisely perhaps the most famously controversial opening in the history of monstrously familiar music, namely the opening harmonic progression of *Tristan*. If the sound of music can ever sensibly be said to represent suspended animation I suppose *Tristan and Isolde* is the crucial case.

I turn to the pair of facts concerning the presentation of the person of Astaire, and first of his walking. Recall to begin with its jauntiness, the slight but distinct exaggeration of his body swinging from side to side as the platform is being paced. Narratively, he is hoping to cheer himself, letting his body, as William James once suggested, tell him what his emotion is. But ontologically, we could say, it is the walk of a man who is known to move in dance exactly like no other man. It is a walk from which, at any step, this man may break into dance—he is known from other contexts to have found dancing called for in the course of driving golf balls, or roller skating, or while swabbing the deck of a ship. Now if his walking does turn into dancing, then isn't what we see of his delivery revealed to have been already dancing, a sort of limiting case, or proto-state, of dancing?

We should readily agree that it *isn't just* walking he is exhibiting. Then what is the relation of dancing to walking (or of singing to talking)? That his song does not here reach unequivocal dancing, as a song-and-dance man's song is normally required to do, that we are for the moment confined, so to speak, to this dance virtuoso's more or less untrained voice, throws the emphasis of interest in this number elsewhere—on the quality of the words and music of course, but specifically on his "delivery" of the song; the walk is part of its delivery. In opera, delivery is essentially a function of voice. What is called "acting" is available to certain operatic presences, but apart from the basis of the voice, the operatic presence is ineffective. In American musical theater, the economy is roughly reversed: unless you are identified as a dancer, or as some kind of clown, your voice will have to be better trained than Astaire's (for all the perfection of its own "manner"); yet apart from the basis of your delivery (as it were mounting the voice), the theatrical presence will be more or less ineffective.

When, in his next routine, Astaire does find his way to dance, it is on New York's former street of theater, 42nd Street, where, continuing his opening adventures in a space that is now an amusement arcade, he stumbles over the outstretched legs of a preoccupied black shoeshine man, responds by singing a tin pan alley tune called "When There's a Shine on your Shoes," and, ascending the shoeshine stand and receiving a transfigurative shine, is invited by the black man—so I invite the encounter to be read—to come to earth and join in the dance. There further unfolds one of the most elaborate and stunning in the history of Astaire routines, one which provides him with an occasion for acknowledging his indebtedness for his existence as a dancer—his deepest identity—to the genius of black dancing. (How fully such an acknowledgment is acceptable is a further question, one that I hope will be considered in connection with the extraordinary details of such a routine as the one in question.) From their pas de deux, Astaire moves into a trancelike solo, quasi dancing, quasi singing, in which his realization that he has found his way (back) to dancing strikes him as having found his feet again, as having refound his body, and his ecstasy is such that when, in his twirling or reeling through the arcade he comes across a coin-operated photograph booth, he happily maneuvers his body in it so as to have the picture taken of his feet (narratively, of the shine on his shoes).

Figure 17.1

Not exactly an abandoned woman but an artist whose public has dispersed, he discovers that for a comeback it is himself that must be singled out, or resingled, by himself. That the discovery of intact existence here expresses itself as ecstasy is linked in my mind with Thoreau's once expressing his recognition of his double existence, say as seer and seen, as a condition of being beside himself, roughly the dictionary definition of ecstasy.

Perhaps out of the experience, or reexperience, of this ode to his feet, we may at some stage remark—after ninety seconds, or as in my case about forty years after having first viewed the film—that the earlier walk we viewed down the train platform is framed in such a way that we never see Astaire's feet, not even when he drops the cigarette that has lasted through the song to the ground and snuffs it out—so we fill in the motion—with his foot; he is throughout cut off between the knee and the thigh, giving that conventional Hollywood form of shot a further determinate life.

Figure 17.2

His feet first appear to us as we cut to him walking into the station, where, also, we hear him repeating or continuing the tune he has just sung to himself, not precisely by humming it, but with the kind of syllabification, or proto-speech, that musicians sometimes use to remind themselves of the exact materialization of a passage of sound, but which can occur, as here, as an unguarded expression of a state of consciousness, in its distraction, disorientation, dispossession: DA; DA, DA DA; DA, DA DA.

Figure 17.3

We should not fail to appropriate this evident triviality for philosophy. That particular consciousness has just been revealed to us (by its delivery along the platform) in concreteness and richness, expressed by whatever is expressed in the song that is still evidently on this fictional figure's mind. Our perception of those syllables (DA, DA, DA), we must bear in mind, is what, is essentially all that, the world has so far witnessed of that consciousness; we are alerted to the fact, or the convention according to which, the opening delivery of the singing was inaudible, and the opening proto-dancing was unnotable, invisible, within its fictional world. Had that crowd of passers-by on the platform been aware of a man doing in their presence what Astaire, or his particular shadow, is doing in ours, they would have felt, let us say, a reportable indecorousness. (A different crowd, under different conventions, might have joined in.) I take the unremarkableness (the missableness), together with the remarkableness (the unmistakability), of Astaire's musical syllabification, and of the routine that renders it so, to emblematize a way of manifesting the ordinary. That the ordinariness in experience is figured in the image of walking is something I have on several occasions found especially worth taking into account.

Let me sketch how we got here another way. It seems right to emphasize that Kant's aesthetic judgment (in radical contrast with his moral judgment) is a form, yet to be specified, of passionate utterance: one person, risking exposure to rebuff, singles out another, through the expression of an emotion, to respond in kind, that is, with appropriate emotion and action (if mainly of speech), here and now. And it seems plausible to assume that if tragedy is the working out of a scene of skepticism, then comedy in contrast works out a festive abatement of skepticism, call it an affirmation of existence. Now the utterance or delivery of Astaire's song and proto-dance has singled me out for a response of pleasure which I propose to read in terms of the concepts of psychic hovering, of dissociation from the body, within a state of ordinary invisibility, which (though you have to take my word for it now) subsequently finds resolution in an acknowledgment of origins which reinstates a relation to an intact body and causes a state of ecstasy. In my wish to share this pleasure I judge a scene of walking and of melodic syllabification as appropriate expressions of the ordinary, as the missable, and the taking of a portrait of a shod foot as an ecstatic attestation of existence. Such proposed touchstones of experience do not, I trust, immediately put the future at stake between us, but they are measures; yet to be assessed, of what the stakes might be.

In bringing these remarks to a close, I pick up my earlier challenge to myself to say why taking skepticism seriously is something more than reveling in its empty fascinations; why the work of a more serious philosophy need not be to take measures to avoid that distraction. I have portrayed the working out of skepticism in *Hamlet*—thinking of this as Hamlet's struggle not to know what he knows—as Hamlet's presiding wish to deny his existence (that ever he was born), made more or less explicit when, in the last act, he proves his existence by announcing, "This is I, Hamlet the Dane," or as Descartes phrases the matter in the Second Meditation, "I am, I exist, is true each time that I say it or think it in my mind." The announcement is undertaken by Hamlet as some preparation, or explanation, for his leap into Ophelia's grave, as if facing the death of love is the condition of announcing one's separate existence. Now what would it mean to advise Hamlet, or for him to have taken measures, to avoid his skepticism, his avoidance of existence, call this his making himself into a ghost? He has been advised to reasonableness by his relations ("Thou know'st 'tis common, all that lives must die. . . . Why seems it so particular with thee?"). And the play contains what I suppose is the most famous scene of such advice we have in our literature. In that scene Polonius's precepts of' moderation are to show his son the way to be unnoticeable, or uninvolved, as far as possible ("Neither borrower nor lender be"). Taken as summarizable by Polonius's phrase "reserve thy judgment," his precepts from a distance echo the chief points of advice in ancient skepticism—to live a customary life (Emerson says conforming) and to suspend judgment. But in the ancient world—and according to some, for a thousand years after—philosophy was identified, hence skepticism as an instance of philosophy was practiced, as a way of life. Was skepticism then livable? Is anything else now livable? What happens to philosophy?

18

The World as Things

Collecting Thoughts on Collecting

[Fleda] took the measure of the poor lady's strange, almost maniacal
disposition to thrust in everywhere the question of "things," to read
all behaviour in the light of some fancied relation to them. "Things"
were of course the sum of the world; and, for Mrs. Gereth, the sum of
the world was rare French furniture and oriental china. She could at a
stretch imagine people's not "having," but she shouldn't imagine their
not wanting and not missing.

> —Henry James, *The Spoils of Poynton* (1897)

The world is the totality of facts, not of things.

> —Ludwig Wittgenstein, *Tractatus Logico-Philosophicus* (1921)

I

NOT THIS OR THAT COLLECTION is my assignment here, but collecting as such, or, as it was also specified for me, the philosophy
of collecting. And presumably not collecting as what dust does on
shelves, or rain in pails, or as what is called a collector on certain roofs does

First published in Bernard Blistene, editor, *Rendezvous: Masterpieces from the Centre Georges
Pompidou and the Guggenheim Museums* (New York: Guggenheim Museum, 1998).

(the one I saw is cylindrical, about the size of a stack of half a dozen coffee cans and made of aluminum, into which are fitted what look like coffee filters), collecting particulates to monitor air pollution; but as someone collects medals, coins, stamps, books, skeletons, jewels, jewel boxes, locks, clocks, armor, vases, sarcophagi, inscriptions, paintings, curiosities of unpredictable kinds. Krzysztof Pomian, in his remarkable study *Collectors and Curiosities*, declares that every human culture has collected and that every movable thing has been collected.[1] As if collecting for possession and display is as primitive as gathering food for survival.

But while we may sensibly speculate, or ask, why certain people collect stamps, jewels, skeletons, and so on, and why different things seem favored for collection by different classes or ranks of society, or different genders or ages, in different historical periods, is it sure that it makes sense to ask (as it hardly makes sense to ask why people gather food) why people collect as such—any more than it makes obvious sense to ask what my relation to things is as such, or my relation to language, or what the point of thinking is?

Yet writers about collecting are characteristically moved precisely to advance some idea of what the point of collecting is as such, as a form of human life. For instance, Jean Baudrillard articulates collecting as an objectifying of oneself in a simulation of death which one symbolically survives within one's life; Pomian begins with the fact of collecting as removing objects from economic circulation and putting them on display, and speaks of a consequent establishment of connection between the visible and the invisible, the realm of religion, made possible (and inevitable?) by the advent of language; Susan Stewart as it were combines the withdrawal of objects from use with the establishment of a commerce between death and life (as if creating a realm of mock exchange [mock religion?]); Robert Opie is one of many who see in collecting an attempt to reproduce and hence preserve or recapture the world; Philip Fisher, concentrating on art museums since the Enlightenment, identifying stages of a history in which an object is removed from its original setting (of use, say, in battle or in prayer), becoming a thing of memory (a souvenir or a relic) and ending up as an object for aesthetic appreciation, arrives at a definition of the museum as a place of the making of art, an institution of practices within which the function of art is operable; Foucault, in the paradigmatic onslaught of his *The Order of Things*, speaks of shifts in our ways of "taming the wild profusion of things."[2] I shall not refrain from certain similar speculations in what follows.

(Then I should note at the outset that an important issue about collections, one that makes news, plays almost no role here, that concerning the right to exhibit, or to own, objects improperly taken from, or identified

with, another culture. My excuse for silence here is that such a conflict is
apt to be poorly discussed apart from a patient account and interpretation
of the forces in play in a concrete historical context, which is not how I
have conceived the form of my contribution. James Clifford, in his
deservedly admired *The Predicament of Culture*, provides such contexts for
several cases, guided by the principle that living cultures worldwide are
inherently appropriating the strange, the evidently predatory no more
than the obviously victimized.)[3]

II

Speculation about the role of collections in human life has been explicit
since at least the problem of the One and the Many, made philosophically
inescapable in Plato's Theory of Forms, or Ideas, according to which the
individual things present to our senses are knowable, are indeed what they
are, by virtue of their "participation" in, or "imitation" of, the realm of
Forms, which provide us with our armature of classification, to put it mildly. The Platonic hierarchy disparages the things, the life, of ordinary sensuous experience, this realm of the transient and the inexact, in contrast
with the perfect, permanent realm of the Ideas. To know a thing in the
lower realm is to know which Ideas it imitates in common with other
things of its kind: there are many chairs, but just one Idea of (the perfect,
hence perfectly knowable) chair; the Form of a chair is what is common to,
the common aspiration of, the collection of the things that are, and are
known as, chairs. Just how the relation between the many and the one (or
as it came to be called in later philosophy, the universal and the particular)
is to be conceived became at once a matter of controversy in the work of
Aristotle, and the problem of the status of universals has not abandoned
philosophy to this day.

But a perplexity other than the relation of universal and particular,
or a more specialized version of the relation of a general term to a singular object, is more pressing for us in the attempt to bring the issue of the
collection into view.

We have in effect said that every collection requires an idea (or universal, or concept). (This seems to presage the fact, testified to by many
writers on collecting, that collections carry narratives with them, ones presumably telling the point of the gathering, the source and adventure of it.)
But can we say the reverse, that every idea requires (posits, names) a collection? This is a form of the question: How can signs refer to what is nonexistent? What do expressions such as "Pegasus," "a round square," "the
present King of France," refer to, and if to nothing, what do they mean,
how can they mean anything, how can anything true be attributed to

them? Bertrand Russell and Edmund Husserl were both caught by the importance of such a question; it was I suppose the last moment at which what has come to be called analytical philosophy and what (consequently?) came to be called Continental philosophy so clearly coincided in concern. It was Russell's solution to the question of the reference of such terms, by means of his theory of descriptions (which evaluates the terms by means of modern logic to demonstrate perspicuously that they do not assert reference to anything), that can be said to have established a preoccupation and determined the style of analytical philosophy, and the style appears to have outlasted that preoccupation.

The preoccupation also outlasts the style. The first section of Wittgenstein's *Philosophical Investigations* announces its first interpretation of the passage from Augustine with which it opens, in which Augustine recalls his learning of language:

> [Augustine's] words give us a particular picture of the essence of human language. It is this: the individual words in language name objects—sentences are combinations of such names.—In this picture of language we find the roots of the following idea: Every word has a meaning. The meaning is correlated with the word. It is the object for which the word stands.[4]

It is a picture of language from which philosophers of both the Anglo-American analytical tradition and the German-French tradition continue to perform, in their different ways, hairbreadth escapes.

Of interest here is that the first example (the first "language-game" of a sort) that Wittgenstein develops in response to this picture materializes not around a single absent object but around a collection.

> I send someone shopping. I give him a slip on which stand the signs "five red apples"; he takes the slip to the shopkeeper, who opens the drawer on which stands the sign "apples"; then he looks up the word "red" in a table and finds a color sample opposite it; then he says the series of cardinal numbers.[5]

Reference—if this means linking a sign to an object—is hardly the chief of the problems revealed in this curious, yet apparently comprehensible, scene. How did the shopper know to whom to present the slip? Does the sign "apple" on his slip refer to the sign "apple" on the shopkeeper's drawer? They may not at all look alike. Would it have secured the linkage to have provided the shopper with a photograph or sketch of the drawer and its sign? How would the shopkeeper know what the point of the photograph or sign is supposed to be? (Perhaps he will hang it on his wall.) Does the sign on the slip rather refer (directly, as it were) to the items inside the closed drawer?

But we are free to imagine that when the shopkeeper opens the drawer it is empty. Did the signs on the slip and on the drawer then become meaningless? And if there were only four apples then would just the word "five" have become meaningless? Do you want an explanation of how it happens that signs retain their meaning under untoward circumstances? Shouldn't you also want an explanation of the fact that the drawer was marked "apples" rather than, say, "red," whereupon the shopkeeper would be expected to look up the word "apple" on a chart of fruits and vegetables (we won't ask how he knows which of his charts to consult)?

Do we know why we classify as we do? In order to know, would we have to memorize what Foucault says about changing conditions of possibility? Wittgenstein's primitive, and studiedly strange, opening example can be taken as stirring such wisps of anxiety among the threads of our common lives that we may wonder, from the outset of thinking, how it is that philosophy, in its craving for explanation, seeks to explain so little, that is to say, how it conceives that so little is mysterious among the untold threads between us that become tangled or broken. Perhaps Wittgenstein may be taken as redressing philosophy's disparagement of the things of sense when late in the *Tractatus* he finds: "It is not *how* things are in the world that is mystical, but *that* it exists."[6]

III

Baudrillard declares:

> [W]hile the appropriation of a "rare" or "unique" object is obviously the perfect culmination of the impulse to possess, it has to be recognized that one can never find absolute proof in the real world that a given object is indeed unique. . . . The singular object never impedes the process of narcissistic projection, which ranges over an indefinite number of objects: on the contrary, it encourages such multiplication whereby the image of the self is extended to the very limits of the collection. Here, indeed, lies the whole miracle of collecting. For it is invariably *oneself* that one collects.[7]

How well do we understand this final claim? Let us consider that one of the most celebrated plays of the middle of this century, Tennessee Williams's *The Glass Menagerie*, depends upon its audience's capacity for a rapt understanding of the daughter Laura's identification with her collection

of fragile glass figures. And this understanding is not broken, but is deepened, when her Gentleman Caller accidentally steps on her favorite piece, a
tiny unicorn, breaking off its horn, and Laura reveals an unexpected independence of spirit, refusing the suggestion of a clumsy castration and instead
observing something like, "It makes him more like other creatures," a state
she also has reason to desire. Another famous work of that period, Orson
Welles's *Citizen Kane*, equally depends upon some identification of a person
by his collection, but here some final interpretation of its meaning appears
rather to be dictated to us by the closing revelation of the childhood snow
sled. I like thinking that when Jay Gatsby is in the course of realizing his fantasy of showing Daisy his house, his showplace, and unfurls his fabulous collection of shirts before her, it is clear that the value he attaches to them, or
to anything, is a function of their value to her. No other object contains him;
he is great.

So let us not be hasty in arriving at very firm conclusions about what
our relation to collections is, hence what relation they may propose concerning our relation to the world of things as such.

It may be worth remembering further here that two of a series of
films breaking all attendance records are about the fatality of a quest for a
unique object, *Raiders of the Lost Ark* and *Indiana Jones and The Last
Crusade*, and that the closing shot of the former, the camera floating over
an unclassifiably colossal collection of crated objects among which, some
unpredictable where, the unique lost object of the quest is anonymously
contained, seems some kind of homage to the closing roving shot of
Citizen Kane, where now the integrity of civilization, not merely of a single unsatisfied millionaire, is at stake.

IV

Both Wittgenstein and Heidegger, in something like opposite directions,
break with the ancient picture of the things of the world as intersections
of universals and particulars. Wittgenstein's way is, characteristically,
almost comically plain and casual.

> Instead of producing something common to all that we call lan-
> guage, I am saying that these phenomena have no one thing in com-
> mon which makes us use the same word for all. . . . Consider for
> example the proceedings that we call "games." I mean board-games,
> card-games, Olympic games, and so on. What is common to them
> all? Don't say: "There *must* be something common, or they would
> not be called 'games' "—but *look and see* whether there is anything
> common to all. . . . [Y]ou will . . . see . . . similarities, relationships,

and a whole series of them at that. . . . I can think of no better expression to characterize these similarities than "family resemblances."[8]

This idea has had the power of conversion for some of its readers—too precipitously to my way of thinking, since it does not account for Wittgenstein's signature play of casualness with profundity. He still wants to be able to articulate the essences of things.

Heidegger's way of breaking with universals is, characteristically, almost comically obscure and portentous. In a seminal essay "The Thing," he opens with the assertion, "All distances in time and space are shrinking," surely a banality we might expect to see in any newspaper.[9] Then he undertakes to show us that, as it were, we do not know the meaning of the banalities of our lives.

> Yet the frantic abolition of all distances brings no nearness; for nearness does not consist in shortness of distance. . . . How can we come to know [the nature of] nearness? . . . Near to us are what we usually call things. But what is a thing? Man has so far given no more thought to the thing as a thing than he has to nearness.[10]

Is Heidegger here constructing a parable of the museum, perhaps a rebuke to those who think art brings things near in the empirical manner of museums? He takes as his most elaborated example that of the jug, which holds water or wine, and he spells out a vision in which the water, retaining its source in the running spring, marries earth and sky, and in which the wine, which may be the gift of a libation, connects mortals and gods. Heidegger concentrates these and other properties of the jug in such words as these: "The thing things. Thinging gathers. Appropriating the fourfold [earth, sky, mortals, gods], it gathers the fourfold's stay, its while, into something that stays for a while: into this thing, that thing."[11] Without giving the German, which has caused a diligent translator recourse to this near-English, I trust one can see the point of my saying that Heidegger, in this text (and it relates to many others variously) is a philosopher of collecting.

What I meant by speaking of the opposite directions taken in Wittgenstein's and Heidegger's perspectives I might express by saying that whereas Heidegger identifies things as implying the setting of the world in which they are and do what they surprisingly are and do, Wittgenstein identifies things as differing in their positions within the system of concepts in which their possibilities are what they surprisingly are. We cannot simply say that Heidegger is concerned with essence ("What, then, is the thing as thing, that its essential nature has never yet been able to appear?")[12] and that Wittgenstein is not so concerned (he in fact

announces that grammar, which provides the medium of his philosophizing, expresses essence.)[13] Nor can we say that Wittgenstein is concerned
with language and Heidegger not, for while Wittgenstein says "Grammar
tells what kind of object anything is"[14] (or more literally, "It is essence that
is articulated in grammar"), Heidegger writes, "It is language that tells us
about the nature of a thing, provided that we respect language's own
nature" ("Building Dwelling Thinking").[15]

If Heidegger is a philosopher of collecting, Wittgenstein composes
his *Investigations* in such a way as to suggest that philosophy is, or has
become for him, a procedure of collecting. Only the first, and longer, of its
two parts was prepared by him for publication and its 172 pages consists
of 693 sections; in his preface he calls the book "really only an album." For
some, me among them, this feature of Wittgenstein's presentation of his
thoughts is essential to them and is part of their attraction. For others it is
at best a distraction. Emerson's writing has also had a liberating effect on
my hopes for philosophical writing, and I have taken the familiar experience of Emerson's writing as leaving the individual sentences to shuffle for
themselves, to suggest that each sentence of a paragraph of his can be
taken to be its topic sentence. I welcome the consequent suggestion that
his essays are collections of equals rather than hierarchies of dependents.

I do not make the world which the thing gathers. I do not system-
atize the language in which the thing differs from all other things of the
world. I testify to both, acknowledge my need of both.

The idea of a series, so essential to the late phase of modernist painting (epitomized in one major form in Michael Fried's *Three American
Painters* catalogue of 1965, on the work of Noland, Stella, and Olitzki)[16]
captures this equipollence in the relation between individual and genus or
genre. These manifestations of participation in an idea may seem exces-
sively specialized, but the implication of their success (granted one is convinced by their success as art) seems justification enough for the existence
of collections and for places in which to exhibit their members in association with one another, as if the conditions of the make-up of the world and
of the knowing of the world are there put on display and find reassurance.

This is an odd point of arrival, this emphasis on knowledge as marking our relation to the world, after a bit of by-play between Heidegger and
Wittgenstein, whose importance to some of us is tied to their throwing
into question, in their radically different ways, philosophy's development
of the question of knowledge as the assessment of claims along the axis of
certainty, certainty taken as its preferred relation to objects.

It is in modern philosophical skepticism, in Descartes and in Hume,
that our relation to the things of the world came to be felt to hang by a

thread of sensuous immediacy, hence to be snapped by a doubt. The wish to defeat skepticism, or to disparage it, has been close to philosophy's heart ever since. To defeat skepticism need not be a declared grounding motive of a philosophical edifice, as it is in Kant; it may simply be declared a bad dream, or bad intellectual manners, as in Quine, who finds skepticism vitiated by science, whose comprehensibility needs from experience only what Quine calls certain measured "check points."[17] Philosophers such as William James and John Dewey were appalled by what their fellow empiricists have been willing to settle for in the name of experience, they steadfastly refusing to give our birthright in return for, it may seem, so specialized a world. (Foucault calls it the world of black and white.)

When Walter Benjamin tracks the impoverishment of our (Western, late capitalist) experience, and relates it to a distance from objects that have become commodified, hence mystified in their measurement for exchange, he does not, so far as I know, relate this experience to philosophy's preoccupation with skepticism, to an enforced distance from the things of the world and others in it by the very means of closing that distance, by the work of my senses. But then Benjamin seems to harbor a fantasy of a future which promises a path—through collecting—to new life, a reformed practicality with, or use for, objects.

> The interior was the place of Art. The collector was the true inhabitant of the interior. He made the glorification of things his concern. To him fell the task of Sisyphus which consisted of stripping things of their commodity character by means of his possession of them. But he conferred on them only a fancier's value, rather than a use-value. The collector dreamed that he was in a world which was not only far-off in distance and time, but which was also a better one, in which to be sure people were just as poorly provided with what they needed as in the world of everyday, but in which things were freed from the bondage of being useful. The interior was not only the private citizen's universe, it was also his casing. Living means leaving traces. In the interior, these were stressed. . . . The detective story appeared, which investigated these traces.[18]

The collector knows that our relation to things should be better, but he does not see this materialized through their more equitable redistribution, or say recollecting. That the interior place of Art, and the collector as its true inhabitant, is registered as past may suggest that the place of Art is altered, or that the time of Art and its private collecting is over, or that interiority is closed, or that these proprieties of experience have vanished together.

Take the formulation "living means leaving traces." In conjunction with the figure of the detective, the implication is that human life, as the privileged life of the interior and its "coverings and antimacassars, boxes and casings," is a crime scene, that (presumably in this period of exclusive comfort) human plans are plans contracted by the guilty. So presumably Benjamin's writing is at once confessing in its existence as traces the guilt of its privilege and at the same time declaring that its obscurity is necessary if it is not to subserve the conditions that insure our guilt toward one another. But the direct allusion to Marx ("[the collector] conferred on [things] only a fancier's value, rather than a use-value"), hence to Marx's derogation of exchange value as a realm of mystery, suggests a mystery in the living of the life of traces that cannot be solved by what are called detectives.

The idea that the evidence of life produced by each of us is of the order of traces, conveys a picture according to which no concatenation of these impressions ever reaches to the origin of these signs of life, call it a self. Then the thrill of the detective story is a function of its warding off the knowledge that we do not know the origins of human plans, why things are made to happen as they do. Traces relate the human body's dinting of the world back to this particular body, but how do we relate this body to what has dinted it? If it was something inside, how do we correlate the events (how compare the sorrow with its manifestation)? If it was something outside, why is *this* the effect (why sorrow instead of contempt or rage)? The discovery of the identity of the criminal is bound to be anticlimactic, something less than we wanted to know.

It does seem brilliant of Poe to have presented the traces of a crime, in *Murders in the Rue Morgue*, early in the genre, so that the solution depends upon realizing that they are not effects of a human action but of those of an ape, as though we no longer have a reliable, instinctive grasp of what the human being is capable of. Was the hand of man therefore not traced in this crime? What brings murder into the world? What detective responds to this evolutionary crossroads?

Beyond this, let's call it, skepticism of traces, I take Benjamin's portrait, or function, of the collector as the true inhabitant of the interior to suggest that the collector himself is without effective or distinctive interiority, without that individuality of the sort he prides himself on. So that when Benjamin goes on to identify the flaneur's search for novelty as engendered by "the collective unconscious" and its craving for fashion,[19] this can be taken to mean that what is interpreted by an individual as his uniqueness is merely an item of impulse in an unobserved collection of such impulses, hence anything but original; call it, after Emerson, the source of conformity, part of the crowd after all.

VI

How did it become fashionable for disparagers of skepticism to tell the story of Dr. Johnson, receiving Bishop Berkeley's "denial" of matter, kicking a stone and replying "Thus I refute you"? People who know nothing of the motives of skepticism know a version of this story. How strange a scene it offers. Why, to begin with, is kicking a hard object more a "refutation" of immateriality than, say, sipping wine, or putting your hand on the arm of a friend, or just walking away on solid ground, or muddy for that matter? Why is a sensation in the toe taken to be closer to the things of the world than one in the throat or in the hand or on the sole of the foot? Does Samuel Johnson take himself to be closer to his foot than to his throat or his hand? Or is it the gesture that is important—the contempt in kicking? Emerson assigns to Johnson the saying that "You remember who last kicked you." Is Johnson's refutation accordingly to be understood as reminding the things of earth who is master, as an allegory of his contempt of philosophy left to its arrogance? Or is it—despite himself—a way of causing himself pain by the things of the world, implying that he knows they exist because he suffers from them? Then had he forgotten when he last kicked them, or brushed them by?

VII

Some I know, otherwise offended than Benjamin by claims to individuality, profess to understand the self—presumably of any period and locality—as some kind of collection of things, as though such a collection is less metaphysically driven on the face of it than the simple and continued self that Hume famously denies, or would deny to all save harmless metaphysicians. Leaving these self-isolating ones aside, Hume "[ventures] to affirm of the rest of mankind, that they are nothing but a bundle or collection of different perceptions."[20] This alternative picture, however, retains relations among the collection such as resemblance, causation, memory, and the incurable capacity of the whole to torment itself with "philosophical melancholy and delirium."[21] Then when Hume confesses here that "I find myself absolutely and necessarily determined to live, and talk, and act like other people, in the common affairs of life,"[22] how are we to take this assertion against his earlier, famous assurance in the section "Of Personal Identity," that "for my part, when I enter most intimately into what I call *myself*, I always stumble on some particular perception or other, of heat or cold, light or shade, love or hatred, pain or pleasure. I never can catch *myself* at any time without a perception"[23] What idea (held or deplored) must we understand Hume to have of "entering most intimately into what

I call myself"—what perception announces to him this entering? And what would count as a pertinent perception he has stumbled on when he declares his "absolute and necessary determination" to live like other people in the common affairs of life—what perception of absoluteness or determination? And is this determination meant to assure himself that he is like other people? Do other people have such a determination to live . . . like themselves? If they do, he is not like them (does not live like them); if they do not, he is not like them (does not think like them).

Hume goes on to say, fascinatingly, that "The mind is a kind of theater," glossing this as emphasizing that "perceptions successively make their appearance, pass, re-pass, glide away, and mingle in an infinite variety of ways. There is properly no *simplicity* in it at one time, nor *identity* in different."[24] But what isn't there? What is the metaphysical proposal that must be denied? Setting aside whatever importance there is to be attached to our "natural propension" to seek some such simplicity or identity, the question Hume posed was "From what impression could [our] idea [of the self] be deriv'd?"[25] I am, for my part, prepared to say that, if we derive from the idea of the mind as a theater the idea that what we witness there are scenes and characters—so impressions of a scene in which characters are in light and dark, expressing love or hatred, manifesting pain or pleasure—these provide precisely impressions or perceptions of myself, revelations of myself, of what I live and die for, wherein I catch myself. They are not—I am happy to report—simple and identical the way impressions of simple, stable things are. They are ones I might miss, as I might miss any other chance at self-discernment. I must discover a narrative for the scene and an identity for the characters and see how to decipher my role in the events. No impression of a thing which failed to relate that thing to itself as a witness or party to its own concerns (or to understand how it fails in a given case in this role) would be an impression of a self, of a thing to which to attribute personhood. Whether what I find is unity or division, simplicity or complicity, depends upon the individual case—both of the one under narration, the collection, or the one doing the narration, call him or her the collector, or adaptor, or ego.

VIII

In his introduction to the *Treatise*, Hume remarks that "'Tis no astonishing reflection to consider, that the application of experimental philosophy to moral subjects should come after that to natural at the distance of above a whole century"—he is constructing his application of Newtonianism to human encounter in the century after Newton's consolidation of the new (corpuscular) science, and considering how long it took Copernicus and the others to arrive at the new science against the reign of Aristotelianism.[26] It took another century and a half after Hume for the Freudian event to arrive with its methodical discoveries of what the "impressions" or "perceptions" are in conjunction with which we catch ourselves. Call the discoveries new laws, or new ideas of laws, of attraction and repulsion and of the distance over which they act. Whether this span is astonishingly long or short depends on where you start counting from— Sophocles, Shakespeare, Schopenhauer. More urgent than determining the time of the achievement is recognizing its fragility. This new knowledge of the self, as Freud explained, perpetually calls down repression upon its self. Since it is these days again under relatively heavy cultural attack (sometimes in conjunction with philosophy, sometimes in the name of philosophy), it is worth asking what would be lost if this knowledge is lost, what aspiration of reason would be abdicated.

That aside, the idea of a self as a collection requiring a narrative locates the idea that what holds a collection together, specifically perhaps in the aspect of its exhibition, is a narrative of some kind. We might think of this idea as the issue of the catalogue, where this refers not simply to the indispensable list of objects and provenances, but to the modern catalogue produced by curators who are as responsible for circulating ideas as for acquiring and preserving objects. Mieke Bal is explicit in positing a narrative among the objects of an exhibition; Susan Stewart more implicitly invokes narrative interaction in her perception of what she calls the animation of a collection; Philip Fisher presents his idea of the effacing and the making of art as a narrative of the stages an object undergoes as it makes its way to the status and stability of a place in a museum of art, a sort of counternarrative, even effecting a certain counteranimation, to that of a collection within itself.[27] The issue of the catalogue is, I think, a pertinent emphasis for Norton Batkin's proposal that an exhibition be informed by its objects' own preoccupations with their fatedness to display, for example, by their relation to the intervention of the theatrical, or to the pervasiveness of the photographic, or, perhaps, later, to what remains of the experience of collage, or of assemblage.[28]

IX

Batkin's concern, evidently, is that the current emphasis on the concept of collecting, on establishing a holding, not come to swamp the concept, and the practices, of the holding's exhibition(s). A shadow of my concern here, rather, has been that the concept of a collection not swamp the concept and perception of the particulars of which it is composed. Both are concerns, I think, that the worth of certain values in the concept of art not be misplaced, that is, lost—for example, that the demand to be seen, call it the demand of experience to be satisfied, however thwarted or deferred, not be settled apart from the responsiveness to the claims of individual objects upon experience.

This says very little, but that little is incompatible with, for example, the recently fashionable tendency among aestheticians in the philosophically analytical mode to let the question of conferring or withholding the status of art upon an object be settled by whether or not someone or some place or other puts it on display (with no Duchampian taste for naughtiness and scenes). If it comes to this, I should prefer to let the status be settled by the persuasiveness of the catalogue. But artists who work in series in effect declare that only art can determine which singularities can sustain, and be identified by, a collection of works of art.

The problem here is already there in Kant's founding of the modern philosophy of art, in his *Critique of Judgment*.[29] His characterization of the aesthetic judgment as placing a universal demand for agreement on the basis of one's own subjectivity in assessing pleasure and purposiveness perhaps draws its extraordinary convincingness from its transferring to the act of judgment what should be understood as the work of the work of art (of as it were—the thing itself), namely, lodging the demand to watch. It is not news that we moderns cannot do or suffer without intellectualizing our experience. Then we should at least make sure that our intellectualizing is after our own hearts. Criticism, which (drawing out the implication of Kant's findings) articulates the grounds in a thing upon which the demand for agreement, after the fact of pleasure, bears a new responsibility for the resuscitation of the world, of our aliveness to it.

It remains tricky. When Thoreau one day at Walden moved all the furniture in his cabin outside in order to clean both the cabin and the furniture, he noticed that his possessions looked much better to him outdoors than they ever had in their proper places. This is an enviable experience, and valuable to hear. But it did not make his possessions works of art. Then recently I read of some new legislation proposed against schemes of price-fixing in certain prominent auction houses, about which a lawyer remarked that the movement of works of art is now being treated to legal constraints designed for deals in milk and cement. I reported this to M. Blistene, my host at the Pompidou Center, as we were about to enter a splendid exhibition there devoted to structures in cement and iron. He replied that he knew a German artist who works with milk.

But in what continues here I shall remain indiscriminate in collecting thoughts of collections in the world of things, leaving the differences in the realm of art mostly to shift for themselves, and perhaps, at times, toward us.

X

The other week, I saw for the first time Chantal Akerman's breakthrough film *Jeanne Dielman/23 quai du Commerce/1080 Bruxelles* (1975), known for the originality of its vision of film and of what film can be about, for its length (three and a half hours), for its director's age (twenty-four years when she made it), and for the performance of Delphine Seyrig. I adduce it here because it can be taken as a study, or materialization, of the self as a collection, in the particular form in which the one who is the subject of the collection is not free (or not moved?) to supply its narrative. I sketch from memory certain events, mostly of its first hour, already knowing that while little happens that in customary terms would be called interesting, the way it is presented, in its very uneventfulness, makes it almost unthinkable to describe what happens in sufficient detail to recount all it is that you notice.

The film opens with a woman standing before a stove, putting on a large pot under which she lights a flame with a match. The camera is unmoving; it will prove never to move, but to be given different posts, always frontal and always taking in most of a person's figure and enough of the environment to locate them, once you know the complete list of their possible locations. It is hard to know whether everything, or whether nothing, is being judged. The camera holds long enough in its opening position that you know you are in a realm of time perhaps unlike any other you have experienced on film. A doorbell sounds, the woman takes off her apron, walks into the hallway to a door which she opens to a man whose face you do not see but whose hat and coat the woman takes and with whom she exchanges one-word greetings, and with whom she disappears into a room. The camera observes the closed door to the room, a change of light indicates the passage of an indefinite span of time, the door opens, the woman returns the coat and hat to the man who now appears in full length. The man takes money out of a wallet and hands it to the woman, says something like "Until next week," and departs. She deposits the money in a decorative vase on what proves to be the dining table, bathes herself, an evident ritual in which each part of her body is as if taken on separately, and then returns to the preparation at the stove. When she is again signaled by the doorbell she opens it to a young man, or school boy. Admitting him, she returns to the kitchen, dishes out the contents of the boiled pot into two bowls, one potato at a time, four potatoes into each bowl, and takes them to the dining room table, where the boy has already taken a seat, and we watch the two of them eat through each of their respective rations of potatoes. Near the beginning of the meal the woman says, "Don't read while you eat"; nothing more is said until the close of the meal when she reports that she has received a letter from her sister in Canada, which she reads, or rather recites, aloud: it is an invitation to visit the sister, saying she has sent a present to her and containing the suggestion that the sister wants to introduce her to a man, since it has been six years since her husband died. She asks the boy—we suppose by now he is her son—whether they should accept the invitation. After dinner she takes out knitting; it is a sweater for the young man; she puts it away after making a few additional knots. Her son meanwhile has been reading; she listens to him recite a poem from Baudelaire, evidently a preparation for school, remarks that his accent is deteriorating, that he doesn't sound like her; they move to the stuffed chair on which the son had been reading and unfold it into a bed. As the woman stands at the door, the boy, now in bed, recites that a friend has told him about erections, orgasm, and conception, which he declares to be disgusting and asks how she can have brought herself to go through it in having him. She replies that that part is not important.

The first day, the screen announces, is over. About an hour of the film has passed. In the remaining two and a half hours the same activities are repeated, with different economies. The second day, for instance, we see the preparation of the potatoes for the soup, watching, of course, each potato being peeled. Kant says that every object which enters our world is given along with all the conditions of its appearance to us. I should like to say: Every action which we enter into our world must satisfy all the conditions of its completion. (Every human action is, as the German says, handled, performed by the creature with hands, the same action in different hands as different, and alike, as different hands.) With this knife with this blade, sitting in this garment at this table, with this heap of potatoes from this bowl, within these walls under this light at this instant, . . . the woman knots herself into the world. Thoreau says the present is the meeting of two eternities, the past and the future. How does a blessing become a curse?

On this second day certain things, or conditions, are not in order— a button is missing from the son's jacket, a wisp of her hair is out of place after finishing with that day's client, she lets the potatoes burn, she cannot get her coffee to taste right, even after going through the process of beginning again, throwing out the old coffee grounds, grinding new beans, and so on. The film feels as if it is nearing its end when on the third day we are not kept outside but accompany her with that day's client into her bedroom. After an abstract scene of intercourse in which she is apparently brought to orgasm despite her air of indifference, she rises, moves about her room to her dressing table to freshen herself, picks up the pair of scissors which we had seen her find and take into her room in order to cut the wrapping of the present just arrived from her sister, walks with the scissors over to the man lying back on her bed, stabs him fatally in the throat, and slides the scissors onto her table as she walks out of the room. In the dining room, without turning on a light, she sits on a chair, still, eyes open, we do not know for how long.

I wish to convey in this selected table of events the sense of how little stands out until the concluding violence, and at the same time that there are so many events taking place that a wholly true account of them could never be completed, and if not in this case, in no case. As for a narrative that amounts to an explanation of the stabbing, it would make sense to say that it was caused by any of the differences between one day and the following—by burning the potatoes or failing to get the coffee to taste right or being unable to decide whether to go to Canada or receiving the gift of a nightgown from her sister or slipping against her will into orgasm. To this equalization of her occupations a narrative feature is brought that is as pervasive and difficult to notice as the camera which never moves of itself but is from time to time displaced. Each time that the woman moves from one room to another room of the apartment (kitchen, bathroom, the woman's bedroom, the dining-sitting-sewing-reading-sleeping room, all connected by a corridor) the woman opens a door and turns out a light and closes the door and opens another door and turns on another light and closes that door (except after the stabbing). The spaces are to be as separate as those in a cabinet of curiosities. (What would happen if they touched? A word for thought would be ignited.)

But if Akerman's film may be brought together with the cabinet of curiosities—an inevitable topic in any discussion of the history of collecting since the Renaissance—it suggests that from the beginning this phenomenon signified both an interest in the variances of the world and at the same time a fear of the loss of interest in the world, a fear of boredom, as though the world might run out of difference, exhaust its possibilities. A space I am trying to designate and leave here is for a consideration of Walter Benjamin's perception of the era of the Baroque as characterized by melancholy, marked by acedia, or depletion of spirit. As the era arguably of Shakespearean tragedy (*Hamlet* is the implicit centerpiece or touchstone of Benjamin's work on the twin of tragedy he calls "the mourning play"),[30] it is marked principally for me as the advent of skepticism. This is no time to try to make this clear; I mention it to go additionally with, for example, Pomian's suggestion that funerary display is at the origin of the idea of collecting, and with Nietzsche's suggestion that it is not God's death that caused churches to turn into mausoleums, but the other way around, that our behavior in these habitations unsuits them for divinity—precisely Emerson's point when he speaks, half a century earlier, of preachers' speaking as if God is dead.

The pivotal role claimed for Akerman's films as events in the unfolding of contemporary feminism would mean, on this account, that she has found women to bear undistractably, however attractively, the marks of supposedly interesting social partitions or dissociations. Her pivotal role in the unfolding of filmmaking is then that she has constructed new means of presenting the world in which these marks perpetuate themselves, and has thereby made them newly visible and discussable. Call this a new discovery of the violence of the ordinary. In this she joins the likes of Beckett and Chekhov, but also Rousseau (in his revelation of mankind so far as free and chained—the easiest thing in the world not to notice), as well as Emerson and Nietzsche (in what the former called conformity and the latter philistinism). That Akerman's camera can as if discover suspense in what is not happening, as if we no longer know what is worth saying or showing, what is remarkable, shows a faith in the sheer existence of film that approaches the prophetic.

XI

That the occasion of the present reflections is the interaction of two great cities, Paris and New York, enacts the fact that major museums and their collections require the concentration of wealth that is to be found, in the modern world, in centers of population and power. I recall that it is in thinking of the connection between what Georg Simmel calls the metropolis and mental life ["*Die Grosstadt und das Geistesleben*"] that he observes:

> There is perhaps no psychic phenomenon which is so unconditionally reserved to the city as the blasé outlook. . . . The essence of the blasé attitude is an indifference toward the distinctions between things. Not in the sense that they are not perceived, as in the case of mental dullness, but rather that the meaning and the value of the distinction between things, and therewith the things themselves, are experienced as meaningless. . . . This psychic mood is the correct subjective reflection of a complete money economy to the extent that money takes the place of all the manifoldness of things and expresses all qualitative distinctions between them in the distinction of "how much." . . . [T]he metropolis is the seat of commerce and it is in it that the purchasability of things [this "altered relation to objects; this coloring, or rather this de-coloring of things"] appears in quite a different aspect than in simpler economies. . . . We see that the self-preservation of certain types of personalities is obtained at the cost of devaluing the entire objective world, ending inevitably in dragging the personality downward into a feeling of its own valuelessness.[31]

Simmel announces the topic of his essay by saying that "The deepest problems of modern life flow from the attempt of the individual to maintain the independence and individuality of his existence against the sovereign powers of the society, against the weight of the historical heritage and the external culture and techniques of life."[32] Call the individual's antagonist here the collective and its heritage and techniques its collections, gathered, it may be, as much like pollutants as like potsherds. Might there be some philosophical cunning that permits us to learn from collections how to oppose their conforming weight?

Benjamin evidently thinks not. From his "Eduard Fuchs, Collector and Historian": "[Culture and history] may well increase the burden of the treasures that are piled up on humanity's back. But it does not give mankind the strength to shake them off, so as to get its hands on them."[33] For whom is this said? It was such a perception that set the early Nietzsche writing against a certain form of history, monumental history he called it; Emerson's first essay in his first *Series of Essays* is "History," written against what he takes us to imagine history to be. Quoting Emerson's essay: "I am ashamed to see what a shallow village tale our so-called History is. How *many* times must we say Rome, and Paris, and Constantinople! What does Rome know of rat and lizard? What are Olympiads and Consulates to these neighboring systems of being? Nay, what food or experience or succor have they for the Esquimaux seal-hunter, for the Kanaka in his canoe, for the fisherman, the stevedore, the porter?"[34] It is part of the concept of my telling another about an event, that I (take myself to) know something about the event that that other fails to know, and might be glad to know, or that I am interested in it in a way that other has not seen and might be interested to see. Emerson opposes a history of events that trades upon their having already received significance, so he demands a recounting of what has hitherto been taken to count. When Freud, in *Civilization and Its Discontents*, introduces the issue of ethics—"the relations of human beings to one another"—into the problem he is bringing before us, "namely, the constitutional inclination of human beings to be aggressive toward one another," he goes on to say:

> The commandment, "Love thy neighbor as thyself," is the strongest defense against human aggressiveness and an excellent example of the unpsychological proceedings of the cultural super-ego. The commandment is impossible to fulfil. . . . What a potent obstacle to civilization aggressiveness must be, if the defense against it [the unshakable super-ego] can cause as much unhappiness as aggressiveness itself! . . . [S]o long as virtue is not rewarded here on earth, ethics will, I fancy, preach in vain. I too think it quite certain that a

real change in the relations of human beings to possessions would be of more help in this direction than any ethical commands; but the recognition of this fact among socialists has been obscured and made useless for practical purposes by a fresh idealistic conception of human nature [namely, that the abolition of private property will eliminate difference that causes aggressiveness].[35]

So you needn't be a socialist to recognize the necessity of a real change in our relation to things. (Lacan in effect develops this thought of Freud's, in the concluding chapters of Seminar VII, *The Ethics of Psychoanalysis*, in, for example, his assertion that the experience and goals of psychoanalysis demand a break with what he calls "the service of goods.")[36] What change in relation to objects might Freud have had in mind? The most prominent model of his own relation to possessions is figured in his well-known collection of some two thousand ancient Greek, Roman, and Asian objects, primarily statuettes. Putting aside psychoanalytically dependent explanations of Freud's tastes (that the statuettes of gods and heroes are father-substitutes, that archeological finds are emblematic of the finds excavated through the methods of psychoanalysis itself), we might consider certain facts of his reported behavior toward these possessions. Baudrillard, among the prominent theorists of collecting, uses Freudian concepts most explicitly, invoking relations to objects he characterizes in connection with oral introjection and anal retention; yet while he concludes "The System of Collecting" by observing that "he who . . . collect[s] can never entirely shake off an air of impoverishment and depleted humanity," he does not, so far as I am aware, express interest in Freud's own collecting.[37] John Forrester's essay "Collector, Naturalist, Surrealist" is indispensable on this topic, relating Freud's psychoanalytic practices throughout as modes of collecting (dreams, slips, symptoms) and emphasizing the life Freud maintained in his collections by adding to them and making gifts of them.[38] It is not easy, in the staid atmosphere of the so-called Freud Museum in London, formed from his residence in London, to imagine what it could be like alone with Freud in his apartment of study and treatment rooms, guarded or regarded by these figures. It is known that new figures, before taking their places within the collection, were initially introduced into the family setting, placed on the table at the communal meal. The suggestion has been that Freud used the collection to mark the separation of his working from his family life, but it seems more pointedly true (but then this should amount only to a redescription of the same fact) to say that it served to mark the separation of his patients' work with him from *their* everyday lives.

What could be more pertinent for a holding environment (to use an idea of D. W. Winnicott's)[39]—in which the claims of ordinary assertions are to be put in suspension (not to stop you, as in philosophical exercises, from saying more than you know, but to free you from stopping saying what you wish, expressing your desire)—than uncounted gods, who have seen and survived the worst and whose medium is revelation through concealment?

To imagine Freud's collecting anything else is like trying to imagine his having a different face (with apologies to Wittgenstein and his example of the ridiculous and embarrassing results in trying to imagine what Goethe would have looked like writing the Ninth Symphony).[40] Neither a series of objects that in themselves are more or less worthless (for example, the series of match boxes mounted in a curved line along a wall that Lacan cites as representing sheer thingness)[41] nor a collection each piece of which may suggest pricelessness (perhaps like the objects in the Frick Museum) fits our idea of Freud. The random voracity of Charles Foster Kane's acquisitiveness, or (somewhat less?) of William Randolph Hearst's at San Simeon, California, on which Orson Welles's *Citizen Kane* was based, seems to fit (indeed to have helped construct) the personas of their acquirers, and to manifest, with touching vulgarity, the proposition—established clinically and theoretically by Melanie Klein,[42] and alluded to in such Romantic narratives as Samuel Taylor Coleridge's "The Rime of the Ancient Mariner" (1798)—that the loss of our first object is never fully compensated for.

XII

Is, then, the value we attach to things ineradicably compromised in its assumption of objectivity? The issue takes on various emphases in moral philosophy. It is essential to John Rawls's *A Theory of Justice* that "[A]s citizens we are to reject the standard of perfection as a political principle, and for the purposes of justice avoid any assessment of the relative value of one another's way of life. . . . This democracy in judging each other's aims is the foundation of self-respect in a well-ordered society."[43] How sure are we that we know what constitutes the aims of the ways of life depicted in *Jeanne Dielman* or in *The Glass Menagerie* or in *The Great Gatsby?* A fundamental implication of the avoidance of relative judgment—call it the rejection of snobbery, that sibling of envy—is that the bearing of another's life cannot be measured (beyond the requirements upon it of justice) without seeing it from that other's perspective. This is emphasized in Christine Korsgaard's Rawlsian/Kantian treatment of the question of the objectivity of value when she takes as an example of questionable value one in which a collection figures essentially.[44] In considering the question whether value is subjective or objective, a Kantian is bound to measure the question by the formulation of the aesthetic judgment in Kant's *Critique of Judgment*, in which the claim to beauty is both subjective and yet necessarily makes a comprehensibly universal claim—necessity and universality being the Kantian marks of the objective. So one can say the issue of conflict between the objective and the subjective (in aesthetic matters, as differently in moral) becomes a matter of how, as rational beings, we are to confront one another.

Korsgaard takes the case of someone who collects pieces of barbed wire—presumably a rarified taste—and asks in effect where the claim, if any, upon my respect for this activity is supposed to lie, in the sincerity of the passion for the wire, or in a property of the wire itself? No one else should be counted on to share the taste, and why be interested in someone who has it? A crucial point of moral order is involved for Korsgaard: our respect for other persons must not await our respect for their ends, but on the contrary, respecting their ends must be a function of respecting them as fellow persons. This must be right. But what does "respecting their ends" come to? Given that it cannot require sharing their ends, as the case of the barbed wire is designed to show, it evidently means something like finding the alien end comprehensible, seeing *how* it may be valued. A good society cannot depend upon our approval of each other's desires but it does depend upon our being able, and being willing, to make ourselves comprehensible to one another. Here is where the idea of a collection plays an essential role. What interest this piece of barbed wire has may only be communicable in associating it with other, competing pieces, to which a given piece may be taken to allude, comparing it with these others, perhaps, in its effectiveness, economy, simplicity, handling, or producibility. This may not succeed. It does seem that some minimum of the sharing of desire is required for reason to prevail. But then respect, or tolerance, should have a way to prevail in the absence of offerable reasons. It seems hard to imagine the members of a society flourishing in which their commitments to one another are based upon sheer indifference toward their differences.

It is to show that a commitment to democracy may have to imagine something like this, and to show the room there is for responsiveness to it, if not quite for offering reasons in it, that I can understand, and be grateful for, Dave Hickey's instruction in his *Overture to Air Guitar*, in our "need [for] so many love songs"—there are so many things to learn, well within the range of justice, about satisfying desire.[45] You needn't share Hickey's taste for Las Vegas, but just a fragment of his love song to it, flying back another time from some respectable art panel—"coming home to the only indigenous visual culture on the North American continent, a town bereft of dead white walls, gray wool carpets, ficus plants, and Barcelona chairs—where there is everything to see and not a single pretentious object demanding to be scrutinized"—and you can rejoice that Las Vegas is, for him, part of the union.[46]

It suggests itself that collecting may serve to allay an anxiety, not exactly that the world can lose its interest, that we may all just disinvest in its differences—but that my interests may make me incomprehensible to others, that safety lies alone in masquerading a conformity with those of others. Early in my reading of Wittgenstein's *Investigations* I summarized my sense of what I (will) come to call his vision of language, and what I might now call the stake of our mutual comprehensibility, in these words:

> We learn and teach words in certain contexts, and then we are expected, and expect others, to be able to project them into further contexts. Nothing insures that this projection will take place (in particular, not the grasping of universals or of books of rules), just as nothing insures that we will make, and understand, the same projections. That on the whole we do is a matter of our sharing routes of interest and feeling, modes of response, senses of humor and of significance and of fulfillment, of what is outrageous, of what is similar to what else, what a rebuke, what forgiveness, of when an utterance is an assertion, when an appeal, when an explanation—all the whirl of organism Wittgenstein calls "forms of life." Human speech and activity, sanity and community, rest upon nothing more, but nothing less, than this. It is a vision as simple as it is difficult, and as difficult as it is (and because it is) terrifying.[47]

Terrifying because this seems to allow that my meaning anything, making sense, depends upon others finding me worth understanding, as if they might just *decide* that I am without sense. Childhood is lived under this threat. It is no wonder Melanie Klein describes the child's world as hedged with madness, negotiating melancholy for paranoia, reparation for destructiveness.[48]

XIII

In *Art and Money*, Marc Shell recounts through a thousand instances the millennial-long controversies in the West over the relation between the status of the representation of value by art and by money, and relates the controversies to life-and-death issues of the materialization and dematerialization of God (for example, over the status of the graven image, over the significance of reproducibility, over the definition of truth as "adequacy" between conception and thing), noting the issue to be alive in minimalist and conceptual art.[49] (Here Michael Fried's "Art and Objecthood" and Clement Greenberg's "Modernist Painting" and "After Abstract Expressionism" are pivotal texts.)[50] But the dematerialization of art and of reality are also at work from Andy Warhol's painted shoes to Martin Heidegger's creepy casualness about our relation to the atom bomb, or as he puts it, ". . . man's staring at what the explosion of the bomb could bring with it. He does not see that the atom bomb and its explosion are the mere final emission of what has long since taken place, has already happened."[51]

What has already happened to us is the loss of distance and ignorance of nearness—our thoughtlessness concerning the nature of the thing—that I glanced at in section IV. Even if, as I am, one is willing to go a considerable way with such signature Heideggerean soundings as "the thing things," there are junctures at the surface around which suspicion should form. What may be dismissed as, let us say, the poor taste of comparing the effects of the atom bomb with a metaphysical process, barely conceals a political claim marked by the careful distinction between the bomb and its explosion. Only one nation has exploded the atom bomb in war, showing "what it could bring with it." And the implication is that there is a metaphysical condition that makes the use of the bomb possible, or thinkable, and that Heidegger's thought has been alone in its efforts to outline and counter this condition on behalf of the globe.

And then there is that matter of Heidegger's exemplary jug, in *What Is Called Thinking*, which is suspiciously folkish—pretechnological, precapitalist, predemocratic—in its extravagant aura.[52] I do not wish here to counter a healthy impulse toward disgust with philosophy. One finds oneself recovering the good of philosophy in one's own time, or not. Yet I will say that to miss Heidegger's narration in which the jug marries earth and sky and its contents form a gift of mortals to gods; and miss the unfolding in which a ring of celebration (alluding surely to Nietzsche's wedding ring of eternal recurrence) among the fourfold (earth, mortals, etc.) is the work of the thing thinging, but a work accessible to us only in stepping back from our millennia of constructions and representations within a heritage of philosophical concepts and leaping free to a form of thinking that is "called by the thing as the thing," and hence understand ourselves as "be-thinged" ("in the strict sense of the German word *bedingt*"), the conditioned ones [dictionary definitions of "bedingt" are "conditionally," "limited," "subject to"], a condition in which "we have left behind us the presumption of all unconditionedness" [unconditionedness for ourselves, as if we were the gods of creation];—to miss this narration of a new relation to things as such is to miss one of the most remarkable in the history of responses to Kant's derivation and puzzle of the thing-in-itself, and accordingly to risk slighting the distinct contribution Heidegger proposes for an understanding of gathering or collecting, namely one that affirms our finitude (the renunciation of our unconditionedness, of an identification with pure spirituality). This forms a counterweight to the impression, variously given in writing about collections, that collecting is a narcissistic, not to say imperialist, effort to incorporate the world. But would Heidegger consider an empirical collection to provide occasion for the event of entering on his new path toward a different gathering of the world? He himself evidently suggests no exercises for this change of heart.

In the sequence of proposals I have made, leading to Heidegger's, meant to account for our valuing of collecting—that we have an interest in learning nearness, in the stability of materiality, in achieving comprehensibility to others, and an interest in the endurance of interest itself—I am continuing a line of thought in earlier moments of my writing that I ask leave to name here: In "Finding as Founding," a reading of Emerson's "Experience," I cite Emerson's search for nearness in terms of his apparent distance from the consciousness of grief over the death of his young son Waldo, standing for all there is to be near to ("I cannot get it nearer to me"), and I observe his discovery that he must thereupon accept the world's nearing itself to him ("indirect" is his word for this direction), an acceptance of a certain revised form of life (philosophy may poorly call it animism) outside himself, outside any human power.[53] This reading goes back to my *The World Viewed*, in which I relate the automatism of Jackson Pollock, and of post-Pollock abstraction (somewhat modifying the concept of automatism as introduced by William Rubin into the discussion of Pollock's work),[54] to the achieving of a candidness, or candor, or uncanniness and incandescence (all etymological developments of the idea of glowing or being white), from which I associate an unexpected, all but paradoxical connection between these nonobjective commitments and the power of photography and of nature's autonomy or self-sufficiency.[55] From here I derive the idea of this painting as facing us (an indebtedness to formative discussions with Michael Fried), as if to perceive them is to turn to them, all at once. This line of thought extends a step further back into my *Senses of Walden* and its discussion of Thoreau's concept of our "nextness" to the world, or our neighboring of it, as the condition of ecstasy.[56] I add here that the idea of automatism in painting leads, in the section that follows in *The World Viewed*, to the invoking of work that essentially exists in series (p. 115), that is, in a collection.[57] (What I referred to a moment ago as philosophy's poor concept of animism, something that dogs, or should, a certain intensity in accounting for the work art does, can be taken, while not named, as a subtext of Heidegger's still formidable "The Origin of the Work of Art," as when he speaks of "let[ting] things encounter us" [p. 25], and claims that "All art is poetry," recalling—I take it—that, as we are forever told, *poesis* means making, but then goes on to ask what it is that art makes happen, and answers in such words as may translate this way: "Art breaks open an open place . . . in such a way that only now, in the midst of beings, the open brings beings to shine and ring out."[58] It does seem sometimes that we are in our period destined to be told things unwelcome either because they are heard too often or because they are too unheard of. As though the world has become immeasurably tactless, inadequately traditional, insufficiently original.)

This line of thought was brought to mind in attending a fine presentation, at the recent meetings of the American Society for Aesthetics, by Stephen Melville, who in taking up the ideas of a painting's candidness and its facing of the beholder, cited among many other matters some of the material I have just alluded to, and startled me (I cannot in this speak for others) with the coup of projecting Andy Warhol's "portrait" of Marilyn Monroe in this context, which presents the image of her in ranks and files of differently tinted replications of the same frontal image.[59] It thus, I suppose, not alone declares the issue of a painting's facing us but posits that we may not see even a singular face in isolation, but only in its repetition, achieving its aura precisely because of its existence as a collective property, as if the mark of the objective now, even of existence, is celebrity.

XIV

What has happened to the idea of the capacity of knowing as our fundamental relation to the world—the capacity so treasured by modern philosophy, thus so exposing itself to its powers of skepticism? We have neglected, and will mostly here continue to neglect, the species of collection which may seem to have been made to inspire the response of, or motive to, knowledge, that of the natural history museum. If there is a decent justification for this neglect it is that such collections are no longer readable as the work of individuals (as in the case of the painting and collecting activities of Charles Willson Peale, given so excellent an account by Susan Stewart in "Death and Life, in That Order"), hence the interest in collecting is apt to shift from the desire of the collector to the quality of the collection, and from the matter of our relation to objects to our relation to that of a theory of the relation of objects to one another, so that classification becomes more fundamental in presenting the collection than juxtaposition.

In both arenas display is essential, but with the things dear to collectors, as is characteristically emphasized (most insistently, perhaps, by Pomian), the object is taken out of circulation (or, to respect Philip Fisher's alliance of the making and the effacing of art, say that the object is put into a different circulation), whereas one could say that in a natural history collection the object (or part or reconstruction) is put into circulation for the first time. Here the status, or life, of the work of art shifts again into view. If it is true, as said earlier, that objects of art are objects from their outset destined to be exhibited (unlike bones and stones), it might also be true that other objects share such a destiny without (quite, yet) being known as objects of art. Was it before or after cultures collected that they also decorated and selected among options, offering themselves grounds for a relation to an object of service not strictly required, or exhausted, by that service? From that moment objects could exist within intersecting circles of circulation.

We should be cautious in saying that with natural objects we know where the next specimen or part fits, whereas with the artifact we have to find where it fits best—cautious because of what we learn from work made most famous in Foucault's texts, especially *The Order of Things*, that knowledge grounded in classification is not a discovery derived from a clear accumulation of facts but itself required a set of intellectual/historical conditions in which a new conception of knowledge (or episteme) was possible, in which a new counting, or order, of facts was made visible. (This is an insight marked as belonging to the same intellectual era in which Thomas Kuhn startled philosophers and historians with the suggestion that physical science, knowledge at its most prestigious, goes through periods of crisis in which accumulation is not driving research, and reconceptualization appears to wish to remake rather than to refine the picture of the world.[60] And of course it was as if we had always known that.)

In both arenas of display death is invoked, even death as present in life, but in collections of art, or artifacts, it is my death that is in question as I enter into the stopped time of the objects (Pomian remarks that their display is as on an altar),[61] whereas the skeletons and parts of natural history speak of the death and the perpetuation of species, of their coexistence and succession, measured within the earth's time (one of Foucault's favorite expressions of the new episteme exemplified by the natural history museum is to say that it displays its items on, or in, a table).[62]

XV

But one event staged within a natural history museum is irresistibly pertinent for an American with a certain philosophical disposition asked to think about a collection being transported from France for a stay in the United States, I mean the declaration Emerson made to his Journal at the time of his visit to Paris in 1833, that he has had something like a revelation in his experience of the great collections in the Jardin des Plantes. In a study that has recently appeared, *The Emerson Museum; Practical Romanticism and the Pursuit of the Whole*, Lee Rust Brown takes that

experience, always remarked on by Emerson's biographers, as more deci-
sively significant than has been recognized before.[63] He proposes that we
understand what floored Emerson by the Paris exhibitions to be their presentation of an image of what he wanted his writing to be. I might formulate the image Brown constructs as one in which Emerson sees that his
words may become specimens of a totality of significance arrived at otherwise than by a system (philosophical or scientific [or narrative?]), of which
Emerson felt incapable. *The Emerson Museum* casts a wide net of social,
philosophical, and historical reference and I do not imagine my formulation to do justice to it. The formulation leaves deliberately open, for example, whether Emerson's "words" refers to single words, to sentences, to
paragraphs, or to essays; and to what the idea of system is to be credited if
not to laws or argument. There should be another time for that. Here I
wish simply to give credit for the insistence that Emerson's experience and
vow in Paris ("I will be a naturalist") is some kind of revelation to him of
his project and practice as a writer. I have myself been too long preoccupied with the sound of the Emersonian sentence not to welcome an addition to its understanding; but too long accustomed to asking how each of
Emerson's essays characterizes its own writing not to be wary of a proposal of any fixed model for them.

This is too important a matter to me not to be a little more specific
about it. Having indicated a connection between the concept of collecting
and that of thinking (as in the history of disappointment with universals),
and with the concept of the self (as in contemporary play with Humean
ideas of the subject), I would not have satisfied my opening sense of my
assignment to think publicly about the philosophical interest of collecting
without including some speculation about its comparable connection with
the concept of philosophical writing, particularly in the cases of Emerson
and of Wittgenstein. An obvious cause for this inclusion at this moment is
to recall Emerson's and Wittgenstein's relation, in their fashionings of discontinuity, to the medium of philosophy as aphorism, in counterpoise to
its medium as system. Wittgenstein is explicit about this, but implicitly
everything about Emerson's practice as a writer bespeaks this sense of
aggregation and juxtaposition—from his culling from his *Journals* for individual essays, to the sense of his sentences as desiring to stand apart from
one another, each saying everything, each starting over.

XVI

The first impulse Emerson records, on 13 July, upon noting that he went
"to the Cabinet of Natural History in the Garden of Plants," is "How

much finer things are in composition than alone. 'Tis wise in man to make Cabinets." Here is some of what he took away with him that day.

> The fancy-colored vests of these elegant beings [in the Ornithological Chambers] make me as pensive as the hues & forms of a cabinet of shells, formerly. It is a beautiful collection & makes the visitor as calm & genial as a bridegroom. The limits of the possible are enlarged, & the real is stranger than the imaginary. Ah said I this is philanthropy, wisdom, taste. . . . The Universe is a more amazing puzzle than ever as you glance along this bewildering series of animated forms . . . the hazy butterflies, the carved shells, the birds, beasts, fishes, insects, snakes,—& the upheaving principle of life everywhere incipient in the very rock aping organized forms. Not a form so grotesque, so sane, nor so beautiful but is an expression of some property inherent in man the observer,—an occult relation between the very scorpions and man. I feel the centipede in me—cayman, carp, eagle, & fox. I am moved by strange sympathies; I say continually "I will be a naturalist."
>
> Walk down the alleys of this flower garden & you come to the enclosures of the animals where almost all that Adam named or Noah preserved are represented. . . . It is very pleasant to walk in this garden.[64]

He does seem at the end of his visit to have well-recovered himself from signs of revelation. The scrupulous editor of this volume of Emerson's *Journals* notes that beneath the ink entry "this is philanthropy, wisdom, taste" is written in faint pencil: *"Le moment ou je parle est déjà loin de moi"*— a learned quotation from Boileau presumably to mark that Emerson is unsure what he has learned.[65]

I think I can see that Emerson's sequence of descriptions of his state at the Jardin des Plantes—being pensive; calm and genial as a bridegroom; inspired as by a perception of philanthropy, wisdom, taste; moved by strange sympathies—produces an outburst of dedication to qualities he wants for his writing. But I am not so far able to see how Lee Rust Brown makes the transfer from, for example, Emerson's description of "a beautiful collection" (of elegant birds) to the way we are to see his sentences hang or perch together. An elegant bird, I should imagine, as Emerson says of a squirrel running over a lawn and up into trees, is not made to go unobserved; linking his writing with a display of bright feathers or a casual virtuosity suggests that Emerson has his own uses for attractiveness. ("You are attracted to the standard of the true man," from the first printing of "Self-Reliance.")[66] And I think I can see, more specifically, Emerson's "Self-Reliance" as describing its own writing when it speaks of thinking as an aversion to conformity; and "The American Scholar" of its own when it speaks of thinking as a process of conversion going forward at every hour; and "Fate" similarly when it describes freedom as resistance or counterstroke; and the so-called Divinity School Address when it speaks of communion; and "Circles" when it speaks of circular forms and seems to imply a circle as an intimate audience; and "Experience" when it speaks of "glancing blows" as opposed to direct grasps as the direction of knowing.[67] (Do we not have a kind of internal gag when "Experience" speaks of originating—as he says Sir Everard Home has discovered the embryo originates "coactively"—from three points, since three points define a circle, three gathered together in an arc.)[68] But I do not know that I have in any case made clear or concrete enough the transfer to Emerson's actual words, or made clear that the process is clear enough as it stands. Enough for what?

Perhaps I am too attached to Thoreau's more explicit interest in literal classification and listing as the basis for self-allegory, as when his series or tables of measurements or soundings in *Walden* show as emblems of the accuracy and systematicity he claims for his words.[69] As when his tabulation of his expenditures on food, in his first chapter "Economy," shows as his "thus publishing his guilt," thus assigning to his writing the power to assess the guilt in acquiring, at who knows what expense to others, the sustenance of his existence; and the writing is the sustenance, declaring that its will is to make itself cost something to read.[70] The Emersonian sound seems different, otherwise, as in the passage cited earlier, in which Emerson expresses his shame of what we know and accept as history: "What does Rome know of rat or lizard?"—these neighboring systems of existence. There is an urgency here of the incessant bearing of unseen processes, to be registered in each sentence, that Thoreau can allow to be suspended across sentences, or chapters, or years. The idea broached earlier of every Emersonian sentence as a self-standing topic sentence of the essay in which it appears, hence of his paragraphs as bundles, collections that may be moved, is linked, in my mind, with Friedrich Schlegel's remark that in good prose it is as if every word is stressed.

XVII

Emerson's visit to the Jardin des Plantes collects (or, more accurately, was itself collected earlier by) another pair of visits there by another translated American, Chris Marker, first as recorded in his film *La Jetée* (1964) and then quoted in his film *Sans Soleil* (1986), that endlessly instructive autobiographical/anthropological meditation on art and technology, and culture and memory, and past and future, and space and time, and words and images, and desire and death, and nearness and distance. The scene from the Jardin des Plantes that Marker uses in the first and quotes in the second of these films is one in which two people are looking and gesturing at a cut from a giant sequoia tree, stood on its side almost to the vertical, inscribed with dates identifying the years for various of its rings, almost facing us, after which, in *Sans Soleil*, Marker continued by quoting the passage from Hitchcock's *Vertigo* on which the shot was based, in which James Stewart and Kim Novak, visiting the Muir Woods near San Francisco, are looking at its sequoia cut covered with historical dates and this woman, pointing, is saying, "There I was born, and there I died." The memory of a memory of a Hitchcock film about the fatality of memory is preserved in the collection of articulations on a tree whose birth preceded French and English and all they have had to forget.

Other collections to be mentioned are present in *Sans Soleil*, which assured that it had to find its place here. Taking the Emerson/ Marker/Hitchcock/California intersection with me to Paris last summer as I went to visit again, for instance, the Jardin des Plantes and the Pompidou Center after a lapse of some years (the Paris sequoia cut is still, or again, on display, but moved inside, into an entrance hall of one of the museum buildings), you may imagine my momentary vertigo on being informed that Chris Marker had accepted an invitation to make a piece to mark the very event of the temporary transfer of its collection that is a cause of these words. When returning to the Center I inquired of M. Blistene whether there were documents recording the ideas with which Marker had been approached for this commission. He replied, "There is something better. Marker is downstairs shooting." What I found him shooting, or having just ceased shooting, was a sequence in which a visitor to the museum is interactively viewing a provisional CD-ROM that Marker had installed on a monitor, mounted on a stand with two chairs before it, in an otherwise empty space. Marker held up the small camera he had been using and said, "I've wanted this all my life. No more waiting for developing, adding tracks. . . . Things like *Sans Soleil* are past. It is why I tore up the poster of *Sans Soleil* before putting it up." I had noticed the collagelike shape on the wall as I entered the installation space, and looking at it again I saw that it appeared to have been torn twice, once lengthwise, then, halves together, once across, then reassembled; the title was still quite legible, and the new form was no doubt more attractive than the original rectangle of the poster would have been. I felt encouraged that this master of his art, or arts, had found elation both in breaking with an old practice (that of the movie camera) and in calling upon an old practice (that of collage) in announcing the fact.

The CD-ROM turned out to be an elaboration of material pertaining to *Sans Soleil*. On one of my routes interacting with it I came upon a voice-over reference to *Vertigo* in which Marker says that he has seen the Hitchcock film—he calls it the best film ever made about time—nineteen times, and that his remarks about the film are for others who also have seen it nineteen times. And, imagined, for those who will see *Sans Soleil* with that attention. (I think here of Susan Howe's wonderful responses to Marker, and others, in her "Sorting Facts; or, Nineteen Ways of Looking at Marker.")[71] This invitation to obsession—must I decide whether it is fetishistic attachment, or honest labor?—is something I have sometimes felt I must ward off. The temptation is, I think, a reason I was struck early by Wittgenstein's self-reflection in the *Investigations*:

> It is not our aim to refine or complete the system of rules for the use of our words in unheard of ways. For the clarity that we are aiming at is indeed *complete* clarity. But this simply means that the philosophical problems should *completely* disappear. The real discovery is the one that makes me capable of breaking off philosophizing when I want to.—The one that gives philosophy peace.[72]

The issue of completeness can haunt discussions of collecting, some writers (for example, Susan Stewart) taking it as essential to the desire in collecting, others (for example, John Forrester) taking it that a collection that is no longer growing is dead.[73] Regarding Wittgenstein's *Investigations* (Part I especially) as a collection, I have described the 693 sections of this work as showing the willingness to come to an end 693 times. Since I have understood the current over-insistence (so I judge it) on the idea of meaning as the deferral of significance to be an expression of the fear of death, I find Wittgenstein's practice here to become a memorable realization of Montaigne's assignment of philosophy as learning how to die. Since Wittgenstein also describes his philosophical practice as "[leading] back words from their metaphysical to their everyday use" (§116), in which, or at which, philosophy brings itself to an end (momentarily?—but how can we know that there will be a further call upon it, a 694th call?), the ordinary, in Wittgenstein's philosophy of the ordinary, is the realm of death, of the life of mortality, subjection to the universal collector.[74]

Does the passion for collecting have something to say about such matters as coming to an end?

XVIII

A number of collections are depicted in the Tokyo sequences of *Sans Soleil*. One toward the beginning is of cat figurines lodged in a temple consecrated to cats; one around the middle is of dolls in a ceremony for the repose of the souls of broken dolls; one toward the end is of the debris collected together from the accessories and decorations of the communal New Year ceremonies.

The ceremony for the broken dolls and the one for the debris both conclude by burning the collections. The film does not make explicit the significance of the burnings, but the suggestion is that debris, whose burning seems fairly natural, has as much right to immortality as the souls of broken dolls do, but the burning of the dolls is shocking. Perhaps one thinks of Kurt Schwitters's collages incorporating debris, as it were tracing a fitful immortality of beauty upon what others have abandoned. There is also to ponder Robert Opie's self-described near mania for collecting and displaying wrappings or packagings, enacting the mad wittiness of retaining and reorganizing precisely what is meant—is it not?—to be discarded.[75] Many collections convey the wish to make the world immortal by so to speak forming a reconstruction or impression or shadowy duplicate of it (what is new about film?); but Opie's idea, in description, projects a sort of defiance of the world's availability, or deliverability.

Thoreau, the philosopher of noncollection, of the way of responsible life as one of disencumbering oneself from false necessity (enacting and extending teachings from Plato and from Rousseau), is struck by a ceremony of burning what he regards as debris, late in the opening chapter of *Walden*.

> Not long since I was present at the auction of a deacon's effects, for his life had not been ineffectual: "The evil that men do lives after them." As usual, a great proportion was trumpery which had begun to accumulate in his father's day. Among the rest was a dried tapeworm. And now, after lying half a century in his garret and other dust holes, these things were not burned; instead of a *bonfire*, or purifying destruction of them, there was an *auction*, or increasing of them. The neighbors eagerly collected to view them, bought them all, and carefully transported them to their garrets and dust holes, to lie there till their estates are settled, when they will start again. When a man dies he kicks the dust.[76]

Thoreau contrasts this ceremony, to its disfavor, with a certain celebration of a "busk" or "feast of first fruits," which Bartram describes as having been the custom of the Mucclasse Indians. Thoreau quotes Bartram: "When a town celebrates the busk, having previously provided themselves with new clothes, new pots, pans, and other household utensils and furniture, they collect all their worn out clothes and other despicable things, sweep and cleanse their houses, squares, and the whole town of their filth, which with all the remaining grain and other old provisions they cast together into one common heap, and consume it with fire."[77]

After adding several further critical details, Thoreau concludes the section by remarking: "I have scarcely heard of a truer sacrament, that is, as the dictionary defines it, 'outward and visible sign of an inward and spiritual grace.' "[78]

This is not quite allowing the debris of life its own right to remembrance, or abandonment. That idea of right is announced by *Sans Soleil* in connection with Sei Shonagon's *Pillow Book* and her passion for lists, lists of elegant things, of distressing things, among them a list of things not worth doing, and one—an enviable mode of composition—of things "to quicken the heart."[79] This passion has, in the film, its own, to my taste, beautiful consequences, inspiring, for instance, ideas of visits to post office boxes without expecting letters but just to honor letters unsent or unwritten; and of pauses at an empty intersection to leave space for the spirits of cars broken there. And when the voice-over adds, to the list of things to be honored in farewell, "All that I'd cut to tidy up" (that is, in completing *Sans Soleil*), I found myself attaching a small prayer for thoughts that have never come, or never been given sufficient appreciation. Priceless uncollecteds.

Thoreau joins in recognizing the necessity to give abandonment, or farewell, to the character of what he calls an event of sacrament (as giving divorce to the character of marriage). But Thoreau's main emphasis falls still farther, to make his leaving even of Walden unceremonious, a step on a way. As if he has so burned himself into every event of Walden's days (the aroma of which is *Walden*) that he can trust both of their existences, entrust them to one another.

If collections can teach this, they may not exempt themselves from the knowledge they impart, that they are to be left. Some people need, or have, as luck would have it, a bequest to leave. Thoreau quite explicitly makes a bequest or deed of each form and depth and nameable object of Walden to whomever wants them properly. Thus he exhibits his obedience to St. Matthew's injunction, "Lay not up for yourself treasures upon earth where moth and Trust doth corrupt." And he can say, evidently, in a worldly register, "A man is rich in proportion to the number of things he can leave alone,"[80] thus humoring the labor theory of possession running, in Locke's formulation: "Whatsoever [any man] removes out of the State that Nature hath provided, and left it in, he hath mixed his Labour with, and joyned to it something that is his own, and thereby makes it his Property."[81] Locke wants something of the kind metaphysically to define ownership, and Marx wants the denial of something of the kind to reveal itself to us in the phantasmagoria of the exchange of commodities; so it is bracing that Thoreau isolates and makes explicit the religious, or animated, bearing of the features of nature left to us, as when he characterizes a lake (in the "Ponds" chapter of *Walden*) as "earth's eye."[82]

But when Walter Benjamin declares, "There is no document of civilization which is not at the same time a document of barbarism," the very power of the perception disguises the fact that it is as much fantasm as insight, an illumination of things indiscriminately in their aspect as spoils or booty.[83] It can be done; in some moods it is irresistible. But in lashing together, say, the Elgin marbles with, perhaps, a collection of old jazz records that preserve treasures of a harsh time, and these, perhaps, with a collection of silver objects of observance which Jews carried from a disguised into an undisguised exile, or with their steamer trunks desperately packed with evening gowns and court slippers for which no future life will call—here is a frenzied invitation to a madness of misanthropy as much as it is an enlightened liberation of conduct. For what is writing responsible? Not to hearten pointlessly; but not to dishearten expansively.

I said earlier that we should encounter again the bearing of Wittgenstein's and of Heidegger's work on the task of leaving or abandonment. In our relation to the things of the world, Heidegger proposes (as he translates a phrase from Parmenides) "letting-lie-before-us" as the mode of thinking to be sought in stepping back from our fantasies of thinking as grasping the world in fixed concepts.[84] Wittgenstein explicitly mentions just once the pertinent idea of leaving, as befits his discontinuous moments of philosophizing about philosophy: "[Philosophy] leaves everything as it is."[85] Perhaps he means to attract the interpretation this has largely received, a confession of philosophy's conservatism. Then one is left with having to put this together with the radical destruction of philosophical tradition that his writing undertakes. The immediate import of the claim is that modes of thought and practice other than the philosophical—for example the political or the economic, as we know them—do *not* leave things as they are, but subject them to violence, the state in which they are given to us. "Our investigation must be turned around the fixed point of our real need."[86] Our thinking is faithless to our desire, oblivious to what it set out to express. Whatever instructs us here is to the good.

"Don't take it as a matter of course, but as a remarkable fact, that pictures and fictitious narratives give us pleasure, occupy our minds."[87] I know of no better initial tip in matters of aesthetics. You are advised to consult yourself as to whether a thing you have taken into your mind, have consented for that time to bear upon your life, gives you pleasure, or perhaps otherwise disturbs you, and if not, to demand of yourself the cause, whether the thing that solicits you is not remarkable or whether you are coarsened in what you can remark, allow to matter to you. Why do we put things together as we do? Why do we put ourselves together with just these things to make a world? What choices have we said farewell to? To put things together differently, so that they quicken the heart, would demand their recollecting.

Notes

1. Krzysztof Pomian, *Collectors and Curiosities: Paris and Venice, 1500–1800,* trans. Elizabeth Wiles-Portier (Cambridge: Polity Press; Cambridge, Mass.: Blackwell, 1990).

2. See Jean Baudrillard, "The System of Collecting," in *The Cultures of Collecting,* ed. John Eisner and Roger Cardinal (Cambridge, Mass.: Harvard University Press, 1994); Pomian, *Collectors and Curiosities;* Susan Stewart, "Death and Life, in That Order, in the Works of Charles Willson Peale," in *The Cultures of Collecting,* Robert Opie, " 'Unless you do these crazy things.' . . . : An Interview with Robert Opie," in ibid.; Philip Fisher, *Making and Effacing Art* (Cambridge, Mass.: Harvard University Press, 1997); Michel Foucault, *The Order of Things: An Archaeology of the Human Sciences* (New York: Vintage, 1994; 1966).

3. See James Clifford, *The Predicament of Culture* (Cambridge, Mass.: Harvard University Press, 1988.

4. Ludwig Wittgenstein, *Philosophical Investigations,* trans. Elizabeth Anscombe, 3d ed. (Oxford: Blackwell, 1958;.1953), § 1.

5. Ibid.

6. Wittgenstein, *Tractatus Logico-Philosophicus,* trans. D. F. Pears and B. F. McGuinness, 2d ed. (London: Routledge & Kegan Paul, 1961; 1921), p. 149.

7. Baudrillard, "The System of Collecting," in *Tlie Cultures of Collecting,* p. 12.

8. Wittgenstein, *Philosophical Investigations,* §§ 65, 66, 67.

9. Martin Heidegger, "The Thing," in *Poetry, Language, Thought,* trans. Albert Hofstadter (New York: Harper & Row, 1975; 1971), p. 165.

10. Ibid., pp. 165, 166.

11. Ibid., p. 174.

12. Ibid., p. 171.

13. Wittgenstein, *Philosophical Investigations,* § 371.

14. Ibid., § 373

15. Heidegger, "Building Dwelling Thinking," in *Poetry, Language, Thought,* p. 146.

16. Michael Fried, *Three American Painters: Kenneth Noland, Jules Olitski, Frank Stella,* exh. cat. (Cambridge, Mass.: Fogg Art Museum, 1965).

17. W. V. Quine, *Pursuit of Truth* (Cambridge, Mass.: Harvard University Press, 1990).

18. Walter Benjamin, *Charles Baudelaire: A Lyric Poet in the Era of High Capitalism,* trans. Harry Zohn (London: Verso, 1983), pp. 168–69.

19. Ibid., p. 172.

20. David Hume, A *Treatise of Human Nature*, ed. L. A. Selby-Bigge, vol. I, iv (Oxford: Oxford University Press, 1951), p. 252.

21. Ibid., p. 269.

22. Ibid.

23. Ibid., p. 252.

24. Ibid., p. 253.

25. Ibid., p. 251.

26. Ibid., p. xx.

27. See Mieke Bal, "Telling Objects: A Narrative Perspective on Collecting," in *The Cultures of Collecting*; Stewart, "Death and Life"; Fisher, *Making and Effacing Art.*"

28. See Norton Batkin, "Conceptualizing the History of the Contemporary Museum: On Foucault and Benjamin," *Philosophical Topics*, vol. 25, no. 1 (spring 1997).

29. Immanuel Kant, *Critique of Judgment*, trans. J. H. Bernard (New York: Hafner, 1951; 1790).

30. Benjamin, *The Origin of German Tragic Drama*, trans. John Osborne (London: NLB, 1977).

31. Georg Simmel, "The Metropolis and Mental Life," in *On Individuality and Social Forms*, ed. Donald N. Levine, trans. Edward A. Shils (Chicago: University of Chicago Press, 1971), pp. 329, 330.

32. Ibid., p. 324.

33. Benjamin, "Eduard Fuchs, Collector and Historian," in *One-Way Street and Other Writings*, trans. Edmund Jephcott and Kingsley Shorter (London and New York: Verso, 1997), sec. 3.

34. Ralph Waldo Emerson, "History," *in Essays and Lectures*, ed. Joel Porte (New York Library of America, 1983).

35. Sigmund Freud, *Civilization and Its Discontents*, ed. and trans. James Strachey, vol. 21 (London: Hogarth, 1961), pp. 142–43.

36. Jacques Lacan, *The Ethics of Psychoanalysis*, Seminar VII (1959–60), trans. Dennis Porter (New York: Norton, 1992).

37. Baudrillard, "The System of Collecting," p. 24.

38 John Forrester, "Collector, Naturalist, Surrealist," in *Dispatches from the Freud Wars* (Cambridge, Mass.: Harvard University Press, 1997), pp. 107–37.

39. For a good introduction to Winnicott's work, see Adam Phillips, *Winnicott* (Cambridge, Mass.: Harvard University Press, 1988).

40. Wittgenstein, *Philosophical Investigations*, §183.

41. Lacan, *The Ethics of Psychoanalysis*, p. 114.

42. See, for example, Melanie Klein, *Envy and Gratitude* (New York: Free Press, 1984).

43. John Rawls, *A Theory of Justice* (Cambridge, Mass.: Harvard University Press, 1971), p. 442.

44. Christine Korsgaard, "The Reasons We Can Share: An Attack on the Distinction between Agent-relative and Agent-neutral Values," in *Creating the Kingdom of Ends* (Cambridge and New York: Cambridge University Press, 1996), pp. 275–310.

45. Dave Hickey, *Air Guitar: Essays on Art and Democracy* (Los Angeles: Art Issues Press, 1997), p. 16.

46. Ibid., p. 23.

47. Stanley Cavell, *Must We Mean What We Say? A Book of Essays* (Cambridge and New York: Cambridge University Press, 1976; 1969), p. 52.

48. Klein, *Envy and Gratitude*.

49. Marc Shell, *Art and Money* (Chicago: University of Chicago Press, 1995).

50. See Fried, "Art and Objecthood" (1967), in *Art and Objecthood* (Chicago: Chicago University Press, 1998); Clement Greenberg, "Modernist Painting" (1960) and "After Abstract Expressionism" (1962), in *Modernism with a Vengeance*, vol. 4, *The Collected Essays and Criticism*, ed. John O'Brian (Chicago: University of Chicago Press, 1993).

51. Heidegger, "The Thing," p. 166.

52. Ibid., pp. 168. Subsequent quotations in this paragraph are from p. 181.

53. Cavell, "Finding as Founding," in *This New Yet Unapproachable America: Lectures after Emerson after Wittgenstein* (Albuquerque: Living Batch, 1989).

54. William Rubin, *Dada, Surrealism and Their Heritage*, exh. cat (New York: Museum of Modern Art, 1968).

55. Cavell, *The World Viewed: Reflections on the Ontology of Film* (Cambridge, Mass., and London: Harvard University Press, 1979; 1971).

56. Cavell, *The Senses of* Walden (Chicago: University of Chicago Press, 1992; 1972), pp. 100–104.

57. Cavell, *The World Viewed*, p. 115.

58. Heidegger, "The Origin of the Work of Art," pp. 25, 72.

59. See, for example, Stephen Melville, *Philosophy Beside Itself: On Deconstruction and Modernism, Theory and History of Literature*, vol. 27 (Minneapolis, 1986).

60. Thomas S. Kuhn, *The Structure of Scientific Revolutions*, 3d ed. (Chicago: University of Chicago Press, 1996; 1962).

61. Pomian, *Collectors and Curiosities*, for example, p. 44.

62. Foucault, *The Order of Things*, p. 131.

63. Lee Rust Brown, The *Emerson Museum: Practical Romanticism and the Pursuit of the Whole* (Cambridge, Mass.: Harvard University Press, 1997).

64. Emerson, *The Journals and Miscellaneous Notebooks of Ralph Waldo Emerson*, vol. 4, ed. Alfred R, Ferguson (Cambridge, Mass.: Belknap, 1964; 1832–34), entry for July 13, 1833.

65. Ibid.

66. Emerson, "Self-Reliance," in *Essays and Essays: Second Series* (Columbus: Merritt, 1969; 1844; 1849), p. 50.

67. Emerson, "The American Scholar," "Fate," "Divinity School Address," "Circles," and "Experience," in *Essays and Lectures*.

68. Emerson, "Experience," in ibid.

69. Henry David Thoreau, *Walden*, ed. Walter Harding (New York: Washington Square Press, 1970; 1854), chap, 1, "Economy," passim.

70. Ibid., p. 43

71. Susan Howe, "Sorting Facts; or, Nineteen Ways of Looking at Marker," in Charles Warren, ed., *Beyond Document: Essays on Non-Fiction Film* (Wesleyan University Press, 1996).

72. Wittgenstein, *Philosophical Investigations*, § 133.

73. Stewart, "Death and life," p. 204; Forrester, "Collector, Naturalist, Surrealist," p. 107.

74. Wittgenstein, *Philosophical Investigations*, § 116.

75. Opie, " 'Unless you do these crazy things' . . ."

76. Thoreau, *Walden*, p. 49.

77. Ibid., p. 50.

78. Ibid.

79. Sei Shonagon, *The Pillow Book*, trans. Ivan Morris (New York: Columbia University Press, 1991).

80. Thoreau, *Walden*, p. 60.

81. John Locke, *The Second Treatise of Government*, in *Locke's Two Treatises of Government*, ed. Peter Laslett, 2d ed. (Cambridge: Cambridge University Press, 1967), chap, v, sec. 27, p. 306.

82. Thoreau, *Walden*, p. 141.

83. Benjamin, "Theses on the Philosophy of History," in *Illuminations: Essays and Reflections*, ed. Hannah Arendt, trans. Harry Zohn (New York: Schocken, 1969), p. 256.

84. Heidegger, *What Is Called Thinking?* trans. J. Glenn Gray (New York: Harper and Row, 1968; 1951–52), pp. 200.

85. Wittgenstein, *Philosophical Investigations*, § 124.

86. Ibid, § 108.

87. Ibid., § 524.

19

Concluding Remarks Presented at Paris Colloquium on *La Projection du monde*

HIS IS A CONCENTRATED moment of pleasure and gratitude for me. I am grateful, as you may imagine, to the organizers of this occasion, Marc Cerisuelo and Sandra Laugier, for conceiving and creating so memorable an event; to the impressive and diverse roster of speakers, for accepting the invitation to participate in it; and to Christian Fournier and Editions Belin for the translation that provides the motive for the occasion. Within this mood and from this perspective I also recapture a sense of gratitude for the existence of the great and still enigmatic art of film, whose history is punctuated as that of no other, by works, small and large, that have commanded the devotion of audiences of all classes, of virtually all ages, and of all spaces around the world in which a projector has been mounted and a screen set up. I hope you will forgive my indulging this mood of thankfulness one step further, as it were a private step, if I thank my lucky stars (I wonder how that will be translated!) which allowed me to write this little book thirty years ago. I published my first book rather late, in my forties, and *The World Viewed* followed it two years later. Such a text was quite uncalled for, in the environment of the Anglo-

---

Originally presented at Colloquium organized by Marc Cerisuelo and Sandra Laugier on the occasion of the publication of *La Projection du monde* (the French translation of *The World Viewed*), University of Paris III, May 1999. Published (in French) as the Conclusion to Marc Cerisuelo and Sandra Laugier, editors, *Stanley Cavell: Cinéma et philosophie* (Presse de la Sorbonne Nouvelle, 2001).

American philosophical world within which I was trained and had found a professional home. It would have been—so it seems to me at this distance, we are speaking of the late 1960s—so easy not to have written it. I must have felt something of this relief even then, for the book opens with an account of what made it urgent for me, of the sense that my history with the experience of film had, for better or worse, been disrupted, by the decline of Hollywood, by the burst of European filmmaking, especially French and Italian, increasingly making its way to American shores from the end of the 1950s, and by the new audiences for film and expectations for the arts generally, demanded by the traumatic social and political events of those times—for us the interaction of the civil rights movement most famously then radiating from Mississippi intersecting with the protests against the war in Vietnam.

A couple of weeks ago at Harvard, at a retrospective of the work of the remarkable so-called experimental filmmaker Stan Brakhage, one of Brakhage's most admiring critics, interviewed in a documentary film about his life and work, in a nostalgic moment inspired by the range of a major artist of film, declared: "Film as we know it is essentially over." It isn't certain what the critic meant, whether that the medium had exhausted its capacity to inspire creativity, or that the photographic medium was as such losing ground to other technologies, or something more. But it struck me not only that some such sense has been recurrent in the modern history of the arts, but specifically that I had felt some such way in writing *The World Viewed*—that an original relation to film, some pretheoretical trust, had been broken, causing a stronger sense of discontinuity than, say, any development since the advent of the talkie. Without trying to define this further now, I report that my sense was of writing as an emissary from another, foreign time, whether from the past or from a missed future is not clear; it is not clear, I mean, whether I was trying to jog the memory or stir the imagination of my noncontemporaries. Either way, the effect of thinking about film on my ambitions for philosophical prose—I have in mind particularly the necessity to become evocative in capturing the moods of faces and motions and settings, in their double existence as transient and as permanent—has proved to leave permanent marks, as I judge it, on the way I write. It was, I believe, more than any other ambition I held, a basis of freedom from the guarded rhythms of philosophy as I had inherited it.

And yet we also know that at any moment a new film can reclaim an untold measure of the history of film's discoveries, or self-revelations. In Terrence Malick's astonishing *The Thin Red Line* (1998), when a pair of soldiers running through a field of waving grass, away from us, are shot and fall, they are hidden by the tall grass which becomes, almost all at once, brilliant with emerging sun, promising at once retribution and redemption, what there is of these; and now I find that I am recalled to think of moments of transcendence in other widely varied temperaments, as when the young woman in Eric Rohmer's *The Green Ray* (sometimes known as *Summer*) (1986) is lost for a transfiguring moment among shivering trees, or at the light in which Hitchcock in *Vertigo* (1958) records the sequoias in the Muir Woods, or at the transfixed prison yard in *The Shawshank Redemption* (1994) over which the women's voices singing the Letter Song from *Figaro* are broadcast. Not everything is possible in every period, but not everything possible in any period is known before its materialization.

There are times when I am unsure whether what I call, in *Pursuits of Happiness*, the genre of remarriage comedy has survived its flowering in the two decades after the introduction of sound. But along comes, quite unforeseen, a piece such as *Moonstruck* (1987), with its open invocations and reversals of *La Bohème*, where the leading woman called Loretta is not Mimi but rather Musetta, and the leading man called Ronnie is not Rodolpho but rather Mimi, with a frozen hand; and their conversations, something more like arias, begin not by identifying themselves for the other tentatively or sentimentally (Rodolpho as a poet, Mimi as a seamstress) but by doing what each, when the time comes, aggressively calls "telling you your life," Loretta revealing Ronnie to himself as a wolf and Ronnie unveiling Loretta to herself as "no lamb." The wit and depth and credibility of these exchanges, something no one else in their world is capable of, mark the pair for one another and take an essential register of remarriage comedy fully and securely into the late 1980s. Why this film at the same time explores the relation of film and opera is a nice question about a large subject which must await another occasion.

The theoretical concepts put in play in *The World Viewed* have seen me, with modifications as critical issues seemed to warrant, through two further books about film, the one on comedy and a companion volume on Hollywood melodrama entitled *Contesting Tears*, and a number of further essays on the subject. Not wanting to argue pointlessly, I have not often contested with theories of film that have been proposed since *The World Viewed* appeared, and I know I have consequently missed valuable opportunities. I did not, for example, yet know when I wrote *Pursuits of Happiness* Walter Benjamin's essay on German Romantic Criticism, with its emphasis on the thesis of that body of work to the effect that what establishes a work as art is its ability to inspire and sustain criticism of a certain sort, one that seeks to articulate the work's idea; what cannot be so criticized is not art. I might not have said this in so many words in *Pursuits of Happiness*, but the thought seems implicit on every page. I treat the seven films principally studied in that book both as representative of the best work of Hollywood's classical period and (hence) as works capable of reflecting critically on the cultural conditions that make them possible. Nor had I read then Benjamin's study of Goethe's *Elective Affinities*, containing the following sentences: "After all, [Goethe] did not want, like [his character] Mittler, to establish a foundation for marriage but wished, rather, to show the forces that arise from its decay. . . . [In] truth, marriage is never justified in law (that is, as an institution) but is justified solely as an expression of continuance in love, which by nature seeks this expression sooner in death than in life." This view of the justification of marriage unnervingly resembles the view taken in my articulation of Hollywood remarriage comedies in *Pursuits of Happiness*, namely that marriage is justified not by law (secular or religious, nor in particular, to cite a more lurid connection with *Elective Affinities*, by the presence of a child), but alone by the will to remarriage. That articulation, however, denies Benjamin's qualification at the end of my citation from him, namely that continuance in love seeks its expression sooner in death than in life (perhaps Benjamin means this as a jab at a Romantic suggestion that it is easier to love eternally than diurnally).

But may I truly find companionability in this connection? My claim about film seems to contravene Benjamin's practice when it comes to his treatment of film, in which his famous speculations concerning the technological medium of film are developed without consulting a film's idea of itself, or undertaking to suppose that one or another may have such a thing. And the example of film featured in Benjamin's "The Work of Art in the Age of Mechanical Reproduction"—in its first version, and not seriously challenged in the later version—is Mickey Mouse. From this exemplification, further links of assumption seem easily acceptable, and confidently to be iterated by Benjamin's readers—that film is essentially a mass art, that film (in the form of cartoons) is to be understood in connection with jazz, that the audience's laughter at the brutalities in slapstick comedy is a sort of homeopathic protection against the psychotic potencies of modern technology (as perfected in the innovations of Henry Ford). Theodor Adorno found it worth reminding Benjamin that "The laughter of the cinema audience is . . . anything but good and revolutionary; it is full of the worst bourgeois sadism." Now the extraordinary Preston Sturges (whose film *The Lady Eve* [1941] is being screened in conjunction with our Colloquium), near the close of his film *Sullivan's Travels* (1941), depicts an audience of chain gang prisoners (and their guards and their community of hosts) laughing at a Mickey Mouse cartoon. It seems an obvious piece of the film's self-reflective proposal for how Sturges takes, or wishes, his film to work, particularly since the film's narrative concerns a Hollywood film director of entertaining films whose desire is to make a dark work for dark times and whose subsequent experiences of dark times show him that people suffering them want to laugh.

I believe the favored way of reading the moment is to take Sturges's film as ratifying a revelation that a Mickey Mouse cartoon was a typical response Hollywood had to offer in the face of social suffering. But mightn't we instead, or in addition, allow the film more of its darkness, or seriousness, and recognize that while men in dark times will sometimes accept a moment's respite in the form of cartoon laughter, the juxtaposition in this film of the faces of brutalized men with brutal cartoon comedy forms a revelation of film's capacity for damning revelations of the unnecessary necessities, call them the unrealized possibilities, of the world?

Consider that Sturges's *Sullivan's Travels* opens with two men fighting on the top of a speeding freight train, a topos emblematic of a Hollywood thriller, which then turns out to be the depiction of the ending of a film recently completed. That the depicted film was at the opening of our film indistinguishable from, as it were, Sturges's film to follow is Sturges's acknowledgment that his film is part of the history or art or technology of film in general, of Hollywood film in particular. That this film in a minute or two proves quite distinguishable from the film it depicts is Sturges's claim that his work makes a difference to this history and this art and this technology: it *raises the question* of the history and the art and the technology that condition the film—a question emblematized by the film's late depiction of another signature Hollywood production, a Mickey Mouse cartoon. I do not imagine that Adorno or Benjamin would have been interested to allow such powers to such productions; nor does Sturges's depicted director seem much moved to formulate such ironies of the medium, of, let us say, the way the medium takes its way beyond the hands of its makers.

But this just suggests that to consider such possibilities of a film requires concentrated and interested criticism. But what—other than poor institutions—requires film to exist in isolation from concentrated and interested criticism?

I close with one word about the translation of *The World Viewed*, specifically about its title. I wanted the title, incorporating a translation of the German *Weltanschauung*, to capture the sense of film as imposing its own conditions of viewing, or revelation. French does not permit this incorporation, and the alternative idea of the world *projected* shifts the location of the conditions of film's existence. So something I liked in the original title was lost. But something was gained. A danger in invoking a *Weltanschauung* for film is the suggestion that film is conditioned by a given set of circumstances and concepts, knowable in advance of the experience and history of film. "Projection," by contrast, captures the sense of the intervention of the work of humans and machines in materializing or rematerializing the world. A danger here is the suggestion that there are psychological and physical processes resulting in some well-understood set of effects which show the subjectivity of film's duplication of the world. But this danger is offset by the invocation of Heidegger's idea of "projection," which speaks of human possibility, and of Freud's idea of "projection," which may alert us to film's capacity to reveal what we would deny. I welcome both registers of the concept.

Multiply these last considerations by several orders of magnitude and one has a sense of the exasperations and elations in translating a sometimes deliberately resistant book. My luck in having translators of my books into French who solve these riddles with efficiency and elegance is a blessing I am, I hope, ever alive to, beginning with the work of Christian Fournier and of Sandra Laugier.

20

On Eric Rohmer's
A Tale of Winter

W HAT IN SHAKESPEARE'S *The Winter's Tale* suggests Eric
Rohmer's *A Tale of Winter* (1992) in response to it? What, from
the point of view of Rohmer's film *A Tale of Winter*, is
Shakespeare's play *The Winter's Tale* about?

Here is one line of answer: Shakespeare's play is about "an art / which
does mend nature—change it rather—but / The art itself is nature" (Act IV,
sc. iv). Applied to film, writing in light and motion, these too-famous words
take on an uncanny literalness. The causal connection between the world
and film is like and unlike the connection between them in the other arts.
Here is another line of answer, perhaps more thematic than formal or gener-
ic: The play is about the separation (or loss) and the reunion with (or finding
of) Perdita (a daughter); together with the disappearance and resurrection of
Hermione (a wife and mother). Rohmer's Félicie is shown as both mother
and daughter, which none of the women in Shakespeare's play is. Now a
Rohmer film is characteristically about how people find one another and
about what constitutes a woman's quest for herself, or her resurrection or
transfiguration. I think expressly of the four tales of the seasons (together
with the film called both *Summer* and *The Green Ray*) (1986), of which the
last, *A Tale of Autumn* (1998), was released last year.

This chapter is a version of a paper presented at a symposium on the films of Eric Rohmer
at the Annual Meeting of the American Society for Aesthetics, October 1999. It provided the
basis for the more extended treatment of *A Tale of Winter* in Chapter 23 of *Cities of Words*.

Here is a brief recital of some of their motifs, to be heard against a sense of certain of the obvious preoccupations of *The Winter's Tale*. All concern demands for, and of, specific places, particularly moving between two places; all are about measuring or marking time, or the lapse of time; and about nature or the normal or the trivial; about coincidence, loneliness or separation, chance, and choice; about impressions you cannot put a word to; and all contain a moment of insight that has transformative power, and some fantastic thing that simply and blankly *happens* (a trick of the setting sun, a sudden onset of wind through high trees, an encounter); and about transcendence entering the everyday. Pervasively they involve explicit discussions of religion, specifically of the difference between true and false religion, or between religion and magic.

I mean this to confirm William Rothman's sense of Rohmer as having a cinematic signature as powerful as Hitchcock's. It suggests Rohmer as a good site to test an idea I proposed to myself a long time ago and have not explicitly followed up very far, namely that for certain films the idea of an *oeuvre* is more pertinent than that of a *genre* in coming to terms with them—a different way of understanding how one work is conceived in the light of others.

But I want to go on here considering the light cast on a film by one of its self-declared sources in another medium, specifically in a Shakespearean romance. The most stunning connection—apart, I mean, from the fact that Rohmer's film actually depicts a scene from Shakespeare's play—is the concluding, miraculously achieved reunion of a man and a woman and of parents and a child, and the way in which belief in the credibility of that achievement, or acceptance of its inevitability, is something that each of the works declares and upon which they stake the powers of their respective arts. I have known superb and famous Shakespeareans who testify that the ending of Shakespeare's *The Winter's Tale* just does not, as they put the matter, "work." How can one know whether the basis for this sense is a function of the performances they have seen? And I should add that the question is live for the film *A Tale of Winter*, where the matter of performance is held constant. Here there is the matter of what I sometimes call "the good encounter" (or the good viewing)—distinguishing the many times nothing much works in a work (of any art) from those times when, as it were, everything happens.

One good encounter is quite enough—if, as I wish to testify, this film can work—for me to insist that with masterpieces nothing should go unaccounted for, including, as Marian Keane particularly notes, the slip or lapse of the mistaken address, even though, or perhaps especially when, a Freudian explanation of some automatic kind seems irrelevant or impertinent.

The point of topological identity between the film and the play is the coincidence of two lines—one in Shakespeare's play: "Perdita is found" [in Act V]; and one in Rohmer's film: "I'm the girl no one can find" [early, in Nevers, as she tells the story of giving her lover, the father of her child, the incorrect address]. Other references or echoes gather in relation to this one, more or less obliquely. (1) In Rohmer's film, Elise (the five-year-old daughter) draws pictures of flowers and a princess and a clown, which I take as references to principal motifs of the pastoral Act IV in Bohemia, where Perdita becomes Queen of the annual sheep-shearing festival. (In Shakespeare's play, a five-year-old son, brother to Perdita, perishes in reaction to his father's outbreak of madness against his mother Hermione in Act I, and is unaccounted for in the rest of the play. Rohmer as it were resurrects both children.) (2) In the film, Félicie's pregnancy is emphasized by its association, as she tells her story, with her realization that she had given the incorrect address. Sandra Laugier stresses this point in her remarkable essay on Rohmer's film. Hermione's pregnancy is dwelt on as the opening fact of the play in my essay on Shakespeare's play (after the prologue, the first spoken phrase is "Nine changes of the watery moon"), associated with the theme of separation. (3) In both the film and the play there is a pointed, explicit discussion of the differences between magic and religion, which rather associates Loic (Félicie's intellectual boyfriend) with Paulina, as she is in Act V (the scene Rohmer excerpts within his film). (4) After the reunion, near the end of the film, Félicie prompts the father to recognize that the daughter looks like him (Leontes' question to his young son is "Art thou my calf? [Act 1, sc. 2], as he is trying to stave off madness). Rohmer's film serves as some reparation for this catastrophe by letting the father rejoice in the similarity, which he accepts at once. (5) Félicie works as a hairdresser in her more brutish boyfriend's beauty parlor in Paris. I note an analogy, not more than implicit, but steady, between sheep shearing and hair dressing: both are associated with festivals and with business. Also Félicie is *out of place* when she moves with the boyfriend to his new hair-dressing salon in Nevers, and returns with her daughter hurriedly to Paris.

All but one of this set of references (the exception is [4], the matter of resembling the father) come from the final two acts of Shakespeare's play; that is, not from the melodrama of jealousy and madness contained in or as the first three acts. You might take Félicie's reference to the madness of true love as a reference to that, essentially omitted, beginning—omitted but with a strand of it epitomized in a prologue Rohmer gives to his film (Shakespeare's play also has a prologue), a sequence of summer love, in which Félicie and her child's lost father are shown playing on the beach, eating a meal he has cooked, and explicitly shown having intercourse—a unique occurrence in the films of Rohmer I know—where, breaking the silence of this opening sequence, the man says, in its closing shot, "You are taking a risk," evidently referring to the possibility of her becoming pregnant, and her response is, oddly, to laugh. If we take this prologue to make explicit the eros and fertility of the sheep-shearing festival, a modern epitome of the idyll of love, this would account for the fact, emphasized by both Rothman and Keane, that Rohmer's film does not seem to concern itself with the skepticism and death-dealing passions of Shakespeare's play, features of it I particularly emphasize in my essay on the play.

Is this informative? It might be, if one could formulate an informative account of Rohmer's interest in, in effect, moving from an epitome of the innocent happiness of Act IV to the mysteries of Act V, which is to say, from the pastoral to the romance of reunion and resurrection, without the skeptical, murderous preparation of Acts I through III.

Take the pastoral setting as an emblem of the everyday, figured as the natural (invoked by Félicie)—life within the turning of the seasons, in its dependence on the earth and the weather, on the powers of mutual amusement and sufficiency, some ancient dream of human happiness and equality—then Rohmer may be understood as posing the following question for his film: Is there some way to take this dream into modern life, as transfigured by a camera?—a way to make credible in what we know as everyday life the quality that the great poets in English articulate in their pastorals?—an immanent transfiguration of human possibility: a way to make it credible that what once required the setting of settled royalty and oracles, is now open to anyone in a populous city of passers-by, mutual now primarily in their being strangers to one another?

That there is such a possibility is glimpsed in Shakespeare's play at the moment when, in Act V, Florizel and the maiden (Perdita) he takes for a shepherdess learn that they have been followed by Florizel's father Polixenes, King of Bohemia, in their escape from Bohemia back to Sicily. It is the moment at which Leontes, King of Sicily, Perdita's father, demands of Florizel, "You are married?" Florizel replies: "We are not, sir, nor are we like to be: / . . . the odds for high and low's alike." That is, the chance for happiness is the same for princes and for poor shepherdesses, and requires the aids of happenstance and good will.

The achievement of this perception of the sameness of odds seems to produce a miracle in the world's responsiveness. As if what has been achieved is an ordinary (on film) that is not in contrast to its denial by skepticism, but is lived with an acceptance not born of resignation and disappointment. Félicie describes such a condition—in the car ride with Loic after their attending the performance of *The Winter's Tale*—as she says, "Not everyone lives with hope." Loic is stunned by her, understanding (truly) what she says not as a sign of hopelessness but, on the contrary, as a sort of, let's say secular, Pascalian wager: this woman has placed her infinite stake in her life not on the theoretical rationality of God's existence, but on the reality of her own desire. She has, as she almost says, found herself. (This is expressed again in her saying to her mother, "There are no good or bad choices," meaning something like: they are mine, they make the sense my life makes. Try telling that to theorists of social choice.)

The Pascalian moment is won for Félicie in her fairly explicitly denying (in all but name) Descartes's call for the cogito, for the proof of one's existence through the force of claiming it, through the implication of thinking it. I am alluding to another moment in the exchange in the car after experiencing *The Winter's Tale*, namely Félicie's response to Loic's rehearsal of the great crux of the play, the one about the narrative of *The Winter's Tale* that everyone is bound at some stage to raise: Did Hermione come back to life, or had she not died? Félicie replies: "You don't get it. Faith brought her back to life." Now this can sound as if it merely begs the question: Loic is asking what that *means*—as if the play has contained no answer for him. Félicie evidently understands the words of the play to provide her with the articulation of an experience which is not only clear but is now a standard of clarity, as it were, for her life.

She describes her experience of prayer the day before, while she was, as it happens, in the church at Nevers, alone with her daughter who was preoccupied with a Nativity scene, a toy of the promise of resurrection. Félicie says it was not praying as she was taught to pray. Loic suggests: "It was a *meditation*"—and she immediately and gratefully agrees. She goes on, among other things, to describe her "excitement in the brain" (an ordinary experience, but this time "a hundred times stronger"), about which she reports: "I didn't think. I saw my thoughts." Now a meditation the mode of which is explicitly a denial of thinking, and the result of which is that a woman comes back to herself, is with herself (I am saying, finds herself), achieving a certainty of her existence that she had, she says, known only once before in her life—this is what I am calling a fair negation of Descartes's cogito. (She describes the experience in terms of "joy." I cannot but assume, working as Rohmer does where and when he does, that in this term, about such matters, Rohmer is here invoking the work of Jacques Lacan.)

You can say she is expressing something like a vision of human existence as an independence from the dictations of the world (of who she is and what it is rational for her to count on happening), expressible also by saying that it does not matter what the calculable odds are against her desire: *finding her desire* is already the answer. This negates Descartes's negation of my dependence on the world: thinking my existence secures my existence by preserving me in the absence of the world; finding my desire exposes me to the world, but whether the world goes on to provide the satisfaction of my desire is a measure not of my existence but of the world's worth.

Formulation here is everything. But I run over the matter thus hurriedly in order to ask—hardly answering—the question I assume Rohmer's film asks of itself: What is film—or, what is the vision of the fact of film— that Rohmer's mode of narration discovers, the mode that allows such a vision as Félicie's to take its place, or to find itself, in everyday existence? Sometimes Rohmer discovers the possibility in the most classical of sources, in an angle of nature—for example, in a tree swaying and hissing in a sudden wind—something others may pass by but which the woman in Rohmer's film called *Summer* (or *The Green Ray*) is shaken by to the point of sobbing. Of course one might on any given viewing dismiss this, pass it, and her, by. But another one, another time, might not. If you do pass it by, then there is nothing much to speak of about such women, yet.

In *A Tale of Winter*—along with other of Rohmer's sorts of cinematic discovery, such as how to capture the interest in the minimal sense of an event in the world, the fact that in each instant, as Samuel Beckett puts the matter, something is taking its course (or in Wittgenstein's *Tractatus*: "Not how the world is, but that it is, is the mystical")—Rohmer discovers the vision or interest in, let's say, a specialized or stylized sense of the *world* as passing by, namely in crowds of strangers passing, in their individual mortal paths, and oneself as a passer-by among others, each working out a stage of human fate. The vision, as I am calling it, is one in which it comes to us that no one of us need have been in precisely this time and place, coincidently with the event or advent of precisely each of the others here and now; yet just this scene of concretion is an immortal fact for each of us, each having come from and each going to different concretions (there are no empty places in the Great Chain of Becoming), each some part of the event of each that passes. Emerson's transcendentalism speaks ahead to Rohmer's, from "Self-Reliance": "Accept the place the divine Providence has found for you; the society of your contemporaries, the connection of events." Some in my hearing have taken Emerson here to be speaking conservatively, as if not, and urging us not, to disturb events (even though he notes a few lines further on that this acceptance is incompatible with our becoming "cowards fleeing before a revolution"). Taking Emerson's words so reads "the place the divine Providence has found for you" as if it said roughly the same as "the place the society of your contemporaries has found for you," a place of conformity rather than a place from which to turn to what it is yours to find.

Which, no doubt, is only to say that in Rohmer's work film has found one of its own ways, among the arts, of marking the intersection of contingency and necessity, of chance and logic. So an initial question in the case of Rohmer's discoveries of his medium is: How has he—for whom has he—found subjects (meaning persons and places and topics) that, on film, render the exploration of such ordinary questions of metaphysics, or such metaphysical questions of the ordinary, representable and of continuous interest?

21

The Image of the Psychoanalyst in Film

FOR ALL THE NOTABLE intimacies between psychoanalysis and cinema—both of them originating in the last decade of the nineteenth century; both bound up, explicitly or implicitly, with the vulnerability and expressiveness of the feminine; each arguably responsible for a greater effect on the human being's perception of itself than any other science or art of the intervening century; neither able to gain the respectability of a stable position within the academic world, in some part due I dare say to the unexhausted subversive reserves of each—I know of no systematic effort to articulate the conditions of these intimacies, however many psychoanalytic interpretations of individual films have been offered and however frequent have been the cinematic presentations of psychoanalysis and psychoanalysts (running into the hundreds in Hollywood alone, especially if one is not asking for a clear differentiation there between psychoanalysis and psychiatry). For someone of my intellectual tastes and debts, a convincing articulation of these intimacies will have to account for the fact that neither psychoanalysis nor cinema has received the measure of attention from philosophy that each calls out for (of course there are exceptions), each calling into question whatever philosophy had hitherto known as representation and reality, pleasure and pain, understanding and

Originally presented at the Freud Museum Film Festival, Vienna, January 2000. Portions of Chapter 12 of *Cities of Words* are adapted from this essay.

295

ignorance, remembering and imagination, intention and desire. I note specifically that I speak, or wish to speak, under the sign of what I have elsewhere called Freud's ambivalence toward philosophy. I do not mean simply the evidence indicated by Freud's taking the trouble to deny that psychoanalysis is philosophy—a trouble expressed in his denying the identity no fewer than twelve times—but I mean as well an all but explicit ambivalence in his speaking, as in chapter 4 of *The Interpretation of Dreams*, of being led to feel "that the interpretation of dreams may enable us to draw conclusions as to the structure of our mental apparatus which we have hoped for in vain from philosophy": the ambivalence may be read equally to mean that our vain waiting for *philosophy* is now to be *replaced* by the positive work of something else, call it psychoanalysis; and/or read to mean that our *waiting* for philosophy is at last no longer vain, that philosophy has now been *fulfilled* in the form of psychoanalysis.

Either way psychoanalysis is seen as some sort of successor of philosophy, but I am rather attracted to the latter, stronger side of the ambivalence, which takes psychoanalysis as some sort of transformation of philosophy—as if, after a millennium or so in which philosophy, as established in Greece, carried on the idea of philosophy as a way of life, constituted in view of the task of caring for the soul, call this philosophy's therapeutic mission, and another millennium or so in which philosophy was prepared to discard this piece of its mission, psychoanalysis had discovered methods that can make good on philosophy's originating goal of liberation (as in Plato's image of our lives as those of chained prisoners in a cave), methods still using dialogue of a kind, but now inflected with injunctions about saying whatever comes to mind, and about free association, and about interventions guided by the progress of transference, which may appear to be antiphilosophical methods, teasing, not training, reason with its dialectics. Then it must be the task of psychoanalysis to show, as Freud says with respect to knowledge, that there is reason and then there is reason.

This shadowing of philosophy within psychoanalysis is pertinent to the image of psychoanalysis, or anyway psychotherapy, sketched in the film I have agreed to take as the focus of my remarks today, *Now, Voyager*, from 1942, one of Bette Davis's most famous and admired roles, supported by Paul Henried and Claude Rains, directed by Irving Rapper, not one of Hollywood's most noted directors, but one who had the talent and the luck to preside over a remarkable, one might even say transcendent combination of script and actors and technicians. But to say how I locate the philosophical pertinence, I have first to place this film, as it comes to me, within as it were two conflicting, or incommensurable, frames of reference.

The received view takes the film as one of what Hollywood named "women's films," rediscovered in the 1980s as part of the emergence of the new feminism as, among other of its intellectual accomplishments, the major unified force within film studies (in the United States at least). This phase of feminism tended fairly uniformly to distrust such films, and the Hollywood that stood behind them, seeing them (even when recognizing their considerable art) as luring their primarily feminine audiences to excessive investments of feeling and identification with their narratives, which have placed themselves in service of a conventional patriarchal hierarchy between men and women, confining women to their roles as mothers and wives when not arraying them as commodities. Here one may be treated to depressing descriptions of the institutions of Hollywood advertising and publicity, which included the phenomenon of the "campaign book" or "press book," which studios distributed along with their films, instructing individual theater owners in ways of marketing the picture they have leased. The principal commodity connections established in the press book for *Now, Voyager*, as those who have seen the film may imagine, are beauty products and fashion tips to make the woman viewer as glamorous as, for example, Bette Davis and therefore loveable to whomever she wishes to be loveable to. But of course it is the point of a kitsch perspective that it can reduce any object or event to kitsch. [Umberto Eco telling the stories of Homer, etc.] It should, to my mind, be of interest to ask how it is that movies as such are vulnerable to such a perspective. It is not enough to say that many movies are in fact works of kitsch. So are many paintings and poems and novels. This does not on the whole tempt us to take up this perspective on all paintings or poems or novels.

Film's critical vulnerability is a question raised by the second of the frames of reference I just mentioned, a view at odds with the received view of the "woman's film." Here I must invoke the two genres of Hollywood film that I have devoted a book each to understanding, one genre I call the comedy of remarriage, the other, derived from that, I call the melodrama of the unknown woman, of which *Now, Voyager* is a definitive example. It is a requirement I impose on the choices of the films I take, from which to develop the laws of each genre, that they be films of cinematic, or say aesthetic, value, by which I mean two things primarily: (1) that I judge them to be of value (in Kant's sense of aesthetic value, the test of which is my declaration that they provide me with a pleasure I am compelled to share with others, a judgment I demand that others agree with, knowing that my subjectivity may be rebuked); (2) that I am prepared to account for my insistent pleasure by a work of criticism (brief or extended) which grounds my experience in the details of the object: in a word, I show that the object is, in the sense Walter Benjamin develops in "The Concept of Criticism in German Romanticism," criticizable, we might say interpretable. What is not criticizable in this sense is not a work of art.

I therefore owe you some examples of gestures of criticism to establish the proposal that, to take our present case, *Now, Voyager* has in it that which resists, or rebukes, reductive description, indeed resists all criticism, in the sense that it invites and contests response, seeking as it were a voice in its judgment. Before discharging that obligation, I add one more comment about the genres of comedy and of melodrama (and certain related films) in relation to the figure of the therapist. Two of the seven core comedies of remarriage and two of the four derived melodramas contain therapist figures. It is true to say of this small sample of films that in the comedies the therapist is a comic, marginal figure, evidently more distorted in character than those he treats (as in *Bringing Up Baby* (1938), with Katharine Hepburn and Cary Grant, and in *His Girl Friday* (1940), with Cary Grant and Rosalind Russell), and in the melodramas the therapist is a serious character, even a leading one (as in *Now, Voyager*, as we shall see, and in *Gaslight* [1944], with Charles Boyer and the young Ingrid Bergman). (The figure of the therapist I identify in *Gaslight* takes the form in this narrative, for interesting reasons, of a young detective, who has an exchange with the maddened central woman in which he confirms the accuracy of her sense perceptions and insists, effectively, that she knows who is causing the ghostly noises overhead in her bedroom. Freud himself, as least as early as 1915, early in the *Introductory Lectures*, compared the scrutiny of an analyst with that of a detective.) In fact I know of no exception to this postulate of the difference in the therapist figure in comedy and in melodrama (except that in film noir, the figure may even be the villain). It is borne out in related melodramas (for example, in *Random Harvest* [1942], with Ronald Colman and Greer Garson, and emphatically in Hitchcock's *Spellbound* [1945]) as well as in related comedies (for example in *Mr. Deeds Goes To Town* [1936], with Gary Cooper and Jean Arthur, where the hero, accused of mental incompetence, is reduced to melancholic silence by a betrayal of trust, and finds his voice again, in a courtroom, by adducing evidence that all human beings, including the psychiatrist, "do silly things when they think," which amounts to the assertion that the creature who thinks, that is to say, the human being, is inherently and inveterately "nervous," or as Freud phrases the matter: "self-betrayal oozes out of every pore," a condition that the motion picture camera feeds upon.

The artistry or "criticizability" of such films suggests determining some explanation for this difference between comic and melodramatic environments. We might say, for example, that in a comic world, where desire is present, joyous, but disruptive, to mistake it for madness is itself comic; it will find its own way out. In a melodramatic world, where desire is denied, or fixated, perhaps a source of horror, liberation must come from outside, from the capacity to attract and tolerate help. In *Now, Voyager*, at the close of the initial interview of Dr. Jaquith and his patient Bette Davis, this guarded, melodramatically suspicious woman is reduced to tears and cries out to the doctor, "Can you help me?" to which he responds mysteriously by saying "You don't need my help." I say mysterious because he is not refusing her plea; but if he is granting it, why isn't his answer a flat lie? She patently does need his help. I take his line as a peculiar compression, meaning something like, "I'll help you come to see that you are not helpless." No doubt we are to understand this man as maintaining a certain mystery about himself, but the writing requires a kind of Hollywood abbreviation or allegorizing in narration that is hard to characterize.

Let's get further into the film *Now, Voyager* by following out what I called its depiction of the initial interview between therapist and patient. It is not literally depicted as such an interview. For one thing it takes place not in the doctor's office but in a Back Bay mansion in Boston, where, in the opening sequence of the film, a concerned family member has brought a prominent psychotherapist to observe her reclusive sister-in-law Charlotte. He has agreed to allow himself to be introduced into the house as a friend, not a doctor, since Charlotte would never agree on her own to seek therapy; but Charlotte's evidently distinguished mother, or matriarch, presented at once as Charlotte's essential problem, will not hear of this, and pointedly calls him doctor when Charlotte appears in the drawing room, upon which Charlotte takes her cue to leave; Dr. Jaquith follows her out of the room. What happens now is what I am calling "the initial interview," to underscore the remarkable fact that what ensues between this pair obeys essentially all the recommendations in Freud's classical statement "On Beginning the Treatment" (1913)—but obeys it backwards, in two respects:

The first half of Freud's paper concerns issues around the scheduling of appointments and money, and it is of the nature of the particular case in question in *Now, Voyager* that the woman in question is not in a position to make such arrangements for herself, but only through the mother. A climax in the relation between this daughter and her mother will turn in part explicitly on the mother's threat to cut off financial support for her unless she returns to her former state of obedience to her mother's wishes, to which the daughter replies, indicating that she has thought of finding an ordinary job, "You see, I'm not afraid, mother," and then is astounded by the simple truth, as it were the originality, of her words.

The second half of Freud's paper concerns the importance of letting the patient do the talking, very much including finding a starting point, throughout the session, except for the analyst's announcing the analytical rule of suppressing nothing that comes to mind. (I have variously noted it as a point of affinity between them that neither philosophy, as I care about it most, nor psychoanalysis, speaks first, that their essential virtue is responsiveness, or else the shunning of response.) But it appears that Dr. Jaquith does almost all of the talking when the two leave the room, as they walk up flights of marble stairs and enter Charlotte's own room where, after further conversation, Charlotte tells, with mounting agitation, a story from her adolescence of a traumatic sea voyage with her mother, a recital that produces the tearful plea for help.

My claim, then, is that one is invited to understand the entire encounter as if Charlotte is initiating the talking, beginning with understanding Jaquith's following Charlotte out of the drawing room as if she has invited him to. (This is no more surprising than the fact that she turns out to permit it.) Then when he says he'd like to be shown around such a house, Charlotte continues walking up the stairs, which might be taken as a refusal of his request but which he takes as an initial response to it: "That's right, I have already seen the ground floor." And when, having been shown an upstairs room, he says, as if it had been offered, he would like to see her room, she mounts another flight, and pauses before a door with a key in her hand saying, "She locks her door, doctor. Significant, isn't it?" (indicating that she's been doing some exploratory reading on her own, another matter her mother will later explicitly deplore). Again he refuses a conventional response—in this case, conventionally Freudian, as it were—saying: "Well, it signifies that it's your door. I've never heard it said that a woman's room is not her castle," which may be taken as a false or conspiratorial gesture of intimacy, but may also be granted as testing the possibility of rapport with this prospective patient; namely one of the principal tasks of the beginning interview as articulated in Freud's paper.

Of course I would not claim, even if I were competent to do so, that these exchanges are literal or mimetic representations of authorized technique; but I emphasize their, so to speak, allegorical aptness, for a pair of reasons: Among the suspicious theorists of Hollywood film alluded to earlier, one notes that *Now, Voyager* does not show us any instance of the implied analytical treatment, but the allegorical abbreviations of analytical purpose I cited, in their accuracy to that purpose seem to me to respect Freud's familiar insistence that one cannot understand psychoanalytical procedures by being shown them, that what one learns, from outside as it were, is hearsay. But there is a further reason for my emphasis on analytical purpose.

The picture of the analyst given in *Now, Voyager* is that of a sage, or say a philosopher; and while that picture is something that suits one dimension of the figure of Freud—one internal, I take it, to the process of analysis—it is one Freud accepted no more than he fought against it (it is surely one of his reasons for wishing to dissociate his work from that of philosophy). Putting aside for the moment Freud's major cultural works, who but a sage, who is at the same time a therapist, would write papers such as "Transience" (1915) and " 'Civilized' Sexual Morality and Modern Nervous Illness" (1908) and the pair entitled "Thoughts for the Times on War and Death" (1915)? The first paper is a contribution to what I would like epistemology to include (a study of our apprehension of the world as nature) as much as it is a perception of the incidence of mourning; the second paper prepares us to recognize that a firmer perception of a balancing must be arrived at between the requirements of instinct and of civilization, for the sake of both, than either can achieve within its own frame; the third (the pair) ends with the line: "If you want to endure life, prepare yourself for death." And who but a therapist who is at the same time a sage would portray a patient as "marooned within her illness" (*Introductory Lectures*, Eighteenth Lecture)—thus casting himself as one who assigns himself the task of discovering her for herself? One of the characteristics of being marooned that Freud specifies is the inability to give gifts; so it is nice to find in *Now, Voyager* that markers on Charlotte's therapeutic path are once the giving and once the receiving of a gift (her gift to Dr. Jaquith of one of the ivory boxes she carves is heavily remarked upon when the two return to the drawing room; her acceptance of a gift from Jerry, the man she is thrown together with on her subsequent sea voyage, is the beginning of their affair).

I could wish that Freud had more systematically theorized the perhaps irreducible function of the sage within the figure of the analyst; it might have clarified how when psychoanalysis is seen as a science, the house of science is modified—as when film is recognized as an art the house of art is modified. Beginning, as an analyst must, from the fact of transference, Lacan has most famously accounted for the element of the sage as "the one supposed to know"; but Lacan seems, to some disgracefully, to have enacted that role as much as he analyzed it. And naturally the extent to which sageness is required in a course of psychotherapy is a function of what one expects of a course of therapy. It is not the least of the affinities of psychoanalysis with philosophy (some strain of philosophy, in my case best represented, perhaps I should say, in the later philosophy of Wittgenstein) that philosophy too, in its way, has to deal with the renunciation of knowledge, with the question whether knowing how to undo false knowledge is itself an extension of what is known.

The overarching image of therapeutic change in *Now, Voyager* is that of metamorphosis: one should not underestimate a narrative that can sustain a pivotal moment in which a stylish, mysterious woman can show an attentive man on the moonlit deck of a ship a photograph of her family and declare, truly, "I am the fat lady with the heavy eyebrows and all the hair."

This is not simply a smart, literary-philosophical moment declaring
human identity to be inherently ambiguous: I still am, whatever you see,
the fat lady with all the hair; and I am not, and never was, however I imagined myself, the fat lady. But there is also evidence that fatness means, and
meant, something to her, say that it is symptomatic, and that we are to
speculate about its meaning. At the end Jerry identifies Tina, his child,
whom Charlotte has befriended and helped when she returned to Jaquith's
clinic, as their child; and we have seen Charlotte comforting Tina in bed,
their bodies spooned together, saying to herself, "This is Jerry's child," as
though she has been delivered of it. But it is her mother whom she says has
caused the fatness, and her mother seems to have been both father and
mother to her. We are not in a position to draw hard conclusions about
how she may imagine a child had been put inside her. But neither need we
accept the idea I have heard expressed that the film wishes us to understand that Charlotte is sexually repressed because of her mother and cured
of this by a love affair (Doane, p. 46). That things must be more complicated is suggested in the early exchange between Charlotte and Jerry,
alone on a midnight hotel terrace some days after their car accident had
isolated them for a night together before a fire. Jerry is already beginning
his song of love and extrication: He has asked: "Are you afraid of happiness?" to which Charlotte replies: "Heavens no. I am immune to happiness." He again: "You weren't immune that night in the mountains." And
she, raising an essential question of the film: "You call that happiness?"
Then his refrain: "A small part. . . . There are other kinds. . . . If I were
free I would spend my life trying to prove to you that you are not immune
to happiness."

Evidently she had found genuine sexual satisfaction with Jerry, and
she will be grateful for that to the end. But why does she find it important
to deny that it brought happiness? I think we know enough about her not
to attribute this to Jerry's conventional imagination of providing her with
what she calls "a man of her own and a home of her own." When she is
called, by her mother, "my ugly duckling," in one of the images the film
provides of transformation, the mother conventionally misinterprets the
image, taking it that Charlotte is in fact ugly and is fated to be a misfit. But
the fantasy of the ugly duckling (fundamental to the film) is not just that a
creature is not ugly, but that she is not a duck at all, but an unrecognized
swan. Charlotte is shown to be capable of physical transformation into a
glamorous presence (is Bette Davis really beautiful? and does it matter?);
but her insistence on immunity to happiness suggests that what she is
remains unrecognized, perhaps unrecognizable. When a proper suitor
later in Boston is courting her he asks why she never lets him send her the
white camellias she habitually wears when they go out in the evening. She

replies, "It's just a personal eccentricity. We're all entitled to them." There is, I think, strong reason to take her to be alluding, among other things, to something like a homosexual side to her make-up. An essential part of the reason for me is my sense that Jerry is attracted precisely to this side of her, to what they both understand as her morbidity. ("I've been sick," she says when she shows him the picture of the fat lady, "and I still am." And in their amorous exchange on the terrace he confesses, "Ever since the night you told me of your illness, I haven't been able to get you out of my mind, or out of my heart.")

The matter of her identity is taken to a new level when, in the sequence preceding the last, Charlotte and Dr. Jaquith are stretched out on the floor of that drawing room in her mansion—itself transformed, after the death of her mother, from a mausoleum into a festival hall full of young people—looking over plans for the new building Charlotte is funding for Jaquith's Cascade, and he stares at her to remark: "Are you the same woman who some months ago hadn't an interest in the world?" And she replies, simply but with Bette Davis mystery, "No." What these two discover together, looking like a couple well along in marriage, is that she is unknown—that the various names and labels that have been applied to her (another pervasive theme of the film) are none of them who she is. That this is a desirable therapeutic result I would like to maintain from a philosophical point of view of what the self is, something which no set of predicates can in principle exhaust.

From this encounter Charlotte moves to her final, famous exchange with Jerry, about which, as far as I know, it is without exception understood that Charlotte sacrifices any new life of her own in favor of a sterile pact with Jerry to remain faithful to the memory of their hopeless love, a view with which I find I thoroughly disagree. It seems to me instead that we are shown that Charlotte perceives Jerry's destructive guilt to be about to cause further destruction, in the form of removing his daughter from Charlotte's protection and love, and shown that he is incapable of responding to Charlotte in her assumption of her freedom and power, and that she accepts the fact that he has reached the limits of his powers of comprehension and allows him to delude himself in peace.

There is no time now to articulate what elsewhere has taken me considerable care to make this claim plausible—including an understanding of the unforgettable closing line of the film: "Oh, Jerry, let's not ask for the moon; we have the stars." So I conclude with the acknowledgment of my awareness that interpretations I find convincing of lines and moments of films that I admire often do not at first find conviction in others. I attribute this—I mean in cases where they are eventually accepted—to a further fact or condition shared by psychoanalysis and by philosophy as I care about philosophy most (the one seeking to do for individual inhabitants of a culture what the other seeks to do for the culture as a whole—and what is this difference?), as manifested in a mode of thinking that wishes to make itself responsible to each of these institutions. What I have in mind here is the sense of impertinence or strain in philosophical or in psycho-analytical interpretation when one is at the moment outside the experience that gives these interventions their life. To me this means that it is the never-ending task of the therapeutic mission, whether in the clarifying and liberating practices of philosophy or of psychoanalysis, to rediscover the reality of such work in one's experience, a reality in each case, therefore, which essentially runs the risk of becoming lost to a culture.

22

Opera in (and As) Film

S TILL IN THE FIRST DECADE OF sound film—talking pictures they were
called, though the first one was a singing picture, Al Jolson's *The Jazz
Singer* (1927)—one of Hollywood's most significant directors, Frank
Capra, in one of his classic comedies, called *Mr. Deeds Goes to Town* (1936)
(with Gary Cooper and Jean Arthur), confesses film's sense of affinity with
opera, often expressed in an impulse of competition with opera. The narrative of this film concerns the consequences of its innocent, provincial hero's
unexpected inheritance of an enormous fortune upon the sudden death of
his rich uncle. This cliché fantasy is evidently well suited to a film made in
the dark years of the economic depression of the 1930s, and the difficulties
in the hero's efforts to aid impoverished farmers with his money is a decisive
part of the narrative. The film is accordingly easy to dismiss as, in a common
phrase, a fairy tale for the depression. But, to go no further, that hardly
accounts for the admiration and affection the film has elicited over the more
than half century since its creation. As soon as Mr. Deeds moves into his
uncle's mansion in New York, he is assaulted by proposals for ways to spend
his fortune. One proposal is from a group informing him that they have
elected him to replace his uncle as President of the Friends of the Opera, an
immediate privilege of which is for him to continue his uncle's annual sub-
sidy of the opera's productions. Mr. Deeds, however (whose name suggests
allegory, perhaps not so clearly as the name Everyman), seems to be one in
a long line of fictional country bumpkins who outwit the schemes of the

Presented at the Vienna State Opera, March 2000.

sophisticated rich, and he asks why the opera company needs so much help, why they don't sell more tickets. When told that their season is always sold out and that everybody understands that ticket sales alone cannot support the undertakings of opera productions, he replies: "Well maybe you're putting on the wrong kind of shows."

It seems plain enough that the film is proposing that the right kind of shows for them to put on are movies, and that it is offering itself as an example. Considering that this is a film in which its title character will refer reverently to the philosopher Henry David Thoreau, and that it is made by a director another of whose leading characters, in another of his films of the period (the grandfather in *You Can't Take it with You* (1938)), refers to Ralph Waldo Emerson, I am not willing to reduce the proposal of a different kind of "show" to the incontestable idea that movies are in some obvious sense economically more viable than operas. What is this film about, that offers itself in the place of opera?

Consider that it is to be understood, so I claim, not simply as depicting a fantasy of inheritance, but that it is *about* the idea of inheritance—the invocation of Thoreau takes place in front of a monument in remembrance of the American Civil War, the tomb of President Grant, a tourist attraction in New York City, where Mr. Deeds is moved to the recognition that America, for all its big buildings, has failed to live up to its promise, its inheritance of noble ideas. Consider further that the film climaxes with a sequence about the idea of expressiveness: the hero Mr. Deeds has, because of his apparent betrayal by the woman he has fallen in love with in New York, fallen silent, into a melancholy, and how he regains his voice, and what his voice is, becomes the subject of the drama. Now I have elsewhere proposed understanding the origins of opera in the first decade of the seventeenth century, namely the same decade as saw the creation of Shakespeare's major tragedies, as marking a cultural trauma having to do with a crisis of expression, with a sense that language as such, reason as such, can no longer be assured of its relation to a world apart from me or to the reality of the passions within me. Nothing less than such a trauma could meet the sense of language as requiring as it were a rescue by music.

This traumatic crisis of expression will be articulated philosophically in the next generation, belatedly—as philosophy is belated—in Descartes's process of doubt, that radical skepticism which heralds the modern era in philosophy. I cannot here go into the readings I have given of Shakespearean tragedy that are meant to demonstrate its working out, in other terms, at other levels, what philosophy knows as the problematic of skepticism, nor can I do more than mention, as I shall in a while, the connection between Shakespearean comedy and a central genre of American comedies. So I must merely assert that such ideas underlie the powers I attribute to film and to opera when I read a moment in Hollywood comedy, the moment of Mr. Deeds refusing a use of his inheritance to support opera, as an argument of film with opera generally about its claims to inherit from opera the flame that preserves the human need, on pain of madness of melancholy, for conviction in its expressions of passion.

The argument has gone on for a long time. Even in the silent era of film, Cecil B. DeMille made a film of *Carmen* as an opera, as if to declare that the expressive powers of silent film are equal to those of music. It seems a perverse undertaking, exacerbating our sense of something missing in silent film, primarily the voice. But DeMille evidently believes in film to the extent that he would measure its power of, let's say, the magnification of gesture against music's intensification of speech in making human expression lucid. In the Marx Brothers' *A Night at the Opera* (1935), the denouement consists of a performance of *Il Trovatore*, or an attempted performance, perpetually interrupted by the manic, subversive intrusions of the Marx Brothers, substituting disruptive pages of music into the score, lowering and raising scenery at the wrong times, giving miscues to the singers, as if to say: they're putting on the wrong kind of show. Only what the brothers turn out to mean is that they are putting on the show wrong, with the wrong people.

The episode trades on the old conundrum that opera's founding convention, which substitutes singing for speaking, is too ludicrous ever to be taken with full seriousness. But the narrative (which Aristotle calls the soul of the drama) says something else; namely, that what they are subverting, or competing with, is this particular production; and the narrative ground of their objection to it is that it has cast the wrong tenor to sing the role of Manrico. The right tenor, in their view, is not simply the better singer, but in life is the true love of the soprano in the role of Leonora, and the Marx Brothers are always on the side of true love. But why is it *this* opera that is the object of their competition? Perhaps most obviously because the libretto of *Trovatore* is famously the example taken by someone in the mood to assert the absurdity of opera plots and words. The well-known opera diva who a few seasons ago introduced a production of *Trovatore* for its broadcast by the New York Metropolitan Opera was herself enacting a cliché when she furthered the education of the members of the television audience by advising them to ignore the words and actions and listen to Verdi's beautiful tunes. It is good to listen to Verdi (though it's hard to know who, presenting themselves for the opera, needs to be encouraged to do it). And how are we to ignore the moment in the plot when Leonora, rushing out into the night in response to the Troubador's song, accosts the cloaked male figure in her path with the words "*Anima mia,*" only to have it prove to be the wrong brother, the one she rejects and who becomes her nemesis? The question is raised concerning how soundly she has chosen the, let's say, right brother—which of them better fits the image of her desire? But the question of articulating the differences and the uneasy relations of brothers is something the Marx Brothers' maniacal routines turn upon, and their film's incorporation of *Trovatore*, or say their homage to it, may be a tip of their hats to a kindred medium whose capacity to thrill audiences is a prize their ambition to move audiences to helpless laughter is worth competing for. It is also characteristic of film that when it incorporates an opera into its narrative, it seeks to divert the tragic ending (Manrico and Leonara are alive and together, so far as we know, at the end of *A Night at the Opera*). We shall see, at greater length, two further instances of this process of diverting death, in the instances of *Tannhäuser* and of *La Bohème*.

Before that, let us get a feel for the variety of ways, in more recent decades, opera and film have intervened in one another, noting three principal ways, each with variations: film can either (1) realize the full performance of an opera, or (2) incorporate an opera essentially within the film's structure, or (3) briefly or intermittently allude to an opera. It is the second of these possibilities—the incorporation of an opera within a film—that I will discuss in a certain amount of detail, so I will begin with the other two possibilities to give some orientation.

Probably the major obvious distinction to be drawn in the first case, the case of film realizing opera in its integrity, is the distinction between a filmed opera and an opera film: a filmed opera is an opera whose independently staged production in a theatrical space is recorded on film; or, an opera film is a film, namely a work whose score—the music and the libretto—is subjected to the conditions of film, to its necessities for real spaces, to the camera's need for movement, to the actor's obliviousness of being seen, to the magnification of detail in the acting. A filmed opera generally has its life on video, whereas an opera film, if made by a significant director of film, may attract a certain public following, as in the case of Ingmar Bergman's *The Magic Flute* (1975) or Joseph Losey's *Don Giovanni* (1979) or Franco Zeffirelli's *Otello* (1986). Here the use of actual locations modifies the effects of the singing and acting differently from anything achievable in the familiar recontextualizing of theatrical settings (for example, Peter Sellars's setting of *Don Giovanni* in the violent ghetto of New York's South Bronx of fifteen years ago, where, for instance, the frenetic "Champagne Aria" ("*Fin ch'han dal vino/Calda la testa*") takes the description of wine heating the head as the cue to have Don Giovanni inject himself with a drug). While making plays into films has long been one of the standard sources of films, too few transformations of operas into films have been attempted for there to be a fair body of evidence of what may eventually emerge in this line. In a play in a theater, the character takes precedence over the actor; in a film the actor is the subject of the camera and takes precedence over the character. What happens in the case of the actor/character whose mode of existence, or self-presentation, is singing? To answer this would require a philosophy of the voice. The only opera film I know to have investigated this matter is Hans-Jürgen Syberberg's *Parsifal* (1982), where voice is sometimes displaced and doubled. (A comic version of such an investigation occurs in a very interesting film, a sort of experimental musical comedy, *Pennies from Heaven* (1981), featuring the American comedian Steve Martin, in which the voices coming from the various actors as they burst into song are as unpredictable as the songs themselves, sometimes sopranos coming out of pompous business men, sometimes baritones out of maidens.)

The case of videos of actual theater productions, on the other hand, of which there are many, and an always increasing number of examples, is I believe creating a new audience for opera. I confess that I find it surprisingly agreeable to experience an opera on video. It goes without saying that it is not the same experience as attending the opera, but it is related to the, as it were, original experience in ways that criticism and theory should take an interest in—for example in the way that the memory of having screened an opera on video is in certain respects surprisingly like the memory of having attended a production of the opera: the original force of transcendence is not there, but fragments catch in the memory, with their involuntary intervention and mystery intact.

The creation of a new or expanded audience for opera, produced by a new technology in the experience of opera, takes its importance, it seems to me, from the well-recognized, if not well-understood, fact that ours is not on the whole an age of awaiting the creation of new operas, but it is an age of awaiting the creation of new *productions* of operas, whose fame comes from what is in effect their new readings of, potentially, the entire heritage of opera.

I think, for example, of my encountering recently the video of the 1986 production of *Wozzeck* by the Vienna State Opera, conducted by Claudio Abbado. What manifests itself in this instance of the now familiar medium of the taped opera is not merely the invaluable documentary record of a great production, but a realization of Alban Berg's setting of Büchner's words that enacts in a new way something essential to that setting. What I mean goes back to my claim that opera enters Western culture at a moment of a crisis of expression, the Shakespearean moment that receives the new science represented in the work and life of Galileo, in which patriarchy and the divine right of kings is challenged by the new empiricism represented in the writing of John Locke, in which early capitalism is under formation. Berg's *Wozzeck* takes into a further dimension of lucidity Büchner's inter- pretation of an insane representative of modern society by showing his maddening, suffocating inexpressiveness (his deprivation of a voice in his history, his poverty of words in which to offer himself for understanding, marked for example in the fragment he can recall of the Lord's Prayer) within a medium of the most intense and continuous expressiveness, achieved in the intricate patterning and the lyricism of his music, insisted upon by the orchestra's continuity of transition between scenes. (In the background of Berg's music and subject lies, of course, Schoenberg's *Moses und Aron*, with its incessant expression of the impossibilities and necessi- ties of speech, figured, as in opera it must be figured, as the impossibility and necessity of singing.) The contribution of the video recording that I point to in the case of *Wozzeck* is that the simple shifts from watching the events on the stage to that of watching, as from the back of the pit, Abaddo conducting the orchestra against a fallen curtain, manifests the new distri- bution of expressive obligation between symphonic organization and vocal gesture that Berg's medium explores. (I speak of "simple shifts" between the video camera's watching the singers and watching the conducting of the orchestra, but those shifts between the fixed positions of television cameras, together with the use of close-ups of the singers, already inter- rupts any simple sense of what a "mere recording" of an, as it were, autonomous opera production does to the experience of that production.) I just mention in passing that the visual emphasis on the orchestra, invit- ed by Berg's compositional choice, puts under review the fundamental aes- thetic vision in Wagner's desire to make the orchestra invisible.

It is time to hear and see something more than poor words being spoken. I begin with a string of five brief excerpts to give an opening sense of the range of opera's invocation in film. The first is from a filmed opera, Peter Sellars's production of *The Marriage of Figaro* from the mid-1980s; the second from the film *Trading Places* (1983), directed by John Landis, starring Eddie Murphy; the third from the remarkable *The Shawshank Redemption* (1994), starring Morgan Freeman and Tim Robbins, a meta- physical as well as brutal reflection on imprisonment; the fourth is also from a filmed opera, a moment from the second act of *Tristan*, sung by Jon Vickers and Roberta Knie, which I screen for the purpose of pairing it with a fifth excerpt, in which that moment from *Tristan* is alluded to in the film *Now, Voyager*, from 1942, starring Bette Davis and Paul Henreid, which plays a key role in a book of mine on Hollywood melodrama. After we screen this set of fragments for less than a minute each I'll say a word about their possible significance.

[SCREENING OF FIVE EXCERPTS]

I don't know which came first of the two uses of the Overture to *Figaro* to set the scene of a drama laid in a big city of the American East, nor whether there is a causal connection between the two. I merely testify—we cannot verify it here—that I find Sellars's use of it the more satisfying. What *Trading Places* seems to want from its reference to *Figaro* is mostly the idea of the resourceful and sociable young and poor overcoming with various disguises the conniving of the unsociable old and rich, but with no sense that the old may be redeemed by a recognition of their faults and no revolutionary desire to see the world formed on a new basis, a desire expressed in the perfection of understanding aspired to in the music. Peter Sellars's opening on New York's Fifth Avenue focuses insistently on the people walking along this famous street of luxurious commodities (rather than, as in *Trading Places*, moving from walkers, to people at work or at play, to architectural landmarks, as though we are assigned the status of tourists), the Sellars accordingly realizing the sense of Mozart's opening figure as a certain registering of human nervousness, where the faces and gaits in the crowds of people individuated by the moving picture camera (a power of the camera noticed by many directors) seem discovered here as each moving toward or away from encounters, their glances and hesitations suggesting their knowledge that the future is impenetrable, its surprises pleasant or wonderful or nasty, a constitutional nervousness that may also be seen as discovered by the motion picture camera.

In the third excerpt, the letter duet from *Figaro*, addressed to the air, is played to fill the air of a prison yard over the loudspeaker reserved for messages from the warden, sent by a prisoner who will serve time in solitary confinement for this subversion of authority. This film stakes and risks its invocation of the human desire for transcendence, or purposefulness, on the conviction that these prisoners hear the realm of the freedom of imagination projected in Mozart's and Da Ponte's unthinkably, to these men, foreign sounds—asking us further to ask ourselves where the true audience of opera might be found.

The fourth and fifth excerpts identify a moment from a classical Hollywood melodrama, reading that moment as encoding the mystery of whether an erotic encounter is to open or close the possibility of mutual existence. The pair in *Now, Voyager* are given several remarkable and extended exchanges, or duets; the significance, even comprehensibility, of their exchange on the subject of happines is a function of what one imagines happened between them one night in an isolated mountain cabin, of which the visual evidence given us by the film is roughly that of a fire dying in a fireplace and a chaste kiss on the cheek delivered by the man to the sleeping woman, both wrapped in clothing against the cold. Take the reference to *Tristan* in evidence and the intensity of the question of their imaginations deepens. That no one of my acquaintances I have asked has remembered this quotation in the film, even when they know the film well, raises obvious questions: How do we determine what the essential elements are of a work of art? What counts as remembering the work? When does a critical intervention in the case of reading a film come too late to be of service? In the case of the great arts it is never too late. You could say—as the young Walter Benjamin almost says—that this is a mark of their greatness. Is film different?

I come to the two somewhat more elaborated cases I wish to illustrate here, ones falling into the second category of relations between opera and film I mentioned at the opening, not that of taped operas or of opera films, both of which realize essentially the full score of an opera, and not that of films which contain an allusion to or a momentary depiction or depictions of an opera, but the category in which a particular opera enters into the substance of a film, where the competition between an opera and the attention given it in the film becomes an essential part of the film's subject; or to say it otherwise, where to understand the relation between the film and the opera to which it weds itself sets the primary task of the understanding of the film. So it is clear that we can in a few minutes at best scratch the surface of what should be said about such cases. My examples, as indicated earlier, are the film *Moonstruck* (1989) (directed by Norman Jewison, starring Cher and Nicolas Cage), in connection with *La Bohème*; and the film *Meeting Venus* (1991) (by the Hungarian director Istvan Szabo, starring Glenn Close) in connection with *Tannhäuser*.

You know something is being arranged for you when, in the opening shot of *Moonstruck*, you see a truck in close-up with the words "Metropolitan Opera Company Scenic Shop" painted tactfully on its side, then watch the truck back into a loading platform to unload, beginning with a canvas flat marked "La Bohème Act One" stenciled on its back, and then see a poster being installed outside the Met announcing a performance of *La Bohème*. Nothing is made of these references as we get to know the principal woman of the film (Cher, Loretta in the film), and learn of her engagement to an uninteresting man, until, as this man (Donnie) is departing to see his mother who is dying in Sicily, he asks the woman to invite his younger brother (Ronnie), to whom he has not spoken in five years, to their wedding. When she goes to see this brother at the bakery he works in and proves to live in an apartment above, he declaims to her, in an extraordinary, we could say operatic, outburst that the "bad blood" with his brother Donnie came when he caused the loss of his, Ronnie's, left hand, which Ronnie shows Loretta is now a gloved piece of wood carved as a hand. Even when this sequence closes with a just perceptible sound of Mimi's suffocation theme from *Bohème*, one would hardly imagine an allusion to Mimi's frozen hand in Ronnie's frozen hand, but the following sequence, in Ronnie's apartment, opens with a close-up of a poster of Act III of *Bohème* as Ronnie is playing a moment from the scene on his turntable, and the sequence closes on that poster, in which interval Ronnie and Loretta fall madly in love, go to his bed, after which Loretta revokes his invitation to the wedding and forbids him to remember what has happened between them, and he agrees, but only on the condition that she come to the opera with him that night, since opera, and now she, Loretta, are the only things in the world he loves. Apart from whether the film is now burlesquing the improbability of opera plots (improbability does not, as Aristotle notes, mean impossibility), references to *Bohème* start coming thick and fast.

I've linked four fragments to screen from *Moonstruck*: (1) Loretta's emergence from the beauty parlor in which she has had her hair redone as part of changing her presentation of herself in preparation for attending her first opera. (2) The pair's meeting outside the Metropolitan Opera House, in which we will hear on the soundtrack the opening of each of the three overtures from *Bohème*. (3) The moment depicting their presence at the performance, in which Mimi and Rudolfo agree they must part, but only when spring comes. (4) The moment walking back from the opera in which Ronnie convinces Loretta to change her mind and accept a happy, if confusing, ending.

[SCREENING OF FOUR EXCERPTS FROM *MOONSTRUCK*]

(1) The music accompanying Loretta's new appearance on the sidewalk outside the beauty parlor is not that of Mimi but is that associated with Musetta, Mimi's unrepressed friend, specifically Musetta's carefree entrance music, which will lead her into her famous waltz ("When I stroll down the street people stare admiringly at me, tip to toe . . ."). This is not to identify Loretta allegorically with Musetta, whose fickle, flirtatious character is anything but Loretta's, but it is to identify one dimension of Loretta's unacknowledged desire and to question what it is to identify someone's character. (2) When she steps out of the cab at the fountain in the plaza in front of the Metropolitan Opera, we first hear the shocking fortissimo unison and the following mysterious pianissimo fifths which open the Overture to Act III of *Bohème*, and then soon hear the opening festive trumpet triads of the Overture to Act II, and, when they are inside and in their seats, we hear the low, agitated descending half-steps signaling the Overture to Act I, a series of musical events virtually announcing

that things are unfolding backwards in the film in its confrontation with this opera. (I haven't, for reasons of time, included that from Act I.) (3) We see the pair experiencing that part of Act III in which, in effect, the poster in his apartment comes to life, and where Loretta, after declaring during the intermission that she doesn't get what's happening, is now shown to be moved to tears. (4) Here Ronnie holds out his false hand to Loretta and speaks truly of the role of desire in human life, when it is allowed to be called forth, as ruining the chances for a calm existence with expected sequences and "right" people to marry, declaring that to "play it safe" in love is the most dangerous thing a woman like Loretta can do.

So where the opera opens with scenes of bohemian celebrations and sentiments and ends with a death and the death of unconventional plans for life, the film, in contrast, opens with a sequence in a mortuary, and a dead hand, and two people who have withdrawn from the dangers of living with desire, and closes with a family celebration in which a conflict of brothers is resolved in joyful invention as one marries the other's betrothed, a union blessed by the isolated brother's permitting the ring he intended, he thought, for his own wedding to be used for that of his redeemed, or resurrected, brother. As the gathered family drinks to the new betrothal, the camera moves away to rest on a photograph of that familiar pairing of the ancestors of an immigrant family, figures whose ways and clothes the young generation barely, if at all, remembers. They are dead—and we remember in the midst of celebration that we all die—but not before they have left, unlike Mimi and Rodolfo, or Musetta and Marcello, progeny in which their hopes have an afterlife. I spoke earlier of film's capacity for diverting the deaths in opera. The most famous work of the century just past which proposes life as a diversion of the desire for the end of desire by discovering detours, or say admitting adventures, which lead to the right death, call it one's own death, is Freud's *Beyond the Pleasure Principle*.

This is not an irrelevant transitional path to a film's account of *Tannhäuser*. The film *Meeting Venus* does not stop with substantive references to *Tannhäuser*, it is a narrative about the preparation of a production of *Tannhäuser* in which the film's leading man is the conductor of the projected production who, like Tannhäuser, is in love both with a profane and with a sanctified object, and who attempts to leave both—in other words, he is a married man who has a liaison with the diva of the production, who however plays the role of Elisabeth. This conflict or division within the perception of women is blatantly announced by Glenn Closes's entrance, in which she theatrically interrupts a rehearsal by marching onto the stage and singing (dubbed by Kiri Te Kanawa) the opening phrases of Elisabeth's entrance aria, "*Dich, teure Halle . . .*" (The amalgamation of roles in the person of Glenn Close is a variation of the idea, as in Gotz Friedrich's

Bayreuth production in the late '70s, of having the same singer (in this case, Gwyneth Jones) sing the parts of both Elisabeth and of Venus. We hear far more of the music, and indeed the words, of Wagner than we heard of Puccini and Da Ponte in *Moonstruck*: taking the excerpts or fragments in the film's order, we hear rehearsals of the fanfare of the arrival of the Landgrave's guests in Act II (or rather we hear on the sound track individuals separately practicing the first and second trumpet parts of the fanfare); we hear fragments of the encounter of the knights with the returning Tannhäuser, in the last scene of Act I, from Wolfram, Biterwolf, and Tannhäuser; we hear the middle section of the Pilgrim's Chorus; Venus's pleading with Tannhäuser in Act I; the Overture to Act I; Elisabeth's aria of homecoming that opens Act II; the Shepherd's song; Tannhäuser's Rome aria in Act III; Venus's signature, excited, rising figure responding to the conductor and the diva running through the afternoon rain in Paris toward their hotel, having discovered their feeling for one another; Tannhäuser and Elisabeth's Love Duet from Act II; the Bacchanal from Act I (evidently using Wagner's revised, Paris version of the score); and various other fragments, including finally the sung Pilgrim's Chorus as the performance, or rather the nonperformance, of the opera is sketched for the penultimate sequence of the film. (Nonperformance literally, since in the film's narrative, showing the difficulties of mounting an opera as an allegory of achieving cooperation among the nations of Europe, the opera cannot be performed since the stage-hand's union, because of a contract dispute, will not allow the safety screen across the front of the stage to be raised, so the musicians declare their loyalty to their art, against politics, by improvising a concert version in front of the screen [rather as though they are suggesting their recognition of the presence of a film screen].)

In short, we hear enough glimpses of the music of the opera as almost to form a program of "Highlights from *Tannhäuser*." The essential difference from such a selection is that every stretch of singing in the film is interrupted, not by the exigencies of rehearsal and practice, but by the narrative decisions of the film. This, to my mind, reflects the fundamental fact that when Tannhäuser principally sings alone, except for the song of the Rome journey, his singing is interrupted: in Act I it is interrupted by himself, when each time he praises Venus he breaks into his cry for freedom, raising the strain a half step on each recurrence; in Act II his praise of love is interrupted by the drawn swords of his outraged fellow contestants. The interruptions in both cases are caused by his singing, as we might put it, always to the wrong woman; in the face of Venus his object is the sanctified one, in the face of Elisabeth he sings the music drawn from him by Venus's. This paradox of desire is reflected in the well-known fact that, as I might put the matter, the opening sounds of the Overture to Act

I realizes the Pilgrim's Chorus in the wrong key, I mean in E, which is
Venus's realm, not in E-flat, which is the key the pilgrims sing it in. The resolution of the paradox of desire in *Meeting Venus* is given in the fantastic
form of the conductor's baton at the end of the nonperformance sprouting
flowers at its tip—fulfilling of course the miracle of a piece of dead wood
flowering, which was the condition imposed by the Pope for the absolution
of Tannhäuser. I no more ask you to accept this miracle of film than I ask
you to accept its allegorical gist, that—let's put it in Nietzsche's early
terms—it is only in the aesthetic that existence may be justified. You would
have to experience the film and determine for yourself whether it has earned
the right to suggest that art and politics both still retain possibilities that are
unattained but not unattainable by human means.

Out of the wealth of choices from *Meeting Venus*, I limit myself to
just the Love Duet from Act II, as Elisabeth and Tannhäuser first reencounter one another. I precede it by recalling for you its sound from the
opera (as in the Bayreuth production mentioned earlier) since for all its
familiarity to you I would like you to experience immediately the uncanny
difference of sound with the male part being sung accurately but without
a trained voice by the conductor in the film and the orchestra sketched on
the piano, as befits coaching rehearsals.

[SCREENING OF LOVE DUETS—
THE OPERA, THEN THE FILM]

I report that when I heard this in the film version for the first time I
seemed not to recognize it and I became quite disoriented, not, I think,
simply because of the presence of the piano, which I am used to, nor
because of the substitution of the baritone register for the tenor, but the
quality of intimacy achieved in the conversational unassertiveness and
attentiveness of the male voice is something all but unheard of in opera
and is among the glories of cinema. Film's capacity for staging an unstaged
moment of absolute communication seemed to realize a promise of
expressiveness denied to opera's very celebration of the transcendent, the
ecstatic achievements of the human voice. Here the unknown intimacy of
the pair suggests an expression which at once predates ecstasy and contains
it afterwards.

I conclude with a further occurrence in a film of a reference to opera
that has again gone unnoticed or rather unremembered by anyone I have
consulted on the issue. This time it is *Tannhäuser*, and it occurs in a
moment from a film of the so-called golden age of Hollywood cinema,
namely the extraordinary director Preston Sturges's *The Lady Eve* (1941,
with Barbara Stanwyck and Henry Fonda). It is one of the films I call

remarriage comedies and study in my book *Pursuits of Happiness*. They
form a set of films (others include *The Philadelphia Story* [1941], *Adam's Rib*
[1949], and *It Happened One Night* [1934], and include such stars as
Katharine Hepburn, Cary Grant, Spencer Tracy, and Clark Gable) that
bear up under exacting critical discussion and are at the same time beloved
by a worldwide audience, a rare combination of conditions notably shared
by a number of operas. To locate the occurrence of *Tannhäuser* in *The Lady
Eve* I must say a word about the genre of the remarriage comedy.

In contrast to the classical romantic form of comedy as established in
the early work of Shakespeare, in which a young pair overcome obstacles
to their union in the form of an older man (usually the young woman's
father—think of *A Midsummer Night's Dream)* who threatens to bring the
law against their desire to be together, in remarriage comedy the couple is
already married, hence somewhat older, confronting inner rather than
outer obstacles that threaten the marriage with divorce, and the narrative
concerns the detours necessary to get the pair together *again, back* together. Among many other features that this alteration of comedy brings with
it, the films generally open in a place of a certain opulence or glamour,
usually New York, and move toward a resolution in a simpler place in the
countryside, most often called, in these films, Connecticut. Uniquely
among the remarriage comedies, Connecticut is not the end of the matter
in *The Lady Eve*, and the bumpy road away from it, on a train in which the
couple are to enjoy their honeymoon night, provides the occasion for
Tannhäuser. If we can say that *Tannhäuser* is about two women who are
opposite aspects of a woman's powers of love, where each promises
redemption and each proves, or threatens to be, lethal, then we can say
that *The Lady Eve* is about one woman who plays two opposite women,
each of whom pretends, and cons the man into believing, that she is the
opposite of what she is. In *The Lady Eve*, as in *Tannhäuser*, the man repeats
an aria-like declaration of love, which he had made to the first woman in
apparent sincerity, with equal sincerity to the second woman (whom we
know to be—do we not?—the same woman). This catastrophic faux pas
also precipitates the man's banishment from which, again, he is redeemed
by the intercession of the very woman to whom he had been apparently
unfaithful in sentiment. The man does not know his sacred bride very
well (above all does not know that he already knows her), as is clear even
from the brief segment we screen of *The Lady Eve*, in which Eve has wait-
ed for the moment of their honeymoon to punish and banish the man for
his repetition of the false song, by confessing a thousand and one tales of
her lurid erotic past. She has just told the first of her tales, and it is her
husband's high-minded speech of wise acceptance that brings *Tannhäuser*
down upon him.

[SCREENING OF SEGMENT FROM *THE LADY EVE*]

Why is *Tannhäuser* invoked in order to mock the hero of the film? Or does it simply mock him? I note that it is played in E here, which I have implied already expresses a kind of deep suspicion or testing of the claim to pious supplication. But let's suppose this is not heard. Another implication is that it is the man who should be in the position of supplicant, for repeating his tale of love which, having been said first to another, presumably refers to that other. The shocking intervention of this Wagnerian air of profundity has become so famous that it inevitably risks banality, so perhaps it is designed here to shock us into posing necessary and banal questions, such as how this man can fail to recognize the woman he has married as the woman he loves, or loved. One answer is that while she has not disguised her appearance she has altered her voice (as Lady Eve she has adopted an English accent). But what about that voice does the man not want to hear? Presumably that he has placed his desire where he loves and that this singular woman is prepared to become an object for him in whom the currents of passion and tenderness can flow together, Freud's recipe for the fullest satisfaction open to human sexuality. Such is this woman's proposal of the reality which prolongs life, or say which diverts death. It is frightening, but the man allows himself foolishness and bewilderment and persistence enough perhaps to welcome it. But why is it through film that such a proposal becomes credible?

Here, for the moment, I answer this question by responding to Mr. Deeds. Even when what were called movie palaces increasingly put on what he implied were the right shows, those picture shows more often than perhaps they knew demanded an inheritance from opera's transcendent powers of communication. And some of us find that movies have proven to deserve that inheritance. To think about the conditions of the inheritance, principally about how film's reflections provide further chapters of opera's life, has afforded me pleasures to which, while strength lasts, I see no end.

23

Philosophy the
Day after Tomorrow

IT WOULD BE A WAY OF INDICATING or instancing something of how I go about the work I do—in response to issues of the standing of knowledge in the inheritance we may claim at the turn of a millennium—to say that I continue to be preoccupied with ideas of what philosophy can do, or has to do, in the aftermath of the Wittgensteinian event in twentieth-century philosophy, emphasizing particularly that one of my early characterizations of Wittgenstein's *Philosophical Investigations* was as a work of instruction. If science is a set of methods of learning—for us the unsurpassable source of paradigms for learning something new about the world—then Wittgenstein's *Investigations*, in what it calls its "methods," takes the paradigms of philosophical instruction to contrast, not to say conflict, with those of science, emphasizing that what we learn from philosophy is precisely not something new.

From *Philosophical Investigations* sec. 89:

> Logical investigation [which includes what Wittgenstein calls grammatical investigation] . . . takes its rise . . . from an urge to understand the basis, or essence, of everything empirical. Not, however, as if to this end we had to hunt out new facts; it is, rather of the essence of our investigation that we do not seek to learn anything *new* by it.

Originally presented at the Einstein Forum, Berlin, November 2000.

We want to *understand* something that is already in plain view. For *this* is what we seem in some sense not to understand.

But—quite apart from the question of which philosophers would accept this as announcing philosophy's aspirations—what does this counterparadigm of learning or understanding come to? Sometimes Wittgenstein says that philosophy's task is to assemble reminders (but so, more or less, for example, do Plato, Heidegger, Levinas, and J. L. Austin, the discoverer of, among other things, the performative theory of speech, or speech act theory). I have taken the following scene, or fantasm, in the *Investigations*, one I call its scene of instruction, to epitomize Wittgenstein's idea of learning and teaching. From sec. 217.

> If I have exhausted the justifications [for following the rules of mathematics or of ordinary language as I do] I have reached bedrock, and my spade is turned. Then I am inclined to say, "This is simply what I do."

How to read this scene is at the core of a disagreement about how to read the *Investigations* quite generally. Saul Kripke, in his influential book *Wittgenstein on Rules and Private Language*, takes the teacher's (or speaker's) gesture of showing what he does to be meant as a show of power, a political gesture, confidently speaking for the community and demanding agreement, threatening rejection. I have taken the gesture oppositely, as acknowledging a necessary weakness, I might call it a creative limitation, in teaching (or socialization), stressing that the arrival at an impasse between teacher and pupil also threatens, and may enlighten, the teacher. This difference of interpretation demands a long story (which I undertake to tell in *Conditions Handsome and Unhandsome*). At the moment I wish to be as uncontroversial as possible and draw a moral from the fact that, whichever way you take the scene of instruction, upon recognizing that she or he has exhausted the justifications, the teacher becomes silent and waits. Satisfaction eludes the teacher, but more words are pointless. Wittgenstein anticipates this inevitable moment of silence in teaching—that the student must at some point go on alone—in the very opening section of the *Investigations*, where he notes, casually but fatefully, "Explanations come to an end somewhere." The moral I draw for Wittgenstein is that an utterance must have a point, whether to inform, amuse, promise, question, insist, beseech—in that sense must be worth saying; and that the point will exceed the saying, is inherently vulnerable, as human action is, to misfortune. (This is a significance of Austin's announcement that every locutionary act—every meaningful utterance—

has both an illocutionary and a perlocutionary force.) And the moral of silence in teaching at the same time implies a task of teaching; namely to demonstrate that informing, amusing, promising, questioning, insisting, beseeching, and so on, must themselves be seen to be worth doing. Quite as if teaching must, as it were, provide a reason for speaking at all. As if we might become appalled by the gift of language, the fatedness to speech, the condition Wittgenstein describes as the life form of talkers, of us.

I have cast matters in this light—some of my colleagues who represent analytical philosophy will I realize find the light somewhat lurid—recently struck by this conjunction of the concepts of a new call for knowledge, or a call for a new idea of knowledge, together with a consequent necessity of silence, followed by the question of the point of speech, in my latest turn, or return, to a text of Nietzsche's (something that seems almost always to happen to me arbitrarily or unpredictably). This time the turn was to *Human, All Too Human*, and especially to the 1886 preface to the original edition of 1878. This preface concludes its preparation for the book to follow—a book that seeks to discover "a knowledge surpassing all previous knowledge [a *knowledge of the conditions of culture*]" (sec. 25)—by declaring, having noted that this book has found its readers abroad but has been *heard* most poorly in Germany, that his philosophy counsels him to be silent, "especially since in certain cases, as the saying suggests, one *remains* a philosopher only by—being silent." The point of speech is then taken up explicitly in the opening sentence of the preface to what came to be Book II of *Human, All Too Human*: "One should speak only where one *must* not be silent. . . . Everything else is chatter [*Geschwätz*; he also calls it "*Literatur*"]." Someone has doubtless before now conjoined this statement with the concluding statement of Wittgenstein's *Tractatus*: "Whereof one cannot speak, thereof one must be silent." [*Wovon man nicht sprechen kann, darüber muss man schweigen.*] The difference seems to turn on the difference between the discovery of speaking in emptiness (chattering) and of speaking meaninglessly (metaphysically). The Wittgenstein of the *Tractatus* departs without considering that his philosophical discovery is bound, as human beings stand, to be ineffective, that human beings (first of all, philosophers) will go on saying, even insisting upon, what cannot be said; whereas the Wittgenstein of the *Investigations* remains obsessed (as Nietzsche, and, let's add, Heidegger and Kierkegaard, are obsessed) with this human vulnerability, or folly, or condition, or, as Nietzsche also puts it, "absence of breeding." This provocative suggestion about his fellow beings, and first his own countrymen, as lacking, let us say, sufficient refinement, may be an allusion to, or as I sometimes say, a rewriting or transfiguration of, as in uncountable other instances, a saying of Emerson's, in this case: "Every word they say chagrins us." These writers sense that they everywhere and nowhere share their native tongue.

I shall not make Nietzsche's affinity for Emerson, hence their endless differences, my principal theme here—I have another direction I wish to pursue—but I note the striking instance of that affinity marked by a phrase in that new preface of Nietzsche's to *Human, All Too Human*, a phrase repeated from his *Beyond Good and Evil*, published the year before that preface, and one that will be repeated again the following year in a new preface to *The Joyful Science*; namely the phrase "a man of tomorrow and the day after tomorrow." This is Nietzsche's characterization of those "free spirits" which the subtitle of *Human, All Too Human* identifies as the desired audience for his words, and which *Beyond Good and Evil* characterizes also as the philosopher (sec. 212), since that "extraordinary furtherer of man . . . has always found himself, and *had* to find himself, in contradiction to his today." Emerson's word for "being in contradiction to his today" is his definition of thinking as being "averse to the demand for conformity." Nietzsche also explicitly in this matter invokes the image of turning, as in Emerson's aversion, challenging his reader to a "reversal [*Umkehrung*] of one's habitual estimation and esteemed habits"; and Wittgenstein, to reinscribe this member of the triangle, speaks of his philosophical investigations as being "turned around the fixed point of our real need." Of course such coincidences can be treated as accidents. Why would a philosopher wish to treat them so, which is to say, wish *not* to treat them, as I assume most will not?

Such connections will, I should imagine, only strike one unforgettably if one is already in the mood of the significance of Nietzsche's lifelong habit of carrying Emerson's essays everywhere with him. Since nothing is easier for most philosophers to ignore, it will also be hard to credit the original of the first of the echoes I mentioned, granted that it is more muffled, when Nietzsche calls upon the free minds of those who are necessarily of tomorrow and the day after tomorrow.

I adapt this characterization of the philosopher for the title of my remarks today to mark that the casual distinction in English between tomorrow and the day after tomorrow translates the German "*Morgen und Übermorgen*," and I claim (again something that I do not know a precedent for) that the prefix "*Über-*," so characteristic a site for Nietzschean inflection, is here in play, as marking a distinction homologous with that between "*Mensch*" and "*Übermensch*." To what end? Take "*Morgen*" in its sense of morning, as well as of tomorrow, and we may discern an idea of an after-, or over-, or super-morning. Why posit such a thing, or event? That it is explicitly posited by Nietzsche is confirmed in the closing sentence of *Human, All Too Human*, where he links the figure of the philosopher with the figure of the wanderer, as one "who has come only in part to a freedom of reason [and hence] cannot feel on earth otherwise than as a wanderer," and he says of such figures: "Born out of the mysteries of the dawn, they ponder how the day can have such a pure, transparent, transfigured and cheerful face between the hours of ten and twelve—they seek the *philosophy of the forenoon* [*des Vormittages*]." I propose this as a rewriting of Emerson's prophecy, in the essay "Circles" (an essay Nietzsche quotes explicitly at the conclusion of his Untimely Meditation on Schopenhauer) that there is always "another dawn risen on mid-noon." It is true that Wordsworth and before him Milton had proposed new dawns at noon; but that it is specifically Emerson's continuation of the thought that is on Nietzsche's mind is, I find, confirmed by the Emersonian tones in which Nietzsche characterizes this further day, namely in the terms "transparent" and "transfigured" and "cheerful." Then the idea is that the further- or over-morning is the day realized, reconceived, by the further- or over-man; and contrariwise, that the over-man is one who realizes such a day.

Thoreau, Emerson's other great reader of the nineteenth century, leans on English as strongly as Nietzsche on German to produce his version of this thought, in the concluding three sentences of *Walden*: "Only that day dawns to which we are awake. There is more day to dawn. The sun is but a morning star." Focusing just on the homonym in the sound "mo(u)rning," meaning both dawning and grieving, we are told that every illumination of the world we have been party to has passed away and is something we must learn to rid ourselves of, to reevaluate. Nietzsche calls this overcoming himself—*Überwinden*, which, in Nietzsche's twist of the old prefix *Über*-, would presumably mean to unwind, unscrew, unbind, straighten, release himself. Conquering oneself then becomes a progress of continuing to free oneself, one might say, pardon oneself.

I pass for the present such echoes of Emerson—still within the eight entries comprising the preface to *Human, All Too Human*—that are captured in its ideas of the lightning flash, of thinking as pregnancy, of immoralism, of one's highest moments, of sitting still spinning patience, of unapproachable questions, of perspective (Emerson says partiality), of our growing upward as a matter of sitting on and climbing the rungs of a ladder (Emerson says we find ourselves on a series of stairs), of being heard poorly (Emerson says being misunderstood). Going further into these conjunctures and differences would likely only serve to make more urgent the question How can we know that taking up such matters in the way I have—matters pertaining to what I have given the name Emersonian Perfectionism—is not merely *Geschwätz*, "*Literatur*"?

Let's test this by calling upon some texts that anyone will accept as self-evidently literary and see how distinction, or say good breeding, manifests itself there. Interesting cases should be provided by the novels of

Jane Austen and of George Eliot, formative texts of English literature and now much on the minds of literary and cultural critics in my part of the world. Their virtues for this experiment are, for example, that they do not carry on their face the philosophical aspirations of the novelistic monsters of European literature, Proust, Joyce, Mann, Musil; again, that they are nevertheless invited into our discussion by its opening emphasis on philosophy's contempt, even horror, of chatter, say of unnecessitated or forced words; and further, more personally, that they are clear precursors of the preoccupations of the two genres of film that I have devoted books to—genres I name the Hollywood comedy of remarriage and the melodrama of the unknown woman. The realization that these films are understandable as studying the possibility of a perfectionist life in a democracy—and I take the comedies to comprise the best comedies of the golden age of Hollywood cinema after the advent of sound—is a pivotal moment in my intellectual path. I pause to emphasize its importance to me, in connection with the issue of perfectionism.

Perfectionism can be said to have been located with Socrates' explanation to Euthyphro that questions which cause hatred and anger—specifically unlike questions of science, or measurement—are disagreements over the question of the just and the unjust (we might say of right and wrong) and of the good and the bad, and of the honorable and the dishonorable. It is still the case that the dominant professional pedagogy in moral philosophy proceeds by taking up the relation of the questions of right and wrong (as most famously presented in Kant), with questions of the good and bad (as in Utilitarianism, exemplified by John Stuart Mill). Issues here tend to emphasize matters of moral choice, of what action is to be done, and the reasons for doing it. The emphasis in Socrates' third pair, the honorable and the dishonorable, tends by contrast to emphasize the evaluation of a way of life. It is this emphasis that I am calling perfectionism, epitomized in Emerson's formulation of our moral aspiration to "our unattained but attainable self." Plato's and Aristotle's perfectionisms, however different, are for the privileged. My claim is that this concession is combated in, among others, Emerson and in Nietzsche, as it is in the films I allude to. (The titles of films are often changed in translation, but they are characterized by the principal couples in them, which include a number of the most famous American stars of the 1930s and 1940s, Katharine Hepburn with Cary Grant, Hepburn with Spencer Tracy, Clark Gable with Claudette Colbert, Barbara Stanwyck with Henry Fonda.) A guiding idea of both the comedies, where marriage is accepted, or reaccepted, and of the related melodramas, where marriage is in fact rejected, is that nothing legitimizes or ratifies marriage—not state, or church, or sex, or gender, or children—apart from the willingness for reaffirmation, which is to say, remarriage (the films open or climax with the threat of divorce), and what makes marriage worth reaffirming is a diurnal devotedness that involves friendship, play, surprise, and mutual education, all expressed in the pair's mode of conversing with one another, expressing an intimacy of understanding often incomprehensible to the rest of the world. The lives depicted in these films have, however, seemed anything but incomprehensible to the generations of viewers, over the world, who treasure the films. Is this not worthy of philosophical reflection?

The education in question is not to provide an increase of learning but a transformation of existence; those who cannot inspire one another to such an education are not married; they do not have the right interest for one another. It is part of the presentation of these films in *Pursuits of Happiness*, where the genre of remarriage comedy is articulated, to determine how the power of this genre of metamorphosis has elicited the power of metamorphosis at the basis of the medium of film.

What invites novels such as Austen's *Pride and Prejudice, Sense and Sensibility, Persuasion, Mansfield Park*, and *Emma* together with George Eliot's *Middlemarch* and *Daniel Deronda* to this discussion is their devotion, in contradiction of philosophy, to the life of the everyday, while at the same time they share, in the texture and turn of every scene, their knowledge of, their craving for, a life lived from what Emerson and Nietzsche call the further self, glimpsed from the perspective of life's higher moments—perfectionist moments. The lives depicted can seem, from a philosophical perspective, too confined or aloof to provide moral inspiration or instruction for a rough world. The experience of the novels is, for many, for me, otherwise. Must either the experience of the novels or else moral perfectionism be renounced?

The connection of these novels with the thinking of Nietzsche is in any case something of a shock, at least to me, and the illumination of the connection works in both directions. When I said that these novels were "invited" by the way I introduced Nietzsche, I had in mind the unarticulated ground on which Nietzsche, or for that matter Emerson, issues his call for the future, for the new day; namely his sickness ("seasickness" Nietzsche calls it in the preface to *Human, All Too Human*) in response to the way humankind lives today. He regards himself, while still participating in that way, as having broken with it (he is at sea) and consequently as in a state of convalescence with respect to it, not ready for, not in possession of a context for, a new way; and he knows—it is the state of knowledge in which he writes—that almost all others remain buried in conformity, in an unrelieved routine of ordinariness, the thing Emerson calls conformity, and Nietzsche calls philistinism in the *Untimely Meditations*.

It is from within some place in this state of conformity, even out of a certain respect for it, for its necessity, or inescapability, that Jane Austen

and George Eliot write, as if out of the obligation to depict for their readers the truth of their condition, hence to awaken and confirm their knowledge of the brutalities of that condition, and to exemplify instances in
which the soul can learn not to be crushed by the force of compromise
modern society still exacts. To manage to maintain faith with one's desires
for an enlightened world, in the face of one's compromises with it, is a recognizable aim of philosophy, as in John Rawls's *A Theory of Justice*. It is a
question for me how one judges whether Rawls's work succeeds in this.

Does this coincidence of aim suggest a philosophical dimension to
the novels I propose to adduce? In today's philosophical climate in the part
of the world I do my work, in which there are more possibilities for philosophy than in the years I was beginning to find my way, I hear it said
that, in thinking about moral issues, novels illuminate imaginatively what
philosophy attempts, if not vainly then limitedly, to articulate conceptually. But here I emphasize that, in confronting everyday life with itself, the
novels I have cited (novels of domesticity or of inhabitation, let's call them,
but we might also call them, etymologically, novels of economy) equally
illustrate antiphilosophy, taking a contrary course to philosophy's chronic
flight from the ordinary, whose philosophical picture of human inhabitation is Plato's Cave. But how could anything, say a novel, or say the study
of a place in nature as in Thoreau's *Walden*, which its writer introduces
explicitly as a work of economy, propose a counter to philosophy without
itself approaching, hence becoming in some part, philosophy?

In compressing matters so severely, hoping to give a sense of the context for my thoughts, I know I run the stranger's risk of becoming merely
odd. My formulation concerning the confronting of the everyday with itself
is meant to allude to the work I understand Wittgenstein to be doing in
Philosophical Investigations. While I regard this aspect of that work as essential to the originality in its contribution to philosophy (or counterphiloso-
phy), I know that the price of the reception of this text, in Anglo-American
philosophizing, is mostly to ignore, or excuse, its emphasis on the ordinary
or everyday, as though that compromises its claims to amount to philosophy.
Part of what I take to constitute its claim to philosophy is that it performs
work that is shown to be necessary to philosophy within Plato's Cave, namely that of confronting its inhabitants with their chains, and suffering their
rage at the offer to free them, which requires that they recognize the irreal-
ity of their condition and turn around, away from illusory pictures. But in
Wittgenstein there is no place essentially elsewhere, high in the open sun,
from which the illuminated philosopher is to return to the everyday. The
change of inhabitation must occur from possibilities within that inhabitation
itself, to which one is complicitous in captivating oneself. In Wittgensteinian
terms, the Cave itself is a picture. Isn't it that in Plato?

I called the connection of Nietzsche with the novels of economy somewhat shocking, sharing I should guess a sense of disproportion in juxtaposing Nietzsche's garish emotionality with, to take the plainer case, Jane Austen's narrator's celebrated surface of lethal calm. Surely her portrait of society is closer to the imagination of the social in Wittgenstein and in Jane's namesake John Austin, whom I mentioned a while ago in passing, than to anything in Nietzsche? I would hardly deny this, but the spiritual distress registered in Nietzsche, and characteristic of his writing, is not inaccurate to something to be felt in Jane Austen's prose. You might say that her prose seeks to minimize the expression of distress in everyday existence no less drastically than Nietzsche's to maximize it.

A trick of the prose, in each case, is to make unassessable the degrees of its seriousness. When I read on the opening page of Austen's *Emma* that its heroine "seemed to unite some of the best blessings of existence" (she is said to be handsome, clever, rich, young), and that "It was on the wedding-day of [her] beloved friend [namely, her governess of sixteen years, said to be her friend and her sister as well as the replacement for the loss of her mother] that Emma first sat in mournful thought of any continuance," I may find that I do not know whether this meditation means that she is vexed not to have her friend to continue their happy mode of existence; or whether it suggests that she is so grief-stricken that she cannot imagine wanting her existence to continue; or whether, as seems to me the case, that Emma herself cannot tell the difference between these states. Distress, vexation, sorrow, and grief, are, in addition to mourning, concepts narratively in play on this first page, and it will take what we may call an education to articulate their differences. The sentence following maintains the, doubtless gentle, irony: "The wedding over and the bride-people gone, her [Emma's] father and herself were left to dine together, with no prospect of a third to cheer a long evening." This suggests, I suppose, that she has intact the thought of the next morning to look forward to, but is there not also a suggestion that she does not know how many cheerless evenings may be in store, nor how the day will be different from the night? The thought is continued on the next page ("many a long October and November evening must be struggled through") where Emma is now said to be "in great danger of suffering from intellectual solitude." How great is this danger—I mean not how likely is it (it is likely) but what order of danger is it?

And is this really to be placed in the same world with the inexpressible loneliness Nietzsche divines in that preface to *Human, All Too Human*?—where he asks "Who today knows what *loneliness* is?" Yet would we really understand Nietzsche's outcries if these instances—Austen's and Nietzsche's—were incommensurable? The sentence of Austen's following the one noting her isolation, defines it further: "She dearly loved her father, but he was no companion for her. He could not meet her in conversation, rational or playful." Now the capacity for rational and playful conversation proves to have its own form of isolation, or say alienation, and to produce its own aspiration for encounter and, let us say, transcendence; and to have the capacity go unmet bespeaks a danger of loneliness not unsuggestive of madness. The father who cannot meet her conversation, like all the fathers in Jane Austen's world, are at the verge of nonexistence, they lack a taste or energy for the world, they are beings for whom everything needs to be done. But what kind of world is it in which, though recognized to be patriarchal, there are no patriarchs? And in these so-called novels of marriage, what is the wager of marriage, where a refusal to marry is apt to mean economic and social destitution and the acceptance of a bad marriage will mean the suffocation of the expression of rationality and playfulness, comedic touchstones of the perfectionist aspiration?

I should confess that I came somewhat late to a fascination with Jane Austen, compared with many of my acquaintance who read her young, who therefore were readier than I to identify with the elation of her novel's conclusions, and with the wit and luck necessary to them (however much I catch their thrill), rather than dwell on the stupidity, the silliness, the emptyheadedness, the quality of being worn out (characteristic predicates of Austen's) of so many of her supporting players, who reveal the character of the social condition which the main characters, of inner aspiration, must overcome in themselves. By the time of *Mansfield Park*, in 1815, there is mostly no one to identify with, and we are free unprotectedly to imagine (as recent critics have) the fact of the Slave Trade, on which the world of that house, as we are repeatedly, if delicately, reminded by Austen, is founded, and recognize that the practice is by the time of the writing of the novel known to be fatally under legislative attack. This is the most lurid of the compromises with an imperfect (to say the least) society shown in Austen's six novels. It seems to me to go with the fact that, among Austen's admirable women, each of whom is flawed, Fanny Price, of *Mansfield Park*, is notable, among other matters, for her unexplained physical weakness, which I confess to wishing to consider as a signal of Nietzschean convalescence, marking one imperfectly fit for the world as it is because in preparation for a further constitution.

The economy of horror invisibly sustaining the main house of *Mansfield Park* makes it harder for us to fail to imagine the unspoken conditions of economy in the other members of the genre Austen made her own. Namely, in a different world from that she depicts in *Emma*, or the same world looked at from a different perspective, in a different disposition or economy, we may take the critical moment she portrays in *Pride and Prejudice* (volume 2, chapter 13), at which self-possessed Elizabeth receives the letter from the fascinating and perplexing Mr. Darcy that overthrows her supposed knowledge of his untrustworthiness and cruelty, rather differently from the way she describes it and, I believe, her audience accepts it. She says to herself that she feels, among other things, that she had been "blind, partial, prejudiced, absurd" and concludes with the recognition: "Till this moment, I never knew myself." That is, she reinterprets her character and goes on to attribute her folly to vanity and prepossession. But, prepared for other levels of anxiety and compromise, we may wish to recognize that what she feels as the initial onset of self-knowledge is the reality for the first time of being known, being acknowledged in her difference, as if until then her existence had been denied—suffered the polite skepticism of everyday life.

Darcy's power to reveal anxiety is present from his early exchanges with Elizabeth. Having been treated to her revelation of herself as an amused student of character, Darcy observes, "The country can in general supply but few subjects for such a study. In a country neighbourhood you move in a very confined and unvarying society." Elizabeth replies: "But people themselves alter so much, that there is something new to be observed in them for ever." Darcy may merely have meant, out of his pride and prejudice, that fashionable society is the more amusing environment. He may, further, have meant to convey a sense that her powers for amusement and for study are, in her situation, confined nearly to the point of paralysis. She deflects both gestures by implying that her powers of observation are more than he imagines, not awaiting but providing her amusement. Now to see something new for ever in an unvarying society is an accurate description of what a writer such as Jane Austen has learned to provide for the world. But this implication of a certain genius shared by Elizabeth at the same time serves more threateningly to seal her isolation, to show her consciousness to be unshareable.

Elizabeth's own recognition of this danger (no longer attributable, I suppose, to any particular social configuration) seems to me to leap out in her impatient concluding reply to her beloved sister Jane's persistent inability to recognize the truth of her (Jane's) feelings for a young man who has wounded her, as Elizabeth interprets those feelings for her. Elizabeth concludes (volume 3 chapter 12): "We all love to instruct, though we can teach only what is not worth knowing." I assume that this is the source of Oscar Wilde's first "Maxim for the Instruction of the Over-Educated": "Education is an admirable thing. But it is well to remember from time to time that nothing that is worth knowing can be taught." Even if both writers took this thought from some common prior source, it would still suggest that a certain Nietzschean pressure is not foreign to Jane Austen's own forces in her novels of the everyday, of the sort Nietzsche describes, almost at the close of *Human All Too Human* (sec 627):

> . . . some individuals know how to treat their experiences (their insignificant everyday experiences) so that these become a plot of ground that bears fruit three times a year; while others (and how many of them!) . . . always stay lightly on the surface, like cork. . . . [the latter], instead of creating the world out of nothing, create nothing out of the world.

I note that "*aus der Welt ein Nichts schaffen*" (more literally, creates a nothing out of the world) seems a fair characterization of nihilism, which I find not too strong an image for what Jane Austen sometimes perceives as the pervasive and silent challenger of her intelligence.

This should be easier to believe in the case of the last great novels of the deeply learned George Eliot, *Middlemarch* and *Daniel Deronda*, which I have left essentially no time to take up now. I shall simply point to an entrance and a path that I find promising to begin with.

Nietzsche, to come back once more to the preface to *Human, All Too Human*, conjectures (sec. 3) that "the decisive event for a spirit in whom the type of the 'free spirit' [*freier Geist*] is one day to ripen to sweet perfection has been a *great separation*, and that before it, he . . . seemed to be chained forever to his corner, to his post." Without now taking up the signal that relates this requirement of separation to Plato's image of chains in his Cave, nor Nietzsche's ensuing description of the separation as a "lightning flash of contempt toward that which was [that spirit's] 'obligation,'" which I cannot but relate to the gleam of light in the opening paragraph of Emerson's "Self-Reliance" meant to instruct the reader in his self-alienation, I now, drawing to a close, ask a question about the separation, and propose a way of answering from George Eliot, and offer a parting moral from within my aspiration for philosophy.

The question: If the perfectionist path exacts the cost of a great separation, is it one that women, of Eliot's, let alone Austen's time, could have afforded? If one dimension of the separation is from society and its pressures toward marriage, or else toward a few alternative posts of respectability (maiden aunt, lady's companion, governess), separation suggests sinking beneath society in massively more cases than it does rising above society. So haven't these historical everydays become impertinent to our modern, or postmodern, achievements?

A proposed way of answering derives from Eliot's *Middlemarch*, written in the early 1870s, the same decade as *Human, All Too Human*. It is to take on Eliot's perception of her era (allowing it to be open how far it differs from ours) as already constituting, at least for women (allowing it to be open how far their fate differs from that of the rest of us), the scene of a great separation. Eliot opens and closes *Middlemarch* with an invocation of Saint Theresa, who several centuries earlier had demanded and found for her passionate, ideal nature expression in an epic life, the reform of a religious order, and she contrasts this history with a new time, in which "many Theresas have been born who found for themselves no epic life; . . . perhaps only a life of mistakes, the offspring of a certain spiritual grandeur ill-matched with the meanness of opportunity." That is the opening page; the closing page, adducing in addition Antigone, announces that "the medium in which their ardent deeds took shape is for ever gone." Nietzsche will observe (*Human, All Too Human*, sec. 223): "The best in us has perhaps been inherited from the feelings of former times, feelings which today can hardly be approached on direct paths; the sun has already set, but our life's sky glows and shines with it still, although we no longer see it." George Eliot's answer, then, to the closing, or setting, of the past of greatness, is to become the novelist of the heroism of everyday life, the life in which "we insignificant people with our daily words and acts are preparing the lives of many Dorotheas [the heroine of *Middlemarch*]," whose unhistoric, hidden acts "the growing good of the world is partly dependent on."

    In her great novels, making such acts visible, readable, memorable, she seems to take her method as one of interpreting myth, and writing the myth to be interpreted—not un-Nietzschean occupations. At least I assume she is describing an aspect of her work in the following exchange from *Daniel Deronda* (chapter 37), where the strange creature Mirah reports to Deronda that a friend had "told a wonderful story of Bouddha giving himself to the famished tigress to save her and her little ones from starving. And he said you were like Bouddha. That is what we all imagine of you." [Deronda objects:] "Pray don't imagine that. . . . Even if it were true that I thought so much of others, it would not follow that I had no wants for myself. When Bouddha let the tigress eat him he might have been very hungry himself." A young girl listening to the exchange asks: "But *was* it beautiful for Bouddha to let the tiger eat him? It would be a bad pattern." A child responds: "The world would get full of fat tigers." Eliot continues: "Deronda laughed, but defended the myth. 'It is like a passionate word,' he said; 'the exaggeration is a flash of fervor. It is an extreme image of what is happening every day—the transmutation of self.' " As if, as Nietzsche also says, the great separation is recapitulated, or resisted, in each life. George Eliot as it were, after Emerson, envisions the democratization of perfectionism, asks for each the right to seek a step toward an unattained possibility of the self, toward a world closer to the heart's desire.

So I am brought to my aspiration for philosophy today. If I ask myself whether Nietzsche's claim of separation is meant primarily as an epistemological or metaphysical or religious or aesthetic or psychic or political or moral task, I find I am glad to reply—glad only to reply—that it is precisely all of these, all the time. But that means to me that every word we utter, or withhold, is an act treading at least these—let me say, unchained—registers. No wonder philosophy lives in fear of the ordinary word. Whether the fear is healthy or unhealthy remains perhaps undecided.

24

The Good of Film

I N AN ERIC ROHMER FILM, *The Green Ray* (1986), sometimes known as *Summer*—clearly related to his four-part masterwork cycle of films, each named for one of the four seasons, of which the last, *A Tale of Autumn* (1998), was released a couple of years ago—a young woman wanders away from an after-dinner conversation with new friends in their garden and in the course of an uneventful walk along country roads finds herself isolated and lost, sobbing among trees shaking in a rising wind. In a recent Jim Jarmusch film, *Ghost Dog* (1997), a young black girl, perhaps eight or nine years old, whom a large, mysterious black man on a park bench had given a book about which he wants her opinion, has just returned the book and given her opinion, whereupon the man is called into the street by a white man who shoots him. The black man, whom we had seen empty his gun, then reaches in his coat for the gun and throws it in the direction of the young girl. The white man shoots twice more and the black man falls dead. As the assassin turns and hurries away, as if frightened by this nonresistance, the young girl picks up her friend's gun and aims and fires it at the back of the assassin. At the click of the empty gun the fleeing man lurches momentarily, then straightens and enters a waiting car. In Howard Hawks's film *His Girl Friday* (1940), a member of a genre of film I call remarriage comedies, a group of reporters covering a politically motivated execution has its cynicism silenced as one of them reads aloud a page of an unfinished account, written from the victim's

---

Presented at Center for Human Values, Princeton University, December 2000.

point of view, left in the typewriter of their newly returned comrade (played by Rosalind Russell) who has left the room with the victim's woman friend whom the male reporters had been taunting. Another reporter enters and observes, "I don't think it's ethical to read other people's work," whereupon another otherwise undistinguished member of the group shoots back, "Where do you get that ethics stuff? You're the only one who'll swipe any of it."

Before the hour of my talk is over, I hope to have shown these moments as belonging among a circle of interests defining what I mean by speaking in my title of the good of film.

In accepting the assignment for this occasion to say something about moral philosophy in relation to film, I have evidently felt free to interpret it somewhat idiosyncratically, not to say personally, since I know of no canonical way of speaking about this relation, that is, as asking me to say how I have been led to think about the matter, and to use the occasion to try to take this thinking a step or two further.

I shall, accordingly, not be speaking about moral problems felt to be raised by the fact of film itself, by its tendencies to violence and to the erotic, and in general by its capacity to create, and demand, extravagant and indiscriminate reactions to obvious events; nor shall I be speaking about front-page moral dilemmas, say about capital punishment (as in *Dead Man Walking* [1995]) or about whistle blowing (as in *The Insider* [1999]) or civil disobedience (as in *Gandhi* [1982]) or informing (as in *The Front* [1976]), or abortion (as in *Love with the Proper Stranger* [1963]), since such films, whatever their considerable merits, tend to obey the law of a certain form of popular engagement that requires the stripping down of moral complexity into struggles between clear good and blatant evil, or ironic reversals of them. Not at all that I think it is uninteresting or unimportant to ask why these tendencies prevail in the medium of film. While there is probably not much moral instruction in asking whether serial killing or cannibalism or volcanic eruptions or burning skyscrapers or sinking ships with insufficient lifeboats or meteors headed toward the earth are good or bad things, it is surely worth knowing what film is that it can maintain grateful connection with a vast audience along such lines. Perhaps it has to do with its power to create spectacular contexts in which the human capacity for improvisation of thought and action is released from the normal constraints of moral judgment.

But my attention has over the years rather been attracted to cases that show film, good films, to have an affinity with a particular conception of the good, a conception somewhat aslant the contrast between Kantian and Utilitarian universes that provides our pedagogically dominant moral theories. So to begin with I have to say something about what I understand a good film to be and give some characterization of this different conception of the good.

My working criterion of a "good film" is one that bears up under criticism of the sort that is invited and expected by serious works within the classical arts, works that attest that film is the latest of the great arts, so works in which an audience's passionate interest, or disinterest, is rewarded with an articulation of the conditions of the interest that illuminates it and expands self-awareness. In the case of film, this capacity to sustain and reward criticism turns out to be realized sometimes by films that have succeeded in maintaining worldwide affection over decades without having tipped the hand of their artistry. It was a revelation to me to discover the intellectual depth and artistic conscience in the Hollywood comedies and melodramas that I have devoted a book each to studying. What I seemed to discover, in a word, was that I had—as American culture generally had—taken my attachment and memories of these films for granted, namely assumed that their value could be accounted for otherwise than by understanding film writers, actors, directors, designers, and photographers to be following and adapting and contesting ancient crafts.

It was for decades a thing unquestioned to understand, for example, the Hollywood melodramas I call those of the unknown woman, as unproblematic instances of what Hollywood called "the woman's film," or "weepies," films like *Letter from an Unknown Woman* (with Joan Fontaine) (1948), *Gaslight* (with Ingrid Bergman and Charles Boyer) (1944), *Now, Voyager* (with Bette Davis and Paul Henreid) (1942), *Stella Dallas* (with Barbara Stanwyck) (1937). Why, or how, such works of film art were taken for granted as routine members of a known form of entertainment is not itself something to be taken for granted. Its explanation awaits, as I see it, an explanation of why film as such remains without a discourse worthy of it, why for example it remains largely unknown to philosophy. Stinting such films is not an innocent matter of not recognizing their aesthetic power, it is an active matter of imposing an understanding of, let us say, their moral outlook. Even the more advanced reading of *Now, Voyager* as embracing patriarchy and uncritically underwriting the excesses of commodified and fetishized late capitalist society is to read the Bette Davis character—in her metamorphosis from what she calls a maiden aunt into a dashing woman of the world—still as sacrificing her life in favor of the Paul Henreid character and his essentially orphaned child. My counterargument begins with noting that the idea of this intelligent, powerful, imaginative woman sacrificing herself for this needy man is precisely and explicitly the view of her taken by that man; so while the view is possible, one may well wish to look elsewhere to determine what her own view of her behavior betokens about her desires, which, according to my reading, has to do with her having outgrown the man, with aspirations that go quite beyond his sense of his trapped inadequacy to rescue her, grateful as she remains for his charming and tactful earlier attentions, which were salubrious. This is where the particular conception of the good for which an indefinitely large class of good films has an affinity comes in. It is the conception found in what I have called Emersonian perfectionism, a conception not given much consideration in today's moral pedagogy compared with the dominant conflict between, say, Kantianism and Utilitarianism.

As a perfectionism it is going to have something to do with being true to oneself, or, in Foucault's title, the caring of the self, hence with a dissatisfaction, sometimes despair, with the self as it stands; so something to do with a progress of self-cultivation and with the presence of a friend of some kind whose words have the power to help guide the progress. Romantics have spoken of the idea as becoming who you are. Perhaps I can most usefully describe the version I call Emersonian by recounting the various origins of my interest in it, since my sense of it is, I trust, still developing.

One origin was my coming to wonder, after finishing a long book much of which is an effort to come to terms with the philosophical event of Wittgenstein's *Philosophical Investigations*, about the experience of something like a moral or a religious fervor in Wittgenstein's text, a fairly obvious feature of it, but one that I believe is characteristically felt by philosophers in our dominant dispensation of philosophy to be something of a pedagogical nuisance. It is true that students who fasten early upon this aspect of that text are apt not to penetrate very deeply into its workings. Now something of the same fervor is to be found in Heidegger's *Being and Time*, so obviously that Heidegger has as it were to stop several times to caution that he is not composing a work of ethics. So I began asking myself what a work is whose ethical import seems pervasive but in which ethics is not understood as a separable field of study, as if it is philosophy itself which is placing moral demands upon its adepts.

A second origin was my puzzled discontent with John Rawls's reading of Nietzsche as representative of an essentially elitist or undemocratic perfectionism, which I found based on what was for Rawls an uncharacteristically incautious reading of a set of citations, ones moreover which showed Nietzsche in his most intimate, quite explicit, association with Emerson. This led me to begin articulating features of a paradigmatic work of elitist perfectionism, Plato's *Republic*, in contrast with the outlook I was moved by in Emerson's writing. In the *Republic* ethics is not a field of study separate from epistemology and metaphysics and aesthetics; the soul is pictured as on a journey toward the good, one which requires a release, dramatized as a turning away, from its everyday life, a transformation initiated and furthered by a kind of painful conversation with a more advanced figure who sets those who approach him on a path of education. In Emerson, agreeing with, or interpreting, most of this, the advanced figure is called, in the famous essay "Self-Reliance," the true man whose standard we are attracted to, and whose educative conversation turns out to be Emerson's conversational text, which, however, Emerson claims to be returning to me my own rejected thoughts; so that the process of reading an Emerson essay is an exercise in coming to oneself, as if one had been in a trance. (Emerson and Heidegger, not surprisingly, actually use the motto of becoming who you are to describe the work they mean their writing to describe and inspire; Wittgenstein in the *Investigations*, not surprisingly, does not, although I have in effect argued that as it were the moral vision of Wittgenstein's text, in what he calls the return to everyday use, pictures us as talking creatures whose words chronically escape us, as if we are, in Kierkegaard's image, "out," that is, not at home, or not reachable, unfound by ourselves.) The decisive difference of Emerson's outlook from that in Plato's *Republic* is that the soul's journey to itself is not pictured as a continuous path directed upward to a known point of completion but rather as a zigzag of discontinuous steps following the lead of what Emerson calls my "unattained but attainable self" (as if there is a sage in each of us), an idea that projects no unique point of arrival but only a willingness for change, directed by specific aspirations that, while rejected, may at unpredictable times return with new power. The path is no more toward incorporation in a given condition of society than it is toward the capacity to judge that condition. The sage in us is what remains after all our social positionings.

A third origin of my interest in perfectionism, the one that encouraged me to think that there may be a set of ideas here worth communicating to others, was my recognition that the genre of Hollywood comedy I had begun studying in the mid-1970s, those I name, in *Pursuits of Happiness*, comedies of remarriage, were working out ideas in Emersonian perfectionism. (Its presence in the genre of melodramas of the unknown woman shows their derivation, as I see it, from its comedic cousin.) I take as the classical instances of remarriage comedy, spanning the years 1934 to 1949, *The Philadelphia Story* (with Katharine Hepburn and Cary Grant) (1940), *Bringing Up Baby* (again with Hepburn and Grant) (1938), *Adam's Rib* (with Hepburn and Spencer Tracy) (1949), *The Awful Truth* (with Grant and Irene Dunne) (1937), *His Girl Friday* (with Grant and Rosalind Russell), *The Lady Eve* (with Barbara Stanwyck and Henry Fonda) (1941), and *It Happened One Night* (with Clark Gable and Claudette Colbert) (1934), each directed by a Hollywood master of the times, Howard Hawks or George Cukor or Leo McCarey or Preston Sturges or Frank Capra.

There seemed to me two immediate touchstones for this conjunction of this comedy and this perfectionism: one is the stress in the films on becoming, or of being changed into, a certain sort of person (the same but different); the other is, in these films whose conversations are among the glories of world cinema, conversations of wit but equally of confrontation and questioning, a notable absence of conversations concerning standard moral problems—quite as if the perplexities of the conditions of ordinary moral life, matters of equality or of the conflict of inclination with duty, or of duty with duty, or of means with ends, pose no intellectual hardships for these people. This, no doubt suspicious, second feature comes out in various ways. It is blatant in the line I quoted in my opening from *His Girl Friday*, "Where do you get that ethics stuff?" Again, in a sequence from *Adam's Rib*, after the husband Adam has left the wife Amanda following a bitter, even violent, quarrel over the differences between men and women, we see Amanda having a drink with her playboy neighbor/client across the hall, whose infatuated addresses to her make no impression upon her, but to whom she is at the moment distractedly voicing her anxious impatience with Adam's sudden inability to live up to their understanding of the equality in marriage. When the neighbor suggests that Adam is just angry because he's losing the law case to her in court, which is the foreground of the film, Amanda turns a withering glance of disdain upon him, and continues with her tirade, as if the attribution of base motives to the actions of the man she married merely reveals a morally stunted sensibility; later in the film, as the principal pair are finding their way back together again, they complete a private exchange they have been conducting intermittently in their accountant's office while they are helping him complete their tax returns, whereupon, to the accountant's astonishment, they hurry out of his office saying over their shoulders, "Oh include it all, we love paying taxes," as if the moral fudging of ordinary sinners is beneath or beyond them.

The other touchstone difference marking the morality of remarriage comedy as perfectionism, that of becoming a new or different person, shows up in everything from Cary Grant's saying to Rosalind Russell, who thinks she has come back to see her former husband to tell him to stop trying to prevent her getting a divorce and marrying another man (when we are invited to see that she has returned precisely, whether she knows it or not, to give him the chance to prevent it): "I took a doll-faced hick and made a newspaper man out of you"—from this to Katharine Hepburn's outcry, in *The Philadelphia Story*, faced with marrying another man after divorcing, again, Cary Grant, "Oh to be of use in the world!" When that other man responds by saying that such a life is not for her but that she should be put in a castle and worshiped, we know his days are numbered. Her outcry was a longing to matter, to count, as though she required being born into the world. Her last words in the film declare that she feels like a human being.

But if these films are studies in perfectionism, then we have a small laboratory for studying moral conversation not as the attempt to persuade someone to a course of action, or as the evaluation of a social institution, but of something I think of sometimes as prior and preparatory to these familiar goals of moral reasoning, sometimes as subsequent and supplementary, namely the responsiveness to and examination of one soul by another. It is prior because it provides us with studies of the standing a moral agent claims in confronting another with his/her judgment; it is subsequent because it provides the space for evaluating the moral framework within which you are reasoning. It was the occlusion of the feature of claiming standing in moral encounter that was, I would say, the principal cause of the dismay and the triumph associated with the dominance, in the 1940s and 1950s in the Anglo-American dispensation of philosophy, of the emotive theory of ethical judgment (an analysis of moral judgment as the attempt to use the expression of feeling as a power to get another to do something or to refrain from doing something). As if there had come upon philosophers thinking of the moral life an amnesia of the fact, or a wish to be free of the fact, that we have claims upon one another, count for one another, matter to one another, sometimes in questionable ways. (It is such a sense of moral amnesia that motivates the chapters on moral philosophy in my *Claim of Reason*. One might say that confronting another morally risks one's identity; otherwise one risks moralism. I think of the moment in *Now, Voyager* in which the Bette Davis character responds to a pious speech from the Paul Henreid character by saying, "I simply don't know you." And of the moment in *The Philadelphia Story* in which Katharine Hepburn halts herself in the middle of a moral rebuke by recognizing that she is repeating the words of someone else, unearned by her. Or of the moment in *Viva Zapata* when Brando's victorious Zapata recognizes that he has become, in office, deaf to the claims for justice instead of their champion.) Perfectionism may be said to concentrate itself on the demand to make ourselves, and to become, intelligible to one another. And I suppose no outlook would count as moral which did not make place for such a demand.

The laboratory of film is one in which the elitism of perfectionism is tested. Any perfectionist tendency in morality will speak of something like self-cultivation, but in my understanding of Emersonian perfectionism, to realize and prove these ideas in the form of a goal of cultivation in the arts or the development of a budget of intellectual or spiritual talents or tastes (I suppose the common current philosophical view of perfectionism) would be as much a debasement of the idea as any of the current popular philosophies that offer to release your potentiality for making a killing in real estate or day trading or to provide you with the means to be all you can be. The Emersonian progress is not from coarseness to sophistication, or from commonness to prominence, but from loss to recovery, or, as Thoreau roughly says, from despair to interest, or as Kierkegaard and Heidegger and Wittgenstein and Lacan more or less put the matter, from chatter to speech. Deontology and Utilitarianism, taking as fundamental the right or the good, are, so to speak, one another's moral competitors. Perfectionism is not a competitor of either, rather assuming that it has a place in both; its competitors are the endless debasements of itself—as philosophy is not in competition with science but with sophistry. (It is Polonius who, as foil to Hamlet's philosophizing, recommends to the young being true to oneself: his announcing of the truth poisons it—does it not?) Nor does, or should, the care of the soul, say the devotion to teaching and learning that Socrates represents, require the drama of Plato's *Apology*, pitting Socrates' standing in this practice of care against the assembled representatives of the city, who threaten him with death for the conversations he lives upon. It is worth being reminded, by this glamorous scene, of the life-and-death importance of moral standing with oneself. But suppose we can see in the laboratory of film the democratization of perfectionism, can recognize what we are capable of in the undramatic, repetitive, daily confrontations to which they call attention. Then we see that in our slights of one another, in an unexpressed or disguised meanness of thought, in a hardness of glance, a willful misconstrual, a shading of loyalty, a dismissal of intention, a casual indiscriminateness of praise or blame—in any of the countless signs of skepticism with respect to the reality, the separateness, of another—we run the risk of suffering, or dealing, little deaths every day.

I note that this way of speaking of skepticism and repetitive little deaths is a kind of characterization of how I think of what Wittgenstein speaks of as the ordinary or everyday, defined or constructed as the place to which, as he more or less says, we lead words back from the violence done them in the insistencies of what he calls the metaphysical. It is the emblem of philosophy's coming, repeatedly, endlessly, to an end, as its illusions of higher meaning each expire. What happens here, where morality is no longer a separate study, is immersion in a moral fervor in which we stake ourselves in every word we utter, as if assuming responsibility for language as such, for the shared world as a whole. No wonder the couples of perfectionist comedy find in one another, only in one another, occasions, also, of superb and raucous playfulness, making themselves incomprehensible to others. (The suggestion here is that the role of art in perfectionism is as much to shield against our moral aspirations—which means, against our despair of reaching them—as to remind us of them.)

What then? Shall we say that we *ought* not to cause little deaths every day, and not use words violently, in estrangement from ourselves, or say that to do so decreases the general good? These theses perhaps seem undeniable, but also unsayable. To whom might they be said? The fact that they express unanswerable observations about our behavior in the world causes a disappointment with the world as a stage for the moral life more harmful to participation in a democracy than moral cynicism. The cynic has the energy to play the game; the discouraged, run down, turn aside. If this disappointment locates a moral outlook it is because within this mood we nevertheless know that there is a further state of the world, or a further world, free of the causes and force of this mood; the world, as Emerson echoes Kant, not that I converse with in the cities and on the farms, but the world I think. (Just how the Kantian intuition of mankind as living in two worlds fits this substitution of a world of disappointment for Kant's world of inclination as the other of the intelligible world is a nice problem. I suppose a way to approach it is from the recognition that in both cases the problem posed is one of making the will practical: in Kant's case thought lacks an incentive to attract the will, in our case the will is repelled by its own ineffectiveness, its powerlessness to effect change. We at least have a glimmer of the direction of a solution, namely that the first move must come from the other. This may seem incompatible with Kant's demand for autonomy. But what then is the power of the exemplar in Kant's book on religion?)

These thoughts are my responses primarily directed to the two small but widely admired genres of film that I have mentioned, one of comedy and one of melodrama, which flourished half a century ago, when half of the population of America went to the movies each week, and moreover, to the same movies. A sequence of questions arises: Are remarriage comedies still made? What might it betoken if they are not? Are other strains of movies being made which suggest further evidence for the idea that film more generally bears an affinity with the morality of perfectionism? If there are, what is the good of them? Let's see where moving through these questions takes us.

I note that I shall not here, except implicitly, reach a certain level of the question of what it is about the medium of film that creates this affinity (having to do with film's power of transformation, its taste for the improvisatory, its registering of the human power of privacy as a person's aliveness to her or himself, its projection of the world as a whole, and so forth), a level that demands the detailed reading of sequences that lectures or chapters devoted to individual films can afford. Here I am trying only to establish the fact of the affinity.

If films with the feel of remarriage comedy are still made—films in which a certain kind of feast of fast talk, never far from the topic of the basis of marriage between a pair who can neither break up nor find a stable mode together, makes them incomprehensible to the rest of the world—they needn't look very much like the classical instances of the genre. How could they, since the fear of divorce has changed, the threat of pregnancy has changed, the male and female stars and the directors and writers who put them in action are gone? Let's recall that the films I take as defining the genre present narratives in which major features of classical comedy are negated: the principal pair or pairs are not young and innocent but older, socially defined and sexually experienced grown ups, whose task is not to get together but to get together again; if the woman's father is present he is on the side of his daughter's desire, not of the law (contrary to, for example, *A Midsummer Night's Dream*); the drama does not feature a threat of death but it in each case comes to a question of a divorce with whose decree the couple threaten the death (or test the life) of their own happiness; the barrier against the marriage accordingly being as it were inner rather than outer, the overcoming of the barrier requires a progress of a particular kind of educative conversation, employing a distinctive play of pleasure and pain. That the couple is (so far?) childless goes with their being subject to certain outbreaks of zaniness or surrealism, one might also call them outbreaks of, reversions to, their own childhood (the couple serenade a leopard on a rooftop; the husband shakes hands with an umbrella; elsewhere, the husband threatens his wife with a licorice pistol). The shadow of violence that shows up in each of the comedies predicts the related genre of melodrama in which women—sisters, I call them, of the women of the comedies—cannot find or will not yield to the men they have encountered with whom such a quest for happiness seemingly might be joined, and opt instead for a life of their own that rejects marriage, such as it is. In the place of educative conversation, the exchanges in the melodramas are filled with stifling irony.

    Some recent films nevertheless try to keep something like a remarriage surface (*As Good As It Gets*, with Helen Hunt and Jack Nicholson [1997]), and at least one that I think of (*The Sure Thing*, with John Cusack [1985]) repeatedly—I counted eight times—alludes to moments or circumstances in *It Happened One Night*. But even while the cultural role of film has for various reasons dwindled, and I myself am a member merely of various fragmented film publics, and do not keep up faithfully with American films, I can recall at once, in this regard, *Moonstruck* (with Nicolas Cage and Cher) (1987), *Tootsie* (with Dustin Hoffman and Jessica Lange) (1982), *Sleepless in Seattle* (with Tom Hanks and Meg Ryan) (1993), *Clueless* (with Alicia Silverstone) (1995), *Groundhog Day* (with Andie

MacDowell and Bill Murray) (1993), *Crocodile Dundee* (with Paul Hogan and Linda Kozloswki) (1986), *Working Girl* (with Harrison Ford and Melanie Griffith) (1990), *Untamed Heart* (with Marisa Tomei and Christian Slater) (1993), *Inventing the Abbotts* (with Joaquin Phoenix and Liv Tyler) (1997), *Four Weddings and a Funeral* (with Hugh Grant and Andie MacDowell) (1994), *My Best Friend's Wedding* (with Cameron Diaz and Julia Roberts) (1997), *Everyone Says I Love You* (with Woody Allen, Goldie Hawn, and Julia Roberts) (1996), *Cookie's Fortune* (Robert Altman's film with Glenn Close, Julianne Moore, and Liv Tyler) (1999), each of which provides an interpretation of one or another feature of remarriage development—for example, each provides a closing sequence worth an ambitious essay on its own. I single out a further pair of films starring John Cusack, *Say Anything* (with Ione Skye) (1989), and *Grosse Pointe Blank* (with Minnie Driver, as black a remarriage comedy as *His Girl Friday*) (1997) as constituting, along with *The Sure Thing*, an effort to explore a quality in the sensibility of a particular actor that is part of the grain of the classical comedies, in them particularly of the leading woman, but that no longer characteristically attends today's isolated film projects.

The Cusack trio also emphasizes a further difference between early and recent remarriage comedy. The recent pairs on the whole seem too young to imagine the future—not unable to imagine *their* future, since after all to live with their future open is the very point of the adventurousness, the readiness for risk, for life without sure, and insured, things, that mark the older remarriage pair, but rather unable to imagine that there will be a habitable social world within which to pursue their own adventure. (I put aside here, if I can, fears of atomic or ecological disaster.) It is an inability to imagine what Nietzsche means by saying that philosophy, if it is to continue, or rather to arrive, must be of the future, what Emerson means, following Wordsworth and Milton, by calling for a new day ("A new dawn at mid-day")—a renewed conviction that genuine change in the conditions of human existence is possible, that they are not fated to will a repetition without change of the institutions, marriage pivotally among them, that have produced the present scene of fixation and joylessness which the older generation has prepared for them.

The older remarriage pair I describe, roughly, as seeking to forgo a narcissistic innocence in return for experience of their own worth having and sharing. The younger pair seem to have no way of insuring their privacy, their mysterious intimacy, without preserving their innocence. Is this a new fragility, or a new sense of the fragility, of youth? It relates to such films in recent years of child (or adolescent) genius as *Little Man Tate* (1991), *Searching for Bobby Fischer* (1993), *Good Will Hunting* (1997), and I think *The Matrix* (1999) makes a contribution here. I understand their interest to lie in presenting genius as a metaphor for singularity, for what I earlier called the sage in each of us, that without which one cannot become the one one is; it is the signal negation of elitism, namely in being universally distributed, if for the most part buried in distraction and conformity.

The joylessness of the world I referred to (parodied in remarriage comedy more than once in the figure of the mother of the man who for a moment seems an alternative to the woman's rightful but exasperating mate) is what I have marked as a disappointment with the world as the setting for a moral life. That we have arrived here at an idea of youth or young genius as an emblem not as a wish for exemption from that moral life, but as a way of being saved for it, brings us to the next question I predicted in store, namely whether there are other current strains of film that tend to suggest some partiality of good films for the outlook of moral perfectionism.

There do seem to me a remarkable number of new films (within my limited experience) that concern a quest for transcendence, a step into an opposite or transformed mood, not so much by becoming another person, or taking a further step in attaining an unattained self, or becoming who you are, as by being recognized at the one you are by having, or giving, access to another world. This is a notable feature of classical remarriage comedies, one I call, after its model in Shakespearean romance, the green world, a place of perspective at which the knots of comic confusion are loosened, a place in four of the seven defining remarriage comedies that, it always pleases me to remember, is called Connecticut, a place more than once shown to be difficult to locate and arrive at. That sequence I opened with from *His Girl Friday*, in a closed press room, is this film's black variation on the placement of the green world. It is a place from which the ordinary world is broken into, out of which beauty and isolation and strangeness intertwine to reveal a glimpse of community and the possibility of change. And here also is where the two other moments I invoked at the opening of my remarks cross paths with this one. The woman in Rohmer's film, as is characteristic of Rohmer's four tales of the seasons, discovers in an apparently uneventful passage and setting of her life an event which we understand to have the power of conversion, what I might call the feel of transcendence, for her—not access to another world necessarily, but a break in the assumptions of this one. The child in the Jarmusch film, in her inflicting as it were an invisible wound upon her friend's killer from within an identification with that dead friend, marks a synchrony of two worlds. That friend had been living the code of what he calls an ancient world, that of the classical samurai (as he has learned of it), and he allows himself to be killed as part of that world, calling it almost extinct; but the child has absorbed, hence renewed, from the friend's friendship and from the text he transmitted to her (a text entitled

Rashomon), the sense that the present world must not be allowed to represent all we desire.

Hollywood has always had a taste for contrasting worlds of the everyday with worlds of the imaginary (playing on the two primordial possibilities of film, realism and fantasy), from *The Wizard of Oz* (1939) and *Lost Horizon* (1937) and *It's A Wonderful Life* (1946) to, in recent years, *The Matrix* (a certain surrealist/Zen version of the Kantian idea of the visible world as illusion and the real intelligible world as holding the truth of its origins), and *Being John Malkovich* (1999) (realizing the contingency of being the one you are by discovering a looking-glass entry into a way of becoming an alternative), and *Fight Club* (1999) (in which the world of the insatiable male identification of aggressiveness with intimacy is permitted expression so constant that, as the individual equivalent of war, it turns against its creation), and *Dogma* (1999) (in which a new disobedience in heaven, made possible by a God who has inadvertently hidden himself too long, threatens to destroy existence), and *Waking the Dead* (2000) (in which the yearning for the love and the aspirations of one's past reaches the point of hallucination, hence of possible madness, reconciled in an acceptance of the continuity of the real and the unreal, or of fact and fantasy), and, as a concluding instance of that yearning, again the influential *Groundhog Day* (in which that yearning is strong enough to earn, and survive, a Nietzschean repetition of days, or of one day, in which the perfection, or say the deed, of an offer of love is seen to require and satisfy an eternal return of steps toward an unattained self)—in all of which (all films of great interest, intelligence, and passion) a crisis is precipitated in the name of demanding a new beginning, another chance. It is perhaps worth adding that three of the five nominees this year for the Oscar for best picture can be understood as dealing with worlds counter to what Emerson calls the world of conformity, namely *American Beauty* (1999) (in which a despairing man's desire for and understanding of America's promise of beauty moves him from a quest for youth to a wish for a transformed power of expression, shown as rose petals not covering the world but issuing from his mouth, and makes him incomprehensible and alarming to America (and in which a young couple, also incomprehensible and alarming, in ways not unlike the way remarriage pairs stand to proper society, depart to be cared for by an underworld of the like-minded in New York, reversing the pattern of moving from New York to the countryside), and *The Sixth Sense* (1999) (in which a child's genius of perceiving/hallucinating another world can only be cured by another who is at home in that other world), and *The Cider House Rules* (1999) (in which rules for a house of migrants, or call them laws for a nation of immigrants, have to be broken if the unwanted and orphaned are to be given a life, as sometimes they can only be, in a place apart populated by the unwanted and orphaned).

Without knowing whether such a set of samples will strike you, in its very randomness, as smacking of mere accidents or as suggestive of an indefinite number of further instances, I recall that I note, in *Pursuits of Happiness*, that remarriage comedy bears a relation to horror movies in view of their both featuring the idea of the transformation of self and world (the idea of which may be either, or both, glorious or ghastly), and remind you that the vast region of the Hollywood musical essentially plays on the idea of the ordinary world as a step away from an ecstatic harmony (a feature especially notable in the routines of Fred Astaire, which so characteristically take their rise from events and objects of everyday life—a walk along a river or down a train platform, taking shelter in a pavilion in the rain, roller skating, golfing, swabbing a floor, tripping over overstuffed chairs).

The films of Eric Rohmer (one of the two surviving great directors of the French New Wave) have an importance for my motivation in pursuing the idea of film's affinity for the transcendental moment that has not come out, namely not alone the fact that such a moment is a signature of his filmmaking but that it goes with his creation of surfaces in which nothing otherwise happens to attract your attention, so it can seem that you may not tell with what interest you follow their narratives, in which so little happens, a visit, a drive, a talk in a shop, a broken appointment over the telephone, an encounter in a train station, a swim. His films seem to me to represent discoveries of the boredom and the menace of the ordinary to match Wittgenstein's sense of philosophy's craving at once to achieve it and to escape it. Since this is so much a part of how I see the motivation to perfectionism, or put otherwise, of how the idea of ethics as a separate study is superseded in works like the *Investigations* and *Being and Time*, and having left no time to follow it now, I console myself, before coming to an ending, by mentioning a direction of inquiry that I had thought of concentrating on for this occasion, namely into the portraits of moral perfectionism and the ordinary which preoccupy the definitive novels of vocation and of domestic life achieved by Jane Austen and George Eliot. As earnest of further work I cite the climactic aria from Austen's *Mansfield Park* in which Edmund reports to Fanny the event that reveals to him the falseness of one object of his love and opens the truth of another, namely Henry Crawford's elopement with Edmund's married sister—or rather the event of Mary Crawford's reaction to that event which demonstrates to Edmund her impossibility as an object of love and marriage. The fault in her is revealed in her anger at her brother for nothing more than the folly of his action. "Guess what I must have felt," Edmund cries out to Fanny. "So voluntarily, so freely, so coolly to canvass it!—No reluctance, no horror, no feminine—shall I say? No modest loathings! . . . She saw it only as folly, and that folly stamped only by exposure. . . . Oh! Fanny, it was the detection, not the offence which she reprobated. It was the imprudence. . . . Hers are faults of principle, Fanny, of blunted delicacy and a corrupted, vitiated mind." In a word, Mary Crawford is repudiated for taking a Utilitarian view of adultery. But Edmund's own somewhat hysterical demand for horror and loathing seems to me to prompt the narrator's suspicion—I shall not say repudiation—of the opposite morality of principle. "Fanny's friendship is all he had to cling to," the same cousin Fanny whom he had known since childhood (a significant feature of remarriage comedy), and whom he had educated to measure the harmony and rapture of life by the test of what they call star gazing. The last paragraph of the novel affirms that Fanny came to judge her and Edmund's life at Mansfield to be "thoroughly perfect." But it is a perfection readers characteristically express some reservation with, as if—in contrast with the other principal marriages concluded in the Austen universe—this one marks the end not the beginning of spiritual adventure, an adventure so dependent upon talking (an obsessive theme of *Mansfield Park*), as the marriage of true minds requires. We no longer sense here what George Eliot calls the defense of the myth, giving it to Daniel Deronda to say that a tale has been "like a passionate word—an extreme image of what is happening every day—the transmutation of self." (In a recent adaptation of *Mansfield Park* for the screen (1999), the surmise that the chastened close of the tale is somehow tied to the fact that its world invisibly rests on an economy of slave trading and labor (a fact mentioned repeatedly throughout the novel) is made garishly visible by a plot change that makes Edmund's brother's illness something contracted by his trip to the family's plantation in the West Indies, from which he returns with a portfolio of sketches of the horrors of slave life uncovered by Fanny as she is caring for the brother in his convalescence. I merely report that, to my surprise, I found the visual explicitness to make excellent sense of something that Austen's prose, after the fact, seems positively to invite.)

The sense in Jane Austen of an undermining of the ordinary brings me to my ending, which is to formulate some initial answer to the question What is the good of that species of film of the transcendental ordinary I distinguish as remarriage comedy? I can give one sort of answer important to me by reinvoking what I spoke of as my dissatisfaction with John Rawls's articulation of Nietzschean perfectionism, adding one further remark about that epochal work. Late in *A Theory of Justice*, Rawls remarks that the adoption of his theory puts one in a position of claiming to be "above reproach," in effect a humane attempt to provide an answer to how we live sanely, knowing that the cry of justice must, in any actual society, to some extent go unanswered, because any actual society exists in a state not of strict but of partial compliance with the principles of justice—*how* partial, or distant from strict compliance, it is up to each of us to judge. (I summarize this idea, in my account of Emersonian perfectionism, by saying that a society is worth our loyalty if it maintains good enough justice to allow criticism of itself, and reform. I discover, to my dismay, that I have been blankly misunderstood as thereby claiming that our present society has as it stands enough justice in it, period. This is an imposition.) I claim that "I am above reproach" is unsayable, or sayable only moralistically, in the conversation of justice. If someone addresses a claim against society out of envy or greed or sloth or anger, and so on, then one can reply to that effect. And if someone denies that our society is possessed of good enough justice to be worthy of loyalty, then one can reply that one continues to consent to it. But this means to me, since consent is then directed to a shared life with justice to some extent unrealized, that one is not claiming to be above reproach but acknowledging that one's social existence is compromised. The lives of remarriage couples, among the films of lives seeking the existence of the transcendental, arrive at a moment in which they have to reaffirm their marriages by taking them intact back into participation in the ordinary world, and attest their faith, or perception, that they consent to their society as one in which a moral life of mutual care is pursuable, and worth the show of happiness sufficient to encourage others to take their lives further, as if happiness in a democracy is a political emotion, and a pair can undertake to represent a general future. The *Republic* asks whether the life of injustice can be happy. Remarriage comedy asks whether the life of good enough justice, of compromise, can be happy enough. That remarriage comedy is still invoked on film, if not exactly continued, is, so I have been suggesting, worth stopping over.

25

Moral Reasoning

Teaching from the Core

D URING MY FIRST YEAR IN the Harvard Philosophy Department's graduate program, fifty years ago this coming fall—having graduated from the University of California at Berkeley with a major in music and then spending three years at UCLA recovering from the crisis of leaving music by continuing to pursue what caused the crisis, namely absorbing myself in other studies, principally philosophy—I would hear from time to time, from fellow students intimidatingly more knowledgeable than I about Harvard, that the bulk of Harvard's resources supported its attention less to graduate than to undergraduate life and education. It was not until that academic year was drawing to a close, and I had passed the Ph.D. qualifying examinations, that I looked around my life, which had pretty thoroughly confined itself to the straightest path between the new graduate dormitories (recently designed by Gropius) and Emerson Hall, home of the Philosophy Department, sufficiently to accept an invitation to dinner that took me beyond Massachusetts Avenue toward the Charles River and thereupon first perceived the contrast between my eight-by-twelve room and the space implied by the chandeliers lighting a company dressed in jackets and ties in the Winthrop House dining hall. I can testify, however, that since my dormitory room had provided me in effect with

Alumni Day Address, Graduate School of Arts and Sciences, Harvard University, 2001. Parts of the introduction to *Cities of Words* are adapted from sections of this piece.

the first efficient basis I had known for bringing order and purpose to my intellectual life, a matter then of considerably more urgency for me than whether I was dining under chandeliers, my perception—while it caused me to accommodate to a new vision of privilege—was merely one of interest, not, so far as I could tell, of disapproval or of envy.

Indeed, what I found I wanted to talk about on the occasion of the Graduate School's Alumni Day, as soon as I received the welcome invitation to participate in it, is a distinctive experience of spending most of a life teaching at Harvard that is a function, to my mind, precisely of the interaction between graduate and undergraduate students, as this happened in the humanities course I and a colleague offered in the old General Education Program when I returned to Harvard to teach in 1963 and more specifically in the Moral Reasoning course I was still offering in the successor program to General Education, namely the Core Curriculum, the year I retired from full-time teaching, in 1997—both of these programs experiments in broadening and bringing coherence to an undergraduate education and community in deeper and more sophisticated terms than imposing distribution requirements. Those programs have marked the distinctiveness of an education in Harvard College, and I recognized as well that they had a distinct effect on the graduate students who were indispensable in conducting the discussion sections into which the large lecture courses were divided once each week. It was an effect I shared and which I treasure. I wonder if in this part of an hour I can give a sense of what its conditions were as I knew them.

I begin with two generalizations—for which each of you will doubtless be able to think of exceptions—that distinguish a humanities course (as I think of that from my angle of philosophy) from a science course, as I know of them. The first generalization is that, unlike scientific ideas, ideas in the humanities are bound up with particular texts, and it is never certain which order of reading the texts is most fruitful for which purposes and which persons—a text from an earlier era can be more decisive in one's experience than yesterday's informed commentary on it. The second generalization is that a text worth devoting part of a course to is apt to be inexhaustible in its implications, so that one would like to give a sense of this richness, and make the most of the idea that it will not be mastered before moving on to the next text.

And I cite two ideas underlying these generalizations. The first is a response to Thomas Kuhn's thesis in *The Structure of Scientific Revolutions* that science does not progress uniformly throughout its history but suffers periods of creative crisis, in which its primary energy is expressed not in a search for new evidence but in radical shifts of conceptualization. Accepting the soundness of this observation, I can speak with confidence in saying that the humanities, where they are creative, never proceed uniformly but are always in crisis—or should be, as long as human life is in crisis. The other underlying idea I cite is from Ludwig Wittgenstein's *Philosophical Investigations*—a book that has influenced me philosophically at least as much any other composed in the past century—where Wittgenstein declares it to be "of the essence of our investigation that we do not seek to learn anything *new* by it. We want to *understand* something that is already in plain view. For this is what we seem in some sense not to understand" (sec. 89). Here Wittgenstein evidently distinguishes philosophy (hence my idea of the humanities) from science, which is for us the unsurpassable source of paradigms for learning something new about the world. This does not mean that philosophy cannot share intimacies with science, any more than the fact that philosophical passages may over various stretches be indistinguishable from literary passages means that the philosophical is identical with the literary. What it means is that one should expect the texts I am apt to choose for the syllabus of a humanities course will be ones engaged in the inexhaustible process of trying to understand themselves as a way of understanding, or making sense, of human lives.

In my practice this has meant that whereas in a strictly conceived philosophy course I assign works intending for us to learn to read as slowly or patiently as possible, in a general humanities course I have tended to assign so much material that you have to learn to read as fast as some initial comprehension will allow—accustoming yourself to the knowledge that one always leaves a text too soon and that the next may tell you more about the one at hand than reading that one again will (at least now). The graduate students who are teaching fellows in such a course are acting less as preprofessional experts checking on a beginner's mastery of a growing body of knowledge, than as older and more experienced guides to texts that they themselves will continue to read indefinitely and that they are prepared, indeed expect, to read with more understanding this time than last. It requires a relationship of tact and trust.

The idea for the particular course I want to talk about (called Moral Reasoning 34: Moral Perfectionism) came from two sources: generally, from my feeling somewhat burnt out from years of responsibility from my General Education course and wanting a new pedagogical departure; and specifically, from my having at that time, in the mid-1980s, recently published a book about a set of seven comedies of the so-called Golden Age of the Hollywood talkie (1934–1949) (I call the book *Pursuits of Happiness*) and only afterwards recognized that the set of moral problems dramatized in the genre of film established by these films (whose narratives concern the threatened breakup of a marriage) were problems whose study suggested a view of the moral life rather at odds with the moral theories that dominated discussion in the then current practice and pedagogy of philosophical moral theory. A favorite way of approaching the field, lent renewed force by the appearance of my colleague John Rawls's epochal work *A Theory of Justice*, was to contrast theories that take the notion of the good as fundamental, deriving from it the notion of right, and that emphasize the consequences or utility of actions (theories of Utilitarianism, represented most famously by David Hume in the eighteenth century and by John Stuart Mill in the nineteenth, with theories that take the notion of the right, or of responsibility, as independent and fundamental, and emphasize the motive to actions (theories associated with the names of Kant and of Hegel, I suppose the two most influential, worldwide, of modern philosophers). But when I thought about these eminent theories in connection with the lives depicted in the grand movies I had been immersed in, the theories and the lives passed one another by, appeared irrelevant to each other. Yet these lives seemed and seem to me ones pursued by thoughtful, mature people, heavily in conversation with one another about the value of their individual or their joint pursuits. I could not understand their interest for me as unrelated to moral reflection. (Just how a course designed to explore this discrepancy between more established moral philosophy and a group of Hollywood films was accepted as a core course is a story on its own.) My book claims for these seven films that they are masterpieces of the art of film, primary instances of America's artistic contribution to world cinema (they remain to this day beloved worldwide), and that their power is bound up in their exploration of a strain of moral urgency for which film's inherent powers of transfiguration and shock and emotionality and intimacy have a particular affinity.

I call the comedies in question remarriage comedies (to mark the fact that unlike classical comedies, the problem of the drama is not to get a young pair past the obstacle of an older figure, usually a father, and see them married (think of *A Midsummer Night's Dream*) but to get a somewhat older pair who are already together past some inner obstacle between them and hence together again, back together; it is a simple difference that turns out to generate a surprising and open-ended set of features shared by the films, for example that the woman of the principal pair is never a mother and never (with one exception that proves the rule) shown to have a mother; and that her father is always on the side of the woman's desire, not of the law; and that the narrative opens in a city and moves at the end to the country, a place of perspective Shakespeare calls the green world; and so on. The seven are *It Happened One Night* (Clark Gable and Claudette Colbert, 1934), *The Awful Truth* (Irene Dunne and Cary Grant, 1937), *Bringing Up Baby* (Cary Grant and Katharine Hepburn, 1938), *His Girl*

Friday (Cary Grant and Rosalind Russell, 1940), *The Philadelphia Story* (Katharine Hepburn, Cary Grant, and James Stewart, 1940), *The Lady Eve* (Barbara Stanwyck and Henry Fonda, 1941), and *Adam's Rib* (Katharine Hepburn and Spencer Tracy, 1949). (Various of these films momentarily appear in rapid sequence of images screened at the opening of the Academy Award ceremony.) There is another play of Shakespeare that I say stands behind these romances, namely *The Winter's Tale*, which is a tale of remarriage to end all such tales.

It is true that these films do not concern front page moral dilemmas, say concerning the death penalty (as in *Dead Man Walking* [1995]) or about whistle blowing (as in *The Insider* [1999]), or informing (as in *The Front* [1976]), or abortion (as in *Cider House Rules* [1999]). Yet one of them does concern a lawyer's effort to *make* front page news (Katharine Hepburn in *Adam's Rib*) by turning a case of assault into a trial of the law's bias against women—but we also know that it is about this lawyer's husband's having broken some unspoken private bargain of equality with her), and another (*The Awful Truth*) is about lack of trust, and *His Girl Friday* is about lack of attention, and *The Lady Eve* is about the difficulty of overcoming moral cynicism.

Just reciting the titles of the remarriage comedies suggests examples of what I mean by speaking of texts in a humanities course as inexhaustible and prompts me to say that I only include films in such a course about which I feel, and undertake to demonstrate, something of that depth. Take just one example. The titles include the names of Adam and of Eve. The film *The Lady Eve* actually features a snake and early shows Barbara Stanwyck draw Henry Fonda's attention to herself by hitting him on the head with an apple. You could think this nothing more than an isolated gag until you realize that the whole film is about the craving for knowledge, and the mischief that knowledge, out of context, can do, and being afraid of being tricked or tempted, and about the refusal of knowledge—all issues pertinent in the Garden of Eden. In that ambience, what shall we make— if anything—of the moment in the opening sequence of *The Awful Truth* when a wife, who seems to have been caught in a compromising situation, plucks an orange from a basket of oranges and tosses it across a room to her wandering husband (Cary Grant)? It's not an apple, and I made nothing of it after repeated viewings of the film over the years. But once it dawned on me that the woman is not *giving* but *returning* the piece of fruit to the man, who had given the basket to her to prove he had been in Florida, whereas the woman notices that the orange has the word CALIFORNIA stamped on it, I found a train of questions to arise about what it is each wants the other to know, and who is to go first in trusting the other, and why they are each perpetually tempted to test the other, not an unreasonable program for a commentary on Adam and Eve.

The question these couples face is formulated less well by questions concerning what they ought to do, what it would be best or right for them to do, than by the question how they shall live their lives, what kind of persons they aspire to be. (To take a central case, we do not feel that the principal pair *ought* not to have divorced, but rather that they *have not*, that they remain in a state of marriage, and that they must, on pain of tragedy, come to recognize this state.) This aspect or moment of morality—one in which a crisis forces an examination of one's life that calls for a transformation or reorienting of it—is the province of what is sometimes called moral perfectionism. It is not an alternative to Kantianism or Utilitarianism (Kant and John Stuart Mill both have deep perfectionist strains in their views) but it emphasizes that aspect of moral choice having to do, as it is sometimes put, with being true to oneself, or as Michel Foucault has put the view, caring for the self.

I am reminded of a passage in an early dialogue of Plato, the *Euthyphro*, where the division of moral questions between those concerning the good and those concerning the right or just (prefiguring those between what I have called Utilitarianism and Kantianism) were, as far as I know, first explicitly distinguished, and where room is made for a further distinction. Here is Socrates speaking to Euthyphro:

> But what kind of disagreement, my friend, causes hatred and anger? . . . If we were to disagree as to the relative size [or weight] of two things, we should measure [or weigh] them and put an end to the disagreement at once, should we not? . . . Is . . . not the question which would make us . . . enemies if we could not come to a settlement . . . the question of the just and unjust, of the honorable and the dishonorable, of the good and the bad?

It is what Socrates is calling the honorable and the dishonorable that I propose points to the issue of perfectionism—not in the sense of conduct expected of high rank and enforceable by others of that rank, but in the sense of conduct perhaps not morally enforceable but which affects your sense of your own worth and of those who in various ways identify or associate themselves with you. When the Cary Grant character in *The Philadelphia Story* (C. K. Dexter Haven), during an exchange with his former wife Tracy Lord (Katharine Hepburn), touches on their past together, he rebukes her for her coldness and moralism, instancing her refusal to tolerate his taste for alcohol; and when she replies that that taste made him unattractive, he returns, "Granted [it was my problem]. But you were no help there. You were a scold," he is not accusing her of some misdeed (as lying, stealing, treachery of some kind) but rather describing her as being unworthy of herself, of what she could be.

Such concerns were paramount in moral thinking at least as early as Plato, who in *The Republic* pictures the soul as on a journey from spiritual slavery to perfectionist enlightenment. In the period since, say, Kant and Hegel, my favorite moral perfectionists are Emerson and Thoreau, to my mind the most underrated philosophical minds (though no doubt often mispraised) to have been produced on this continent. In Emerson there is no question of reaching a final state of the soul but of endlessly taking the next step to "an unattained but attainable self," a step that turns us not from bad to good or wrong to right but from confusion and constriction toward self-knowledge and sociability. In this period moral perfectionism is identified less with canonical moral philosophers than with figures who work between philosophy and literature, such, beyond Emerson, and indebted to him, as Nietzsche, or literary figures such as George Eliot, Matthew Arnold, Ibsen, and Bernard Shaw, who look back to such writers as Montaigne, Pascal, Rousseau, Goethe, and Wordsworth. Partly because of this shift in the division of intellectual labor, perfectionism has not been much esteemed among philosophers in my part of the philosophical forest, a lack of esteem climaxed when Rawls in *A Theory of Justice* identified moral perfectionism, in its strongest form, with Nietzsche and in effect ruled it out as a serious contender among views of the just life (since it asks for higher rewards for higher lives). I have argued that Rawls's judgment was based on an uncharacteristically (for him) ungenerous reading of Nietzsche's admittedly distressed and distressing sound, and moreover specifically of a passage in which Nietzsche shows most openly his indebtedness to Emerson. So of course I would protect this moment if I could. (Nietzsche does say things like, "Your life [can] retain the highest value . . . only by your living for the good of the rarest and most valuable examples." What I am calling ungenerous in Rawls's reading is his taking this to mean that the business of most of us is to live for others. Nietzsche also says: "Anyone who believes in culture is thereby saying: 'I see above me something higher and more human than I am; let everyone help me to attain it, as I will help everyone who knows and suffers as I do.' " In a word, the valuable example I am to live for (any I who cares) is my future self, exemplary in its efforts at perfection, self-transformation. My stake in this protection is deepened in recognizing that two of the most influential, if problematical, philosophers of the middle third of the twentieth century, and beyond, namely Martin Heidegger and Ludwig Wittgenstein, neither of whom wrote works specifically identified as of ethics, but whose central texts (Heidegger's *Being and Time* and Wittgenstein's *Philosophical*

Investigations) may be seen to advance claims for a way of life, of a transformation of one's life, demanded by philosophy as such and which is characterizable as perfectionist.

Socrates wished to protect the philosopher from the unjust city, in his pursuit of the question the *Republic* asks: Can the unjust man be happy? John Rawls's *A Theory of Justice* in effect asks the next question: Can—to what extent can—the *just* man be happy? (compromised as he inevitably is in an, at best, imperfectly just world). I have elsewhere expressed a pang of uneasiness with that part of Rawls's answer which is supposed to allow us to claim (at least to ourselves), in a society that we judge close enough to compliance with the principles of justice to be worth consenting to, that we are, in Rawls's phrase, above reproach. There is, I argue, no such position to be claimed, so that our question becomes, rather, whether a given dispensation is worth suffering reproach for. To be able to withstand and answer this reproach is a way of seeing the value of perfectionism to democracy, a willingness for change analogous with society's commitment to reform toward greater justice [what is justice to the self? to its desires]. That happiness is possible in the place called America—not by insulation from it (say by wealth or power) but by participation in it—is how I understand the idiosyncratic happiness sought by the principal pairs of the remarriage comedies.

I have mentioned the bulk of the texts from among which a set, with some variation in successive years, was assigned for the course, about one (or a portion of one) each week, paired with a film—setting the stage with Kant, Mill, and Rawls, continuing with Plato and Aristotle, with John Locke and (for a reason yet to be mentioned) John Milton, and with Emerson, perhaps some of *Walden*, and Nietzsche, and interspersed among them Matthew Arnold, Ibsen, Bernard Shaw, the opening chapters of Genesis, and *The Winter's Tale*. I cannot deny that in the opening weeks of the course many students were bewildered by the pace of reading and viewing and by the range of different voices in the texts. It took all the skill of accomplished and dedicated teaching fellows to keep them confident. But I can report that—with no higher rate of disaffection than would be expected in any large course—there came a time when the general air of comprehension and satisfaction and accomplishment became palpable—it is what makes teaching worth a lifetime.

We have a little further to go before I can describe how the experience of giving that course has affected me. Go back to Cary Grant's accusation of Hepburn as having been a scold. It is an accusation less of what is said than a rejection of a way of speaking as such. Dexter Haven is saying that Tracy Lord is incapable of rational (what Jane Austen calls amiable) conversation, which she also calls conversation fit for a rational society. That is, for these films, an absolutely radical charge. The wit and intelligence of the conversation in these films is widely appreciated as one of the glories of American cinema. And it is a chief claim of my book on the subject that a certain capacity for conversation is related specifically to the basis of marriage. The basis is unforgettably formulated in John Milton's revolutionary tract *The Doctrine and Discipline of Divorce*. Milton invokes, as is traditional in Protestantism, the passage from Genesis justifying marriage ("And the Lord said: 'It is not good that the man be alone. I shall make an helpmeet for him' ") and interprets this to define a fit marriage partner; in Milton's words such a partner is one with whom a "meet and cheerful conversation" is possible (where "conversation" refers not alone to words but to a mode of interaction generally; our term "intercourse" uses both ranges). Dexter Haven's accusing Tracy Lord of being a "scold" thus precisely accuses her of being unfit for marriage.

To justify the demand for conversation, let's say to make oneself intelligible to others, to oneself, is essential for any moral theory—to say how and why we owe words to one another. In moral perfectionism this demand becomes the principal object of study. In case it seems that marriage is too specialized an issue to bear up under the thinking represented in the list of texts I have given, I have a double response: First, marriage is an allegory in these films of what philosophers since Aristotle think about under the title of friendship, what it is that gives value to personal relations. Second, the idea I want conveyed is that the moral life is constituted not alone by consideration of isolated judgments of striking moral and political problems but is a life whose texture is a weave of cares and commitments in which one is bound to become muddled and to need the friendly perception of others in order to find one's way, in which at any time a choice may present itself (whether, as in *It Happened One Night*, to break an engagement to be married on what will seem frivolous grounds; or whether, or when, as in *The Lady Eve*, to confess an indiscretion; or whether, as in *The Awful Truth*, to take offense at an indiscretion), in pondering which you will have to decide whose view of you is most valuable to you.

These films can give the impression of regarding the more outstanding issues of moral perplexity (abortion, euthanasia, poverty, taxation, capital punishment) as matters that will take care of themselves for people of good will. For example, in *His Girl Friday*, the woman reporter (Rosalind Russell) at one point leaves an unfinished story in her typewriter when an emergency calls her away from the press room, and it is read aloud by another reporter to the rest of the group. One of them observes, "I don't think it's ethical to read other people's writing without asking," to which another responds, "Where do you get that ethics stuff? You're the only one who'll swipe any of it." Or again, in *Adam's Rib*, Hepburn, after Spencer Tracy has in a rage packed a bag and left their apartment, is giving legal advice to a client who lives across the hall and who admires her, and she suddenly stops reading the document in her hand and says to no one, "That was wrong of Adam" and the admirer replies, "He's just getting even for having lost the case to you in court," whereupon Hepburn silently turns a gaze of high disdain on this creature who can imagine that the man she married could act on a base motive. The perpetual moral risk run by the principal pair of these comedies is that of snobbery. This is a reason the narrative of the films inevitably provides each of the pair with a moment of being humbled, or humiliated, and consequent insight.

Now, in conclusion, what has all this to do with graduate and undergraduate education? I wanted to create a pedagogical environment in which great texts of moral reasoning, whose power to inspire thought and insight has been proven over decades and centuries and millennia, would be put in touch with a body of films whose experience has been found to survive the changing tastes of generations and which minimizes the degree of expertise required to respond to them intelligently, so that the differences between generations can become interesting and discussible from all sides; in particular, in which the half-decade of difference between being an undergraduate and a graduate student is both minimized and maximized. Put otherwise, in which undergraduate students, perhaps still searching for the vocation meant for them, or perhaps beginning to doubt that an earlier choice is as clear as it once seemed, can see more unobstructedly what the commitment to the humanities can look like a few years down the road, and in which graduate students, steeped in taking on the necessary confinements of a profession, can remember unprotectedly what their motivation was for converting so much freedom into responsibility.

From my own perspective, I hope I was able to enact, and to speak to, both sides of this exchange. But there was something else inspiring to me in taking on this course, something I associate with the particular fortune of teaching at Harvard through the final four decades of the century just past. I had the feeling sometimes, lecturing to such a group, committed to forming around these materials its transitory identity, of this size and this proportion of ages, regularly supplemented by visitors and auditors, often graduate students from the various humanities who were in sight of finishing their doctoral dissertations and were faced with the prospect of perhaps offering such a course themselves, wanting to observe an example of it, perhaps to modify or perhaps reject—I had the feeling that one could say anything one had it at heart to say about major moments of our shared culture, and if one got it clear enough and interesting enough, one would be understood, and not just by this group but by what the group represented for me, the body of citizens of good will with time for thought and imagination. This permanently affected the way I write books. And it provided a happy, stabilizing influence in my relation to the country, when I felt it was doing itself harm. There is a recurrent happiness, and anxiety, that is perhaps more intense at Harvard than virtually at any comparable place, in the thought that anyone, destined for any achievement, may be a member of the group sitting in your classroom, weighing the value of what you have to offer. But the steadier happiness I speak of comes rather from my sense that the group, as it stood each year, then and there, and developed throughout the months of these shared experiences, was calling on the best of myself. I am forever grateful for that inspiration.

26

Crossing Paths

C ELEBRATIONS INSPIRE reminiscences and those that follow are as
much concerned with keeping similar paths from crossing as they
are with recognizing the fact that different paths have crossed and
keep crossing. Arthur Danto and I are perhaps the American philosophers
of our generation—I know of no others—about whom the following four
descriptions can all be said to be true: first, our itineraries contain a period, beginning in our youths, in which our lives had been devoted to the
practice of an art—painting and print making in Arthur's case, composing
music in mine—and we discovered philosophy as if by accident, after moving to the east coast for college, or postcollege; second, on the basis of an
education in analytical philosophy, and without ever forgoing an
identification with the dispensation of American philosophy, we both came
to spend extraordinary amounts of liberating, productive time writing, in
ways whose philosophicality we had explicitly to insist upon (in the introduction to a collection of his articles as art critic for *The Nation*, Arthur
calls this writing also a contribution to literature, and I sometimes describe
some of what I do as calling for philosophy), in part meant for those
beyond the world of professional philosophy who were invested in one or
other of the arts, or to what we had to insist were arts, perhaps ones that
revised the idea of art; third, we each found ourselves in important part
philosophizing in connection with work intimately connected with the
place we had moved eastward to and found also to be home—for Arthur,

Version of a paper read at a colloquium on the work of Arthur Danto, Columbia University,
October 2002.

the exploding world of painting in the 1960s in New York, for me the remote world of Emerson and Thoreau in Cambridge and Concord; and fourth, a recurrent motivation in Danto's writing about art after modernism, and in my writing about film, was to express both admiration for the achievement of Clement Greenberg as the dominant theorist of modernism, and at the same time a fundamental dissatisfaction, and break (in my case building on conversations with, and in reading, Michael Fried), with Greenberg's idea of the essence of the medium of art represented as painting, and most particularly with his identification of that essence with the use of paint on a two dimensional flat surface—a dissatisfaction, and break, precipitated, however differently understood by us, by a kind of revelation of a break in the history of the arts that linked the fate of art with that of philosophy.

Yet for all the affinities suggested in these four descriptions, and in great measure because of different accents in our inheritances of the discourse of philosophy, we may not often have seemed to find details of help in each other's writing. But Arthur had begun publishing books years earlier than I, and his example of independence of mind was a signal encouragement in my beginning years of a certain strife with the difficult and indispensable profession of philosophy, and the spirit of my contributing to these days of celebration is to express my sense of gratitude for his achievement.

It pleases me, in that spirit, before noting certain differences in our work made interesting to me by those similarities, brought home to me in my recent weeks of renewed companionship with Danto's writing, to commemorate two early encounters in which our paths literally crossed, in 1964 and 1965, years decisive for each of us in determining the ensuing decades of our writing. They were the years in which Danto's *The Transfiguration of the Commonplace* was prepared, in which Andy Warhol's *Brillo* box revelation had played a defining role in demonstrating for Danto that there are no sensuous criteria for distinguishing art objects from what he called ordinary or mere real objects. They were also principal years of my writing or drafting the bulk of the essays making up my first book, *Must We Mean What We Say?* In those essays, the significance of the ordinary for philosophy was confessed as a revelation for me, especially in the work of J. L. Austin, and the problematizing of the ordinary (sometimes meaning the commonplace)—as it was made extraordinary in, for example, the writing of Samuel Beckett's *Endgame* and shown tragically unachievable in Shakespeare's *King Lear*—struck me as literature's taking on the condition of philosophy's self-criticism, and at the same time as philosophy's chance, or obligation, to face the return of the repressed (both in the form of literature's contesting of philosophy's early dominance, in Plato, in assessing the state of the soul, and of philosophy's contempt for, or impatience with, the everyday).

The first of the encounters I have in mind was the result of a phone call—I cannot remember whether it was from Arthur or from Sydney Morgenbesser—saying that they were both driving up to Cambridge in the company of a philosophy student of theirs who was a filmmaker and who wanted, as part of a film he was working on, to shoot a scene of philosophers having an informal philosophical exchange in a location in the countryside near Cambridge, and that they would all like me to join them. Moved by the idea of these teachers wanting to spend a vigorous weekend helping a student with a project that, while in an extended sense in service of philosophy, risked making fools of themselves, I found the invitation irresistible. The idea of the film, I vaguely recall, seemed to be, beginning on the west coast, to follow a young man's spiritual adventures hitchhiking across the country, ending on Cape Cod; the late adventure, in or near Cambridge, consisted in being given a lift by three philosophers who were driving to a philosophy conference, and who would persist in pursuing an impassioned philosophical conversation regardless of their surroundings. It would turn out that virtually all of the footage shot that day had been technically, unusably flawed. The screening of it I attended, one midnight in Boston, did include ten or fifteen seconds of blurred red footage capturing three almost recognizable grown men inexplicably playing kicking-the-can in a large meadow. So three careers as film stars vanished like a dream. But something else that remains from that day is my impression that each of the philosophers, in the exoticism of the event, had found pleasure in the sheer sound as well as in the fact of earnest and playful philosophical conversation, and were willing to go, by academic standards, to extravagant lengths to convey this to strangers. It seems to me that I have been finding an enviable, refined version of such a willingness, or say generosity, in the outpouring of Danto's work as a philosophical critic of art, and of the concept of art—the aspect of his work that I will confine myself to on this occasion.

This fluency relates to the second of our early encounters, again in a car, this time as Arthur was driving the two of us, the summer we both taught classes at the University of California at Santa Barbara, to a roundtable discussion on, as it happens, philosophy and film. Out of the blue, Arthur said, getting better acquainted: "You haven't published much, have you?" I admitted glumly that I had not. He persisted: "What's the matter Stanley, don't you *like* to write?" This version of shock therapy, I have come to think, going over it more than once, had a beneficial effect upon me. I could not protest that I had written more than I had published, because I seemed to recognize that that might only prove the truth of

Arthur's surmise, not that I hadn't in some sense written, but that what kept me from offering it to strangers was not simply my fear that it wasn't good enough but, compounded with that, the fear that my pleasure in it would show, which for some reason would constitute a worse exposure. I guess it is not news that philosophy is as forbidding as it is attractive.

Perhaps the central cause of difference, of paths parting, within the similarities I have described, can be articulated by taking the circumstance Danto describes in his later essay, "The Philosopher as Andy Warhol," in the following way:

> It is perhaps of some value to pause and reflect on some parallels between what Warhol was doing and what some of the advanced philosophers of the time were doing. The latter, largely under the influence of the late philosophy of Wittgenstein, were making a certain return to ordinary language the center of their thought; precisely, the language of the marketplace, the nursery, and the street, the language everybody knows how to use in the commonplace situations that define the common life. This requires some explanation. In the period up to and following World War II, philosophical attitudes toward common sense and common speech were by and large contemptuous. . . . The task of philosophy was to construct an impeccable ideal language suited to house the truths of science, and mathematical logic offered a magnificent tool for this rational reconstruction. . . . All this changed abruptly in the 1950s, in a shift as dramatic and as climactic as the shift later in that decade from abstract expressionism to pop. . . . There was nothing internal to either art or philosophy that explains the shift—it seems to have come from outside, from exactly "the spirit of the times." All at once the prospect of an ideal language seemed as preposterous as the claims of the New York School seemed pretentious. (*Philosophizing Art*, pp. 77–78)

Let's remember that there was a further element often playing a role in the characteristic reception of each of these two shifts, or turns, namely the sense of the ending of something—in the case of art, of the end, or inertia, of painting; in the case of the work of Wittgenstein and of Austin, of the end of philosophy. I did not share this quite widespread feeling about the significance of these philosophers, and if I did not find Danto's articulation of the subsequent course of art perfectly satisfying, I was less satisfied by what various of his philosophical critics were saying in response to him. Even if I had been moved, and free, to enter into that debate then, it would have been pointless (I felt) apart from living a New

York life, I mean living with the work, and with conversations about the work, that Danto was responding to.

But in fact I was not free, since what was claiming my attention was that other half of the coincidence of developments in art and in philosophy that Danto had pointed to, namely the attempt to inherit what seemed to me right, and irreversibly innovative, in the work of the later Wittgenstein and in that of my teacher Austin. (I am not relying on the report, and in fact I do not know what to make of it, in a volume of interviews of American philosophers done in the 1990s in which Danto and I both participated, of his saying "The later Wittgenstein strikes me as hazy: it is beautifully written, marvelous thought, but philosophically of no significance whatsoever." (in G. Borradori, *The American Philosopher*, University of Chicago Press, 1994, p. 90).

Writing philosophy has not, I believe, presented itself as an open *problem* for Danto, philosophically or artistically, as making art has done; a new age of philosophy did not beckon to him still to be articulated as he felt drawn to articulate a new age of what he called pluralism in art, against, primarily, Greenberg's monism; a new language did not have to be invented in which to understand and participate in what one found new in philosophical thinking, as he found to be called for by the new art. (I think here of Danto's repeated expression of his devotion to analytical philosophy as expressed in the writing of it he most admires, principally that of Russell and of Quine.) It was essential to my attraction to the work of Wittgenstein that for him philosophy is an incessant problem, in a sense is the essential problem of philosophy, expressed in its quintessential human wish to escape the conditions of human knowing and speaking, to escape, as I sometimes put the matter, the human. (It is not science that Wittgenstein contrasts with the ordinary, but metaphysics, especially as an answer to skepticism.) Wittgenstein was not the first to see this predicament of human self-dissatisfaction. Kant built systematic bulwarks against it, perhaps increasing the temptations but at the same time diagnosing and locating the points at which human restlessness, let us say, makes its gravest assaults upon reason (in metaphysics, in skepticism, in magic, in fanaticism). Wittgenstein's innovation, to my mind, was to perceive this as a drama enacted in philosophy's dissatisfaction with or disappointment with ordinary language, one in which ordinary language both rejects itself and assumes the obligation to come to itself. In this way of looking at things, the "return" to ordinary language is rather seen as a return *of* it, not as to a place of stability, but as of a place of inevitable loss. In particular it is not to a place of common sense or shared belief—the thing Emerson calls conformity—but is equally to be understood as an attack on settled beliefs. It is the possibility, or necessity, of this self-dissatisfaction, this battle of the human with itself, that creates the possibility, and necessity, in philosophy, of skepticism.

I express this in the first part of *The Claim of Reason*, in chapters adapted in a later decade from my doctoral dissertation, as the discovery of the absence of criteria for distinguishing the real from the imaginary, Descartes says from dreams, I say also from simulacra (though I did not use the word): characteristic examples I employ (taken from Wittgenstein and from Austin) were that of pretended pain, and of a painted goldfinch, which must exhibit the same criteria of identity as real pain and a real goldfinch, since otherwise it would not be *pain* that was pretended and not a *goldfinch* that was painted. The conclusion I drew from such cases was, unlike all other accounts of *Philosophical Investigations* that I knew of then, that Wittgenstein had not in fact or in intention provided a refutation of skepticism but had articulated a source of it. Human language is such that dissatisfaction with it can never be stilled; the question is not so much whether we can live within our finite means (which those who have respected skepticism have in different ways recommended, from the ancient Greeks to thinkers through Descartes and Hume to such as Bertrand Russell) as whether we can become responsible for our infinite desires.

Danto somewhere uses the term *skepticism* once, as I recall, as an instance of what he calls the duplication that Warhol and Duchamp had introduced into art, making explicit the inherent philosophicality of art. I might ask: Has Danto shown Warhol, first among others, to have made art, in linking its fate with philosophy, at the same time an illustration of a form of skepticism? Put it another way: Is the discovery that real things and their images (in perception or dream) are, in Bishop Berkeley's phrase, sensuously indistinguishable, a general version of the specific discovery that a real thing and a work of art are sensuously indistinguishable?

One difference is that, in skepticism we discover that we know less than we thought we knew, indeed perhaps nothing; whereas in Danto's proposal we know as it were twice as much as everything we thought we knew, that any and every object (or artifact, any object that reflects the hand of man or woman) may be a work of art. This is a proposal whose power I do not question—Danto has, I believe, been convincing to others beyond any predicting in realizing his desire to show the postmodernist world of art accessible to philosophical criticism—that is, in his wish to do for postmodernism what Greenberg did for modernism, and to do it by turning art and the ordinary toward each other. I have said that I have never felt sufficiently experienced in the world of that development of art to, even if I had wanted to, debate his achievement. A reason I might have wanted to is my sense of not sharing what I might call his taste for the objects he champions; but there again I cannot dismiss the doubt that the same lack of experience disqualifies this sense of mine from serious attention. (It is a lack magnified by the fact that my main experience of art has been with literature and music, in neither of which has modernism, however challenged, been thought to be eclipsed by a worldwide movement that tends to make, say, Schoenberg or Bartok or Proust or Joyce unlistenable or unreadable.)

Of course *I* have to take my lack, which is to say, my experience, seriously. So I notice the number of times, in response to Danto's assertion, or revelation, that there need be no sensuous mark distinguishing an art object from a real or mere object, that I have felt the question begged: his assertion would be true on the condition that there *is* an object of art here, which however is just what is contested. Perhaps it will be replied that that is just the point, to show that art now begs the question of art. But in this mood, Danto's suggested two criteria for the existence of art—namely that the object is "about" something and "embodies" what it is about—seem quite elastic enough to fit equally well how one is to take modernist, not alone postmodernist, works. The series of paintings called Unfurled, by the modernist Morris Louis, is for example about blankness and diagonals and corners, and embodies these. But at some stage I realize that Danto, or anyone I have read who follows his thought, never, or almost never, puts things as I have been doing, speaking of distinguishing an art object, or a work of art, from a real or mere object.

Danto speaks rather of the presence of an "artwork," sensuously indistinguishable from, for example, this box or this snow shovel or this bottle rack or, most lingeringly, this urinal. I do not know the provenance of this use of the English word "artwork" (which those born before a fairly recent date would have taken to mean the visual material, other than written copy, say in a glossy magazine or on a printer's layout; or perhaps what Desdemona means by saying of the terrific handkerchief that she had thought to have the "work ta'en out," that is, its design or decoration copied), nor whether that revised use has been part of a familiar discussion that has passed me by. So—in any case—what? What could be more familiar than the introduction of a new word, or new use of a word, into our language?

But is that what has happened—that "artwork" has taken on an additional use as what Quine calls an individuating noun in contrast with its established existence as a bulk or mass noun, so that in addition to speaking of needing or copying *some* or more artwork we can speak of *an* artwork and hence of a *different* artwork? Such a use doesn't quite seem to capture Danto's sense that what happened—with a "Blam!"—when in the 1960s painting came to (something like) an end, but art continued, was that art was suddenly replaced by incidents of artwork, as though the visual world, so far as the hand of man or woman was discernible, and as far as the eye can see, had taken on the value of decoration. His idea, beyond this, is that things were still being made, or shown, that had the power to transform the beholder or participant, or the experience of the beholder or participant. Danto never tires of speaking of his own transformation in realizing this condition. But that leaves the matter of the kind of transformation in question.

While I seem unable in general to endow the realm of objects Danto has philosophically rescued for art with the interest or fascination he expresses (from which it perhaps follows that I am unable to allow them to transform my conception of the house of art), I think I may not altogether be a stranger to moments of intensity and gratitude in relation to them, which keeps their form of existence a question for me. I cite two instances, one in connection with an installation, the other in connection with a series of lecture/performances by John Cage, a composer Danto is not alone in associating with the art he champions. It is from such instances, or touchstones, I sometimes say good encounters, that I would attempt to test the extent to which I have been abandoned by history.

The installation I have in mind, which I encountered on a visit to Caracas in its Museum of Fine Art several years ago, was made by the Venezuelan performance artist Antonieta Sosa. I excerpt a few sentences here from notes I made the following day and read as a preface to one of the several lectures I gave in the museum during my week's stay.

Sosa's installation is a sort of representation or facsimile or simulacrum or abstraction of what some title card identified as her own apartment. It is a real space, with real, smallish rooms that one walks through. I asked myself what such a piece is doing in a museum in which, for instance, there are Chinese porcelain vases that take your breath away with their beauty; classically scaled sculptures set in gardens or on a terrace that overlooks the city; and suddenly, set in a niche at the turning of a ramp, ancient tiny gold and silver ornaments of fascination. Is an installation a beautiful or imposing or fascinating thing; is it an ignorable thing, or a thing about the ignorable? What is it about the space of the installation that questions whether it is out of place, or arbitrarily in place, in the space of a museum? Sosa's installation incorporated a window of the museum as a window within its installed, self-defined space. Is this some declaration that this installation of an apartment shows our dwellings, our houses as they are, to be museums themselves of some sort? Then what do they exhibit, or remember, or collect? At the same time the installation questions the idea that what there is in a museum is collected, since it itself obviously cannot be collected—questions the idea, that is to say, *if* it turns out that it itself does indeed *belong* there, that is to say, if we accept its presence there in the right spirit, and it is not for some reason, for example, being stored there, which may or may not serve to discourage that spirit. Antonieta Sosa's bed is empty, but there are traces of someone's having lain on its sheets. The impressions are like prints left by something immaterial, as if some ghost had (or has) fallen asleep in that bed. Other traces struggle against the idea of the immaterial. At about eye level, or a bit higher, along the walls of the installation's opening room, there is a continuous horizontal line of dozens of small, tidy, transparent packets of dust, each with a meticulous label giving the date on which its portion of dust was collected in this apartment. In one packet there is a torn theater ticket, in another a broken hair clip. That theater ticket is the only thing that has color in the whole region of the wall, a red ticket that appeals to your attention and to your imagination of the life beyond these walls. Dust, the very type of insignificance, worthlessness, triviality—ranking with Plato's mud, for which it is doubtful that there is a corresponding type or Platonic Form, rendering it fit for recognition, redeeming its imperfection—is here being granted lucid space to participate in our self-discovery. Sosa is of course not the first artist to elevate, or sublate, and incorporate the debris or leavings of life into a work of art. (For example, Chris Marker's film *Sans Soleil* [1982] takes as essential to its study of eternity and impermanence the importance of respecting the residue, say the consequences, of what we do, as well as of what we have left undone, wastes of actions and of possibilities of actions; and I have no way of doubting that this film is a masterpiece of art.) Yet Thoreau's text about Walden, which Sosa's installation brought to mind, urges us to get rid of our debris, which he names dust, which for him includes the bulk of our possessions, on the ground that we fail to know what is of real interest and importance to us, what we live for. I phrase this so as to allude also to a moment of Wittgenstein's self-portrait in *Philosophical Investigations* as he lets himself inspire the question "Where does our investigation get its importance from, since it seems to destroy everything interesting, that is, all that is great and important?" (*Investigations*, sec. 118). His answer is, in effect, that whatever we, after him, seem to destroy was already of the value of dust. (I had a chance, the day after reading the lecture these remarks preface, to ask Antonieta Sosa if she had read Thoreau. She answered in excellent English that she had read enough to know that she was still too young to study it more thoroughly—though she was, even if her dancer's body made her seem younger, surely close to Thoreau's age when he died. I detected no grain of irony in anything she said or did.)

I am reminded that I have neglected a pervasive feature of moving through Antonieta Sosa's rooms. Because the walls of her rooms are apparently no different, in color and texture, from those of the museum, you enter them before you know you are there, I mean you expect (I expected) that what is exhibited there is *on* its walls, not that the walls *themselves* are on exhibit, along with everything they enclose, if anything. Then the recognition perhaps dawns that you are yourself enclosed there, hence exhibited while the music of your presence lasts, hence (since you are a human being) that you are a subject of interrogation. So the question why this installation is here becomes the question why you are here, what interests you here, hence perhaps exhibits your confusion. It is philosophy's invitation.

This brings me to the other of the good encounters I mentioned with the artwork world, namely John Cage's Charles Eliot Norton Lectures delivered at Harvard in 1988–89. The six lectures, so called—he titles them, for short I–VI—were constructed by establishing (as what composers for a while called precompositional assumptions) a set of what Cage would use as source texts, namely ones from which, by various chance procedures, sentences and parts of sentences were extracted and joined together for the length of whatever length a lecture may be. The resulting lecture-texts consisted of chains sometimes of near gibberish, sometimes of what almost seemed sense, and sometimes of a whole English phrase or sentence (sometimes one perfectly familiar—Thoreau, and Emerson, and Wittgenstein, I am happy to report, were prominent among Cage's source texts). These constructions were read by Cage sitting before a table on the lit platform/stage of a dimmed Victorian quasi amphitheater with a balcony running through a full semicircle, the hall seating better than a thousand people, reading from what I recall as an ordinary notebook in a clear, fluent, rather sing-song tenor voice, at a steady pace, never looking up from his text. I found myself charmed, my overall mood as of hovering in a sort of active peacefulness, freed from the demands either of sense or of silence, punctuated from time to time by the wonder whether something intelligible had found its way to speech, and more rarely, but striking with the force of revelation, by a completely pure, unmistakable sentence, after which I actively for a while held myself in readiness for another such incredible gift. I became almost joyful as I took in the joke (Danto asserts that a postmodern object works in the region of metaphysical jokes) that, apart from the sensuous pleasure of the event, it was almost mimetic, a simulacrum, of an ordinary lecture, of one of those uncountable hours in which audiences have sat without effective complaint through an hour-long talk, so much of so many of which are recyclings of personal or cultural source texts, parts of which are unintelligible, other parts as if almost intelligible, with here and there perhaps memorable leaps or slips of clarity. Cage's imperturbability seemed to question how much of any of this is taken into the sum of one's happiness, and whether that matters. A more disreputable part of my joy, or fun, no doubt, was witnessing the spectacle of members of the audience, from high and low, leaving early, some shyly, as if out of regret and respect, but others brazenly, as if insulted or mildly outraged, without realizing that they were equally and inevitably part of the theater Cage had created of the occasion, that their leaving was in effect predicted in Cage's preparations, which produced a construction to be delivered in independence of the audience's expectations, or responses, or needs (except those of audibility and physical comfort), that in his eyes leaving his performance may or may not have been as accurate and telling a response to his work as staying would have been. Why are you there? Or in Thoreau's way of speaking, Where do you live?

I attended the next week's lecture to see what a second experience would reveal, and, doubtless, to count the house. I would not guess who sat through all of all six lectures, or who could distinguish one from the others. I am reminded of Danto's recurring in various of his pieces to Warhol's film *Sleep* (1963), a roughly six-hour string of shots, often repeated, of a man sleeping. Danto confesses that he did not sit through it all (or did he say this about Warhol's *Empire* [1963]?). Was leaving the screening artistic bad faith or faint-heartedness on Danto's part? Part of the background of the joke here is that eight hours is typically and wisely said to be the span of a good night's sleep. Is a span of six hours good enough? What is any good about watching a moving picture of such periods of sleep (undrugged, and not for the purpose of studying sleep)? Here I do not feel like asking whether the object is art, but whether it is a film, which Danto does not question, or, I believe, take the film to question. To say it is a bad or boring film would seem not to be in on the depth of the joke; and how would one support such a judgment? After Hitchcock experimented in his film *Rope* (1948) by using no editing, shooting each reel of film in one take, he concluded that a film, meaning a good film, had to be edited, that is, cut. Does Warhol's *Empire* challenge that judgment? Only on the condition that it is, and is accepted as, a good film.

To view, or watch, or scan, or stare at all but unvarying motion picture footage of the Empire State Building for just over eight hours will cause various states of consciousness. Where would the interest lie? How does the fact of unvarying motion picture footage *hold* interest as a projected still slide would not, and as the building itself does not?—anyway not in a form that would be expressed by fixing oneself at the place of Warhol's camera and staring at the building for eight hours (what would count as *watching* it?)—or at any other still artifact out of doors. As a declaration or exploration of motion and still photography, or of demanding awareness of the fact of viewing film, the concluding sequence of fixed camera shots of empty cityscapes that concludes Antonioni's roughly contemporary *Eclipse* (1962) is a thousand times more interesting and pleasant to view than (I wager) *Empire*. Perhaps that is precisely what *Empire* implies is dangerously beguiling in such a film as *Eclipse*. Here is an instance of what has caused me to speak of modernist art as, over a couple of centuries, calling increasingly in some new way for philosophy.

A test of artistic worth announced by Wordsworth is the desire to *return* to a work, to behold it again. This seems all but fantastic to consider in the case of experiencing the Cage lectures or the Warhol films. Yet what if I go on to suggest that we take *Sleep* as a comment on an old motif of sculpture and painting, even forming a test (whether by confirming or mocking it may be left open) specifically of a thesis of Michael Fried's about the development of modern painting in discovering that overcoming an unwanted theatricality requires denying the presence of the beholder, effected in depicting an otherwise absorbed, oblivious subject? Has Warhol's film shown that this is true or untrue of film more generally?

What do these recent comments of mine, or readings, at best amount to? They do not count as what Kant defines as aesthetic judgment, because they do not claim to speak with necessity and universality, an essential mark of which for Kant is that I am willing to impose them as demands that others share my pleasure in the objects, see that what I see in them is as if there to see. I find that I am not vividly interested in whether others agree with me about Warhol's films, or perhaps no more interested than I would be in whether they understand and like a joke I like, which may be no small matter. But this is not the role I have counted on from the great arts, which is rather to prepare my experience for judgment, by making experience mine, and to show the world, I might say show the justice of the world, to deserve judgment. Yet I remain grateful to the artwork or artworld objects, as it were, for their still strange interest to me, and particularly, I think, for making me voluble, loosening my tongue, expressing myself. This is also no small matter. On my reading of Wittgenstein's *Investigations*, it is concerned with the human terror of inexpressiveness, of suffocation, alternating with an equal terror of exposure, as if speech threatens to become unable perfectly to refer to objects of my interest or to give expression to my states of being, or else to refer and give expression so fully as to give myself away. It is the version, or threat, of skepticism that I claim Wittgenstein's *Investigations* stakes itself on identifying and dispersing, ceaselessly.

But here I seem to be proposing a way to distinguish the objects Danto calls postmodern from ones most would call modernist—among which I count Wittgenstein's *Investigations* itself—not by whether one contains a set of properties (sensuous or conceptually derived) that the other lacks, but by the role they play in our lives, by how we treat them, by whether, for example, I have, in order to allow myself and the object to be revealed to each other, to do the thing Wittgenstein calls "turning my investigation around," which I understand as having to turn myself around, reorient my life with the object. I do not have a list of criteria that distinguish these addresses to objects from what Danto means by speaking of our "participating" in performances and installations and being "transformed" by them. So I conclude with a further example.

Godard's film *Two or Three Things I Know about Her*, from 1967, takes place in a cityscape of demonic juxtaposition, with equal parts of decay, junk, and construction amid a growing forest of babbling one- or two-word signs, done with big letters in primary colors, made as if for giant children who will learn nothing beyond them. It is the sort of scene Danto has declared himself struck by as wonderful (an experience not foreign to me), and which Godard seems to despise and to admire America for bringing into the world. The film contains Godard's early figure of the housewife/prostitute, symbolizing late capitalism, surrounded in her modern kitchen by every familiarly garish product purchasable from a supermarket, underscored by a sound track sometimes unyielding with its sounds of cans being opened and of pots carelessly slammed on a stovetop and, outside the windows, of trucks and cars and trains spelling out our dependence upon them. But suddenly, from nowhere, the opening phrase, or quasi fragment, of Beethoven's last String Quartet is heard, lasting some three seconds. The modified repetition and the responding phrase do not follow. This happens again in the film. The ache for the responding phrase is so strong as for a moment to convince us that we are apt for prayer. Grant that the Godard film is a masterpiece of postmodernist filmmaking, at any rate one that positions itself against a tradition of complacent, derivative modernism and humanism and liberalism and the rest, as strongly as any postmodern object. How do we understand the gesture of its quoting the Beethoven, this Beethoven? Is it to emphasize the lastness of the quartet? Is it to say that its opening fragment is to be regarded as complete, in other words, that there is no established way of going on from it, to an answering fragment? Does this mean that there is hope for us in learning how to go on, or that there is not? T. J. Clark, in *Farewell to an Idea*, speaks of Beethoven as Jacques-Louis David's brother, both of them sources of a long period of modernism that is over. Is Godard's quotation of Beethoven taunting us with the memory of an experience we can no longer have, or trust? Or is he proposing that we learn from it, if such an experience is any longer open to us, that we shall have to find it in unheard-of forms, within landscapes of ideals that seem merely blasted? It is in opting for the unheard of that I have from .my first credible encounter with

Wittgenstein's *Investigations* undertaken to inherit that work as an achievement of modernism, from which it follows that I have come to understand
some future of philosophy, however else, and without supposing that any
separate field of philosophy will continue to be known as aesthetics, to be
itself irreducibly aesthetic.

27

After Half a Century

ROBERT WARSHOW'S *The Immediate Experience* is one of those books whose discovery, early or late, can create so specific a feeling of personal gratitude for its existence that it is almost a surprise to learn that others know how good it is. That is how I account for my recurrent feeling—despite recognizing that individual essays within the book have been repeatedly anthologized, in college textbooks on writing, in celebratory collections of essays—that the book remains neglected. Partly the feeling is that the writing is so lucid and so peculiarly valuable that *everyone* should read it who cares about coming to terms with her or his relation to our culture; partly the feeling is that the writing is so consistent and urgent that its collection advances claims upon attention going beyond anything to be expected from a sequence of essays so many of which are devoted to mere movies—even though no one in our culture has written better about movies than Robert Warshow. A paradoxical expression of the feeling is that one wishes at once to make a present of the book to friends and to strangers, and at the same time to keep it private, as if playing for time to work out one's own relation to it. My effort in this epilogue is to begin to understand, in some measure to realize, both of these wishes, taking myself as an emissary from another time, a time specified by the association of the appearance of the earliest of the essays in this book with the arrival in my life of the not unfamiliar crisis of reconstituting one's education.

First published as an epilogue to Robert Warshow, *The Immediate Experience: Movies, Comics, Theatre and Other Aspects of Popular Culture* (Cambridge and London: Harvard University Press, 2001).

From the fall of 1948 through the summer of 1951, I bought, or rather seized and laid trembling money on the counter for, each number of the quarterlies *Partisan Review* and *Hudson Review* and *Sewanee Review* as they appeared in the elegant little bookstore in Westwood Village, several square blocks of shops adjacent to UCLA that were mostly too expensive or irrelevant for me and the other graduate students I knew to enter. Supplemented by the new periodical *Commentary*, which as I recall the bookstore did not carry, this was almost the only reading I allowed myself in those years to take me away from the regime of philosophical studies I had found my way to after graduating from Berkeley a year earlier, having majored in music and read no philosophy. I had spent most of the intervening year in New York, the last months avoiding my composition lessons at Juilliard, very often, afternoons and evenings, at the movies. In *Hudson* and *Sewanee* one could expect essays by all the major names associated with the New Criticism (it is easy to remember, for example, finding Empson on Wordsworth, and R. P. Blackmur on Eliot and Flaubert, and Allen Tate on Poe), and in *Partisan* as well as in *Commentary*, the figures of those who will later be called the New York Jewish intellectuals and who were at the height of their powers—a given issue could contain fiction by Saul Bellow and Isaac Rosenfeld (even if rather more Chicago than New York), a piece on painting by Clement Greenberg, an essay by Lionel Trilling, and something odd, perhaps on movies, by a certain Robert Warshow. The trembling anticipation I note was distinctly, but only partly, directed to the pleasures I knew the reading would afford me. It was equally directed to my daily reminders that these pleasures were not welcome in the profession of philosophy, at any rate not then and there, when English and continental analytical philosophy were its dominant modes, together with American pragmatism. Contrariwise, my consciousness was alerted to the fact that philosophy, in any form, was essentially absent from the cultural commitments, literary or political, of any of the quarterlies. I was having too much trouble recognizing the subjects I was being expertly taught as essential to what I had imagined I wanted from the study of philosophy— something, let's say, that spoke to my crisis in giving up music—to welcome having to face the fact that my America was one in which philosophy and the life of literature were forbidden to each other.

Robert Warshow was the principal writer constituting my strict diet of extracurricular reading who was asking what America is, and specifically what his relation to American culture is. This explicitly meant not only following his sense that film, and popular culture more generally, were key manifestations in which to read this relation, but also his awareness at the same time that his upbringing and education had given him no way in which to articulate this sense with honesty and interest and conviction—

the culture's power to reveal itself, even at its most blatant, could not break free of its capacity to keep itself concealed. Perhaps Warshow's knack for interesting himself in what Lionel Trilling in his introduction calls "objects unworthy of his attention" contributes to the notion (mine at any rate) that Warshow, or his sensibility, was of a younger, or I might say later, generation than most of the writers with whom he was appearing. This youthful cast of mind, marked by a fresh, irritated, but undisappointed sagacity, seems to go with other distinguishing characteristics of his writing, among them the fact that he cites few major literary figures as touchstones of ideas. His official reason for this is that while the likes of T. S. Eliot and Henry James (whom he names but does not, I believe, discuss or quote) are great artists, unlike those who create the comic strip *Krazy Kat* and write Broadway plays and make Hollywood movies, the latter say things he (also) wants to hear, or rather things he (also) can and must understand his relation to; this relation manifests the way he lives, his actual life of culture. He concludes that to say what he finds in these more everyday concerns he needs to write personally, but it seems clear that the reverse is equally true, that he wants to attend to them because that attention demands of him writing that is personal, and inspires him to it. And why would this way of writing seem to him of such importance?

He expresses his sense of the necessarily personal in various ways in his opening essay ("The Legacy of the Thirties")—namely, a sense of the writer's having to invent his own audience (p. 9), of the writer's having to invent all the meanings of experience (p. 16), of the modern intellectual's "facing the necessity of describing and clarifying an experience which has itself deprived him of the vocabulary he requires to deal with it" (p. 9). What experience has caused this devastation?

Before giving his answer, I note the magnitude of the claim. It expresses an isolation (he is without an audience) so extreme as to deprive him not only of meaningful speech (as if he is effectively aphasic) but also of that access to recognizable experience of his own that is the cause of meaningful speech. Something of this sense of inexpressiveness or suffocation is how I would come, two decades later, to characterize a fundamental philosophical motive of Wittgenstein's *Philosophical Investigations*, to teach us to return to ourselves the language that philosophy, in response to modern culture, would repudiate, the ordinary language in which we can recognize our desire. ("Ordinary language philosophy" has proven to be an unfortunate title for this mode of philosophizing, because it has been taken to contrast with extraordinary, or sometimes with literary, language. What it contrasts with, rather, is a fixated *philosophical* language which precisely would preempt the extraordinary from disturbing customary experience.) The sense of being unexpressed, or as Warshow also puts the matter, of lacking "an adequate emotional and moral response to experience" (p. 17), is an intimate tie of this mode of philosophizing with the motivation to psychoanalysis. I take it as a significant gesture of the *Investigations* that Wittgenstein begins with a description or memory (from Augustine's *Confessions*) of a child learning language; and I take it as a mark of Warshow's philosophicality that the only conversations in which he actually depicts himself engaged are ones with his then eleven-year-old son Paul (in "Paul, the Horror Comics, and Dr. Wertham"), and there is even a footnoted transcription of an exchange when Paul was four.

It is hard to perceive such matters (the relation to American culture, the relation to one's own speech) as the bases for marking an affinity I felt with Warshow's work that distinguished my sense of it from what I was learning from his more renowned companions in the pages of those quarterlies. And even when I came to be moved, out of my own work, to take up the presence of film (for philosophical reasons, and consciously as well for the claims its powers placed upon the description of experience), and even to assign Warshow's path-breaking essays on the gangster film and the Western in the first seminar I offered on the aesthetics of film, at Harvard in 1963, it was another dozen years before Warshow's example manifested its fuller effect upon me—something which took the form of adducing, in what eventually appeared in an essay appended to my book *Pursuits of Happiness* ("Film in the University"), the fascinating coincidences of concepts that thinking about film had produced between the writing of Warshow and the writing of Walter Benjamin (whom I am assuming Warshow had not read).

In that essay I emphasize that both refuse to exempt themselves from the common response elicited by film, yet both insist that film poses a revolutionary problem for criticism and aesthetics. Both demand the legitimization of film as an object of (philosophical, theoretical) study, a study that must modify the concept of art, hence of what we mean by the popular and what we mean by the exclusive. And the more I explore the writing of Benjamin, the more interesting I find the occasional conjunction of it with the wildly different pages of Warshow. I had not, for example, in my first thoughts of the conjunction, recognized that something like Warshow's sense of the loss of access to his own experience was what produced the centrality for Benjamin of Baudelaire's access to the experience of the modern.

Is this sufficient ground for insisting on so unlikely a conjunction, which might prompt, if not disbelief, exaggeration? I bring it up now mainly as a spur to ask whether the current extreme prestige of Benjamin and the comparative neglect of Warshow, even within the realm of the academic study of film, is a reasonable measure of their comparative value. The point of this gesture is not to suggest that something needs to be done about this disparity but to ask what it betokens about our relation to our own experience. Here is a place from which to give Warshow's answer to the question I postponed, concerning the cause of the devastation of culture (of audience, of language, of experience) and the consequent sense of isolation within which Warshow understands the serious American intellectual of his time to have to work.

Warshow calls the cause the "mass culture of Stalinist liberalism" (p. 16), a development to which he attributes the corruption of American radicalism and the "vulgarization of intellectual life" (p. 3), whose sign is that "alienation from reality" which is "the characteristic experience of our age" (p. 9). Warshow writes as one to whom becoming a socialist had been the expected step of having grown up in New York with a lifelong socialist immigrant Jewish father, hence one for whom, while "the *issue* of Stalinism" is settled (though the danger is not), "the *experience* of Stalinism remains [with its "peculiar complexity"] . . . the most important of our time" (p. 6). And of our place. "The Communists could never completely set the tone of thinking in Europe" because in Europe the Communist movement, while "at once more serious and more popular" than in America, "was still only one current in intellectual life." In this country, by contrast, "there was a time when virtually all intellectual vitality was derived . . . from the Communist party," whether you existed within its "wide orbit" or "maintained yourself in opposition," resulting in "a disastrous vulgarization of intellectual life" (p. 3). Robert Warshow's father, like Walter Benjamin's, was a businessman, but Benjamin's was much more successful in amassing wealth, alienated from Berlin high bourgeois life only (*only*) because he was a Jew. Benjamin separated from him as a result of perpetual, mutual grievances. Yet for all the incommensurabilities in the weaves of the sensibilities of Benjamin and of Warshow, the issue of the Communist movement, and in particular of what Stalinism can be taken to signify, was as unsettled an issue in Benjamin's writing, in its way, as it was in Warshow's, in its different way. It was the issue over which Benjamin and his old friend Gershom Scholem were fatefully at odds.

Still, why insist on what is incommensurable, also, in importance? The conflicts within an incontestably great European intellectual such as Walter Benjamin become part of subsequent intellectual history in the West; the conflicts of a talented young American thinker, whose early death stopped short his exploration of his gifts, die with him—unless perhaps given life in the work of some later such young. I have a variety of reasons for the insistence. First, I want to emphasize not so much that Warshow is as immediate for us as Benjamin is, as that Benjamin is no less remote than Warshow is, that each is writing from memories that should not deprive us of our differing memories, that an inescapable autobiographical moment in philosophizing ("we," as I remarked a long time ago, is still first-person) is inseparable from an autopolitical task, letting the polis reflect upon itself, define itself. In Benjamin's case, film has to bear up under a proof of its usefulness to social aspiration; in Warshow's case film's powers are seen, for example in transforming Charles Chaplin's Tramp into Monsieur Verdoux and thence (in *Limelight*) into Calvero, to test whether our reception of socialist aspiration can bear up under the observations of irony: the former requires high theory, for which Warshow was engaging to prepare himself; the latter requires high criticism of individual objects, to which, in the case of movies, Benjamin never turned himself.

Second, Warshow's revulsion and anger at the devastation of national radical politics by the absorption into an international popular front creates passages some will find hard in the critic's portrait of Julius and Ethel Rosenberg's exchange of stilted messages in prison and in his contempt for Arthur Miller's *Death of a Salesman*, which half a century later was chosen for celebration by a production in China. But these passages of Warshow's, in the candor and complexity of their expression, are measures of the effort of imagination called upon to reach the reality of an old story, and of what is perhaps the continuing story—of the movement of so many American intellectuals from left to right, and of the mutual contempt of older and newer lefts.

Third, the conjunction is meant to counter an impression perhaps left by the understandable editorial decision, in originally collecting Warshow's writings, to use as the book's "Author's Preface" (rather than, say, as an appendix) Warshow's project statement for a Guggenheim Fellowship application to prepare a study of movies. Together with the subtitle (I assume also an editorial decision)—"Movies, Comics, Theatre and Other Aspects of Popular Culture"—the decision encourages the sense that Warshow was identifying movies as a part of a wider and quite well-known phenomenon named popular culture, whereas it strikes me as closer to what Warshow evidently regards as his unheard-of efforts, to say that they explode what we think we know of the natures of movies and of popular culture, manifested, for example, in the fact that the viewing of a pair of Chaplin films inspires from Warshow sustained and powerful and moving instances of the criticism of human creativity (what Henry James wickedly calls "appreciations" of it), whereas looking through comic books produces from him intelligent and concerned thoughts about how we are to protect the integrity of each, evidently necessary, side of a loving but tricky generational impasse. The tact and range of such exercises convey the promise of, and provide instances of, a sophistication of intellectual life whose luster, as idea and achievement, has not dimmed.

By the fall of 1951, a fellowship took me to graduate study at Harvard and an even more exclusive concentration on philosophy. While I still had not found a voice in philosophy, I could allow myself some association with the dissident voices within it that traditions inevitably create. Although Pascal, Nietzsche, and Kierkegaard, for example, were still not part of an accepted philosophy curriculum, they were not exactly dismissed as philosophy when discreetly inserted in term papers. Then, a short decade after Warshow's death in 1955, another radicalism emerged in connection with a revived civil rights movement and, bewilderingly rapidly, a catastrophic chain of misjudgments concerning Vietnam, precipitating a new culture of popular music that defied familiar forms of criticism. New Criticism and the New York intellectual life could seem now, suddenly, impertinent, an impertinence that some will take to be confirmed theoretically in the late 1960s by the onslaught of the French transfiguration into English-speaking academic life of (largely) German philosophy. Was this reasonable? It could be said that old and new revolutions in philosophy (and their uneven effects on literary theory, and for that matter social science) were not being allowed time to work out their own implications and demises; even apart from wars, persistent thoughts derived from Vienna (logical positivism) and then from Cambridge (the later Wittgenstein) and from Oxford (Austin and the unfortunately named ordinary language philosophy) and later from Paris (with stunning indiscriminateness, sometimes of acceptance, sometimes of rejection) kept—keep—rubbing one another wrong.

I allude to these immediate forces active in the ways I work in order to note that one issue that has remained throughout their as yet uncharted and incalculable cultural effects is that of movies, almost as foreign to professional philosophy as it has always been. The issue had itself intensified at the beginning of the 1960s with the decline of Hollywood and the importing of the outburst of new (and a new awareness of earlier) filmmaking in Italy and France and Sweden and Japan. Foreign films were no longer foreign. And Warshow's words about movies, and more than movies, remain, the words' very distance (but distinction) bespeaking an intellectual conscience that is wary of saying less than it feels, or more than it knows. An admirable aspiration for philosophy.

My emphasis, intended to follow Warshow's, on his reclaiming and challenging his experience may still strike some as a craving for metaphysical presence. To convince oneself, on the contrary, that he wrote in recoil from metaphysical abduction, I recommend the exercise of tracking the term "experience" as it makes its inevitable appearance in each of his essays. From out of his sense, so far as he can determine it, of the powers that offer to substitute attitudes in place of his experience, he seeks it as a measure, for example, of his young son's restriction of experience, anxious over the poor preparation it affords for life's surprises (cf. p. 63); of the *New Yorker's* vulgarity in insisting upon the tasteful in the face of the unconscionable (cf. p. 75); of the memory at his father's funeral of the disappointment that constituted his father's experience (cf. p. 91); of Hollywood's power to discourage thoughtfulness (cf. p. 126); of the Westerner's imperviousness to experience (cf. p. 120); of Arthur Miller's slighting of experience (cf. p. 158) or freezing of it (cf. p. 170) in *The Crucible*; of Dreyer's blocking of it in *Days of Wrath* (cf. p. 234); of an American posture of affirmation that comfortably assumes one's adequacy to any experience (cf. p. 225); and goes so far as to attempt, noting his probable insufficiency, to measure the experience, or rather the shutting off from experience (cf. p. 215), of the Jews in Europe who survived Hitler. To me this itinerary, along with the other turns I have cited, suggests an enactment of that responsiveness to events and to others as they present themselves (awake when everyone else has fallen asleep)—counting again, for ourselves, what the world has counted for us, presuming to assign the significance of our experiences for us—that marks philosophy as I care about it most.

Index